Medical Essays

Oliver Wendell Holmes, Sr.

Contents

PREFACE.	7
A SECOND PREFACE.	11
PREFACE TO THE NEW EDITION.	12
HOMOEOPATHY AND ITS KINDRED DELUSIONS	16
THE CONTAGIOUSNESS OF PUERPERAL FEVER	86
THE CONTAGIOUSNESS OF PUERPERAL FEVER.	103
CURRENTS AND COUNTER-CURRENTS IN	134
MEDICAL SCIENCE.	134
BORDER LINES OF KNOWLEDGE IN SOME	158
PROVINCES OF MEDICAL SCIENCE.	158
SCHOLASTIC AND BEDSIDE TEACHING.	200
THE MEDICAL PROFESSION IN MASSACHUSETTS.	227
THE YOUNG PRACTITIONER	264
MEDICAL LIBRARIES.	283
SOME OF MY EARLY TEACHERS	299
APPENDUM	314

MEDICAL ESSAYS

BY

Oliver Wendell Holmes, Sr.

PREFACE.

The character of the opposition which some of these papers have met with suggests the inference that they contain really important, but unwelcome truths. Negatives multiplied into each other change their sign and become positives. Hostile criticisms meeting together are often equivalent to praise, and the square of fault-finding turns out to be the same thing as eulogy.

But a writer has rarely so many enemies as it pleases him to believe. Self-love leads us to overrate the numbers of our negative constituency. The larger portion of my limited circle of readers must be quite indifferent to, if not ignorant of, the adverse opinions which have been expressed or recorded concerning any of these Addresses or Essays now submitted to their own judgment. It is proper, however, to inform them, that some of the positions maintained in these pages have been unsparingly attacked, with various degrees of ability, scholarship, and good-breeding. The tone of criticism naturally changes with local conditions in different parts of a country extended like our own, so that it is one of the most convenient gauges of the partial movements in the direction of civilization. It is satisfactory to add, that the views assailed have also been unflinchingly defended by unsought champions, among the ablest of whom it is pleasant to mention, at this moment of political alienation, the Editor of the Charleston Medical Journal.

"Currents and Counter-Currents" was written and delivered as an Oration, a florid rhetorical composition, expressly intended to secure the attention of an audience not easy to hold as listeners. It succeeded in doing this, and also in being as curiously misunderstood and misrepresented as if it had been a political harangue. This gave it more local notoriety than it might otherwise have attained, so that, as I learn, one ingenious person made use of its title as an advertisement to a production of his own.

The commonest mode of misrepresentation was this: qualified propositions, the whole meaning of which depended on the qualifications, were stripped of these and taken as absolute. Thus, the attempt to establish a presumption against giving poisons to sick persons was considered as equivalent to condemning the use of these substances. The only important inference the writer has been able to draw from the greater number of the refutations of his opinions which have been kindly sent him, is that the preliminary education of the Medical Profession is not always what it ought to be.

One concession he is willing to make, whatever sacrifice of pride it may involve. The story of Massasoit, which has furnished a coral, as it were, for some teething critics, when subjected to a powerful logical analysis, though correct in its essentials, proves to have been told with exceptionable breadth of statement, and therefore (to resume the metaphor) has been slightly rounded off at its edges, so as to be smoother for any who may wish to bite upon it hereafter. In other respects the Discourse has hardly been touched. It is only an individual's expression, in his own way, of opinions entertained by hundreds of the Medical Profession in every civilized country, and has nothing in it which on revision the writer sees cause to retract or modify. The superstitions it attacks lie at the very foundation of Homoeopathy, and of almost every form of medical charlatanism. Still the mere routinists and unthinking artisans in most callings dislike whatever shakes the dust out of their traditions, and it may be unreasonable to expect that Medicine will always prove an exception to the rule. One half the opposition which the numerical system of Louis has met with, as applied to the results of treatment, has been owing to the fact that it showed the movements of disease to be far more independent of the kind of practice pursued than was agreeable to the pride of those whose self-confidence it abated.

The statement, that medicines are more sparingly used in physicians' families than in most others, admits of a very natural explanation, without putting a harsh construction upon it, which it was not intended to admit. Outside pressure is less felt in the physician's own household; that is all. If this does not sometimes influence him to give medicine, or what seems to be medicine, when among those who have more confidence in drugging than his own family commonly has, the learned Professor Dunglison is hereby requested to apologize for his definition of the word

Placebo, or to expunge it from his Medical Dictionary.

One thing is certain. A loud outcry on a slight touch reveals the weak spot in a profession, as well as in a patient. It is a doubtful policy to oppose the freest speech in those of our own number who are trying to show us where they honestly believe our weakness lies. Vast as are the advances of our Science and Art, may it not possibly prove on examination that we retain other old barbarisms beside the use of the astrological sign of Jupiter, with which we endeavor to insure good luck to our prescriptions? Is it the act of a friend or a foe to try to point them out to our brethren when asked to address them, and is the speaker to subdue the constitutional habit of his style to a given standard, under penalty of giving offence to a grave assembly?

"Homoeopathy and its Kindred Delusions" was published nearly twenty years ago, and has been long out of print, so that the author tried in vain to procure a copy until the kindness of a friend supplied him with the only one he has had for years. A foolish story reached his ears that he was attempting to buy up stray copies for the sake of suppressing it. This edition was in the press at that very time.

Many of the arguments contained in the Lectures have lost whatever novelty they may have possessed. All its predictions have been submitted to the formidable test of time. They appear to have stood it, so far, about as well as most uninspired prophecies; indeed, some of them require much less accommodation than certain grave commentators employ in their readings of the ancient Prophets.

If some statistics recently published are correct, Homoeopathy has made very slow progress in Europe.

In all England, as it appears, there are hardly a fifth more Homoeopathic practitioners than there are students attending Lectures at the Massachusetts Medical College at the present time. In America it has undoubtedly proved more popular and lucrative, yet how loose a hold it has on the public confidence is shown by the fact that, when a specially valued life, which has been played with by one of its agents, is seriously threatened, the first thing we expect to hear is that a regular practitioner is by the patient's bed, and the Homoeopathic counsellor overruled or discarded. Again, how many of the ardent and capricious persons who embraced Homoeopathy have run the whole round of pretentious novelties;--have been boarded at water-cure establishments, closeted with uterine and other specialists, and finally wandered over seas to put themselves in charge of foreign celebrities, who dosed them as lustily as they were ever dosed before they took to globules! It will surprise many to learn to what a shadow of a shade Homoeopathy has dwindled in the hands of many of its noted practitioners. The itch-doctrine is treated with contempt. Infinitesimal doses are replaced by full ones whenever the fancy-practitioner chooses. Good Homoeopathic reasons can be found for employing anything that anybody wants to employ. Homoeopathy is now merely a name, an unproved theory, and a box of pellets pretending to be specifics, which, as all of us know, fail ignominiously in those cases where we would thankfully sacrifice all our prejudices and give the world to have them true to their promises.

Homoeopathy has not died out so rapidly as Tractoration. Perhaps it was well that it should not, for it has taught us a lesson of the healing faculty of Nature which was needed, and for which many of us have made proper acknowledgments. But it probably does more harm than good to medical science at the present time, by keeping up the delusion of treating everything by specifics,--the old barbarous notion that sick people should feed on poisons [Lachesis, arrow-poison, obtained from a serpent (Pulte). Crotalus horridus, rattlesnake's venom (Neidhard). The less dangerous Pediculus capitis is the favorite remedy of Dr. Mure, the English "Apostle of Homoeopathy." These are examples of the retrograde current setting towards barbarism] against which a part of the Discourse at the beginning of this volume is directed. The infinitesimal globules have not become a curiosity as yet, like Perkins's Tractors. But time is a very elastic element in Geology and Prophecy. If Daniel's seventy weeks mean four hundred and ninety years, as the learned Prideaux and others have settled it that they do, the "not many years" of my prediction may be stretched out a generation or two beyond our time, if necessary, when the prophecy will no doubt prove true.

It might be fitting to add a few words with regard to the Essay on the Contagiousness of Puerperal Fever. But the whole question I consider to be now transferred from the domain of medical inquiry to the consideration of Life Insurance agencies and Grand Juries. For the justification of this somewhat sharply accented language I must refer the reader to the paper itself for details which I regret to have been forced to place on permanent record.

BOSTON, January, 1861.

A SECOND PREFACE.

These Lectures and Essays are arranged in the order corresponding to the date of their delivery or publication. They must, of course, be read with a constant reference to these dates, by such as care to read them. I have not attempted to modernize their aspect or character in presenting them, in this somewhat altered connection, to the public. Several of them were contained in a former volume which received its name from the Address called "Currents and Counter-Currents." Some of those contained in the former volume have been replaced by others. The Essay called "Mechanism of Vital Actions" has been transferred to a distinct collection of Miscellaneous essays, forming a separate volume.

I had some intention of including with these papers an Essay on Intermittent Fever in New England, which received one of the Boylston prizes in 1837, and was published in the following year. But as this was upon a subject of local interest, chiefly, and would have taken up a good deal of room, I thought it best to leave it out, trusting that the stray copies to be met with in musty book-shops would sufficiently supply the not very extensive or urgent demand for a paper almost half a century old.

Some of these papers created a little stir when they first fell from the press into the pool of public consciousness. They will slide in very quietly now in this new edition, and find out for themselves whether the waters are those of Lethe, or whether they are to live for a time as not wholly unvalued reminiscences.

March 21, 1883.

PREFACE TO THE NEW EDITION.

These Essays are old enough now to go alone without staff or crutch in the shape of Prefaces. A very few words may be a convenience to the reader who takes up the book and wishes to know what he is likely to find in it.

HOMOEOPATHY AND ITS KINDRED DELUSIONS.

Homoeopathy has proved lucrative, and so long as it continues to be so will surely exist,--as surely as astrology, palmistry, and other methods of getting a living out of the weakness and credulity of mankind and womankind. Though it has no pretensions to be considered as belonging among the sciences, it may be looked upon by a scientific man as a curious object of study among the vagaries of the human mind. Its influence for good or the contrary may be made a matter of calm investigation. I have studied it in the Essay before the reader, under the aspect of an extravagant and purely imaginative creation of its founder. Since that first essay was written, nearly half a century ago, we have all had a chance to witness its practical working. Two opposite inferences may be drawn from its doctrines and practice. The first is that which is accepted by its disciples. This is that all diseases are "cured" by drugs. The opposite conclusion is drawn by a much larger number of persons. As they see that patients are very commonly getting well under treatment by infinitesimal drugging, which they consider equivalent to no medication at all, they come to disbelieve in every form of drugging and put their whole trust in "nature." Thus experience,

"From seeming evil still educing good,"

has shown that the dealers in this preposterous system of pseudo-therapeutics have cooperated with the wiser class of practitioners in breaking up the system of over-dosing and over-drugging which has been one of the standing reproaches of medical practice. While keeping up the miserable delusion that diseases were all to be "cured" by drugging, Homoeopathy has been unintentionally showing that they would very generally get well without any drugging at all. In the mean time the newer doctrines of the "mind cure," the "faith cure," and the rest are encroaching on the territory so long monopolized by that most ingenious of the pseudo-sciences. It would not be surprising if its whole ground should be taken possession of by these new claimants with their flattering appeals to the imaginative class of persons open to such attacks. Similia similabus may prove fatally true for once, if Homoeopathy is killed out by its new-born rivals.

It takes a very moderate amount of erudition to unearth a charlatan like the supposed father of the infinitesimal dosing system. The real inventor of that specious trickery was an Irishman by the name of Butler. The whole story is to be found in the "Ortus Medicinm" of Van Helmont. I have given some account of his chapter "Butler" in different articles, but I would refer the students of our Homoeopathic educational institutions to the original, which they will find very interesting and curious.

CURRENTS AND COUNTER-CURRENTS

My attack on over-drugging brought out some hostile comments and treatment. Thirty years ago I expressed myself with more vivacity than I should show if I were writing on the same subjects today. Some of my more lively remarks called out very sharp animadversion. Thus my illustration of prevention as often better than treatment in the mother's words to her child which had got a poisonous berry in its mouth,--"Spit it out!" gave mortal offence to a well-known New York practitioner and writer, who advised the Massachusetts Medical Society to spit out the offending speaker. Worse than this was my statement of my belief that if a ship-load of miscellaneous drugs, with certain very important exceptions,--drugs, many of which were then often given needlessly and in excess, as then used "could be sunk to the bottom of the sea, it would be all the better for mankind and all the worse for the fishes." This was too bad. The sentence was misquoted, quoted without its qualifying conditions, and frightened some of my worthy professional brethren as much as if I had told them to throw all physic to the dogs. But for the epigrammatic sting the sentiment would have been unnoticed as a harmless overstatement at the very worst.

Since this lecture was delivered a great and, as I think, beneficial change has taken place in the practice of medicine. The habit of the English "general practitioner" of making his profit out of the pills and potions he administered was ruinous to professional advancement and the dignity of the physician. When a half-starving medical man felt that he must give his patient draught and boluses for which he could charge him, he was in a pitiable position and too likely to persuade himself that his drugs were useful to his patient because they were profitable to him. This practice has prevailed a good deal in America, and was doubtless the source in some measure of the errors I combated.

THE CONTAGIOUSNESS OF PUERPERAL FEVER.

This Essay was read before a small Association called "The Society for Medical Improvement," and published in a Medical Journal which lasted but a single year. It naturally attracted less attention than it would have done if published in such a periodical as the "American Journal of Medical Sciences." Still it had its effect, as I have every reason to believe. I cannot doubt that it has saved the lives of many young mothers by calling attention to the existence and propagation of "Puerperal Fever as a Private Pestilence," and laying down rules for taking the necessary precautions against it. The case has long been decided in favor of the views I advocated, but, at the time when I wrote two of the most celebrated professors of Obstetrics in this country opposed my conclusions with all the weight of their experience and position.

This paper was written in a great heat and with passionate indignation. If I touched it at all I might trim its rhetorical exuberance, but I prefer to leave it all its original strength of expression. I could not, if I had tried, have disguised the feelings with which I regarded the attempt to put out of sight the frightful facts which I brought forward and the necessary conclusions to which they led. Of course the whole matter has been looked at in a new point of view since the microbe as a vehicle of contagion has been brought into light, and explained the mechanism of that which was plain enough as a fact to all who were not blind or who did not shut their eyes.

O. W. H.
BEVERLY Farms, Mass., August 3, 1891

HOMOEOPATHY AND ITS KINDRED DELUSIONS

[Two lectures delivered before the Boston Society for the Diffusion of Useful Knowledge. 1842.]

[When a physician attempts to convince a person, who has fallen into the Homoeopathic delusion, of the emptiness of its pretensions, he is often answered by a statement of cases in which its practitioners are thought to have effected wonderful cures. The main object of the first of these Lectures is to show, by abundant facts, that such statements, made by persons unacquainted with the fluctuations of disease and the fallacies of observation, are to be considered in general as of little or no value in establishing the truth of a medical doctrine or the utility of a method of practice.

Those kind friends who suggest to a person suffering from a tedious complaint, that he "Had better try Homoeopathy," are apt to enforce their suggestion by adding, that "at any rate it can do no harm." This may or may not be true as regards the individual. But it always does very great harm to the community to encourage ignorance, error, or deception in a profession which deals with the life and health of our fellow-creatures. Whether or not those who countenance Homoeopathy are guilty of this injustice towards others, the second of these Lectures may afford them some means of determining.

To deny that good effects may happen from the observance of diet and regimen when prescribed by Homoeopathists as well as by others, would be very unfair to them. But to suppose that men with minds so constituted as to accept such statements and embrace such doctrines as make up the so-called science of Homoeopathy are more competent than others to regulate the circumstances which influence the human body in health and disease, would be judging very harshly the average capacity of ordinary practitioners.

To deny that some patients may have been actually benefited through the influence exerted upon their imaginations, would be to refuse to Homoeopathy what all are willing to concede to every one of those numerous modes of practice known to all intelligent persons by an opprobrious title.

So long as the body is affected through the mind, no audacious device, even of the most manifestly dishonest character, can fail of producing occasional good to those who yield it an implicit or even a partial faith. The argument founded on this occasional good would be as applicable in justifying the counterfeiter and giving circulation to his base coin, on the ground that a spurious dollar had often relieved a poor man's necessities.

Homoeopathy has come before our public at a period when the growing spirit of eclecticism has prepared many ingenious and honest minds to listen to all new doctrines with a candor liable to degenerate into weakness. It is not impossible that the pretended evolution of great and mysterious virtues from infinitely attenuated atoms may have enticed a few over-refining philosophers, who have slid into a vague belief that matter subdivided grows less material, and approaches nearer to a spiritual nature as it requires a more powerful microscope for its detection.

However this may be, some persons seem disposed to take the ground of Menzel that the Laity must pass formal judgment between the Physician and the Homoeopathist, as it once did between Luther and the Romanists. The practitioner and the scholar must not, therefore, smile at the amount of time and labor expended in these Lectures upon this shadowy system; which, in the calm and serious judgment of many of the wisest members of the medical profession, is not entitled by anything it has ever said or done to the notoriety of a public rebuke, still less to the honors of critical martyrdom.]

I

I have selected four topics for this lecture, the first three of which I shall touch but slightly, the last more fully. They are

1. The Royal cure of the King's Evil, or Scrofula.
2. The Weapon Ointment, and its twin absurdity, the Sympathetic Powder.
3. The Tar-water mania of Bishop Berkeley.

4. The History of the Metallic Tractors, or Perkinism.

The first two illustrate the ease with which numerous facts are accumulated to prove the most fanciful and senseless extravagances.

The third exhibits the entire insufficiency of exalted wisdom, immaculate honesty, and vast general acquirements to make a good physician of a great bishop.

The fourth shows us the intimate machinery of an extinct delusion, which flourished only forty years ago; drawn in all its details, as being a rich and comparatively recent illustration of the pretensions, the arguments, the patronage, by means of which windy errors have long been, and will long continue to be, swollen into transient consequence. All display in superfluous abundance the boundless credulity and excitability of mankind upon subjects connected with medicine.

"From the time of Edward the Confessor to Queen Anne, the monarchs of England were in the habit of touching those who were brought to them suffering with the scrofula, for the cure of that distemper. William the Third had good sense enough to discontinue the practice, but Anne resumed it, and, among her other patients, performed the royal operation upon a child, who, in spite of his, disease, grew up at last into Samuel Johnson. After laying his hand upon the sufferers, it was customary for the monarch to hang a gold piece around the neck of each patient. Very strict precautions were adopted to prevent those who thought more of the golden angel hung round the neck by a white ribbon, than of relief of their bodily infirmities, from making too many calls, as they sometimes attempted to do. According to the statement of the advocates and contemporaries of this remedy, none ever failed of receiving benefit unless their little faith and credulity starved their merits. Some are said to have been cured immediately on the very touch, others did not so easily get rid of their swellings, until they were touched a second time. Several cases are related, of persons who had been blind for several weeks, and months, and obliged even to be led to Whitehall, yet recovered their sight immediately upon being touched, so as to walk away without any guide." So widely, at one period, was the belief diffused, that, in the course of twelve years, nearly a hundred thousand persons were touched by Charles the Second. Catholic divines; in disputes upon the orthodoxy of their church, did not deny that the power had descended to protestant princes;--Dr. Harpsfield, in his "Ecclesiastical History of England," admitted it, and in Wiseman's words, "when Bishop Tooker would make use of this

Argument to prove the Truth of our Church, Smitheus doth not thereupon go about to deny the Matter of fact; nay, both he and Cope acknowledge it." "I myself," says Wiseman, the best English surgical writer of his day,[Edinburgh Medical and Surgical Journal, vol. iii. p. 103.]--"I my self have been a frequent Eye-witness of many hundred of Cures performed by his Majesties Touch alone, without any assistance of Chirurgery; and those, many of them such as had tired out the endeavours of able Chirurgeons before they came hither. It were endless to recite what I myself have seen, and what I have received acknowledgments of by Letter, not only from the severall parts of this Nation, but also from Ireland, Scotland, Jersey, Garnsey. It is needless also to remember what Miracles of this nature were performed by the very Bloud of his late Majesty of Blessed memory, after whose decollation by the inhuman Barbarity of the Regicides, the reliques of that were gathered on Chips and in Handkerchieffs by the pious Devotes, who could not but think so great a suffering in so honourable and pious a Cause, would be attended by an extraordinary assistance of God, and some more then ordinary a miracle: nor did their Faith deceive them in this there point, being so many hundred that found the benefit of it." [Severall Chirurgicall Treatises. London.1676. p. 246.]

Obstinate and incredulous men, as he tells us, accounted for these cures in three ways: by the journey and change of air the patients obtained in coming to London; by the influence of imagination; and the wearing of gold.

To these objections he answers, 1st. That many of those cured were inhabitants of the city. 2d. That the subjects of treatment were frequently infants. 3d. That sometimes silver was given, and sometimes nothing, yet the patients were cured.

A superstition resembling this probably exists at the present time in some ignorant districts of England and this country. A writer in a Medical Journal in the year 1807, speaks of a farmer in Devonshire, who, being a ninth son of a ninth son, is thought endowed with healing powers like those of ancient royalty, and who is accustomed one day in every week to strike for the evil.

I remember that one of my schoolmates told me, when a boy, of a seventh son of a seventh son, somewhere in Essex County, who touched for the scrofula, and who used to hang a silver fourpence halfpenny about the neck of those who came to him, which fourpence halfpenny it was solemnly affirmed became of a remarkably black color after having been some time worn, and that his own brother had been subjected to this extraordinary treatment; but I must add that my schoolmate drew a bow of remarkable length, strength, and toughness for his tender years.

One of the most curious examples of the fallacy of popular belief and the uncertainty of asserted facts in medical experience is to be found in the history of the UNGUENTUM ARMARIUM, or WEAPON OINTMENT.

Fabricius Hildanus, whose name is familiar to every surgical scholar, and Lord Bacon, who frequently dipped a little into medicine, are my principal authorities for the few circumstances I shall mention regarding it. The Weapon Ointment was a preparation used for the healing of wounds, but instead of its being applied to them, the injured part was washed and bandaged, and the weapon with which the wound was inflicted was carefully anointed with the unguent. Empirics, ignorant barbers, and men of that sort, are said to have especially employed it. Still there were not wanting some among the more respectable members of the medical profession who supported its claims. The composition of this ointment was complicated, in the different formulae given by different authorities; but some substances addressed to the imagination, rather than the wound or weapon, entered into all. Such were portions of mummy, of human blood, and of moss from the skull of a thief hung in chains.

Hildanus was a wise and learned man, one of the best surgeons of his time. He was fully aware that a part of the real secret of the Unguentum Armarium consisted in the washing and bandaging the wound and then letting it alone. But he could not resist the solemn assertions respecting its efficacy; he gave way before the outcry of facts, and therefore, instead of denying all their pretensions, he admitted and tried to account for them upon supernatural grounds. As the virtue of those applications, he says, which are made to the weapon cannot reach the wound, and as they can produce no effect without contact, it follows, of necessity, that the Devil must have a hand in the business; and as he is by far the most long headed and experienced of practitioners, he cannot find this a matter of any great difficulty. Hildanus himself reports, in detail, the case of a lady who had received a moderate wound, for which the Unguentum Armarium was employed without the slightest use. Yet instead of receiving this flat case of failure as any evidence against the remedy, he accounts for its not succeeding by the devout character of the lady, and her freedom from that superstitious and over-imaginative tendency which the Devil requires in those who are to be benefited by his devices.

Lord Bacon speaks of the Weapon Ointment, in his Natural History, as having in its favor the testimony of men of credit, though, in his own language, he himself "as yet is not fully inclined to believe it." His remarks upon the asserted facts respecting it show a mixture of wise suspicion and partial belief. He does not like the precise directions given as to the circumstances under which the animals from which some of the materials were obtained were to be killed; for he thought it looked like a provision for an excuse in case of failure, by laying the fault to the omission of some of these circumstances. But he likes well that "they do not observe the confecting of the Ointment under any certain constellation; which is commonly the excuse of magical medicines, when they fail, that they were not made under a fit figure of heaven." [This was a mistake, however, since the two recipes given by Hildanus are both very explicit as to the aspect of the heavens required for different stages of the process.] "It was pretended that if the offending weapon could not be had, it would serve the purpose to anoint a wooden one made like it." "This," says Bacon, "I should doubt to be a device to keep this strange form of cure in request and use; because many times you cannot come by the weapon itself." And in closing his remarks on the statements of the advocates of the ointment, he says, "Lastly, it will cure a beast as well as a man, which I like best of all the rest, because it subjecteth the matter to an easy trial." It is worth remembering, that more than two hundred years ago, when an absurd and fantastic remedy was asserted to possess wonderful power, and when sensible persons ascribed its pretended influence to imagination, it was boldly answered that the cure took place when the wounded party did not know of the application made to the weapon, and even when a brute animal was the subject of the experiment, and that this assertion, as we all know it was, came in such a shape as to shake the incredulity of the keenest thinker of his time. The very same assertion has been since repeated in favor of Perkinism, and, since that, of Homoeopathy.

The same essential idea as that of the Weapon Ointment reproduced itself in the still more famous SYMPATHETIC POWDER. This Powder was said to have the faculty, if applied to the blood-stained garments of a wounded person, to cure his injuries, even though he were at a great distance at the time. A friar, returning from the East, brought the recipe to Europe somewhat before the middle of the seventeenth century. The Grand Duke of Florence, in which city the friar was residing, heard of his cures, and tried, but without success, to obtain his secret. Sir Kenehn Digby, an Englishman well known to fame, was fortunate enough to do him a favor, which wrought upon his feelings and induced him to impart to his benefactor the composition of his extraordinary Powder. This English knight was at different periods of his life an admiral, a theologian, a critic, a metaphysician, a politician, and a disciple of Alchemy. As is not unfrequent with versatile and inflammable people, he caught fire at the first spark of a new medical discovery, and no sooner got home to England than he began to spread the conflagration.

An opportunity soon offered itself to try the powers of the famous powder. Mr. J. Howell, having been wounded in endeavoring to part two of his friends who were fighting a duel, submitted himself to a trial of the Sympathetic Powder. Four days after he received his wounds, Sir Kenehn dipped one of Mr. Howell's gaiters in a solution of the Powder, and immediately, it is said, the wounds, which were very painful, grew easy, although the patient, who was conversing in a corner of the chamber, had not, the least idea of what was doing with his garter. He then returned home, leaving his garter in the hands of Sir Kenelm, who had hung it up to dry, when Mr. Howell sent his servant in a great hurry to tell him that his wounds were paining him horribly; the garter was therefore replaced in the solution of the Powder, "and the patient got well after five or six days of its continued immersion."

King James First, his son Charles the First, the Duke of Buckingham, then prime minister, and all the principal personages of the time, were cognizant of this fact; and James himself, being curious to know the secret of this remedy, asked it of Sir Kenelm, who revealed it to him, and his Majesty had the opportunity of making several trials of its efficacy, "which all succeeded in a surprising manner." [Dict. des Sciences Medieales.]

The king's physician, Dr. Mayerne, was made master of the secret, which he carried to France and communicated to the Duke of Mayenne, who performed many cures by means of it, and taught it to his surgeon, who, after the Duke's death, sold it to many distinguished persons, by whose agency it soon ceased to be a secret. What was this wonderful substance which so astonished kings, princes, dukes, knights, and doctors? Nothing but powdered blue vitriol. But it was made to undergo several processes that conferred on it extraordinary virtues. Twice or thrice it was to be dissolved, filtered, and crystallized. The crystals were to be laid in the sun during the months of June, July, and August, taking care to turn them carefully that all should be exposed. Then they were to be powdered, triturated, and again exposed to the sun, again reduced to a very fine powder, and secured in a vessel, while hot, from the sunshine. If there seem anything remarkable in the fact of such astonishing properties being developed by this process, it must be from our shortsightedness, for common salt and charcoal develop powers quite as marvellous after a certain number of thumps, stirs, and shakes, from the hands of modern workers of miracles. In fact the Unguentum Armarium and Sympathetic Powder resemble some more recent prescriptions; the latter consisting in an infinite dilution of the common dose in which remedies are given, and the two former in an infinite dilution of the common distance at which they are applied.

Whether philosophers, and more especially metaphysicians, have any peculiar tendency to dabble in drugs and dose themselves with physic, is a question which might suggest itself to the reader of their biographies.

When Bishop Berkeley visited the illustrious Malebranche at Paris, he found him in his cell, cooking in a small pipkin a medicine for an inflammation of the lungs, from which he was suffering; and the disease, being unfortunately aggravated by the vehemence of their discussion, or the contents of the pipkin, carried him off in the course of a few days. Berkeley himself afforded a remarkable illustration of a truth which has long been known to the members of one of the learned professions, namely, that no amount of talent, or of acquirements in other departments, can rescue from lamentable folly those who, without something of the requisite preparation, undertake to experiment with nostrums upon themselves and their neighbors. The exalted character of Berkeley is thus drawn by Sir James Mackintosh: Ancient learning, exact science, polished society, modern literature, and the fine arts, contributed to adorn and enrich the mind of this accomplished man. All his contemporaries agreed with the satirist in ascribing

"'To Berkeley every virtue under heaven.'

"Even the discerning, fastidious, and turbulent Atterbury said, after an interview with him, 'So much understanding, so much knowledge, so much innocence, and such humility, I did not think had been the portion of any but angels, till I saw this gentleman.'"

But among the writings of this great and good man is an Essay of the most curious character, illustrating his weakness upon the point in question, and entitled, "Siris, a Chain of Philosophical Reflections and Inquiries concerning the Virtues of TAR WATER, and divers other Subjects,"--an essay which begins with a recipe for his favorite fluid, and slides by gentle gradations into an examination of the sublimest doctrines of Plato. To show how far a man of honesty and benevolence, and with a mind of singular acuteness and depth, may be run away with by a favorite notion on a subject which his habits and education do not fit him to investigate, I shall give a short account of this Essay, merely stating that as all the supposed virtues of Tar Water, made public in successive editions of his treatise by so illustrious an author, have not saved it from neglect and disgrace, it may be fairly assumed that they were mainly imaginary.

The bishop, as is usual in such cases, speaks of himself as indispensably obliged, by the duty he owes to mankind, to make his experience public. Now this was by no means evident, nor does it follow in general, that because a man has formed a favorable opinion of a person or a thing he has not the proper means of thoroughly understanding, he shall be bound to print it, and thus give currency to his impressions, which may be erroneous, and therefore injurious. He would have done much better to have laid his impressions before some experienced physicians and surgeons, such as Dr. Mead and Mr. Cheselden, to have asked them to try his experiment over again, and have been guided by their answers. But the good bishop got excited; he pleased himself with the thought that he had discovered a great panacea; and having once tasted the bewitching cup of self-quackery, like many before and since his time, he was so infatuated with the draught that he would insist on pouring it down the throats of his neighbors and all mankind.

The precious fluid was made by stirring a gallon of water with a quart of tar, leaving it forty-eight hours, and pouring off the clear water. Such was the specific which the great metaphysician recommended for averting and curing all manner of diseases. It was, if he might be believed, a preventive of the small-pox, and of great use in the course of the disease. It was a cure for impurities of the blood, coughs, pleurisy, peripneumony, erysipelas, asthma, indigestion, carchexia, hysterics, dropsy, mortification, scurvy, and hypochondria. It was of great use in gout and fevers, and was an excellent preservative of the teeth and gums; answered all the purpose of Elixir Proprietatis, Stoughton's drops, diet drinks, and mineral waters; was particularly to be recommended to sea-faring persons, ladies, and men of studious and sedentary lives; could never be taken too long, but, on the contrary, produced advantages which sometimes did not begin to show themselves for two or three months.

"From my representing Tar Water as good for so many things," says Berkeley, "some perhaps may conclude it is good for nothing. But charity obligeth me to say what I know, and what I think, however it may be taken. Men may censure and object as they please, but I appeal to time and experiment. Effects misimputed, cases wrong told, circumstances overlooked, perhaps, too, prejudices and partialities against truth, may for a time prevail and keep her at the bottom of her well, from whence nevertheless she emergeth sooner or later, and strikes the eyes of all who do not keep them shut." I cannot resist the temptation of illustrating the bishop's belief in the wonderful powers of his remedy, by a few sentences from different parts of his essay. "The hardness of stubbed vulgar constitutions renders them insensible of a thousand things that fret and gall those delicate people, who, as if their skin was peeled off, feel to the quick everything that touches them. The tender nerves and low spirits of such poor creatures would be much relieved by the use of Tar Water, which might prolong and cheer their lives." "It [the Tar Water] may be made stronger for brute beasts, as horses, in whose disorders I have found it very useful." "This same water will also give charitable relief to the ladies, who often want it more than the parish poor; being many of them never able to make a good meal, and sitting pale, puny, and forbidden, like ghosts, at their own table, victims of vapors and indigestion." It does not appear among the virtues of Tar Water that "children cried for it," as for some of our modern remedies, but the bishop says, "I have known children take it for above six months together with great benefit, and without any inconvenience; and after long and repeated experience I do esteem it a most excellent diet drink, fitted to all seasons and ages." After mentioning its usefulness in febrile complaints, he says: "I have had all this confirmed by my own experience in the late sickly season of the year one thousand seven hundred and forty-one, having had twenty-five fevers in my own family cured by this medicinal water, drunk copiously." And to finish these extracts with a most important suggestion for the improvement of the British nation: "It is much to be lamented that our Insulars who act and think so much for themselves, should yet, from grossness of air and diet, grow stupid or doat sooner than other people, who, by virtue of elastic air, water-drinking, and light food, preserve their faculties to extreme old age; an advantage which may perhaps be approached, if not equaled, even in these regions, by Tar Water, temperance, and early hours."

Berkeley died at the age of about seventy; he might have lived longer, but his fatal illness was so sudden that there was not time enough to stir up a quart of the panacea. He was an illustrious man, but he held two very odd opinions; that tar water was everything, and that the whole material universe was nothing.

Most of those present have at some time in their lives heard mention made of the METALLIC TRACTORS, invented by one Dr. Perkins, an American, and formerly enjoying great repute for the cure of various diseases. Many have seen or heard of a satirical poem, written by one of our own countrymen also, about forty years since, and called "Terrible Tractoration." The Metallic Tractors are now so utterly abandoned that I have only by good fortune fallen upon a single one of a pair, to show for the sake of illustration. For more than thirty years this great discovery, which was to banish at least half the evils which afflict humanity, has been sleeping undisturbed in the grave of oblivion. Not a voice has, for this long period, been raised in its favor; its noble and learned patrons, its public institutions, its eloquent advocates, its brilliant promises are all covered with the dust of silent neglect; and of the generation which has sprung up since the period when it flourished, very few know anything of its history, and hardly even the title which in its palmy days it bore of PERKINISM. Taking it as settled, then, as no one appears to answer for it, that Perkinism is entirely dead and gone, that both in public and private, officially and individually, its former adherents even allow it to be absolutely defunct, I select it for anatomical examination. If this pretended discovery was made public; if it was long kept before the public; if it was addressed to the people of different countries; if it was formally investigated by scientific men, and systematically adopted by benevolent persons, who did everything in their power to diffuse the knowledge and practice of it; if various collateral motives, such as interest and vanity, were embarked in its cause; if, notwithstanding all these things, it gradually sickened and died, then the conclusion seems a fair one, that it did not deserve to live. Contrasting its failure with its high pretensions, it is fair to call it an imposition; whether an expressly fraudulent contrivance or not, some might be ready to question. Everything historically shown to have happened concerning the mode of promulgation, the wide diffusion, the apparent success of this delusion, the respectability and enthusiasm of its advocates, is of great interest in showing to what extent and by what means a considerable part of the community may be led into the belief of that which is to be eventually considered' as an idle folly. If there is any existing folly, fraudulent or innocent in its origin, which appeals to certain arguments for its support; provided that the very same arguments can be shown to have been used for Perkinism with as good reason, they will at once fall to the ground. Still more, if it shall appear that the general course of any existing delusion bears a strong resemblance to that of Perkinism, that the former is most frequently advocated by the same class of persons who were conspicuous in behalf of the latter, and treated with contempt or opposed by the same kind of persons who thus treated Perkinism; if the facts in favor of both have a similar aspect; if the motives of their originators and propagators may be presumed to have been similar; then there is every reason to suppose that the existing folly will follow in the footsteps of the past, and after displaying a given amount of cunning and credulity in those deceiving and deceived, will drop from the public view like a fruit which has ripened into spontaneous rottenness, and be succeeded by the fresh bloom of some other delusion required by the same excitable portion of the community.

Dr. Elisha Perkins was born at Norwich, Connecticut, in the year 1740. He had practised his profession with a good local reputation for many years, when he fell upon a course of experiments, as it is related, which led to his great discovery. He conceived the idea that metallic substances might have the effect of removing diseases, if applied in a certain manner; a notion probably suggested by the then recent experiments of Galvani, in which muscular contractions were found to be produced by the contact of two metals with the living fibre. It was in 1796 that his discovery was promulgated in the shape of the Metallic Tractors, two pieces of metal, one apparently iron and the other brass, about three inches long, blunt at one end and pointed at the other. These instruments were applied for the cure of different complaints, such as rheumatism, local pains, inflammations, and even tumors, by drawing them over the affected part very lightly for about twenty minutes. Dr. Perkins took out a patent for his discovery, and travelled about the country to diffuse the new practice. He soon found numerous advocates of his discovery, many of them of high standing and influence. In the year 1798 the tractors had crossed the Atlantic, and were publicly employed in the Royal Hospital at Copenhagen. About the same time the son of the inventor, Mr. Benjamin Douglass Perkins, carried them to London, where they soon attracted attention. The Danish physicians published an account of their cases, containing numerous instances of alleged success, in a respectable octavo volume. In the year 1804 an establishment, honored with the name of the Perkinean Institution, was founded in London. The transactions of this institution were published in pamphlets, the Perkinean Society had public dinners at the Crown and Anchor, and a poet celebrated their medical triumph in strains like these:

> "See, pointed metals, blest with power t' appease
> The ruthless rage of merciless disease,
> O'er the frail part a subtle fluid pour,
> Drenched with invisible Galvanic shower,
> Till the arthritic staff and crutch forego,
> And leap exulting like the bounding roe!"

While all these things were going on, Mr. Benjamin Douglass Perkins was calmly pocketing money, so that after some half a dozen years he left the country with more than ten thousand pounds, which had been paid him by the believers in Great Britain. But in spite of all this success, and the number of those interested and committed in its behalf, Perkinism soon began to decline, and in 1811 the Tractors are spoken of by an intelligent writer as being almost forgotten. Such was the origin and duration of this doctrine and practice, into the history of which we will now look a little more narrowly.

Let us see, then, by whose agency this delusion was established and kept up; whether it was principally by those who were accustomed to medical pursuits, or those whose habits and modes of reasoning were different; whether it was with the approbation of those learned bodies usually supposed to take an interest in scientific discoveries, or only of individuals whose claims to distinction were founded upon their position in society, or political station, or literary eminence; whether the judicious or excitable classes entered most deeply into it; whether, in short, the scientific men of that time were deceived, or only intruded upon, and shouted down for the moment by persons who had no particular call to invade their precincts.

Not much, perhaps, was to be expected of the Medical Profession in the way of encouragement. One Dr. Fuller, who wrote in England, himself a Perkinist, thus expressed his opinion: "It must be an extraordinary exertion of virtue and humanity for a medical man, whose livelihood depends either on the sale of drugs, or on receiving a guinea for writing a prescription, which must relate to those drugs, to say to his patient, 'You had better purchase a set of Tractors to keep in your family; they will cure you without the expense of my attendance, or the danger of the common medical practice.' For very obvious reasons medical men must never be expected to recommend the use of Perkinism. The Tractors must trust for their patronage to the enlightened and philanthropic out of the profession, or to medical men retired from practice, and who know of no other interest than the luxury of relieving the distressed. And I do not despair of seeing the day when but very few of this description as well as private families will be without them."

Whether the motives assigned by this medical man to his professional brethren existed or not, it is true that Dr. Perkins did not gain a great deal at their hands. The Connecticut Medical Society expelled him in 1797 for violating their law against the use of nostrums, or secret remedies. The leading English physicians appear to have looked on with singular apathy or contempt at the miracles which it was pretended were enacting in the hands of the apostles of the new practice. In looking over the reviews of the time, I have found little beyond brief occasional notices of their pretensions; the columns of these journals being occupied with subjects of more permanent interest. The state of things in London is best learned, however, from the satirical poem to which I have already alluded as having been written at the period referred to. This was entitled, "Terrible Tractoration!! A Poetical Petition against Galvanizing Trumpery and the Perkinistic Institution. Most respectfully addressed to the Royal College of Physicians, by Christopher Caustic, M. D., LL. D., A. S. S., Fellow of the Royal College of Physicians, Aberdeen, and Honorary Member of no less than nineteen very learned Societies." Two editions of this work were published in London in the years 1803 and 1804, and one or two have been published in this country.

"Terrible Tractoration" is supposed, by those who never read it, to be a satire upon the follies of Perkins and his followers. It is, on the contrary, a most zealous defence of Perkinism, and a fierce attack upon its opponents, most especially upon such of the medical profession as treated the subject with neglect or ridicule. The Royal College of Physicians was the more peculiar object of the attack, but with this body, the editors of some of the leading periodicals, and several physicians distinguished at that time, and even now remembered for their services to science and humanity, were involved in unsparing denunciations. The work is by no means of the simply humorous character it might be supposed, but is overloaded with notes of the most seriously polemical nature. Much of the history of the subject, indeed, is to be looked for in this volume.

It appears from this work that the principal members of the medical profession, so far from hailing Mr. Benjamin Douglass Perkins as another Harvey or Jenner, looked very coldly upon him and his Tractors; and it is now evident that, though they were much abused for so doing, they knew very well what they had to deal with, and were altogether in the right. The delusion at last attracted such an amount of attention as to induce Dr. Haygarth and some others of respectable standing to institute some experiments which I shall mention in their proper place, the result of which might have seemed sufficient to show the emptiness of the whole contrivance.

The Royal Society, that learned body which for ages has constituted the best tribunal to which Britain can appeal in questions of science, accepted Mr. Perkins's Tractors and the book written about them, passed the customary vote of thanks, and never thought of troubling itself further in the investigation of pretensions of such an aspect. It is not to be denied that a considerable number of physicians did avow themselves advocates of the new practice; but out of the whole catalogue of those who were publicly proclaimed as such, no one has ever been known, so far as I am aware, to the scientific world, except in connection with the short-lived notoriety of Perkinism. Who were the people, then, to whose activity, influence, or standing with the community was owing all the temporary excitement produced by the Metallic Tractors?

First, those persons who had been induced to purchase a pair of Tractors. These little bits of brass and iron, the intrinsic value of which might, perhaps, amount to ninepence, were sold at five guineas a pair! A man who has paid twenty-five dollars for his whistle is apt to blow it louder and longer than other people. So it appeared that when the "Perkinean Society" applied to the possessors of Tractors in the metropolis to concur in the establishment of a public institution for the use of these instruments upon the poor, "it was found that only five out of above a hundred objected to subscribe, on account of their want of confidence in the efficacy of the practice; and these," the committee observes, "there is reason to believe, never gave them a fair trial, probably never used them in more than one case, and that perhaps a case in which the Tractors had never been recommended as serviceable." "Purchasers of the Tractors," said one of their ardent advocates, "would be among the last to approve of them if they had reason to suppose themselves defrauded of five guineas." He forgot poor Moses, with his "gross of green spectacles, with silver rims and shagreen cases." "Dear mother," cried the boy, "why won't you listen to reason? I had them a dead bargain, or I should not have bought them. The silver rims alone will sell for double the money."

But it is an undeniable fact, that many persons of considerable standing, and in some instances holding the most elevated positions in society, openly patronized the new practice. In a translation of a work entitled "Experiments with the Metallic Tractors," originally published in Danish, thence rendered successively into German and English, Mr. Benjamin Perkins, who edited the English edition, has given a copious enumeration of the distinguished individuals, both in America and Europe, whose patronage he enjoyed. He goes so far as to signify that ROYALTY itself was to be included among the number. When the Perkinean Institution was founded, no less a person than Lord Rivers was elected President, and eleven other individuals of distinction, among them Governor Franklin, son of Dr. Franklin, figured as Vice-Presidents. Lord Henniker, a member of the Royal Society, who is spoken of as a man of judgment and talents, condescended to patronize the astonishing discovery, and at different times bought three pairs of Tractors. When the Tractors were introduced into Europe, a large number of testimonials accompanied them from various distinguished characters in America, the list of whom is given in the translation of the Danish work referred to as follows:

"Those who have individually stated cases, or who have presented their names to the public as men who approved of this remedy, and acknowledged themselves instrumental in circulating the Tractors, are fifty-six in number; thirty-four of whom are physicians and surgeons, and many of them of the first eminence, thirteen clergymen, most of whom are doctors of divinity, and connected with the literary institutions of America; among the remainder are two members of Congress, one professor of natural philosophy in a college, etc., etc." It seemed to be taken rather hardly by Mr. Perkins that the translators of the work which he edited, in citing the names of the advocates of the Metallic Practice, frequently omitted the honorary titles which should have been annexed. The testimonials were obtained by the Danish writer, from a pamphlet published in America, in which these titles were given in full. Thus one of these testimonials is from "John Tyler, Esq., a magistrate in the county of New London, and late Brigadier-General of the militia in that State." The "omission of the General's title" is the subject of complaint, as if this title were sufficient evidence of the commanding powers of one of the patrons of tractoration. A similar complaint is made when "Calvin Goddard, Esq., of Plainfield, Attorney at Law, and a member of the Legislature of the State of Connecticut," is mentioned without his titular honors, and even on account of the omission of the proper official titles belonging to "Nathan Pierce, Esq., Governor and Manager of the Almshouse of Newburyport." These instances show the great importance to be attached to civil and military dignities, in qualifying their holders to judge of scientific subjects, a truth which has not been overlooked by the legitimate successors of the Perkinists. In Great Britain, the Tractors were not less honored than in America, by the learned and the illustrious. The "Perkinistic Committee" made this statement in their report: "Mr. Perkins has annually laid before the public a large collection of new cases communicated to him for that purpose by disinterested and intelligent characters, from almost every quarter of Great Britain. In regard to the competency of these vouchers, it will be sufficient simply to state that, amongst others whose names have been attached to their communications, are eight professors, in four different universities, twenty-one regular Physicians, nineteen Surgeons, thirty Clergymen, twelve of whom are Doctors of Divinity, and numerous other characters of equal respectability."

It cannot but excite our notice and surprise that the number of clergymen both in America and Great Britain who thrust forward their evidence on this medical topic was singularly large in proportion to that of the members of the medical profession. Whole pages are contributed by such worthies as the Rev. Dr. Trotter of Hans Place, the Rear. Waring Willett, Chaplain to the Earl of Dunmore, the Rev. Dr. Clarke, Chaplain to the Prince of Wales. The style of these theologico-medical communications may be seen in the following from a divine who was also professor in one of the colleges of New England. "I have used the Tractors with success in several other cases in my own family, and although, like Naaman the Syrian, I cannot tell why the waters of Jordan should be better than Abana and Pharpar, rivers of Damascus; yet since experience has proved them so, no reasoning can change the opinion. Indeed, the causes of all common facts are, we think, perfectly well known to us; and it is very probable, fifty or a hundred years hence, we shall as well know why the Metallic Tractors should in a few minutes remove violent pains, as we now know why cantharides and opium will produce opposite effects, namely, we shall know very little about either excepting facts." Fifty or a hundred years hence! if he could have looked forward forty years, he would have seen the descendants of the "Perkinistic" philosophers swallowing infinitesimal globules, and knowing and caring as much about the Tractors as the people at Saratoga Springs do about the waters of Abana and Pharpar.

I trust it will not be thought in any degree disrespectful to a profession which we all honor, that I have mentioned the great zeal of many clergymen in the cause of Perkinism. I hope, too, that I may without offence suggest the causes which have often led them out of their own province into one to which their education has no special reference. The members of that profession ought to be, and commonly are, persons of benevolent character. Their duties carry them into the midst of families, and particularly at times when the members of them are suffering from bodily illness. It is natural enough that a strong desire should be excited to alleviate sufferings which may have defied the efforts of professional skill; as natural that any remedy which recommends itself to the belief or the fancy of the spiritual physician should be applied with the hope of benefit; and perfectly certain that the weakness of human nature, from which no profession is exempt, will lead him to take the most flattering view of its effects upon the patient; his own sagacity and judgment being staked upon the success of the trial. The inventor of the Tractors was aware of these truths. He therefore sent the Tractors gratuitously to many clergymen, accompanied with a formal certificate that the holder had become entitled to their possession by the payment of five guineas. This was practised in our own neighborhood, and I remember finding one of these certificates, so presented, which proved that amongst the risks of infancy I had to encounter Perkins's Tractors. Two clergymen of Boston and the vicinity, both well known to local fame, gave in their testimony to the value of the instruments thus presented to them; an unusually moderate proportion, when it is remembered that to the common motives of which I have spoken was added the seduction of a gift for which the profane public was expected to pay so largely.

It was remarkable, also, that Perkinism, which had so little success with the medical and scientific part of the community, found great favor in the eyes of its more lovely and less obstinate portion. "The lady of Major Oxholin,"--I quote from Mr. Perkins's volume,--"having been lately in America, had seen and heard much of the great effects of Perkinism. Influenced by a most benevolent disposition, she brought these Tractors and the pamphlet with her to Europe, with a laudable desire of extending their utility to her suffering countrymen." Such was the channel by which the Tractors were conveyed to Denmark, where they soon became the ruling passion. The workmen, says a French writer, could not manufacture them fast enough. Women carried them about their persons, and delighted in bringing them into general use. To what extent the Tractors were favored with the patronage of English and American ladies, it is of course not easy to say, except on general principles, as their names were not brought before the public. But one of Dr. Haygarth's stories may lead us to conjecture that there was a class of female practitioners who went about doing good with the Tractors in England as well as in Denmark. A certain lady had the misfortune to have a spot as big as a silver penny at the corner of her eye, caused by a bruise, or some such injury. Another lady, who was a friend of hers, and a strong believer in Perkinism, was very anxious to try the effects of tractoration upon this unfortunate blemish. The patient consented; the lady "produced the instruments, and, after drawing them four or five times over the spot, declared that it changed to a paler color, and on repeating the use of them a few minutes longer, that it had almost vanished, and was scarcely visible, and departed in high triumph at her success." The lady who underwent the operation assured the narrator "that she looked in the glass immediately after, and that not the least visible alteration had taken place."

It would be a very interesting question, what was the intellectual character of those persons most conspicuous in behalf of the Perkinistic delusion? Such an inquiry might bring to light some principles which we could hereafter apply to the study of other popular errors. But the obscurity into which nearly all these enthusiasts have subsided renders the question easier to ask than to answer. I believe it would have been found that most of these persons were of ardent temperament and of considerable imagination, and that their history would show that Perkinism was not the first nor the last hobby-horse they rode furiously. Many of them may very probably have been persons of more than common talent, of active and ingenious minds, of versatile powers and various acquirements. Such, for instance, was the estimable man to whom I have repeatedly referred as a warm defender of tractoration, and a bitter assailant of its enemies. The story tells itself in the biographical preface to his poem. He went to London with the view of introducing a hydraulic machine, which he and his Vermont friends regarded as a very important invention. He found, however, that the machine was already in common use in that metropolis. A brother Yankee, then in London, had started the project of a mill, which was to be carried by the water of the Thames. He was sanguine enough to purchase one fifth of this concern, which also proved a failure. At about the same period he wrote the work which proved the great excitement of his mind upon the subject of the transient folly then before the public. Originally a lawyer, he was in succession a mechanician, a poet, and an editor, meeting with far less success in each of these departments than usually attends men of less varied gifts, but of more tranquil and phlegmatic composition. But who is ignorant that there is a class of minds characterized by qualities like those I have mentioned; minds with many bright and even beautiful traits; but aimless and fickle as the butterfly; that settle upon every gayly-colored illusion as it opens into flower, and flutter away to another when the first has dropped its leaves, and stands naked in the icy air of truth!

Let us now look at the general tenor of the arguments addressed by believers to sceptics and opponents. Foremost of all, emblazoned at the head of every column, loudest shouted by every triumphant disputant, held up as paramount to all other considerations, stretched like an impenetrable shield to protect the weakest advocate of the great cause against the weapons of the adversary, was that omnipotent monosyllable which has been the patrimony of cheats and the currency of dupes from time immemorial,--Facts! Facts! Facts! First came the published cases of the American clergymen, brigadier-generals, almshouse governors, representatives, attorneys, and esquires. Then came the published cases of the surgeons of Copenhagen. Then followed reports of about one hundred and fifty cases published in England, "demonstrating the efficacy of the metallic practice in a variety of complaints both upon the human body and on horses, etc." But the progress of facts in Great Britain did not stop here. Let those who rely upon the numbers of their testimonials, as being alone sufficient to prove the soundness and stability of a medical novelty, digest the following from the report of the Perkinistic Committee. "The cases published [in Great Britain] amounted, in March last, the date of Mr. Perkins's last publication, to about five thousand. Supposing that not more than one cure in three hundred which the Tractors have performed has been published, and the proportion is probably much greater, it will be seen that the number, to March last, will have exceeded one million five hundred thousand!"

Next in order after the appeal to what were called facts, came a series of arguments, which have been so long bruised and battered round in the cause of every doctrine or pretension, new, monstrous, or deliriously impossible, that each of them is as odiously familiar to the scientific scholar as the faces of so many old acquaintances, among the less reputable classes, to the officers of police.

No doubt many of my hearers will recognize, in the following passages, arguments they may have heard brought forward with triumphant confidence in behalf of some doctrine not yet extinct. No doubt some may have honestly thought they proved something; may have used them with the purpose of convincing their friends, or of silencing the opponents of their favorite doctrine, whatever that might be. But any train of arguments which was contrived for Perkinism, which was just as applicable to it as to any other new doctrine in the same branch of science, and which was fully employed against its adversaries forty years since, might, in common charity, be suffered to slumber in the grave of Perkinism. Whether or not the following sentences, taken literally from the work of Mr. Perkins, were the originals of some of the idle propositions we hear bandied about from time to time, let those who listen judge.

The following is the test assumed for the new practice: "If diseases are really removed, as those persons who have practised extensively with the Tractors declare, it should seem there would be but little doubt of their being generally adopted; but if the numerous reports of their efficacy which have been published are forgeries, or are unfounded, the practice ought to be crushed." To this I merely add, it has been crushed.

The following sentence applies to that a priori judging and uncandid class of individuals who buy their dinners without tasting all the food there is in the market. "On all discoveries there are persons who, without descending to any inquiry into the truth, pretend to know, as it were by intuition, that newly asserted facts are founded in the grossest errors. These were those who knew that Harvey's report of the circulation of the blood was a preposterous and ridiculous suggestion, and in latter later days there were others who knew that Franklin deserved reproach for declaring that points were preferable to balls for protecting buildings from lightning."

Again: "This unwarrantable mode of offering assertion for proof, so unauthorized and even unprecedented except in the condemnation of a Galileo, the persecution of a Copernicus, and a few other acts of inquisitorial authority, in the times of ignorance and superstition, affords but a lamentable instance of one of his remarks, that this is far from being the Age of Reason."

"The most valuable medicines in the Materia Medica act on principles of which we are totally ignorant. None have ever yet been able to explain how opium produces sleep, or how bark cures intermittent fevers; and yet few, it is hoped, will be so absurd as to desist from the use of these important articles because they know nothing of the principle of their operations." Or if the argument is preferred, in the eloquent language of the Perkinistic poet:

"What though the CAUSES may not be explained,

> Since these EFFECTS are duly ascertained,
> Let not self-interest, prejudice, or pride,
> Induce mankind to set the means aside;
> Means which, though simple, are by
> Heaven designed to alleviate the woes of human kind."

This course of argument is so often employed, that it deserves to be expanded a little, so that its length and breadth may be fairly seen. A series of what are called facts is brought forward to prove some very improbable doctrine. It is objected by judicious people, or such as have devoted themselves to analogous subjects, that these assumed facts are in direct opposition to all that is known of the course of nature, that the universal experience of the past affords a powerful presumption against their truth, and that in proportion to the gravity of these objections, should be the number and competence of the witnesses. The answer is a ready one. What do we know of the mysteries of Nature? Do we understand the intricate machinery of the Universe? When to this is added the never-failing quotation,

> "There are more things in heaven and earth, Horatio,
> Than are dreamt of in your philosophy,"--
> the question is thought to be finally disposed of.

Take the case of astrology as an example. It is in itself strange and incredible that the relations of the heavenly bodies to each other at a given moment of time, perhaps half a century ago, should have anything to do with my success or misfortune in any undertaking of to-day. But what right have I to say it cannot be so? Can I bind the sweet influences of Pleiades, or loose the bands of Orion? I do not know by what mighty magic the planets roll in their fluid paths, confined to circles as unchanging as if they were rings of steel, nor why the great wave of ocean follows in a sleepless round upon the skirts of moonlight; nor cam I say from any certain knowledge that the phases of the heavenly bodies, or even the falling of the leaves of the forest, or the manner in which the sands lie upon the sea-shore, may not be knit up by invisible threads with the web of human destiny. There is a class of minds much more ready to believe that which is at first sight incredible, and because it is incredible, than what is generally thought reasonable. Credo quia impossibile est,--"I believe, because it is impossible,"--is an old paradoxical expression which might be literally applied to this tribe of persons. And they always succeed in finding something marvellous, to call out the exercise of their robust faith. The old Cabalistic teachers maintained that there was not a verse, line, word, or even letter in the Bible which had not a special efficacy either to defend the person who rightly employed it, or to injure his enemies; always provided the original Hebrew was made use of. In the hands of modern Cabalists every substance, no matter how inert, acquires wonderful medicinal virtues, provided it be used in a proper state of purity and subdivision.

I have already mentioned the motives attributed by the Perkinists to the Medical Profession, as preventing its members from receiving the new but unwelcome truths. This accusation is repeated in different forms and places, as, for instance, in the following passage: "Will the medical man who has spent much money and labor in the pursuit of the arcana of Physic, and on the exercise of which depends his support in life, proclaim the inefficacy of his art, and recommend a remedy to his patient which the most unlettered in society can employ as advantageously as himself? and a remedy, too, which, unlike the drops, the pills, the powders, etc., of the Materia Medica, is inconsumable, and ever in readiness to be employed in successive diseases?"

As usual with these people, much indignation was expressed at any parallel between their particular doctrine and practice and those of their exploded predecessors. "The motives," says the disinterested Mr. Perkins, "which must have impelled to this attempt at classing the METALLIC PRACTICE with the most paltry of empyrical projects, are but too thinly veiled to escape detection."

To all these arguments was added, as a matter of course, an appeal to the feelings of the benevolent in behalf of suffering humanity, in the shape of a notice that the poor would be treated gratis. It is pretty well understood that this gratuitous treatment of the poor does not necessarily imply an excess of benevolence, any more than the gratuitous distribution of a trader's shop-bills is an evidence of remarkable generosity; in short, that it is one of those things which honest men often do from the best motives, but which rogues and impostors never fail to announce as one of their special recommendations. It is astonishing to see how these things brighten up at the touch of Mr. Perkins's poet:

> "Ye worthy, honored, philanthropic few,
> The muse shall weave her brightest wreaths for you,
> Who in Humanity's bland cause unite,
> Nor heed the shaft by interest aimed or spite;
> Like the great Pattern of Benevolence,
> Hygeia's blessings to the poor dispense;
> And though opposed by folly's servile brood,
> ENJOY THE LUXURY OF DOING GOOD."

Having thus sketched the history of Perkinism in its days of prosperity; having seen how it sprung into being, and by what means it maintained its influence, it only remains to tell the brief story of its discomfiture and final downfall. The vast majority of the sensible part of the medical profession were contented, so far as we can judge, to let it die out of itself. It was in vain that the advocates of this invaluable discovery exclaimed over their perverse and interested obstinacy,--in vain that they called up the injured ghosts of Harvey, Galileo, and Copernicus to shame that unbelieving generation; the Baillies and the Heberdens,--men whose names have come down to us as synonymous with honor and wisdom,--bore their reproaches in meek silence, and left them unanswered to their fate. There were some others, however, who, believing the public to labor under a delusion, thought it worth while to see whether the charm would be broken by an open trial of its virtue, as compared with that of some less hallowed formula. It must be remembered that a peculiar value was attached to the Metallic Tractors, as made and patented by Mr. Perkins. Dr. Haygarth, of Bath, performed various experiments upon patients afflicted with different complaints,--the patients supposing that the real five-guinea Tractors were employed. Strange to relate, he obtained equally wonderful effects with Tractors of lead and of wood; with nails, pieces of bone, slate pencil, and tobacco-pipe. Dr. Alderson employed sham Tractors made of wood, and produced such effects upon five patients that they returned solemn thanks in church for their cures. A single specimen of these cases may stand for all of them. Ann Hill had suffered for some months from pain in the right arm and shoulder. The Tractors (wooden ones) were applied, and in the space of five minutes she expressed herself relieved in the following apostrophe: "Bless me! why, who could have thought it, that them little things could pull the pain from one. Well, to be sure, the longer one lives, the more one sees; ah, dear!"

These experiments did not result in the immediate extinction of Perkinism. Doubtless they were a great comfort to many obstinate unbelievers, and helped to settle some sceptical minds; but for the real Perkinistic enthusiasts, it may be questioned whether they would at that time have changed their opinion though one had risen from the dead to assure them that it was an error. It perished without violence, by an easy and natural process. Like the famous toy of Mongolfier, it rose by means of heated air,--the fevered breath of enthusiastic ignorance,--and when this grew cool, as it always does in a little while, it collapsed and fell.

And now, on reviewing the whole subject, how shall we account for the extraordinary prevalence of the belief in Perkinism among a portion of what is supposed to be the thinking part of the community?

Could the cures have been real ones, produced by the principle of ANIMAL MAGNETISM? To this it may be answered that the Perkinists ridiculed the idea of approximating Mesmer and the founder of their own doctrine, that nothing like the somnambulic condition seems to have followed the use of the Tractors, and that neither the exertion of the will nor the powers of the individual who operated seem to have been considered of any consequence. Besides, the absolute neglect into which the Tractors soon declined is good evidence that they were incapable of affording any considerable and permanent relief in the complaints for the cure of which they were applied.

Of course a large number of apparent cures were due solely to nature; which is true under every form of treatment, orthodox or empirical. Of course many persons experienced at least temporary relief from the strong impression made upon their minds by this novel and marvellous method of treatment.

Many, again, influenced by the sanguine hopes of those about them, like dying people, who often say sincerely, from day to day, that they are getting better, cheated themselves into a false and short-lived belief that they were cured; and as happens in such cases, the public never knew more than the first half of the story.

When it was said to the Perkinists, that whatever effects they produced were merely through the imagination, they declared (like the advocates of the ROYAL TOUCH and the UNGUENTUM ARMARIUM) that this explanation was sufficiently disproved by the fact of numerous and successful cures which had been witnessed in infants and brute animals. Dr. Haygarth replied to this, that "in these cases it is not the Patient, but the Observer, who is deceived by his own imagination," and that such may be the fact, we have seen in the case of the good lady who thought she had conjured away the spot from her friend's countenance, when it remained just as before.

As to the motives of the inventor and vender of the Tractors, the facts must be allowed to speak for themselves. But when two little bits of brass and iron are patented, as an invention, as the result of numerous experiments, when people are led, or even allowed, to infer that they are a peculiar compound, when they are artfully associated with a new and brilliant discovery (which then happened to be Galvanism), when they are sold at many hundred times their value, and the seller prints his opinion that a Hospital will suffer inconvenience, "unless it possesses many sets of the Tractors, and these placed in the hands of the patients to practise on each other," one cannot but suspect that they were contrived in the neighborhood of a wooden nutmeg factory; that legs of ham in that region are not made of the best mahogany; and that such as buy their cucumber seed in that vicinity have to wait for the fruit as long as the Indians for their crop of gunpowder.

The succeeding lecture will be devoted to an examination of the doctrines of Samuel Hahnemann and his disciples; doctrines which some consider new and others old; the common title of which is variously known as Ho-moeopathy, Homoe-op-athy, Homoeo-paith-y, or Hom'pathy, and the claims of which are considered by some as infinitely important, and by many as immeasurably ridiculous.

I wish to state, for the sake of any who may be interested in the subject, that I shall treat it, not by ridicule, but by argument; perhaps with great freedom, but with good temper and in peaceable language; with very little hope of reclaiming converts, with no desire of making enemies, but with a firm belief that its pretensions and assertions cannot stand before a single hour of calm investigation.

II.

It may be thought that a direct attack upon the pretensions of HOMOEOPA-THY is an uncalled-for aggression upon an unoffending doctrine and its peaceful advocates.
But a little inquiry will show that it has long assumed so hostile a position with respect to the Medical Profession, that any trouble I, or any other member of that profession, may choose to bestow upon it may be considered merely as a matter of self-defence. It began with an attempt to show the insignificance of all existing medical knowledge. It not only laid claim to wonderful powers of its own, but it declared the common practice to be attended with the most positively injurious effects, that by it acute diseases are aggravated, and chronic diseases rendered incurable. It has at various times brought forward collections of figures having the air of statistical documents, pretending to show a great proportional mortality among the patients of the Medical Profession, as compared with those treated according to its own rules. Not contented with choosing a name of classical origin for itself, it invented one for the whole community of innocent physicians, assuring them, to their great surprise, that they were all ALLOPATHISTS, whether they knew it or not, and including all the illustrious masters of the past, from Hippocrates down to Hunter, under the same gratuitous title. The line, then, has been drawn by the champions of the new doctrine; they have lifted the lance, they have sounded the charge, and are responsible for any little skirmishing which may happen.

But, independently of any such grounds of active resistance, the subject involves interests so disproportioned to its intrinsic claims, that it is no more than an act of humanity to give it a public examination. If the new doctrine is not truth, it is a dangerous, a deadly error. If it is a mere illusion, and acquires the same degree of influence that we have often seen obtained by other illusions, there is not one of my audience who may not have occasion to deplore the fatal credulity which listened to its promises.

I shall therefore undertake a sober examination of its principles, its facts, and some points of its history. The limited time at my disposal requires me to condense as much as possible what I have to say, but I shall endeavor to be plain and direct in expressing it. Not one statement shall be made which cannot be supported by unimpeachable reference: not one word shall be uttered which I am not as willing to print as to speak. I have no quibbles to utter, and I shall stoop to answer none; but, with full faith in the sufficiency of a plain statement of facts and reasons, I submit the subject to the discernment of my audience.

The question may be asked in the outset,--Have you submitted the doctrines you are professing to examine to the test of long-repeated and careful experiment; have you tried to see whether they were true or not? To this I answer, that it is abundantly evident, from what has often happened, that it would be of no manner of use for me to allege the results of any experiments I might have instituted. Again and again have the most explicit statements been made by the most competent persons of the utter failure of all their trials, and there were the same abundant explanations offered as used to be for the Unguentum Armarium and the Metallic Tractors. I could by no possibility perform any experiments the result of which could not be easily explained away so as to be of no conclusive significance. Besides, as arguments in favor of Homoeopathy are constantly addressed to the public in journals, pamphlets, and even lectures, by inexperienced dilettanti, the same channel must be open to all its opponents.

It is necessary, for the sake of those to whom the whole subject may be new, to give in the smallest possible compass the substance of the Homoeopathic Doctrine. Samuel Hahnemann, its founder, is a German physician, now living in Paris, [Hahnemann died in 1843.] at the age of eighty-seven years. In 1796 he published the first paper containing his peculiar notions; in 1805 his first work on the subject; in 1810 his somewhat famous "Organon of the Healing Art;" the next year what he called the "Pure Materia Medica;" and in 1828 his last work, the "Treatise on Chronic Diseases." He has therefore been writing at intervals on his favorite subject for nearly half a century.

The one great doctrine which constitutes the basis of Homoeopathy as a system is expressed by the Latin aphorism,

"SIMILIA SIBILIBUS CURANTUR,"

or like cures like, that is, diseases are cured by agents capable of producing symptoms resembling those found in the disease under treatment. A disease for Hahnemann consists essentially in a group of symptoms. The proper medicine for any disease is the one which is capable of producing a similar group of symptoms when given to a healthy person.

It is of course necessary to know what are the trains of symptoms excited by different substances, when administered to persons in health, if any such can be shown to exist. Hahnemann and his disciples give catalogues of the symptoms which they affirm were produced upon themselves or others by a large number of drugs which they submitted to experiment.

The second great fact which Hahnemann professes to have established is the efficacy of medicinal substances reduced to a wonderful degree of minuteness or dilution. The following account of his mode of preparing his medicines is from his work on Chronic Diseases, which has not, I believe, yet been translated into English. A grain of the substance, if it is solid, a drop if it is liquid, is to be added to about a third part of one hundred grains of sugar of milk in an unglazed porcelain capsule which has had the polish removed from the lower part of its cavity by rubbing it with wet sand; they are to be mingled for an instant with a bone or horn spatula, and then rubbed together for six minutes; then the mass is to be scraped together from the mortar and pestle, which is to take four minutes; then to be again rubbed for six minutes. Four minutes are then to be devoted to scraping the powder into a heap, and the second third of the hundred grains of sugar of milk to be added. Then they are to be stirred an instant and rubbed six minutes,--again to be scraped together four minutes and forcibly rubbed six; once more scraped together for four minutes, when the last third of the hundred grains of sugar of milk is to be added and mingled by stirring with the spatula; six minutes of forcible rubbing, four of scraping together, and six more (positively the last six) of rubbing, finish this part of the process.

Every grain of this powder contains the hundredth of a grain of the medicinal substance mingled with the sugar of milk. If, therefore, a grain of the powder just prepared is mingled with another hundred grains of sugar of milk, and the process just described repeated, we shall have a powder of which every grain contains the hundredth of the hundredth, or the ten thousandth part of a grain of the medicinal substance. Repeat the same process with the same quantity of fresh sugar of milk, and every grain of your powder will contain the millionth of a grain of the medicinal substance. When the powder is of this strength, it is ready to employ in the further solutions and dilutions to be made use of in practice.

A grain of the powder is to be taken, a hundred drops of alcohol are to be poured on it, the vial is to be slowly turned for a few minutes, until the powder is dissolved, and two shakes are to be given to it. On this point I will quote Hahnemann's own words. "A long experience and multiplied observations upon the sick lead me within the last few years to prefer giving only two shakes to medicinal liquids, whereas I formerly used to give ten." The process of dilution is carried on in the same way as the attenuation of the powder was done; each successive dilution with alcohol reducing the medicine to a hundredth part of the quantity of that which preceded it. In this way the dilution of the original millionth of a grain of medicine contained in the grain of powder operated on is carried successively to the billionth, trillionth, quadrillionth, quintillionth, and very often much higher fractional divisions. A dose of any of these medicines is a minute fraction of a drop, obtained by moistening with them one or more little globules of sugar, of which Hahnemann says it takes about two hundred to weigh a grain.

As an instance of the strength of the medicines prescribed by Hahnemann, I will mention carbonate of lime. He does not employ common chalk, but prefers a little portion of the friable part of an oystershell. Of this substance, carried to the sextillionth degree, so much as one or two globules of the size mentioned can convey is a common dose. But for persons of very delicate nerves it is proper that the dilution should be carried to the decillionth degree. That is, an important medicinal effect is to be expected from the two hundredth or hundredth part of the millionth of the millionth of the millionth of the millionth of the millionth of the millionth of the millionth of the millionth of the millionth of the millionth of a grain of oystershell. This is only the tenth degree of potency, but some of his disciples profess to have obtained palpable effects from "much higher dilutions."

The third great doctrine of Hahnemann is the following. Seven eighths at least of all chronic diseases are produced by the existence in the system of that infectious disorder known in the language of science by the appellation of PSORA, but to the less refined portion of the community by the name of ITCH. In the words of Hahnemann's "Organon," "This Psora is the sole true and fundamental cause that produces all the other countless forms of disease, which, under the names of nervous debility, hysteria, hypochondriasis, insanity, melancholy, idiocy, madness, epilepsy, and spasms of all kinds, softening of the bones, or rickets, scoliosis and cyphosis, caries, cancer, fungua haematodes, gout,--yellow jaundice and cyanosis, dropsy,--"

["The degrees of DILUTION must not be confounded with those of POTENCY. Their relations may be seen by this table:

1st dilution,--One hundredth of a drop or grain.
2d " One ten thousandth.
3d " One millionth, marked I.
4th " One hundred millionth.
5th " One ten thousand millionth.
6th " One million millionth, or one billionth, marked II.
7th " One hundred billionth.
8th " One ten thousand billionth.
9th " One million billionth, or one trillionth, marked III.
10th " One hundred trillionth.
11th " One ten thousand trillionth.
12th " One million trillionth, or one quadrillionth, marked

IV.,--and so on indefinitely.

The large figures denote the degrees of POTENCY.]

"gastralgia, epistaxis, haemoptysis,--asthma and suppuration of the lungs,--megrim, deafness, cataract and amaurosis,--paralysis, loss of sense, pains of every kind, etc., appear in our pathology as so many peculiar, distinct, and independent diseases."

For the last three centuries, if the same authority may be trusted, under the influence of the more refined personal habits which have prevailed, and the application of various external remedies which repel the affection from the skin; Psora has revealed itself in these numerous forms of internal disease, instead of appearing, as in former periods, under the aspect of an external malady.

These are the three cardinal doctrines of Hahnemann, as laid down in those standard works of Homoeopathy, the "Organon" and the "Treatise on Chronic Diseases."

Several other principles may be added, upon all of which he insists with great force, and which are very generally received by his disciples.

1. Very little power is allowed to the curative efforts of nature. Hahnemann goes so far as to say that no one has ever seen the simple efforts of nature effect the durable recovery of a patient from a chronic disease. In general, the Homoeopathist calls every recovery which happens under his treatment a cure.

2. Every medicinal substance must be administered in a state of the most perfect purity, and uncombined with any other. The union of several remedies in a single prescription destroys its utility, and, according to the "Organon," frequently adds a new disease.

3. A large number of substances commonly thought to be inert develop great medicinal powers when prepared in the manner already described; and a great proportion of them are ascertained to have specific antidotes in case their excessive effects require to be neutralized.

4. Diseases should be recognized, as far as possible, not by any of the common names imposed upon them, as fever or epilepsy, but as individual collections of symptoms, each of which differs from every other collection.

5. The symptoms of any complaint must be described with the most minute exactness, and so far as possible in the patient's own words. To illustrate the kind of circumstances the patient is expected to record, I will mention one or two from the 313th page of the "Treatise on Chronic Diseases,"--being the first one at which I opened accidentally.

"After dinner, disposition to sleep; the patient winks."

"After dinner, prostration and feeling of weakness (nine days after taking the remedy)."

This remedy was that same oyster-shell which is to be prescribed "fractions of the sextillionth or decillionth degree." According to Hahnemann, the action of a single dose of the size mentioned does not fully display itself in some cases until twenty-four or even thirty days after it is taken, and in such instances has not exhausted its good effects until towards the fortieth or fiftieth day,--before which time it would be absurd and injurious to administer a new remedy.

So much for the doctrines of Hahnemann, which have been stated without comment, or exaggeration of any of their features, very much as any adherent of his opinions might have stated them, if obliged to compress them into so narrow a space.

Does Hahnemann himself represent Homoeopathy as it now exists? He certainly ought to be its best representative, after having created it, and devoted his life to it for half a century. He is spoken of as the great physician of the time, in most, if not all Homoeopathic works. If he is not authority on the subject of his own doctrines, who is? So far as I am aware, not one tangible discovery in the so-called science has ever been ascribed to any other observer; at least, no general principle or law, of consequence enough to claim any prominence in Homoeopathic works, has ever been pretended to have originated with any of his illustrious disciples. He is one of the only two Homoeopathic writers with whom, as I shall mention, the Paris publisher will have anything to do upon his own account. The other is Jahr, whose Manual is little more than a catalogue of symptoms and remedies. If any persons choose to reject Hahnemann as not in the main representing Homoeopathy, if they strike at his authority, if they wink out of sight his deliberate and formally announced results, it is an act of suicidal rashness; for upon his sagacity and powers of observation, and experience, as embodied in his works, and especially in his Materia Medica, repose the foundations of Homoeopathy as a practical system.

So far as I can learn from the conflicting statements made upon the subject, the following is the present condition of belief.

1. All of any note agree that the law Similia similibus is the only fundamental principle in medicine. Of course if any man does not agree to this the name Homoeopathist can no longer be applied to him with propriety.

2. The belief in and employment of the infinitesimal doses is general, and in some places universal, among the advocates of Homoeopathy; but a distinct movement has been made in Germany to get rid of any restriction to the use of these doses, and to employ medicines with the same license as other practitioners.

3. The doctrine of the origin of most chronic diseases in Psora, notwithstanding Hahnemann says it cost him twelve years of study and research to establish the fact and its practical consequences, has met with great neglect and even opposition from very many of his own disciples.

It is true, notwithstanding, that, throughout most of their writings which I have seen, there runs a prevailing tone of great deference to Hahnemann's opinions, a constant reference to his authority, a general agreement with the minor points of his belief, and a pretence of harmonious union in a common faith. [Those who will take the trouble to look over Hull's Translation of Jahr's Manual may observe how little comparative space is given to remedies resting upon any other authority than that of Hahnemann.]

Many persons, and most physicians and scientific men, would be satisfied with the statement of these doctrines, and examine them no further. They would consider it vastly more probable that any observer in so fallacious and difficult a field of inquiry as medicine had been led into error, or walked into it of his own accord, than that such numerous and extraordinary facts had really just come to light. They would feel a right to exercise the same obduracy towards them as the French Institute is in the habit of displaying when memoirs or models are offered to it relating to the squaring of the circle or perpetual motion; which it is the rule to pass over without notice. They would feel as astronomers and natural philosophers must have felt when, some half a dozen years ago, an unknown man came forward, and asked for an opportunity to demonstrate to Arago and his colleagues that the moon and planets were at a distance of a little more than a hundred miles from the earth. And so they would not even look into Homoeopathy, though all its advocates should exclaim in the words of Mr. Benjamin Douglass Perkins, vender of the Metallic Tractors, that "On all discoveries there are persons who, without descending to any inquiry into the truth, pretend to know, as it were by intuition, that newly asserted facts are founded in the grossest errors." And they would lay their heads upon their pillows with a perfectly clear conscience, although they were assured that they were behaving in the same way that people of old did towards Harvey, Galileo, and Copernicus, the identical great names which were invoked by Mr. Benjamin Douglass Perkins.

But experience has shown that the character of these assertions is not sufficient to deter many, from examining their claims to belief. I therefore lean but very slightly on the extravagance and extreme apparent singularity of their pretensions. I might have omitted them, but on the whole it seemed more just to the claims of my argument to suggest the vast complication of improbabilities involved in the statements enumerated. Every one must of course judge for himself as to the weight of these objections, which are by no means brought forward as a proof of the extravagance of Homoeopathy, but simply as entitled to a brief consideration before the facts of the case are submitted to our scrutiny.

The three great asserted discoveries of Hahnemann are entirely unconnected with and independent of each other. Were there any natural relation between them it would seem probable enough that the discovery of the first would have led to that of the others. But assuming it to be a fact that diseases are cured by remedies capable of producing symptoms like their own, no manifest relation exists between this fact and the next assertion, namely, the power of the infinitesimal doses. And allowing both these to be true, neither has the remotest affinity to the third new doctrine, that which declares seven eighths of all chronic diseases to be owing to Psora.

This want of any obvious relation between Hahnemann's three cardinal doctrines appears to be self-evident upon inspection. But if, as is often true with his disciples, they prefer the authority of one of their own number, I will refer them to Dr. Trinks's paper on the present state of Homoeopathy in Europe, with which, of course, they are familiar, as his name is mentioned as one of the most prominent champions of their faith, in their American official organ. It would be a fact without a parallel in the history, not merely of medicine, but of science, that three such unconnected and astonishing discoveries, each of them a complete revolution of all that ages of the most varied experience had been taught to believe, should spring full formed from the brain of a single individual.

Let us look a moment at the first of his doctrines. Improbable though it may seem to some, there is no essential absurdity involved in the proposition that diseases yield to remedies capable of producing like symptoms. There are, on the other hand, some analogies which lend a degree of plausibility to the statement. There are well-ascertained facts, known from the earliest periods of medicine, showing that, under certain circumstances, the very medicine which, from its known effects, one would expect to aggravate the disease, may contribute to its relief. I may be permitted to allude, in the most general way, to the case in which the spontaneous efforts of an overtasked stomach are quieted by the agency of a drug which that organ refuses to entertain upon any terms. But that every cure ever performed by medicine should have been founded upon this principle, although without the knowledge of a physician; that the Homoeopathic axiom is, as Hahnemann asserts, "the sole law of nature in therapeutics," a law of which nothing more than a transient glimpse ever presented itself to the innumerable host of medical observers, is a dogma of such sweeping extent, and pregnant novelty, that it demands a corresponding breadth and depth of unquestionable facts to cover its vast pretensions.

So much ridicule has been thrown upon the pretended powers of the minute doses that I shall only touch upon this point for the purpose of conveying, by illustrations, some shadow of ideas far transcending the powers of the imagination to realize. It must be remembered that these comparisons are not matters susceptible of dispute, being founded on simple arithmetical computations, level to the capacity of any intelligent schoolboy. A person who once wrote a very small pamphlet made some show of objecting to calculations of thus kind, on the ground that the highest dilutions could easily be made with a few ounces of alcohol. But he should have remembered that at every successive dilution he lays aside or throws away ninety-nine hundredths of the fluid on which he is operating, and that, although he begins with a drop, he only prepares a millionth, billionth, trillionth, and similar fractions of it, all of which, added together, would constitute but a vastly minute portion of the drop with which he began. But now let us suppose we take one single drop of the Tincture of Camomile, and that the whole of this were to be carried through the common series of dilutions.

A calculation nearly like the following was made by Dr. Panvini, and may be readily followed in its essential particulars by any one who chooses.

For the first dilution it would take 100 drops of alcohol.

For the second dilution it would take 10;000 drops, or about a pint.

For the third dilution it would take 100 pints.

For the fourth dilution it would take 10,000 pints, or more than 1,000 gallons, and so on to the ninth dilution, which would take ten billion gallons, which he computed would fill the basin of Lake Agnano, a body of water two miles in circumference. The twelfth dilution would of course fill a million such lakes. By the time the seventeenth degree of dilution should be reached, the alcohol required would equal in quantity the waters of ten thousand Adriatic seas. Trifling errors must be expected, but they are as likely to be on one side as the other, and any little matter like Lake Superior or the Caspian would be but a drop in the bucket.

Swallowers of globules, one of your little pellets, moistened in the mingled waves of one million lakes of alcohol, each two miles in circumference, with which had been blended that one drop of Tincture of Camomile, would be of precisely the strength recommended for that medicine in your favorite Jahr's Manual, "against the most sudden, frightful, and fatal diseases!" [In the French edition of 1834, the proper doses of the medicines are mentioned, and Camomile is marked IV. Why are the doses omitted in Hull's Translation, except in three instances out of the whole two hundred remedies, notwithstanding the promise in the preface that "some remarks upon the doses used may be found at the head of each medicine"? Possibly because it makes no difference whether they are employed in one Homoeopathic dose or another; but then it is very singular that such precise directions were formerly given in the same work, and that Hahnemann's "experience" should have led him to draw the nice distinctions we have seen in a former part of this Lecture (p. 44).]

And proceeding on the common data, I have just made a calculation which shows that this single drop of Tincture of Camomile, given in the quantity ordered by Jahr's Manual, would have supplied every individual of the whole human family, past and present, with more than five billion doses each, the action of each dose lasting about four days.

Yet this is given only at the quadrillionth, or fourth degree of potency, and various substances are frequently administered at the decillionth or tenth degree, and occasionally at still higher attenuations with professed medicinal results. Is there not in this as great an exception to all the hitherto received laws of nature as in the miracle of the loaves and fishes? Ask this question of a Homoeopathist, and he will answer by referring to the effects produced by a very minute portion of vaccine matter, or the extraordinary diffusion of odors. But the vaccine matter is one of those substances called morbid poisons, of which it is a peculiar character to multiply themselves, when introduced into the system, as a seed does in the soil. Therefore the hundredth part of a grain of the vaccine matter, if no more than this is employed, soon increases in quantity, until, in the course of about a week, it is a grain or more, and can be removed in considerable drops. And what is a very curious illustration of Homoeopathy, it does not produce its most. characteristic effects until it is already in sufficient quantity not merely to be visible, but to be collected for further use. The thoughtlessness which can allow an inference to be extended from a product of disease possessing this susceptibility of multiplication when conveyed into the living body, to substances of inorganic origin, such as silex or sulphur, would be capable of arguing that a pebble may produce a mountain, because an acorn can become a forest.

As to the analogy to be found between the alleged action of the infinitely attenuated doses, and the effects of some odorous substances which possess the extraordinary power of diffusing their imponderable emanations through a very wide space, however it may be abused in argument, and rapidly as it evaporates on examination, it is not like that just mentioned, wholly without meaning. The fact of the vast diffusion of some odors, as that of musk or the rose, for instance, has long been cited as the most remarkable illustration of the divisibility of matter, and the nicety of the senses. And if this were compared with the effects of a very minute dose of morphia on the whole system, or the sudden and fatal impression of a single drop of prussic acid, or, with what comes still nearer, the poisonous influence of an atmosphere impregnated with invisible malaria, we should find in each of these examples an evidence of the degree to which nature, in some few instances, concentrates powerful qualities in minute or subtle forms of matter. But if a man comes to me with a pestle and mortar in his hand, and tells me that he will take a little speck of some substance which nobody ever thought to have any smell at all, as, for instance, a grain of chalk or of charcoal, and that he will, after an hour or two of rubbing and scraping, develop in a portion of it an odor which, if the whole grain were used, would be capable of pervading an apartment, a house, a village, a province, an empire, nay, the entire atmosphere of this broad planet upon which we tread; and that from each of fifty or sixty substances he can in this way develop a distinct and hitherto unknown odor: and if he tries to show that all this is rendered quite reasonable by the analogy of musk and roses, I shall certainly be justified in considering him incapable of reasoning, and beyond the reach of my argument. What if, instead of this, he professes to develop new and wonderful medicinal powers from the same speck of chalk or charcoal, in such proportions as would impregnate every pond, lake, river, sea, and ocean of our globe, and appeals to the same analogy in favor of the probability of his assertion.

All this may be true, notwithstanding these considerations. But so extraordinary would be the fact, that a single atom of substances which a child might swallow without harm by the teaspoonful could, by an easy mechanical process, be made to develop such inconceivable powers, that nothing but the strictest agreement of the most cautious experimenters, secured by every guaranty that they were honest and faithful, appealing to repeated experiments in public, with every precaution to guard against error, and with the most plain and peremptory results, should induce us to lend any credence to such pretensions.

The third doctrine, that Psora, the other name of which you remember, is the cause of the great majority of chronic diseases, is a startling one, to say the least. That an affection always recognized as a very unpleasant personal companion, but generally regarded as a mere temporary incommodity, readily yielding to treatment in those unfortunate enough to suffer from it, and hardly known among the better classes of society, should be all at once found out by a German physician to be the great scourge of mankind, the cause of their severest bodily and mental calamities, cancer and consumption, idiocy and madness, must excite our unqualified surprise. And when the originator of this singular truth ascribes, as in the page now open before me, the declining health of a disgraced courtier, the chronic malady of a bereaved mother, even the melancholy of the love-sick and slighted maiden, to nothing more nor less than the insignificant, unseemly, and almost unmentionable ITCH, does it not seem as if the very soil upon which we stand were dissolving into chaos, over the earthquake-heaving of discovery?

And when one man claims to have established these three independent truths, which are about as remote from each other as the discovery of the law of gravitation, the invention of printing, and that of the mariner's compass, unless the facts in their favor are overwhelming and unanimous, the question naturally arises, Is not this man deceiving himself, or trying to deceive others?

I proceed to examine the proofs of the leading ideas of Hahnemann and his school.

In order to show the axiom, similia similibus curantur (or like is cured by like), to be the basis of the healing art,--"the sole law of nature in therapeutics,"--it is necessary,

1. That the symptoms produced by drugs in healthy persons should be faithfully studied and recorded.

2. That drugs should be shown to be always capable of curing those diseases most like their own symptoms.

3. That remedies should be shown not to cure diseases when they do not produce symptoms resembling those presented in these diseases.

1. The effects of drugs upon healthy persons have been studied by Hahnemann and his associates. Their results were made known in his Materia Medica, a work in three large volumes in the French translation, published about eight years ago. The mode of experimentation appears to have been, to take the substance on trial, either in common or minute doses, and then to set down every little sensation, every little movement of mind or body, which occurred within many succeeding hours or days, as being produced solely by the substance employed. When I have enumerated some of the symptoms attributed to the power of the drugs taken, you will be able to judge how much value is to be ascribed to the assertions of such observers.

The following list was taken literally from the Materia Medica of Hahnemann, by my friend M. Vernois, for whose accuracy I am willing to be responsible. He has given seven pages of these symptoms, not selected, but taken at hazard from the French translation of the work. I shall be very brief in my citations.

"After stooping some time, sense of painful weight about the head upon resuming the erect posture."

"An itching, tickling sensation at the outer edge of the palm of the left hand, which obliges the person to scratch." The medicine was acetate of lime, and as the action of the globule taken is said to last twenty-eight days, you may judge how many such symptoms as the last might be supposed to happen.

Among the symptoms attributed to muriatic acid are these: a catarrh, sighing, pimples; "after having written a long time with the back a little bent over, violent pain in the back and shoulder-blades, as if from a strain,"--"dreams which are not remembered,--disposition to mental dejection,--wakefulness before and after midnight."

I might extend this catalogue almost indefinitely. I have not cited these specimens with any view to exciting a sense of the ridiculous, which many others of those mentioned would not fail to do, but to show that the common accidents of sensation, the little bodily inconveniences to which all of us are subject, are seriously and systematically ascribed to whatever medicine may have been exhibited, even in the minute doses I have mentioned, whole days or weeks previously.

To these are added all the symptoms ever said by anybody, whether deserving confidence or not, as I shall hereafter illustrate, to be produced by the substance in question.

The effects of sixty-four medicinal substances, ascertained by one or both of these methods, are enumerated in the Materia Medica of Hahnemann, which may be considered as the basis of practical Homoeopathy. In the Manual of Jahr, which is the common guide, so far as I know, of those who practise Homoeopathy in these regions, two hundred remedies are enumerated, many of which, however, have never been employed in practice. In at least one edition there were no means of distinguishing those which had been tried upon the sick from the others. It is true that marks have been added in the edition employed here, which serve to distinguish them; but what are we to think of a standard practical author on Materia Medica, who at one time omits to designate the proper doses of his remedies, and at another to let us have any means of knowing whether a remedy has ever been tried or not, while he is recommending its employment in the most critical and threatening diseases?

I think that, from what I have shown of the character of Hahnemann's experiments, it would be a satisfaction to any candid inquirer to know whether other persons, to whose assertions he could look with confidence, confirm these pretended facts. Now there are many individuals, long and well known to the scientific world, who have tried these experiments upon healthy subjects, and utterly deny that their effects have at all corresponded to Hahnemann's assertions.

I will take, for instance, the statements of Andral (and I am not referring to his well-known public experiments in his hospital) as to the result of his own trials. This distinguished physician is Professor of Medicine in the School of Paris, and one of the most widely known and valued authors upon practical and theoretical subjects the profession can claim in any country. He is a man of great kindness of character, a most liberal eclectic by nature and habit, of unquestioned integrity, and is called, in the leading article of the first number of the "Homoepathic Examiner," "an eminent and very enlightened allopathist." Assisted by a number of other persons in good health, he experimented on the effects of cinchona, aconite, sulphur, arnica, and the other most highly extolled remedies. His experiments lasted a year, and he stated publicly to the Academy of Medicine that they never produced the slightest appearance of the symptoms attributed to them. The results of a man like this, so extensively known as one of the most philosophical and candid, as well as brilliant of instructors, and whose admirable abilities and signal liberality are generally conceded, ought to be of great weight in deciding the question.

M. Double, a well-known medical writer and a physician of high standing in Paris, had occasion so long ago as 1801, before he had heard of Homoeopathy, to make experiments upon Cinchona, or Peruvian bark. He and several others took the drug in every kind of dose for four months, and the fever it is pretended by Hahnemann to excite never was produced.

M. Bonnet, President of the Royal Society of Medicine of Bordeaux, had occasion to observe many soldiers during the Peninsular War, who made use of Cinchona as a preservative against different diseases, but he never found it to produce the pretended paroxysms.

If any objection were made to evidence of this kind, I would refer to the express experiments on many of the Homoeopathic substances, which were given to healthy persons with every precaution as to diet and regimen, by M. Louis Fleury, without being followed by the slightest of the pretended consequences. And let me mention as a curious fact, that the same quantity of arsenic given to one animal in the common form of the unprepared powder, and to another after having been rubbed up into six hundred globules, offered no particular difference of activity in the two cases.

This is a strange contradiction to the doctrine of the development of what they call dynamic power, by means of friction and subdivision.

In 1835 a public challenge was offered to the best known Homoeopathic physician in Paris to select any ten substances asserted to produce the most striking effects; to prepare them himself; to choose one by lot without knowing which of them he had taken, and try it upon himself or any intelligent and devoted Homoeopathist, and, waiting his own time, to come forward and tell what substance had been employed. The challenge was at first accepted, but the acceptance retracted before the time of trial arrived.

From all this I think it fair to conclude that the catalogues of symptoms attributed in Homoeopathic works to the influence of various drugs upon healthy persons are not entitled to any confidence.

2. It is necessary to show, in the next place, that medicinal substances are always capable of curing diseases most like their own symptoms. For facts relating to this question we must look to two sources; the recorded experience of the medical profession in general, and the results of trials made according to Homoeopathic principles, and capable of testing the truth of the doctrine.

No person, that I am aware of, has ever denied that in some cases there exists a resemblance between the effects of a remedy and the symptoms of diseases in which it is beneficial. This has been recognized, as Hahnemann himself has shown, from the time of Hippocrates. But according to the records of the medical profession, as they have been hitherto interpreted, this is true of only a very small proportion of useful remedies. Nor has it ever been considered as an established truth that the efficacy of even these few remedies was in any definite ratio to their power of producing symptoms more or less like those they cured.

Such was the state of opinion when Hahnemann came forward with the proposition that all the cases of successful treatment found in the works of all preceding medical writers were to be ascribed solely to the operation of the Homoeopathic principle, which had effected the cure, although without the physician's knowledge that this was the real secret. And strange as it may seem, he was enabled to give such a degree of plausibility to this assertion, that any person not acquainted somewhat with medical literature, not quite familiar, I should rather say, with the relative value of medical evidence, according to the sources whence it is derived, would be almost frightened into the belief, at seeing the pages upon pages of Latin names he has summoned as his witnesses.

It has hitherto been customary, when examining the writings of authors of preceding ages, upon subjects as to which they were less enlightened than ourselves, and which they were very liable to misrepresent, to exercise some little discretion; to discriminate, in some measure, between writers deserving confidence and those not entitled to it. But there is not the least appearance of any such delicacy on the part of Hahnemann. A large majority of the names of old authors he cites are wholly unknown to science. With some of them I have been long acquainted, and I know that their accounts of diseases are no more to be trusted than their contemporary Ambroise Pare's stories of mermen, and similar absurdities. But if my judgment is rejected, as being a prejudiced one, I can refer to Cullen, who mentioned three of Hahnemann's authors in one sentence, as being "not necessarily bad authorities; but certainly such when they delivered very improbable events;" and as this was said more than half a century ago, it could not have had any reference to Hahnemann. But although not the slightest sign of discrimination is visible in his quotations,-- although for him a handful of chaff from Schenck is all the same thing as a measure of wheat from Morgagni,--there is a formidable display of authorities, and an abundant proof of ingenious researches to be found in each of the great works of Hahnemann with which I am familiar. [Some painful surmises might arise as to the erudition of Hahnemann's English Translator, who makes two individuals of "Zacutus, Lucitanus," as well as respecting that of the conductors of an American Homoeopathic periodical, who suffer the name of the world-renowned Cardanus to be spelt Cardamus in at least three places, were not this gross ignorance of course attributable only to the printer.]

It is stated by Dr. Leo-Wolf, that Professor Joerg, of Leipsic, has proved many of Hahnemann's quotations from old authors to be adulterate and false. What particular instances he has pointed out I have no means of learning. And it is probably wholly impossible on this side of the Atlantic, and even in most of the public libraries of Europe, to find anything more than a small fraction of the innumerable obscure publications which the neglect of grocers and trunkmakers has spared to be ransacked by the all-devouring genius of Homoeopathy. I have endeavored to verify such passages as my own library afforded me the means of doing. For some I have looked in vain, for want, as I am willing to believe, of more exact references. But this I am able to affirm, that, out of the very small number which I have been able, to trace back to their original authors, I have found two to be wrongly quoted, one of them being a gross misrepresentation.

The first is from the ancient Roman author, Caelius Aurelianus; the second from the venerable folio of Forestus. Hahnemann uses the following expressions,-- if he is not misrepresented in the English Translation of the 'Organon': "Asclepiades on one occasion cured an inflammation of the brain by administering a small quantity of wine." After correcting the erroneous reference of the Translator, I can find no such case alluded to in the chapter. But Caelius Aurelianus mentions two modes of treatment employed by Asclepiades, into both of which the use of wine entered, as being "in the highest degree irrational and dangerous." [Caelius Aurel. De Morb. Acut. et Chron. lib. I. cap. xv. not xvi. Amsterdam. Wetstein, 1755.]

In speaking of the oil of anise-seed, Hahnemann says that Forestus observed violent colic caused by its administration. But, as the author tells the story, a young man took, by the counsel of a surgeon, an acrid and virulent medicine, the name of which is not given, which brought on a most cruel fit of the gripes and colic. After this another surgeon was called, who gave him oil of anise-seed and wine, "which increased his suffering." [Observ. et Curat. Med. lib. XXI obs. xiii. Frankfort, 1614.] Now if this was the Homoeopathic remedy, as Hahnemann pretends, it might be a fair question why the young man was not cured by it. But it is a much graver question why a man who has shrewdness and learning enough to go so far after his facts, should think it right to treat them with such astonishing negligence or such artful unfairness.

Even if every word he had pretended to take from his old authorities were to be found in them, even if the authority of every one of these authors were beyond question, the looseness with which they are used to prove whatever Hahnemann chooses is beyond the bounds of credibility. Let me give one instance to illustrate the character of this man's mind. Hahnemann asserts, in a note annexed to the 110th paragraph of the "Organon," that the smell of the rose will cause certain persons to faint. And he says in the text that substances which produce peculiar effects of this nature on particular constitutions cure the same symptoms in people in general. Then in another note to the same paragraph he quotes the following fact from one of the last sources one would have looked to for medical information, the Byzantine Historians.

"It was by these means (i.e. Homoeopathically) that the Princess Eudosia with rose-water restored a person who had fainted!"

Is it possible that a man who is guilty of such pedantic folly as this,--a man who can see a confirmation of his doctrine in such a recovery as this,--a recovery which is happening every day, from a breath of air, a drop or two of water, untying a bonnet-string, loosening a stay-lace, and which can hardly help happening, whatever is done,--is it possible that a man, of whose pages, not here and there one, but hundreds upon hundreds are loaded with such trivialities, is the Newton, the Columbus, the Harvey of the nineteenth century!

The whole process of demonstration he employs is this. An experiment is instituted with some drug upon one or more healthy persons. Everything that happens for a number of days or weeks is, as we have seen, set down as an effect of the medicine. Old volumes are then ransacked promiscuously, and every morbid sensation or change that anybody ever said was produced by the drug in question is added to the list of symptoms. By one or both of these methods, each of the sixty-four substances enumerated by Hahnemann is shown to produce a very large number of symptoms, the lowest in his scale being ninety-seven, and the highest fourteen hundred and ninety-one. And having made out this list respecting any drug, a catalogue which, as you may observe in any Homoeopathic manual, contains various symptoms belonging to every organ of the body, what can be easier than to find alleged cures in every medical author which can at once be attributed to the Homoeopathic principle; still more if the grave of extinguished credulity is called upon to give up its dead bones as living witnesses; and worst of all, if the monuments of the past are to be mutilated in favor of "the sole law of Nature in therapeutics"?

There are a few familiar facts of which great use has been made as an entering wedge for the Homoeopathic doctrine. They have been suffered to pass current so long that it is time they should be nailed to the counter, a little operation which I undertake, with perfect cheerfulness, to perform for them.

The first is a supposed illustration of the Homoeopathic law found in the precept given for the treatment of parts which have been frozen, by friction with snow or similar means. But we deceive ourselves by names, if we suppose the frozen part to be treated by cold, and not by heat. The snow may even be actually warmer than the part to which it is applied. But even if it were at the same temperature when applied, it never did and never could do the least good to a frozen part, except as a mode of regulating the application of what? of heat. But the heat must be applied gradually, just as food must be given a little at a time to those perishing with hunger. If the patient were brought into a warm room, heat would be applied very rapidly, were not something interposed to prevent this, and allow its gradual admission. Snow or iced water is exactly what is wanted; it is not cold to the part; it is very possibly warm, on the contrary, for these terms are relative, and if it does not melt and let the heat in, or is not taken away, the part will remain frozen up until doomsday. Now the treatment of a frozen limb by heat, in large or small quantities, is not Homoeopathy.

The next supposed illustration of the Homoeopathic law is the alleged successful management of burns, by holding them to the fire. This is a popular mode of treating those burns which are of too little consequence to require any more efficacious remedy, and would inevitably get well of themselves, without any trouble being bestowed upon them. It produces a most acute pain in the part, which is followed by some loss of sensibility, as happens with the eye after exposure to strong light, and the ear after being subjected to very intense sounds. This is all it is capable of doing, and all further notions of its efficacy must be attributed merely to the vulgar love of paradox. If this example affords any comfort to the Homoeopathist, it seems as cruel to deprive him of it as it would be to convince the mistress of the smoke-jack or the flatiron that the fire does not literally "draw the fire out," which is her hypothesis.

But if it were true that frost-bites were cured by cold and burns by heat, it would be subversive, so far as it went, of the great principle of Homoeopathy.

For you will remember that this principle is that Like cures Like, and not that Same cures Same; that there is resemblance and not identity between the symptoms of the disease and those produced by the drug which cures it, and none have been readier to insist upon this distinction than the Homoeopathists themselves. For if Same cures Same, then every poison must be its own antidote,--which is neither a part of their theory nor their so-called experience. They have been asked often enough, why it was that arsenic could not cure the mischief which arsenic had caused, and why the infectious cause of small-pox did not remedy the disease it had produced, and then they were ready enough to see the distinction I have pointed out. O no! it was not the hair of the same dog, but only of one very much like him!

A third instance in proof of the Homoeopathic law is sought for in the acknowledged efficacy of vaccination. And how does the law apply to this? It is granted by the advocates of Homoeopathy that there is a resemblance between the effects of the vaccine virus on a person in health and the symptoms of small-pox. Therefore, according to the rule, the vaccine virus will cure the small-pox, which, as everybody knows, is entirely untrue. But it prevents small-pox, say the Homoeopathists. Yes, and so does small-pox prevent itself from ever happening again, and we know just as much of the principle involved in the one case as in the other. For this is only one of a series of facts which we are wholly unable to explain. Small-pox, measles, scarlet-fever, hooping-cough, protect those who have them once from future attacks; but nettle-rash and catarrh and lung fever, each of which is just as Homoeopathic to itself as any one of the others, have no such preservative power. We are obliged to accept the fact, unexplained, and we can do no more for vaccination than for the rest.

I come now to the most directly practical point connected with the subject, namely,--

What is the state of the evidence as to the efficacy of the proper Homoeopathic treatment in the cure of diseases.

As the treatment adopted by the Homoeopathists has been almost universally by means of the infinitesimal doses, the question of their efficacy is thrown open, in common with that of the truth of their fundamental axiom, as both are tested in practice.

We must look for facts as to the actual working of Homoeopathy to three sources.

1. The statements of the unprofessional public.
2. The assertions of Homoeopathic practitioners.
3. The results of trials by competent and honest physicians, not pledged to the system.

I think, after what we have seen of medical facts, as they are represented by incompetent persons, we are disposed to attribute little value to all statements of wonderful cures, coming from those who have never been accustomed to watch the caprices of disease, and have not cooled down their young enthusiasm by the habit of tranquil observation. Those who know nothing of the natural progress of a malady, of its ordinary duration, of its various modes of terminating, of its liability to accidental complications, of the signs which mark its insignificance or severity, of what is to be expected of it when left to itself, of how much or how little is to be anticipated from remedies, those who know nothing or next to nothing of all these things, and who are in a great state of excitement from benevolence, sympathy, or zeal for a new medical discovery, can hardly be expected to be sound judges of facts which have misled so many sagacious men, who have spent their lives in the daily study and observation of them. I believe that, after having drawn the portrait of defunct Perkinism, with its five thousand printed cures, and its million and a half computed ones, its miracles blazoned about through America, Denmark, and England; after relating that forty years ago women carried the Tractors about in their pockets, and workmen could not make them fast enough for the public demand; and then showing you, as a curiosity, a single one of these instruments, an odd one of a pair, which I obtained only by a lucky accident, so utterly lost is the memory of all their wonderful achievements; I believe, after all this, I need not waste time in showing that medical accuracy is not to be looked for in the florid reports of benevolent associations, the assertions of illustrious patrons, the lax effusions of daily journals, or the effervescent gossip of the tea-table.

Dr. Hering, whose name is somewhat familiar to the champions of Homoeopathy, has said that "the new healing art is not to be judged by its success in isolated cases only, but according to its success in general, its innate truth, and the incontrovertible nature of its innate principles."

We have seen something of "the incontrovertible nature of its innate principles," and it seems probable, on the whole, that its success in general must be made up of its success in isolated cases. Some attempts have been made, however, to finish the whole matter by sweeping statistical documents, which are intended to prove its triumphant success over the common practice.

It is well known to those who have had the good fortune to see the "Homoeopathic Examiner," that this journal led off, in its first number, with a grand display of everything the newly imported doctrine had to show for itself. It is well remarked, on the twenty-third page of this article, that "the comparison of bills of mortality among an equal number of sick, treated by divers methods, is a most poor and lame way to get at conclusions touching principles of the healing art." In confirmation of which, the author proceeds upon the twenty-fifth page to prove the superiority of the Homoeopathic treatment of cholera, by precisely these very bills of mortality. Now, every intelligent physician is aware that the poison of cholera differed so much in its activity at different times and, places, that it was next to impossible to form any opinion as to the results of treatment, unless every precaution was taken to secure the most perfectly corresponding conditions in the patients treated, and hardly even then. Of course, then, a Russian Admiral, by the name of Mordvinov, backed by a number of so-called physicians practising in Russian villages, is singularly competent to the task of settling the whole question of the utility of this or that kind of treatment; to prove that, if not more than eight and a half per cent. of those attacked with the disease perished, the rest owed their immunity to Hahnemann. I can remember when more than a hundred patients in a public institution were attacked with what, I doubt not, many Homoeopathic physicians (to say nothing of Homoeopathic admirals) would have called cholera, and not one of them died, though treated in the common way, and it is my firm belief that, if such a result had followed the administration of the omnipotent globules, it would have been in the mouth of every adept in Europe, from Quin of London to Spohr of Gandersheim. No longer ago than yesterday, in one of the most widely circulated papers of this city, there was published an assertion that the mortality in several Homoeopathic Hospitals was not quite five in a hundred, whereas, in what are called by the writer Allopathic Hospitals, it is said to be eleven in a hundred. An honest man should be ashamed of such an argumentum ad ignorantiam. The mortality of a hospital depends not merely on the treatment of the patients, but on the class of diseases it is in the habit of receiving, on the place where it is, on the season, and many other circumstances. For instance, there are many hospitals in the great cities of Europe that receive few diseases of a nature to endanger life, and, on the other hand, there are others where dangerous diseases are accumulated out of the common proportion. Thus, in the wards of Louis, at the Hospital of La Pitie, a vast number of patients in the last stages of consumption were constantly entering, to swell the mortality of that hospital. It was because he was known to pay particular attention to the diseases of the chest that patients laboring under those fatal affections to an incurable extent were so constantly coming in upon him. It is always a miserable appeal to the thoughtlessness of the vulgar, to allege the naked fact of the less comparative mortality in the practice of one hospital or of one physician than another, as an evidence of the superiority of their treatment. Other things being equal, it must always be expected that those institutions and individuals enjoying to the highest degree the confidence of the community will lose the largest proportion of their patients; for the simple reason that they will naturally be looked to by those suffering from the gravest class of diseases; that many, who know that they are affected with mortal disease, will choose to die under their care or shelter, while the subjects of trifling maladies, and merely troublesome symptoms, amuse themselves to any extent among the fancy practitioners. When, therefore, Dr. Mublenbein, as stated in the "Homoeopathic Examiner," and quoted in yesterday's "Daily Advertiser," asserts that the mortality among his patients is only one per cent. since he has practised Homoeopathy, whereas it was six per cent. when he employed the common mode of practice, I am convinced by this, his own statement, that the citizens of Brunswick, whenever they are seriously sick, take good care not to send for Dr. Muhlenbein!

It is evidently impossible that I should attempt, within the compass of a single lecture, any detailed examination of the very numerous cases reported in the Homoeopathic Treatises and Journals. Having been in the habit of receiving the French "Archives of Homoeopathic Medicine" until the premature decease of that Journal, I have had the opportunity of becoming acquainted somewhat with the style of these documents, and experiencing whatever degree of conviction they were calculated to produce. Although of course I do not wish any value to be assumed for my opinion, such as it is, I consider that you are entitled to hear it. So far, then, as I am acquainted with the general character of the cases reported by the Homoeopathic physicians, they would for the most part be considered as wholly undeserving a place in any English, French, or American periodical of high standing, if, instead of favoring the doctrine they were intended to support, they were brought forward to prove the efficacy of any common remedy administered by any common practitioner. There are occasional exceptions to this remark; but the general truth of it is rendered probable by the fact that these cases are always, or almost always, written with the single object of showing the efficacy of the medicine used, or the skill of the practitioner, and it is recognized as a general rule that such cases deserve very little confidence. Yet they may sound well enough, one at a time, to those who are not fully aware of the fallacies of medical evidence. Let me state a case in illustration. Nobody doubts that some patients recover under every form of practice. Probably all are willing to allow that a large majority, for instance, ninety in a hundred, of such cases as a physician is called to in daily practice, would recover, sooner or later, with more or less difficulty, provided nothing were done to interfere seriously with the efforts of nature.

Suppose, then, a physician who has a hundred patients prescribes to each of them pills made of some entirely inert substance, as starch, for instance. Ninety of them get well, or if he chooses to use such language, he cures ninety of them. It is evident, according to the doctrine of chances, that there must be a considerable number of coincidences between the relief of the patient and the administration of the remedy. It is altogether probable that there will happen two or three very striking coincidences out of the whole ninety cases, in which it would seem evident that the medicine produced the relief, though it had, as we assumed, nothing to do with it. Now suppose that the physician publishes these cases, will they not have a plausible appearance of proving that which, as we granted at the outset, was entirely false? Suppose that instead of pills of starch he employs microscopic sugarplums, with the five' million billion trillionth part of a suspicion of aconite or pulsatilla, and then publishes his successful cases, through the leaden lips of the press, or the living ones of his female acquaintances,--does that make the impression a less erroneous one? But so it is that in Homoeopathic works and journals and gossip one can never, or next to never, find anything but successful cases, which might do very well as a proof of superior skill, did it not prove as much for the swindling advertisers whose certificates disgrace so many of our newspapers. How long will it take mankind to learn that while they listen to "the speaking hundreds and units," who make the world ring with the pretended triumphs they have witnessed, the "dumb millions" of deluded and injured victims are paying the daily forfeit of their misplaced confidence!

I am sorry to see, also, that a degree of ignorance as to the natural course of diseases is often shown in these published cases, which, although it may not be detected by the unprofessional reader, conveys an unpleasant impression to those who are acquainted with the subject. Thus a young woman affected with jaundice is mentioned in the German "Annals of Clinical Homoeopathy" as having been cured in twenty-nine days by pulsatilla and nux vomica. Rummel, a well-known writer of the same school, speaks of curing a case of jaundice in thirty-four days by Homoeopathic doses of pulsatilla, aconite, and cinchona. I happened to have a case in my own household, a few weeks since, which lasted about ten days, and this was longer than I have repeatedly seen it in hospital practice, so that it was nothing to boast of.

Dr. Munneche of Lichtenburg in Saxony is called to a patient with sprained ankle who had been a fortnight under the common treatment. The patient gets well by the use of arnica in a little more than a month longer, and this extraordinary fact is published in the French "Archives of Homoeopathic Medicine."

In the same Journal is recorded the case of a patient who with nothing more, so far as any proof goes, than inluenza, gets down to her shop upon the sixth day.

And again, the cool way in which everything favorable in a case is set down by these people entirely to their treatment, may be seen in a case of croup reported in the "Homoeopathic Gazette" of Leipsic, in which leeches, blistering, inhalation of hot vapor, and powerful internal medicine had been employed, and yet the merit was all attributed to one drop of some Homoeopathic fluid.

I need not multiply these quotations, which illustrate the grounds of an opinion which the time does not allow me to justify more at length; other such cases are lying open before me; there is no end to them if more were wanted; for nothing is necessary but to look into any of the numerous broken-down Journals of Homoeopathy, the volumes of which may be found on the shelves of those curious in such matters.

A number of public trials of Homoeopathy have been made in different parts of the world. Six of these are mentioned in the Manifesto of the "Homoeopathic Examiner." Now to suppose that any trial can absolutely silence people, would be to forget the whole experience of the past. Dr. Haygarth and Dr. Alderson could not stop the sale of the five-guinea Tractors, although they proved that they could work the same miracles with pieces of wood and tobacco-pipe. It takes time for truth to operate as well as Homoeopathic globules. Many persons thought the results of these trials were decisive enough of the nullity of the treatment; those who wish to see the kind of special pleading and evasion by which it is attempted to cover results which, stated by the "Homoeopathic Examiner" itself, look exceedingly like a miserable failure, may consult the opening flourish of that Journal. I had not the intention to speak of these public trials at all, having abundant other evidence on the point. But I think it best, on the whole, to mention two of them in a few words,--that instituted at Naples and that of Andral.

There have been few names in the medical profession, for the last half century, so widely known throughout the world of science as that of M. Esquirol, whose life was devoted to the treatment of insanity, and who was without a rival in that department of practical medicine. It is from an analysis communicated by him to the "Gazette Medicale de Paris" that I derive my acquaintance with the account of the trial at Naples by Dr. Panvini, physician to the Hospital della Pace. This account seems to be entirely deserving of credit. Ten patients were set apart, and not allowed to take any medicine at all,--much against the wish of the Homoeopathic physician. All of them got well, and of course all of them would have been claimed as triumphs if they had been submitted to the treatment. Six other slight cases (each of which is specified) got well under the Homoeopathic treatment, none of its asserted specific effects being manifested.

All the rest were cases of grave disease; and so far as the trial, which was interrupted about the fortieth day, extended, the patients grew worse, or received no benefit. A case is reported on the page before me of a soldier affected with acute inflammation in the chest, who took successively aconite, bryonia, nux vomica, and pulsatilla, and after thirty-eight days of treatment remained without any important change in his disease. The Homoeopathic physician who treated these patients was M. de Horatiis, who had the previous year been announcing his wonderful cures. And M. Esquirol asserted to the Academy of Medicine in 1835, that this M. de Horatiis, who is one of the prominent personages in the "Examiner's" Manifesto published in 1840, had subsequently renounced Homoeopathy. I may remark, by the way, that this same periodical, which is so very easy in explaining away the results of these trials, makes a mistake of only six years or a little more as to the time when this at Naples was instituted.

M. Andral, the "eminent and very enlightened allopathist" of the "Homoeopathic Examiner," made the following statement in March, 1835, to the Academy of Medicine: "I have submitted this doctrine to experiment; I can reckon at this time from one hundred and thirty to one hundred and forty cases, recorded with perfect fairness, in a great hospital, under the eye of numerous witnesses; to avoid every objection--I obtained my remedies of M. Guibourt, who keeps a Homoeopathic pharmacy, and whose strict exactness is well known; the regimen has been scrupulously observed, and I obtained from the sisters attached to the hospital a special regimen, such as Hahnemann orders. I was told, however, some months since, that I had not been faithful to all the rules of the doctrine. I therefore took the trouble to begin again; I have studied the practice of the Parisian Homoeopathists, as I had studied their books, and I became convinced that they treated their patients as I had treated mine, and I affirm that I have been as rigorously exact in the treatment as any other person."

And he expressly asserts the entire nullity of the influence of all the Homoeopathic remedies tried by him in modifying, so far as he could observe, the progress or termination of diseases. It deserves notice that he experimented with the most boasted substances,--cinchona, aconite, mercury, bryonia, belladonna. Aconite, for instance, he says he administered in more than forty cases of that collection of feverish symptoms in which it exerts so much power, according to Hahnemann, and in not one of them did it have the slightest influence, the pulse and heat remaining as before.

These statements look pretty honest, and would seem hard to be explained away, but it is calmly said that he "did not know enough of the method to select the remedies with any tolerable precision." ["Homoeopathic Examiner, vol. i. p. 22.]

"Nothing is left to the caprice of the physician." (In a word, instead of being dependent upon blind chance, that there is an infallible law, guided by which; the physician MUST select the proper remedies.') ['Ibid.,' in a notice of Menzel's paper.] Who are they that practice Homoeopathy, and say this of a man with the Materia Medica of Hahnemann lying before him? Who are they that send these same globules, on which he experimented, accompanied by a little book, into families, whose members are thought competent to employ them, when they deny any such capacity to a man whose life has been passed at the bedside of patients, the most prominent teacher in the first Medical Faculty in the world, the consulting physician of the King of France, and one of the most renowned practical writers, not merely of his nation, but of his age? I leave the quibbles by which such persons would try to creep out from under the crushing weight of these conclusions to the unfortunates who suppose that a reply is equivalent to an answer.

Dr. Baillie, one of the physicians in the great Hotel Dieu of Paris, invited two Homoeopathic practitioners to experiment in his wards. One of these was Curie, now of London, whose works are on the counters of some of our bookstores, and probably in the hands of some of my audience. This gentleman, whom Dr. Baillie declares to be an enlightened man, and perfectly sincere in his convictions, brought his own medicines from the pharmacy which furnished Hahnemann himself, and employed them for four or five months upon patients in his ward, and with results equally unsatisfactory, as appears from Dr. Baillie's statement at a meeting of the Academy of Medicine. And a similar experiment was permitted by the Clinical Professor of the Hotel Dieu of Lyons, with the same complete failure.

But these are old and prejudiced practitioners. Very well, then take the statement of Dr. Fleury, a most intelligent young physician, who treated homoeopathically more than fifty patients, suffering from diseases which it was not dangerous to treat in this way, taking every kind of precaution as to regimen, removal of disturbing influences, and the state of the atmosphere, insisted upon by the most vigorous partisans of the doctrine, and found not the slightest effect produced by the medicines. And more than this, read nine of these cases, which he has published, as I have just done, and observe the absolute nullity of aconite, belladonna, and bryonia, against the symptoms over which they are pretended to exert such palpable, such obvious, such astonishing influences. In the view of these statements, it is impossible not to realize the entire futility of attempting to silence this asserted science by the flattest and most peremptory results of experiment. Were all the hospital physicians of Europe and America to devote themselves, for the requisite period, to this sole pursuit, and were their results to be unanimous as to the total worthlessness of the whole system in practice, this slippery delusion would slide through their fingers without the slightest discomposure, when, as they supposed, they had crushed every joint in its tortuous and trailing body.

3. I have said, that to show the truth of the Homoeopathic doctrine, as announced by Hahnemann, it would be necessary to show, in the third place, that remedies never cure diseases when they are not capable of producing similar symptoms! The burden of this somewhat comprehensive demonstration lying entirely upon the advocates of this doctrine, it may be left to their mature reflections.

It entered into my original plan to treat of the doctrine relating to Psora, or itch,--an almost insane conception, which I am glad to get rid of, for this is a subject one does not care to handle without gloves. I am saved this trouble, however, by finding that many of the disciples of Hahnemann, those disciples the very gospel of whose faith stands upon his word, make very light of his authority on this point, although he himself says, "It has cost me twelve years of study and research to trace out the source of this incredible number of chronic affections, to discover this great truth, which remained concealed from all my predecessors and contemporaries, to establish the basis of its demonstration, and find out, at the same time, the curative medicines that were fit to combat this hydra in all its different forms."

But, in the face of all this, the following remarks are made by Wolff, of Dresden, whose essays, according to the editor of the "Homoeopathic Examiner," "represent the opinions of a large majority of Homoeopathists in Europe."

"It cannot be unknown to any one at all familiar with Homoeopathic literature, that Hahnemann's idea of tracing the large majority of chronic diseases to actual itch has met with the greatest opposition from Homoeopathic physicians themselves." And again, "If the Psoric theory has led to no proper schism, the reason is to be found in the fact that it is almost without any influence in practice."

We are told by Jahr, that Dr. Griesselich, "Surgeon to the Grand Duke of Baden," and a "distinguished" Homocopathist, actually asked Hahnemann for the proof that chronic diseases, such as dropsy, for instance, never arise from any other cause than itch; and that, according to common report, the venerable sage was highly incensed (fort courrouce) with Dr. Hartmann, of Leipsic, another "distinguished" Homoeopathist, for maintaining that they certainly did arise from other causes.

And Dr. Fielitz, in the "Homoeopathic Gazette" of Leipsic, after saying, in a good-natured way, that Psora is the Devil in medicine, and that physicians are divided on this point into diabolists and exorcists, declares that, according to a remark of Hahnemann, the whole civilized world is affected with Psora. I must therefore disappoint any advocate of Hahnemann who may honor me with his presence, by not attacking a doctrine on which some of the disciples of his creed would be very happy to have its adversaries waste their time and strength. I will not meddle with this excrescence, which, though often used in time of peace, would be dropped, like the limb of a shell-fish, the moment it was assailed; time is too precious, and the harvest of living extravagances nods too heavily to my sickle, that I should blunt it upon straw and stubble.

I will close the subject with a brief examination of some of the statements made in Homoeopathic works, and more particularly in the brilliant Manifesto of the

"Examiner," before referred to. And first, it is there stated under the head of "Homoeopathic Literature," that "SEVEN HUNDRED volumes have been issued from the press developing the peculiarities of the system, and many of them possessed of a scientific character that savans know well how to respect." If my assertion were proper evidence in the case, I should declare, that, having seen a good many of these publications, from the year 1834, when I bought the work of the Rev. Thomas Everest, [Dr. Curie speaks of this silly pamphlet as having been published in 1835.] to within a few weeks, when I received my last importation of Homaeopathic literature, I have found that all, with a very few exceptions, were stitched pamphlets varying from twenty or thirty pages to somewhat less than a hundred, and generally resembling each other as much as so many spelling-books.

But not being evidence in the case, I will give you the testimony of Dr. Trinks, of Dresden, who flourishes on the fifteenth page of the same Manifesto as one of the most distinguished among the Homoeopathists of Europe. I translate the sentence literally from the "Archives de la Medecine Homoeopathique."

"The literature of Homoeopathy, if that honorable name must be applied to all kinds of book-making, has been degraded to the condition of the humblest servitude. Productions without talent, without spirit, without discrimination, flat and pitiful eulogies, exaggerations surpassing the limits of the most robust faith, invectives against such as dared to doubt the dogmas which had been proclaimed, or catalogues of remedies; of such materials is it composed! From distance to distance only, have appeared some memoirs useful to science or practice, which appear as so many green oases in the midst of this literary desert."

It is a very natural as well as a curious question to ask, What has been the success of Homoeopathy in the different countries of Europe, and what is its present condition?

The greatest reliance of the advocates of Homoeopathy is of course on Germany. We know very little of its medical schools, its medical doctrines, or its medical men, compared with those of England and France. And, therefore, when an intelligent traveller gives a direct account from personal inspection of the miserable condition of the Homoeopathic hospital at Leipsic, the first established in Europe, and the first on the list of the ever-memorable Manifesto, it is easy enough answer or elude the fact by citing various hard names of "distinguished" practitioners, which sound just as well to the uninformed public as if they were Meckel, or Tiedemann, or Langenbeck. Dr. Leo-Wolf, who, to be sure, is opposed to Homoeopathy, but who is a scholar, and ought to know something of his own countrymen, assures us that "Dr. Kopp is the only German Homoeopathist, if we can call him so, who has been distinguished as an author and practitioner before he examined this method." And Dr. Lee, the same gentleman in whose travels the paragraph relating to the Leipsic Hospital is to be found, says the same thing. And I will cheerfully expose myself to any impertinent remark which it might suggest, to assure my audience that I never heard or saw one authentic Homoeopathic name of any country in Europe, which I had ever heard mentioned before as connected with medical science by a single word or deed sufficient to make it in any degree familiar to my ears, unless Arnold of Heidelberg is the anatomist who discovered a little nervous centre, called the otic ganglion. But you need ask no better proof of who and what the German adherents of this doctrine must be, than the testimony of a German Homoeopathist as to the wretched character of the works they manufacture to enforce its claims.

As for the act of this or that government tolerating or encouraging Homoeopathy, every person of common intelligence knows that it is a mere form granted or denied according to the general principles of policy adopted in different states, or the degree of influence which some few persons who have adopted it may happen to have at court. What may be the value of certain pompous titles with which many of the advocates of Homoeopathy are honored, it might be disrespectful to question. But in the mean time the judicious inquirer may ponder over an extract which I translate from a paper relating to a personage well known to the community as Williams the Oculist, with whom I had the honor of crossing the Atlantic some years since, and who himself handed me two copies of the paper in question.

"To say that he was oculist of Louis XVIII. and of Charles X., and that he now enjoys the same title with respect to His Majesty, Louis Philippe, and the King of the Belgians, is unquestionably to say a great deal; and yet it is one of the least of his titles to public confidence. His reputation rests upon a basis more substantial even than the numerous diplomas with which he is provided, than the membership of the different medical societies which have chosen him as their associate," etc., etc.

And as to one more point, it is time that the public should fully understand that the common method of supporting barefaced imposture at the present day, both in Europe and in this country, consists in trumping up "Dispensaries," "Colleges of Health," and other advertising charitable clap-traps, which use the poor as decoy-ducks for the rich, and the proprietors of which have a strong predilection for the title of "Professor." These names, therefore, have come to be of little or no value as evidence of the good character, still less of the high pretensions of those who invoke their authority. Nor does it follow, even when a chair is founded in connection with a well-known institution, that it has either a salary or an occupant; so that it may be, and probably is, a mere harmless piece of toleration on the part of the government if a Professorship of Homoeopathy is really in existence at Jena or Heidelberg. And finally, in order to correct the error of any who might suppose that the whole Medical Profession of Germany has long since fallen into the delusions of Hahnemann, I will quote two lines which a celebrated anatomist and surgeon (whose name will occur again in this lecture in connection with a very pleasing letter) addressed to the French Academy of Medicine in 1835. "I happened to be in Germany some months since, at a meeting of nearly six hundred physicians; one of them wished to bring up the question of Homoeopathy; they would not even listen to him." This may have been very impolite and bigoted, but that is not precisely the point in reference to which I mention the circumstance.

But if we cannot easily get at Germany, we can very easily obtain exact information from France and England. I took the trouble to write some months ago to two friends in Paris, in whom I could place confidence, for information upon the subject. One of them answered briefly to the effect that nothing was said about it. When the late Curator of the Lowell Institute, at his request, asked about the works upon the subject, he was told that they had remained a long time on the shelves quite unsalable, and never spoken of.

The other gentleman, [Dr. Henry T. Bigelow, now Professor of Surgery in Harvard University] whose name is well known to my audience, and who needs no commendation of mine, had the kindness to procure for me many publications upon the subject, and some information which sets the whole matter at rest, so far as Paris is concerned. He went directly to the Baillieres, the principal and almost the only publishers of all the Homoeopathic books and journals in that city. The following facts were taken by him from the account-books of this publishing firm. Four Homoeopathic Journals have been published in Paris; three of them by the

Baillieres.

The reception they met with may be judged of by showing the number of subscribers to each on the books of the publishing firm.

A Review published by some other house, which lasted one year, and had about fifty subscribers, appeared in 1834, 1835.

There were only four Journals of Homoeopathy ever published in Paris. The Baillieres informed my correspondent that the sale of Homoeopathic books was much less than formerly, and that consequently they should undertake to publish no new books upon the subject, except those of Jahr or Hahnemann. "This man," says my correspondent,--referring to one of the brothers,--"the publisher and headquarters of Homoeopathy in Paris, informs me that it is going down in England and Germany as well as in Paris." For all the facts he had stated he pledged himself as responsible.

Homoeopathy was in its prime in Paris, he said, in 1836 and 1837, and since then has been going down.

Louis told my correspondent that no person of distinction in Paris had embraced Homoeopathy, and that it was declining. If you ask who Louis is, I refer you to the well-known Homoeopathist, Peschier of Geneva, who says, addressing him, "I respect no one more than yourself; the feeling which guides your researches, your labors, and your pen, is so honorable and rare, that I could not but bow down before it; and I own, if there were any allopathist who inspired me with higher veneration, it would be him and not yourself whom I should address."

Among the names of "Distinguished Homoeopathists," however, displayed in imposing columns, in the index of the "Homoeopathic Examiner," are those of MARJOLIN, AMUSSAT, and BRESCHET, names well known to the world of science, and the last of them identified with some of the most valuable contributions which anatomical knowledge has received since the commencement of the present century. One Dr. Chrysaora, who stands sponsor for many facts in that Journal, makes the following statement among the rest: "Professors, who are esteemed among the most distinguished of the Faculty (Faculty de Medicine), both as to knowledge and reputation, have openly confessed the power of Homoeopathia in forms of disease where the ordinary method of practice proved totally insufficient. It affords me the highest pleasure to select from among these gentlemen, Marjolin,

Amussat, and Breschet."

Here is a literal translation of an original letter, now in my possession, from one of these Homoeopathists to my correspondent:--

"DEAR SIR, AND RESPECTED PROFESSIONAL BROTHER:

"You have had the kindness to inform me in your letter that a new American Journal, the 'New World,' has made use of my name in support of the pretended Homoeopathic doctrines, and that I am represented as one of the warmest partisans of Homoeopathy in France.

"I am vastly surprised at the reputation manufactured for me upon the new continent; but I am obliged, in deference to truth, to reject it with my whole energy. I spurn far from me everything which relates to that charlatanism called Homoeopathy, for these pretended doctrines cannot endure the scrutiny of wise and enlightened persons, who are guided by honorable sentiments in the practice of the noblest of arts.

"PARIS, 3d November, 1841
"I am, etc., etc.,
"G. BRESCHET,

"Professor in the Faculty of Medicine, Member of the Institute, Surgeon of Hotel Dieu, and Consulting Surgeon to the King, etc." [I first saw M. Breschet's name mentioned in that Journal]

Concerning Amussat, my correspondent writes, that he was informed by Madame Hahnemann, who converses in French more readily than her husband, and therefore often speaks for him, that "he was not a physician, neither Homoeopathist nor Allopathist, but that he was the surgeon of their own establishment; that is, performed as a surgeon all the operations they had occasion for in their practice."

I regret not having made any inquiries as to Marjolin, who, I doubt not, would strike his ponderous snuff-box until it resounded like the Grecian horse, at hearing such a doctrine associated with his respectable name. I was not aware, when writing to Paris, that this worthy Professor, whose lectures I long attended, was included in these audacious claims; but after the specimens I have given of the accuracy of the foreign correspondence of the "Homoeopathic Examiner," any further information I might obtain would seem so superfluous as hardly to be worth the postage.

Homoeopathy may be said, then, to be in a sufficiently miserable condition in Paris. Yet there lives, and there has lived for years, the illustrious Samuel Hahnemann, who himself assured my correspondent that no place offered the advantages of Paris in its investigation, by reason of the attention there paid to it.

In England, it appears by the statement of Dr. Curie in October, 1839, about eight years after its introduction into the country, that there were eighteen Homoeopathic physicians in the United Kingdom, of whom only three were to be found out of London, and that many of these practised Homoeopathy in secret.

It will be seen, therefore, that, according to the recent statement of one of its leading English advocates, Homoeopathy had obtained not quite half as many practical disciples in England as Perkinism could show for itself in a somewhat less period from the time of its first promulgation in that country.

Dr. Curie's letter, dated London, October 30, 1839, says there is "one in Dublin, Dr. Luther; at Glasgow, Dr. Scott." The "distinguished" Chrysaora writes from Paris, dating October 20, 1839, "On the other hand, Homoeopathy is commencing to make an inroad into England by the way of Ireland. At Dublin, distinguished physicians have already embraced the new system, and a great part of the nobility and gentry of that city have emancipated themselves from the English fashion and professional authority."

But the Marquis of Anglesea and Sir Edward Lytton Bulwer patronize Homoeopathy; the Queen Dowager Adelaide has been treated by a Homoeopathic physician. "Jarley is the delight of the nobility and gentry." "The Royal Family are the patrons of Jarley."

Let me ask if a Marquis and a Knight are better than two Lords, and if the Dowager of Royalty is better than Royalty itself, all of which illustrious dignities were claimed in behalf of Benjamin Douglass Perkins?

But if the balance is thought too evenly suspended in this case, another instance can be given in which the evidence of British noblemen and their ladies is shown to be as valuable in establishing the character of a medical man or doctrine, as would be the testimony of the Marquis of Waterford concerning the present condition and prospects of missionary enterprise. I have before me an octavo volume of more than four hundred pages, in which, among much similar matter, I find highly commendatory letters from the Marchioness of Ormond, Lady Harriet Kavanagh, the Countess of Buckinghamshire, the Right Hon. Viscount Ingestre, M. P., and the Most Noble, the Marquis of Sligo,--all addressed to "John St. John Long, Esq," a wretched charlatan, twice tried for, and once convicted of, manslaughter at the Old Bailey.

This poor creature, too, like all of his tribe, speaks of the medical profession as a great confederation of bigoted monopolists. He, too, says that "If an innovator should appear, holding out hope to those in despair, and curing disorders which the faculty have recorded as irremediable, he is at once, and without inquiry, denounced as an empiric and an impostor." He, too, cites the inevitable names of Galileo and Harvey, and refers to the feelings excited by the great discovery of Jenner. From the treatment of the great astronomer who was visited with the punishment of other heretics by the ecclesiastical authorities of a Catholic country some centuries since, there is no very direct inference to be drawn to the medical profession of the present time. His name should be babbled no longer, after having been placarded for the hundredth time in the pages of St. John Long. But if we are doomed to see constant reference to the names of Harvey and Jenner in every worthless pamphlet containing the prospectus of some new trick upon the public, let us, once for all, stare the facts in the face, and see how the discoveries of these great men were actually received by the medical profession.

In 1628, Harvey published his first work upon the circulation. His doctrines were a complete revolution of the prevailing opinions of all antiquity. They immediately found both champions and opponents; of which last, one only, Riolanus, seemed to Harvey worthy of an answer, on account of his "rank, fame, and learning." Controversy in science, as in religion, was not, in those days, carried on with all the courtesy which our present habits demand, and it is possible that some hard words may have been applied to Harvey, as it is very certain that he used the most contemptuous expressions towards others.

Harvey declares in his second letter to Riolanus, "Since the first discovery of the circulation, hardly a day, or a moment, has passed without my hearing it both well and ill spoken of; some attack it with great hostility, others defend it with high encomiums; one party believe that I have abundantly proved the truth of the doctrine against all the weight of opposing arguments, by experiments, observations, and dissections; others think it not yet sufficiently cleared up, and free from objections." Two really eminent Professors, Plempius of Louvain, and Walaeus of Leyden, were among its early advocates.

The opinions sanctioned by the authority of long ages, and the names of Hippocrates and Galen, dissolved away, gradually, but certainly, before the demonstrations of Harvey. Twenty-four years after the publication of his first work, and six years before his death, his bust in marble was placed in the Hall of the College of Physicians, with a suitable inscription recording his discoveries.

Two years after this he was unanimously invited to accept the Presidency of that body; and he lived to see his doctrine established, and all reputable opposition withdrawn.

There were many circumstances connected with the discovery of Dr. Jenner which were of a nature to excite repugnance and opposition. The practice of inoculation for the small-pox had already disarmed that disease of many of its terrors. The introduction of a contagious disease from a brute creature into the human system naturally struck the public mind with a sensation of disgust and apprehension, and a part of the medical public may have shared these feelings. I find that Jenner's discovery of vaccination was made public in June, 1798. In July of the same year the celebrated surgeon, Mr. Cline, vaccinated a child with virus received from Dr. Jenner, and in communicating the success of this experiment, he mentions that Dr. Lister, formerly of the Small-Pox Hospital, and himself, are convinced of the efficacy of the cow-pox. In November of the same year, Dr. Pearson published his "Inquiry," containing the testimony of numerous practitioners in different parts of the kingdom, to the efficacy of the practice. Dr. HAYGARTH, who was so conspicuous in exposing the follies of Perkinism, was among the very earliest to express his opinion in favor of vaccination. In 1801, Dr. Lettsom mentions the circumstance "as being to the honor of the medical professors, that they have very generally encouraged this salutary practice, although it is certainly calculated to lessen their pecuniary advantages by its tendency to extirpate a fertile source of professional practice."

In the same year the Medical Committee of Paris spoke of vaccination in a public letter, as "the most brilliant and most important discovery of the eighteenth century." The Directors of a Society for the Extermination of the Small-Pox, in a Report dated October 1st, 1807, "congratulate the public on the very favorable opinion which the Royal College of Physicians of London, after a most minute and laborious investigation made by the command of his Majesty, have a second time expressed on the subject of vaccination, in their Report laid before the House of Commons, in the last session of Parliament; in consequence of which the sum of twenty thousand pounds was voted to Dr. Jenner, as a remuneration for his discovery, in addition to ten thousand pounds before granted." (In June, 1802.)

These and similar accusations, so often brought up against the Medical Profession, are only one mode in which is manifested a spirit of opposition not merely to medical science, but to all science, and to all sound knowledge. It is a spirit which neither understands itself nor the object at which it is aiming. It gropes among the loose records of the past, and the floating fables of the moment, to glean a few truths or falsehoods tending to prove, if they prove anything, that the persons who have passed their lives in the study of a branch of knowledge the very essence of which must always consist in long and accurate observation, are less competent to judge of new doctrines in their own department than the rest of the community. It belongs to the clown in society, the destructive in politics, and the rogue in practice.

The name of Harvey, whose great discovery was the legitimate result of his severe training and patient study, should be mentioned only to check the pretensions of presumptuous ignorance. The example of Jenner, who gave his inestimable secret, the result of twenty-two years of experiment and researches, unpurchased, to the public,--when, as was said in Parliament, he might have made a hundred thousand pounds by it as well as any smaller sum,--should be referred to only to rebuke the selfish venders of secret remedies, among whom his early history obliges us reluctantly to record Samuel Hahnemann. Those who speak of the great body of physicians as if they were united in a league to support the superannuated notions of the past against the progress of improvement, have read the history of medicine to little purpose. The prevalent failing of this profession has been, on the contrary, to lend a too credulous ear to ambitious and plausible innovators. If at the present time ten years of public notoriety have passed over any doctrine professing to be of importance in medical science, and if it has not succeeded in raising up a powerful body of able, learned, and ingenious advocates for its claims, the fault must be in the doctrine and not in the medical profession.

Homoeopathy has had a still more extended period of trial than this, and we have seen with what results. It only remains to throw out a few conjectures as to the particular manner in which it is to break up and disappear.

1. The confidence of the few believers in this delusion will never survive the loss of friends who may die of any acute disease, under a treatment such as that prescribed by Homoeopathy. It is doubtful how far cases of this kind will be trusted to its tender mercies, but wherever it acquires any considerable foothold, such cases must come, and with them the ruin of those who practise it, should any highly valued life be thus sacrificed.

2. After its novelty has worn out, the ardent and capricious individuals who constitute the most prominent class of its patrons will return to visible doses, were it only for the sake of a change.

3. The Semi-Homoeopathic practitioner will gradually withdraw from the rotten half of his business and try to make the public forget his connection with it.

4. The ultra Homoeopathist will either recant and try to rejoin the medical profession; or he will embrace some newer and if possible equally extravagant doctrine; or he will stick to his colors and go down with his sinking doctrine. Very few will pursue the course last mentioned.

A single fact may serve to point out in what direction there will probably be a movement of the dissolving atoms of Homoeopathy. On the 13th page of the too frequently cited Manifesto of the "Examiner" I read the following stately paragraph:

"Bigelius, M. D., physician to the Emperor of Russia, whose elevated reputation is well known in Europe, has been an acknowledged advocate of Hahnemann's doctrines for several years. He abandoned Allopathia for Homoeopathia." The date of this statement is January, 1840. I find on looking at the booksellers' catalogues that one Bigel, or Bigelius, to speak more classically, has been at various times publishing Homoeopathic books for some years.

Again, on looking into the "Encyclographie des Sciences Medicales" for April, 1840, I find a work entitled "Manual of HYDROSUDOPATHY, or the Treatment of Diseases by Cold Water, etc., etc., by Dr. Bigel, Physician of the School of Strasburg, Member of the Medico-Chirurgical Institute of Naples, of the Academy of St. Petersburg,--Assessor of the College of the Empire of Russia, Physician of his late

Imperial Highness the Grand Duke Constantine, Chevalier of the Legion of Honor, etc." Hydrosudopathy or Hydropathy, as it is sometimes called, is a new medical doctrine or practice which has sprung up in Germany since Homoeopathy, which it bids fair to drive out of the market, if, as Dr. Bigel says, fourteen physicians afflicted with diseases which defied themselves and their colleagues came to Graefenberg, in the year 1836 alone, and were cured. Now Dr. Bigel, "whose elevated reputation is well known in Europe," writes as follows: "The reader will not fail to see in this defence of the curative method of Graefenberg a profession of medical faith, and he will be correct in so doing." And his work closes with the following sentence, worthy of so distinguished an individual: "We believe, with religion, that the water of baptism purifies the soul from its original sin; let us believe also, with experience, that it is for our corporeal sins the redeemer of the human body." If Bigel, Physician to the late Grand Duke Constantine, is identical with Bigel whom the "Examiner" calls Physician to the Emperor of Russia, it appears that he is now actively engaged in throwing cold water at once upon his patients and the future prospects of Homoeopathy.

If, as must be admitted, no one of Hahnemann's doctrines is received with tolerable unanimity among his disciples, except the central axiom, Similia similibus curantur; if this axiom itself relies mainly for its support upon the folly and trickery of Hahnemann, what can we think of those who announce themselves ready to relinquish all the accumulated treasures of our art, to trifle with life upon the strength of these fantastic theories? What shall we think of professed practitioners of medicine, if, in the words of Jahr, "from ignorance, for their personal convenience, or through charlatanism, they treat their patients one day Homoeopathically and the next Allopathically;" if they parade their pretended new science before the unguarded portion of the community; if they suffer their names to be coupled with it wherever it may gain a credulous patient; and deny all responsibility for its character, refuse all argument for its doctrines, allege no palliation for the ignorance and deception interwoven with every thread of its flimsy tissue, when they are questioned by those competent to judge and entitled to an answer?

Such is the pretended science of Homoeopathy, to which you are asked to trust your lives and the lives of those dearest to you. A mingled mass of perverse ingenuity, of tinsel erudition, of imbecile credulity, and of artful misrepresentation, too often mingled in practice, if we may trust the authority of its founder, with heartless and shameless imposition. Because it is suffered so often to appeal unanswered to the public, because it has its journals, its patrons, its apostles, some are weak enough to suppose it can escape the inevitable doom of utter disgrace and oblivion. Not many years can pass away before the same curiosity excited by one of Perkins's Tractors will be awakened at the sight of one of the Infinitesimal Globules. If it should claim a longer existence, it can only be by falling into the hands of the sordid wretches who wring their bread from the cold grasp of disease and death in the hovels of ignorant poverty.

As one humble member of a profession which for more than two thousand years has devoted itself to the pursuit of the best earthly interests of mankind, always assailed and insulted from without by such as are ignorant of its infinite perplexities and labors, always striving in unequal contest with the hundred-armed giant who walks in the noonday, and sleeps not in the midnight, yet still toiling, not merely for itself and the present moment, but for the race and the future, I have lifted my voice against this lifeless delusion, rolling its shapeless bulk into the path of a noble science it is too weak to strike, or to injure.

THE CONTAGIOUSNESS OF PUERPERAL FEVER

Printed in 1843; reprinted with additions, 1855.
THE POINT AT ISSUE.
THE AFFIRMATIVE.
"The disease known as Puerperal Fever is so far contagious as to be frequently carried from patient to patient by physicians and nurses." O. W. Holmes, 1843.
THE NEGATIVE.
"The result of the whole discussion will, I trust, serve, not only to exalt your views of the value and dignity of our profession, but to divest your minds of the overpowering dread that you can ever become, especially to woman, under the extremely interesting circumstances of gestation and parturition, the minister of evil; that you can ever convey, in any possible manner, a horrible virus, so destructive in its effects, and so mysterious in its operations as that attributed to puerperal fever."--Professor Hodge, 1852.

"I prefer to attribute them to accident, or Providence, of which I can form a conception, rather than to a contagion of which I cannot form any clear idea, at least as to this particular malady."--Professor Meigs, 1852.

"... in the propagation of which they have no more to do, than with the propagation of cholera from Jessore to San Francisco, and from Mauritius to St. Petersburg."--Professor Meigs, 1854.

"I arrived at that certainty in the matter, that I could venture to foretell what women would be affected with the disease, upon hearing by what midwife they were to be delivered, or by what nurse they were to be attended, during their lying-in; and, almost in every instance, my prediction was verified."--Gordon, 1795.

"A certain number of deaths is caused every year by the contagion of puerperal fever, communicated by the nurses and medical attendants." Farr, in Fifth Annual Report of Registrar-General of England, 1843.

"... boards of health, if such exist, or, without them, the medical institutions of a country, should have the power of coercing, or of inflicting some kind of punishment on those who recklessly go from cases of puerperal fevers to parturient or puerperal females, without using due precaution; and who, having been shown the risk, criminally encounter it, and convey pestilence and death to the persons they are employed to aid in the most interesting and suffering period of female existence." --Copland's Medical Dictionary, Art. Puerperal States and Diseases, 1852.

"We conceive it unnecessary to go into detail to prove the contagious nature of this disease, as there are few, if any, American practitioners who do not believe in this doctrine."--Dr. Lee, in Additions to Article last cited.

[INTRODUCTORY NOTE.] It happened, some years ago, that a discussion arose in a Medical Society of which I was a member, involving the subject of a certain supposed cause of disease, about which something was known, a good deal suspected, and not a little feared. The discussion was suggested by a case, reported at the preceding meeting, of a physician who made an examination of the body of a patient who had died with puerperal fever, and who himself died in less than a week, apparently in consequence of a wound received at the examination, having attended several women in confinement in the mean time, all of whom, as it was alleged, were attacked with puerperal fever.

Whatever apprehensions and beliefs were entertained, it was plain that a fuller knowledge of the facts relating to the subject would be acceptable to all present. I therefore felt that it would be doing a good service to look into the best records I could find, and inquire of the most trustworthy practitioners I knew, to learn what experience had to teach in the matter, and arrived at the results contained in the following pages.

The Essay was read before the Boston Society for Medical Improvement, and, at the request of the Society, printed in the "New England Quarterly Journal of Medicine and Surgery" for April, 1843. As this Journal never obtained a large circulation, and ceased to be published after a year's existence, and as the few copies I had struck off separately were soon lost sight of among the friends to whom they were sent, the Essay can hardly be said to have been fully brought before the Profession.

The subject of this Paper has the same profound interest for me at the present moment as it had when I was first collecting the terrible evidence out of which, as it seems to me, the commonest exercise of reason could not help shaping the truth it involved. It is not merely on account of the bearing of the question,--if there is a question,--on all that is most sacred in human life and happiness, that the subject cannot lose its interest. It is because it seems evident that a fair statement of the facts must produce its proper influence on a very large proportion of well-constituted and unprejudiced minds. Individuals may, here and there, resist the practical bearing of the evidence on their own feelings or interests; some may fail to see its meaning, as some persons may be found who cannot tell red from green; but I cannot doubt that most readers will be satisfied and convinced, to loathing, long before they have finished the dark obituary calendar laid before them.

I do not know that I shall ever again have so good an opportunity of being useful as was granted me by the raising of the question which produced this Essay. For I have abundant evidence that it has made many practitioners more cautious in their relations with puerperal females, and I have no doubt it will do so still, if it has a chance of being read, though it should call out a hundred counterblasts, proving to the satisfaction of their authors that it proved nothing. And for my part, I had rather rescue one mother from being poisoned by her attendant, than claim to have saved forty out of fifty patients to whom I had carried the disease. Thus, I am willing to avail myself of any hint coming from without to offer this paper once more to the press. The occasion has presented itself, as will be seen, in a convenient if not in a flattering form.

I send this Essay again to the MEDICAL PROFESSION, without the change of a word or syllable. I find, on reviewing it, that it anticipates and eliminates those secondary questions which cannot be entertained for a moment until the one great point of fact is peremptorily settled. In its very statement of the doctrine maintained it avoids all discussion of the nature of the disease "known as puerperal fever," and all the somewhat stale philology of the word contagion. It mentions, fairly enough, the names of sceptics, or unbelievers as to the reality of personal transmission; of Dewees, of Tonnelle, of Duges, of Baudelocque, and others; of course, not including those whose works were then unwritten or unpublished; nor enumerating all the Continental writers who, in ignorance of the great mass of evidence accumulated by British practitioners, could hardly be called well informed on this subject. It meets all the array of negative cases,--those in which disease did not follow exposure,--by the striking example of small-pox, which, although one of the most contagious of diseases, is subject to the most remarkable irregularities and seeming caprices in its transmission. It makes full allowance for other causes besides personal transmission, especially for epidemic influences. It allows for the possibility of different modes of conveyance of the destructive principle. It recognizes and supports the belief that a series of cases may originate from a single primitive source which affects each new patient in turn; and especially from cases of Erysipelas. It does not undertake to discuss the theoretical aspect of the subject; that is a secondary matter of consideration. Where facts are numerous, and unquestionable, and unequivocal in their significance, theory must follow them as it best may, keeping time with their step, and not go before them, marching to the sound of its own drum and trumpet. Having thus narrowed its area to a limited practical platform of discussion, a matter of life and death, and not of phrases or theories, it covers every inch of it with a mass of evidence which I conceive a Committee of Husbands, who can count coincidences and draw conclusions as well as a Synod of Accoucheurs, would justly consider as affording ample reasons for an unceremonious dismissal of a practitioner (if it is conceivable that such a step could be waited for), after five or six funerals had marked the path of his daily visits, while other practitioners were not thus escorted. To the Profession, therefore, I submit the paper in its original form, and leave it to take care of itself.

To the MEDICAL STUDENTS, into whose hands this Essay may fall, some words of introduction may be appropriate, and perhaps, to a small number of them, necessary. There are some among them who, from youth, or want of training, are easily bewildered and confused in any conflict of opinions into which their studies lead them. They are liable to lose sight of the main question in collateral issues, and to be run away with by suggestive speculations. They confound belief with evidence, often trusting the first because it is expressed with energy, and slighting the latter because it is calm and unimpassioned. They are not satisfied with proof; they cannot believe a point is settled so long as everybody is not silenced. They have not learned that error is got out of the minds that cherish it, as the taenia is removed from the body, one joint, or a few joints at a time, for the most part, rarely the whole evil at once. They naturally have faith in their instructors, turning to them for truth, and taking what they may choose to give them; babes in knowledge, not yet able to tell the breast from the bottle, pumping away for the milk of truth at all that offers, were it nothing better than a Professor's shrivelled forefinger.

In the earliest and embryonic stage of professional development, any violent impression on the instructor's mind is apt to be followed by some lasting effect on that of the pupil. No mother's mark is more permanent than the mental naevi and moles, and excrescences, and mutilations, that students carry with them out of the lecture-room, if once the teeming intellect which nourishes theirs has been scared from its propriety by any misshapen fantasy. Even an impatient or petulant expression, which to a philosopher would be a mere index of the low state of amiability of the speaker at the moment of its utterance, may pass into the young mind as an element of its future constitution, to injure its temper or corrupt its judgment. It is a duty, therefore, which we owe to this younger class of students, to clear any important truth which may have been rendered questionable in their minds by such language, or any truth-teller against whom they may have been prejudiced by hasty epithets, from the impressions such words have left. Until this is done, they are not ready for the question, where there is a question, for them to decide. Even if we ourselves are the subjects of the prejudice, there seems to be no impropriety in showing that this prejudice is local or personal, and not an acknowledged conviction with the public at large. It may be necessary to break through our usual habits of reserve to do this, but this is the fault of the position in which others have placed us.

Two widely-known and highly-esteemed practitioners, Professors in two of the largest Medical Schools of the Union, teaching the branch of art which includes the Diseases of Women, and therefore speaking with authority; addressing in their lectures and printed publications large numbers of young men, many of them in the tenderest immaturity of knowledge, have recently taken ground in a formal way against the doctrine maintained in this paper:

On the Non-Contagious Character of Puerperal Fever: An Introductory Lecture. By Hugh L. Hodge, M. D., Professor of Obstetrics in the University of Pennsylvania. Delivered Monday, October 11, 1852. Philadelphia, 1852.

On the Nature, Signs, and Treatment of Childbed Fevers: in a Series of Letters addressed to the Students of his Class. By Charles D. Meigs, M. D., Professor of Midwifery and the Diseases of Women and Children in Jefferson Medical College, Philadelphia, etc., etc. Philadelphia, 1854. Letter VI.

The first of the two publications, Dr. Hodge's Lecture, while its theoretical considerations and negative experiences do not seem to me to require any further notice than such as lay ready for them in my Essay written long before, is, I am pleased to say, unobjectionable in tone and language, and may be read without offence.

This can hardly be said of the chapter of Dr. Meigs's volume which treats of Contagion in Childbed Fever. There are expressions used in it which might well put a stop to all scientific discussions, were they to form the current coin in our exchange of opinions. I leave the "very young gentlemen," whose careful expositions of the results of practice in more than six thousand cases are characterized as "the jejune and fizenless dreamings of sophomore writers," to the sympathies of those "dear young friends," and "dear young gentlemen," who will judge how much to value their instructor's counsel to think for themselves, knowing what they are to expect if they happen not to think as he does.

One unpalatable expression I suppose the laws of construction oblige me to appropriate to myself, as my reward for a certain amount of labor bestowed on the investigation of a very important question of evidence, and a statement of my own practical conclusions. I take no offence, and attempt no retort. No man makes a quarrel with me over the counterpane that covers a mother, with her new-born infant at her breast. There is no epithet in the vocabulary of slight and sarcasm that can reach my personal sensibilities in such a controversy. Only just so far as a disrespectful phrase may turn the student aside from the examination of the evidence, by discrediting or dishonoring the witness, does it call for any word of notice.

I appeal from the disparaging language by which the Professor in the Jefferson

School of Philadelphia world dispose of my claims to be listened to. I appeal, not to the vote of the Society for Medical Improvement, although this was an unusual evidence of interest in the paper in question, for it was a vote passed among my own townsmen; nor to the opinion of any American, for none know better than the Professors in the great Schools of Philadelphia how cheaply the praise of native contemporary criticism is obtained. I appeal to the recorded opinions of those whom I do not know, and who do not know me, nor care for me, except for the truth that I may have uttered; to Copland, in his "Medical Dictionary," who has spoken of my Essay in phrases to which the pamphlets of American "scribblers" are seldom used from European authorities; to Ramsbotham, whose compendious eulogy is all that self-love could ask; to the "Fifth Annual Report" of the Registrar-General of England, in which the second-hand abstract of my Essay figures largely, and not without favorable comment, in an important appended paper. These testimonies, half forgotten until this circumstance recalled them, are dragged into the light, not in a paroxysm of vanity, but to show that there may be food for thought in the small pamphlet which the Philadelphia Teacher treats so lightly. They were at least unsought for, and would never have been proclaimed but for the sake of securing the privilege of a decent and unprejudiced hearing.

I will take it for granted that they have so far counterpoised the depreciating language of my fellow-countryman and fellow-teacher as to gain me a reader here and there among the youthful class of students I am now addressing. It is only for their sake that I think it necessary to analyze, or explain, or illustrate, or corroborate any portion of the following Essay. But I know that nothing can be made too plain for beginners; and as I do not expect the practitioner, or even the more mature student, to take the trouble to follow me through an Introduction which I consider wholly unnecessary and superfluous for them, I shall not hesitate to stoop to the most elementary simplicity for the benefit of the younger student. I do this more willingly because it affords a good opportunity, as it seems to me, of exercising the untrained mind in that medical logic which does not seem to have been either taught or practised in our schools of late, to the extent that might be desired.

I will now exhibit, in a series of propositions reduced to their simplest expression, the same essential statements and conclusions as are contained in the Essay, with such commentaries and explanations as may be profitable to the inexperienced class of readers addressed.

I. It has been long believed, by many competent observers, that Puerperal Fever (so called) is sometimes carried from patient to patient by medical assistants.

II. The express object of this Essay is to prove that it is so carried.

III. In order to prove this point, it is not necessary to consult any medical theorist as to whether or not it is consistent with his preconceived notions that such a mode of transfer should exist.

IV. If the medical theorist insists on being consulted, and we see fit to indulge him, he cannot be allowed to assume that the alleged laws of contagion, deduced from observation in other diseases, shall be cited to disprove the alleged laws deduced from observation in this. Science would never make progress under such conditions. Neither the long incubation of hydrophobia, nor the protecting power of vaccination, would ever have been admitted, if the results of observation in these affections had been rejected as contradictory to the previously ascertained laws of contagion.

V. The disease in question is not a common one; producing, on the average, about three deaths in a thousand births, according to the English Registration returns which I have examined.

VI. When an unusually large number of cases of this disease occur about the same time, it is inferred, therefore, that there exists some special cause for this increased frequency. If the disease prevails extensively over a wide region of country, it is attributed without dispute to an epidemic influence. If it prevails in a single locality, as in a hospital, and not elsewhere, this is considered proof that some local cause is there active in its production.

VII. When a large number of cases of this disease occur in rapid succession, in one individual's ordinary practice, and few or none elsewhere, these cases appearing in scattered localities, in patients of the same average condition as those who escape under the care of others, there is the same reason for connecting the cause of the disease with the person in this instance, as with the place in that last mentioned.

VIII. Many series of cases, answering to these conditions, are given in this Essay, and many others will be referred to which have occurred since it was written.

IX. The alleged results of observation may be set aside; first, because the so-called facts are in their own nature equivocal; secondly, because they stand on insufficient authority; thirdly, because they are not sufficiently numerous. But, in this case, the disease is one of striking and well-marked character; the witnesses are experts, interested in denying and disbelieving the facts; the number of consecutive cases in many instances frightful, and the number of series of cases such that I have no room for many of them except by mere reference.

X. These results of observation, being admitted, may, we will suppose, be interpreted in different methods. Thus the coincidences may be considered the effect of chance. I have had the chances calculated by a competent person, that a given practitioner, A., shall have sixteen fatal cases in a month, on the following data: A. to average attendance upon two hundred and fifty births in a year; three deaths in one thousand births to be assumed as the average from puerperal fever; no epidemic to be at the time prevailing. It follows, from the answer given me, that if we suppose every one of the five hundred thousand annual births of England to have been recorded during the last half-century, there would not be one chance in a million million million millions that one such series should be noted. No possible fractional error in this calculation can render the chance a working probability. Applied to dozens of series of various lengths, it is obviously an absurdity. Chance, therefore, is out of the question as an explanation of the admitted coincidences.

XI. There is, therefore, some relation of cause and effect between the physician's presence and the patient's disease.

XII. Until it is proved to what removable condition attaching to the attendant the disease is owing, he is bound to stay away from his patients so soon as he finds himself singled out to be tracked by the disease. How long, and with what other precautions, I have suggested, without dictating, at the close of my Essay. If the physician does not at once act on any reasonable suspicion of his being the medium of transfer, the families where he is engaged, if they are allowed to know the facts, should decline his services for the time. His feelings on the occasion, however interesting to himself, should not be even named in this connection. A physician who talks about ceremony and gratitude, and services rendered, and the treatment he got, surely forgets himself; it is impossible that he should seriously think of these small matters where there is even a question whether he may not carry disease, and death, and bereavement into any one of "his families," as they are sometimes called.

I will now point out to the young student the mode in which he may relieve his mind of any confusion, or possibly, if very young, any doubt, which the perusal of Dr. Meigs's Sixth Letter may have raised in his mind.

The most prominent ideas of the Letter are, first, that the transmissible nature of puerperal fever appears improbable, and, secondly, that it would be very inconvenient to the writer. Dr. Woodville, Physician to the Small-Pox and Inoculation Hospital in London, found it improbable, and exceedingly inconvenient to himself, that cow pox should prevent small-pox; but Dr. Jenner took the liberty to prove the fact, notwithstanding.

I will first call the young student's attention to the show of negative facts (exposure without subsequent disease), of which much seems to be thought. And I may at the same time refer him to Dr. Hodge's Lecture, where he will find the same kind of facts and reasoning. Let him now take up Watson's Lectures, the good sense and spirit of which have made his book a universal favorite, and open to the chapter on Continued Fever. He will find a paragraph containing the following sentence: "A man might say, 'I was in the battle of Waterloo, and saw many men around me fall down and die, and it was said that they were struck down by musket-balls; but I know better than that, for I was there all the time, and so were many of my friends, and we were never hit by any musket-balls. Musket-balls, therefore, could not have been the cause of the deaths we witnessed.' And if, like contagion, they were not palpable to the senses, such a person might go on to affirm that no proof existed of there being any such thing as musket-balls." Now let the student turn back to the chapter on Hydrophobia in the same volume. He will find that John Hunter knew a case in which, of twenty-one persons bitten, only one died of the disease. He will find that one dog at Charenton was bitten at different times by thirty different mad dogs, and outlived it all. Is there no such thing, then, as hydrophobia? Would one take no especial precautions if his wife, about to become a mother, had been bitten by a rabid animal, because so many escape? Or let him look at "Underwood on Diseases of Children," [Philadelphia, 1842, p. 244, note.] and he will find the case of a young woman who was inoculated eight times in thirty days, at the same time attending several children with smallpox, and yet was not infected. But seven weeks afterwards she took the disease and died.

It would seem as if the force of this argument could hardly fail to be seen, if it were granted that every one of these series of cases were so reported as to prove that there could have been no transfer of disease. There is not one of them so reported, in the Lecture or the Letter, as to prove that the disease may not have been carried by the practitioner. I strongly suspect that it was so carried in some of these cases, but from the character of the very imperfect evidence the question can never be settled without further disclosures.

Although the Letter is, as I have implied, principally taken up with secondary and collateral questions, and might therefore be set aside as in the main irrelevant, I am willing, for the student's sake, to touch some of these questions briefly, as an illustration of its logical character.

The first thing to be done, as I thought when I wrote my Essay, was to throw out all discussions of the word contagion, and this I did effectually by the careful wording of my statement of the subject to be discussed. My object was not to settle the etymology or definition of a word, but to show that women had often died in childbed, poisoned in some way by their medical attendants. On the other point, I, at least, have no controversy with anybody, and I think the student will do well to avoid it in this connection. If I must define my position, however, as well as the term in question, I am contented with Worcester's definition; provided always this avowal do not open another side controversy on the merits of his Dictionary, which Dr. Meigs has not cited, as compared with Webster's, which he has.

I cannot see the propriety of insisting that all the laws of the eruptive fevers must necessarily hold true of this peculiar disease of puerperal women. If there were any such propriety, the laws of the eruptive fevers must at least be stated correctly. It is not true, for instance, as Dr. Meigs states, that contagion is "no respecter of persons;" that "it attacks all individuals alike." To give one example: Dr. Gregory, of the Small-Pox Hospital, who ought to know, says that persons pass through life apparently insensible to or unsusceptible of the small-pox virus, and that the same persons do not take the vaccine disease.

As to the short time of incubation, of which so much is made, we have no right to decide beforehand whether it shall be long or short, in the cases we are considering. A dissection wound may produce symptoms of poisoning in six hours; the bite of a rabid animal may take as many months.

After the student has read the case in Dr. Meigs's 136th paragraph, and the following one, in which he exclaims against the idea of contagion, because the patient, delivered on the 26th of December, was attacked in twenty-four hours, and died on the third day, let him read what happened at the "Black Assizes" of 1577 and 1750. In the first case, six hundred persons sickened the same night of the exposure, and three hundred more in three days. [Elliotson's Practice, p. 298.] Of those attacked in the latter year, the exposure being on the 11th of May, Alderman Lambert died on the 13th, Under-Sheriff Cox on the 14th, and many of note before the 20th. But these are old stories. Let the student listen then to Dr. Gerhard, whose reputation as a cautious observer he may be supposed to know. "The nurse was shaving a man, who died in a few hours after his entrance; he inhaled his breath, which had a nauseous taste, and in an hour afterwards was taken with nausea, cephalalgia, and singing of the ears. From that moment the attack began, and assumed a severe character. The assistant was supporting another patient, who died soon afterwards; he felt the pungent heat upon his skin, and was taken immediately with the symptoms of typhus." [Am. Jour. Med. Sciences, Feb. 1837, p. 299.] It is by notes of cases, rather than notes of admiration, that we must be guided, when we study the Revised Statutes of Nature, as laid down from the curule chairs of Medicine.

Let the student read Dr. Meigs's 140th paragraph soberly, and then remember, that not only does he infer, suspect, and surmise, but he actually asserts (page 154), "there was poison in the house," because three out of five patients admitted into a ward had puerperal fever and died. Have I not as much right to draw a positive inference from "Dr. A.'s" seventy exclusive cases as he from the three cases in the ward of the Dublin Hospital? All practical medicine, and all action in common affairs, is founded on inferences. How does Dr. Meigs know that the patients he bled in puerperal fever would not have all got well if he had not bled them?

"You see a man discharge a gun at another; you see the flash, you hear the report, you see the person fall a lifeless corpse; and you infer, from all these circumstances, that there was a ball discharged from the gun, which entered his body and caused his death, because such is the usual and natural cause of such an effect. But you did not see the ball leave the gun, pass through the air, and enter the body of the slain; and your testimony to the fact of killing is, therefore, only inferential,--in other words, circumstantial. It is possible that no ball was in the gun; and we infer that there was, only because we cannot account for death on any other supposition." [Chief Justice Gibson, in Am. Law Journal, vol. vi. p. 123.]

"The question always comes to this: Is the circumstance of intercourse with the sick followed by the appearance of the disease in a proportion of cases so much greater than any other circumstance common to any portion of the inhabitants of the place under observation, as to make it inconceivable that the succession of cases occurring in persons having that intercourse should have been the result of chance? If so, the inference is unavoidable, that that intercourse must have acted as a cause of the disease. All observations which do not bear strictly on that point are irrelevant, and, in the case of an epidemic first appearing in a town or district, a succession of two cases is sometimes sufficient to furnish evidence which, on the principle I have stated, is nearly irresistible."

Possibly an inexperienced youth may be awe-struck by the quotation from Cuvier. These words, or their equivalent, are certainly to be found in his Introduction. So are the words "top not come down"! to be found in the Bible, and they were as much meant for the ladies' head-dresses as the words of Cuvier were meant to make clinical observation wait for a permit from anybody to look with its eyes and count on its fingers. Let the inquiring youth read the whole Introduction, and he will see what they mean.

I intend no breach of courtesy, but this is a proper place to warn the student against skimming the prefaces and introductions of works for mottoes and embellishments to his thesis. He cannot learn anatomy by thrusting an exploring needle into the body. He will be very liable to misquote his author's meaning while he is picking off his outside sentences. He may make as great a blunder as that simple prince who praised the conductor of his orchestra for the piece just before the overture; the musician was too good a courtier to tell him that it was only the tuning of the instruments.

To the six propositions in the 142d paragraph, and the remarks about "specific" diseases, the answer, if any is necessary, seems very simple. An inflammation of a serous membrane may give rise to secretions which act as a poison, whether that be a "specific" poison or not, as Dr. Homer has told his young readers, and as dissectors know too well; and that poison may produce its symptoms in a few hours after the system has received it, as any may see in Druitt's "Surgery," if they care to look. Puerperal peritonitis may produce such a poison, and puerperal women may be very sensible to its influences, conveyed by contact or exhalation. Whether this is so or not, facts alone can determine, and to facts we have had recourse to settle it.

The following statement is made by Dr. Meigs in his 142d paragraph, and developed more at length, with rhetorical amplifications, in the 134th. "No human being, save a pregnant or parturient woman, is susceptible to the poison." This statement is wholly incorrect, as I am sorry to have to point out to a Teacher in Dr. Meigs's position. I do not object to the erudition which quotes Willis and Fernelius, the last of whom was pleasantly said to have "preserved the dregs of the Arabs in the honey of his Latinity." But I could wish that more modern authorities had not been overlooked. On this point, for instance, among the numerous facts disproving the statement, the "American Journal of Medical Sciences," published not far from his lecture-room, would have presented him with a respectable catalog of such cases. Thus he might refer to Mr. Storrs's paper "On the Contagious Effects of Puerperal Fever on the Male Subject; or on Persons not Childbearing" (Jan. 1846), or to Dr. Reid's case (April, 1846), or to Dr. Barron's statement of the children's dying of peritonitis in an epidemic of puerperal fever at the Philadelphia Hospital (Oct. 1842), or to various instances cited in Dr. Kneeland's article (April, 186). Or, if he would have referred to the "New York Journal," he might have seen Prof. Austin Flint's cases. Or, if he had honored my Essay so far, he might have found striking instances of the same kind in the first of the new series of cases there reported and elsewhere. I do not see the bearing of his proposition, if it were true. But it is one of those assertions that fall in a moment before a slight examination of the facts; and I confess my surprise, that a professor who lectures on the Diseases of Women should have ventured to make it.

Nearly seven pages are devoted to showing that I was wrong in saying I would not be "understood to imply that there exists a doubt in the mind of any well-informed member of the medical profession as to the fact that puerperal fever is sometimes communicated from one person to another, both directly and indirectly." I will devote seven lines to these seven pages, which seven lines, if I may say it without offence, are, as it seems to me, six more than are strictly necessary.

The following authors are cited as sceptics by Dr. Meigs: Dewees.--I cited the same passage. Did not know half the facts. Robert Lee.--Believes the disease is sometimes communicable by contagion. Tonnelle, Baudelocque. Both cited by me. Jacquemier.--Published three years after my Essay. Kiwisch. "Behindhand in knowledge of Puerperal Fever." [B. & F. Med. Rev. Jan. 1842.] Paul Dubois.--Scanzoni.

These Continental writers not well informed on this point.[See Dr. Simpson's Remarks at Meeting of Edin. Med. Chir. Soc. (Am. Jour. Oct. 1851.)]

The story of Von Busch is of interest and value, but there is nothing in it which need perplex the student. It is not pretended that the disease is always, or even, it may be, in the majority of cases, carried about by attendants; only that it is so carried in certain cases. That it may have local and epidemic causes, as well as that depending on personal transmission, is not disputed. Remember how small-pox often disappears from a community in spite of its contagious character, and the necessary exposure of many persons to those suffering from it; in both diseases contagion is only one of the coefficients of the disease.

I have already spoken of the possibility that Dr. Meigs may have been the medium of transfer of puerperal fever in some of the cases he has briefly catalogued. Of Dr. Rutter's cases I do not know how to speak. I only ask the student to read the facts stated by Dr. Condie, as given in my Essay, and say whether or not a man should allow his wife to be attended by a practitioner in whose hands "scarcely a female that has been delivered for weeks past has escaped an attack," "while no instance of the disease has occurred in the patients of any other accoucheur practising in the same district." If I understand Dr. Meigs and Dr. Hodge, they would not warn the physician or spare the patient under such circumstances. They would "go on," if I understand them, not to seven, or seventy, only, but to seventy times seven, if they could find patients. If this is not what they mean, may we respectfully ask them to state what they do mean, to their next classes, in the name of humanity, if not of science!

I might repeat the question asked concerning Dr. Rutter's cases, with reference to those reported by Dr. Roberton. Perhaps, however, the student would like to know the opinion of a person in the habit of working at matters of this kind in a practical point of view. To satisfy him on this ground, I addressed the following question to the President of one of our principal Insurance Companies, leaving Dr. Meigs's book and my Essay in his hands at the same time.

Question. "If such facts as Roberton's cases were before you, and the attendant had had ten, or even five fatal cases, or three, or two even, would you, or would you not, if insuring the life of the next patient to be taken care of by that attendant, expect an extra premium over that of an average case of childbirth?"

Answer. "Of course I should require a very large extra premium, if I would take take risk at all."

But I do not choose to add the expressions of indignation which the examination of the facts before him called out. I was satisfied from the effect they produced on him, that if all the hideous catalogues of cases now accumulated were fully brought to the knowledge of the public, nothing, since the days of Burke and Hare, has raised such a cry of horror as would be shrieked in the ears of the Profession.

Dr. Meigs has elsewhere invoked "Providence" as the alternative of accident, to account for the "coincidences." ("Obstetrics," Phil. 1852, p. 631.) If so, Providence either acts through the agency of secondary causes, as in other diseases, or not. If through such causes, let us find out what they are, as we try to do in other cases. It may be true that offences, or diseases, will come, but "woe unto him through whom they come," if we catch him in the voluntary or careless act of bringing them! But if Providence does not act through secondary causes in this particular sphere of etiology, then why does Dr. Meigs take such pains to reason so extensively about the laws of contagion, which, on that supposition, have no more to do with this case than with the plague which destroyed the people after David had numbered them? Above all, what becomes of the theological aspect of the question, when he asserts that a practitioner was "only unlucky in meeting with the epidemic cases?" (Op. cit. p. 633.) We do not deny that the God of battles decides the fate of nations; but we like to have the biggest squadrons on our side, and we are particular that our soldiers should not only say their prayers, but also keep their powder dry. We do not deny the agency of Providence in the disaster at Norwalk, but we turn off the engineer, and charge the Company five thousand dollars apiece for every life that is sacrificed.

Why a grand jury should not bring in a bill against a physician who switches off a score of women one after the other along his private track, when he knows that there is a black gulf at the end of it, down which they are to plunge, while the great highway is clear, is more than I can answer. It is not by laying the open draw to Providence that he is to escape the charge of manslaughter.

To finish with all these lesser matters of question, I am unable to see why a female must necessarily be unattended in her confinement, because she declines the services of a particular practitioner. In all the series of cases mentioned, the death-carrying attendant was surrounded by others not tracked by disease and its consequences. Which, I would ask, is worse,--to call in another, even a rival practitioner, or to submit an unsuspecting female to a risk which an Insurance Company would have nothing to do with?

I do not expect ever to return to this subject. There is a point of mental saturation, beyond which argument cannot be forced without breeding impatient, if not harsh, feelings towards those who refuse to be convinced. If I have so far manifested neither, it is well to stop here, and leave the rest to those younger friends who may have more stomach for the dregs of a stale argument.

The extent of my prefatory remarks may lead some to think that I attach too much importance to my own Essay. Others may wonder that I should expend so many words upon the two productions referred to, the Letter and the Lecture. I do consider my Essay of much importance so long as the doctrine it maintains is treated as a question, and so long as any important part of the defence of that doctrine is thought to rest on its evidence or arguments. I cannot treat as insignificant any opinions bearing on life, and interests dearer than life, proclaimed yearly to hundreds of young men, who will carry them to their legitimate results in practice.

The teachings of the two Professors in the great schools of Philadelphia are sure to be listened to, not only by their immediate pupils, but by the Profession at large. I am too much in earnest for either humility or vanity, but I do entreat those who hold the keys of life and death to listen to me also for this once. I ask no personal favor; but I beg to be heard in behalf of the women whose lives are at stake, until some stronger voice shall plead for them.

I trust that I have made the issue perfectly distinct and intelligible. And let it be remembered that this is no subject to be smoothed over by nicely adjusted phrases of half-assent and half-censure divided between the parties. The balance must be struck boldly and the result declared plainly. If I have been hasty, presumptuous, ill-informed, illogical; if my array of facts means nothing; if there is no reason for any caution in the view of these facts; let me be told so on such authority that I must believe it, and I will be silent henceforth, recognizing that my mind is in a state of disorganization. If the doctrine I have maintained is a mournful truth; if to disbelieve it, and to practise on this disbelief, and to teach others so to disbelieve and practise, is to carry desolation, and to charter others to carry it, into confiding families, let it be proclaimed as plainly what is to be thought of the teachings of those who sneer at the alleged dangers, and scout the very idea of precaution. Let it be remembered that persons are nothing in this matter; better that twenty pamphleteers should be silenced, or as many professors unseated, than that one mother's life should be taken. There is no quarrel here between men, but there is deadly incompatibility and exterminating warfare between doctrines. Coincidences meaning nothing, though a man have a monopoly of the disease for weeks or months; or cause and effect, the cause being in some way connected with the person; this is the question. If I am wrong, let me be put down by such a rebuke as no rash declaimer has received since there has been a public opinion in the medical profession of America; if I am right, let doctrines which lead to professional homicide be no longer taught from the chairs of those two great Institutions. Indifference will not do here; our Journalists and Committees have no right to take up their pages with minute anatomy and tediously detailed cases, while it is a question whether or not the "blackdeath" of child-bed is to be scattered broadcast by the agency of the mother's friend and adviser. Let the men who mould opinions look to it; if there is any voluntary blindness, any interested oversight, any culpable negligence, even, in such a matter, and the facts shall reach the public ear; the pestilence-carrier of the lying-in chamber must look to God for pardon, for man will never forgive him.

THE CONTAGIOUSNESS OF PUERPERAL FEVER.

In collecting, enforcing, and adding to the evidence accumulated upon this most serious subject, I would not be understood to imply that there exists a doubt in the mind of any well-informed member of the medical profession as to the fact that puerperal fever is sometimes communicated from one person to another, both directly and indirectly. In the present state of our knowledge upon this point I should consider such doubts merely as a proof that the sceptic had either not examined the evidence, or, having examined it, refused to accept its plain and unavoidable consequences. I should be sorry to think, with Dr. Rigby, that it was a case of "oblique vision;" I should be unwilling to force home the argumentum ad hominem of Dr. Blundell, but I would not consent to make a question of a momentous fact which is no longer to be considered as a subject for trivial discussions, but to be acted upon with silent promptitude. It signifies nothing that wise and experienced practitioners have sometimes doubted the reality of the danger in question; no man has the right to doubt it any longer. No negative facts, no opposing opinions, be they what they may, or whose they may, can form any answer to the series of cases now within the reach of all who choose to explore the records of medical science.

If there are some who conceive that any important end would be answered by recording such opinions, or by collecting the history of all the cases they could find in which no evidence of the influence of contagion existed, I believe they are in error. Suppose a few writers of authority can be found to profess a disbelief in contagion,--and they are very few compared with those who think differently,--is it quite clear that they formed their opinions on a view of all the facts, or is it not apparent that they relied mostly on their own solitary experience? Still further, of those whose names are quoted, is it not true that scarcely a single one could by any possibility have known the half or the tenth of the facts bearing on the subject which have reached such a frightful amount within the last few years? Again, as to the utility of negative facts, as we may briefly call them,--instances, namely, in which exposure has not been followed by disease,--although, like other truths, they may be worth knowing, I do not see that they are like to shed any important light upon the subject before us. Every such instance requires a good deal of circumstantial explanation before it can be accepted. It is not enough that a practitioner should have had a single case of puerperal fever not followed by others. It must be known whether he attended others while this case was in progress, whether he went directly from one chamber to others, whether he took any, and what precautions. It is important to know that several women were exposed to infection derived from the patient, so that allowance may be made for want of predisposition. Now if of negative facts so sifted there could be accumulated a hundred for every one plain instance of communication here recorded, I trust it need not be said that we are bound to guard and watch over the hundredth tenant of our fold, though the ninety and nine may be sure of escaping the wolf at its entrance. If any one is disposed, then, to take a hundred instances of lives endangered or sacrificed out of those I have mentioned, and make it reasonably clear that within a similar time and compass ten thousand escaped the same exposure, I shall thank him for his industry, but I must be permitted to hold to my own practical conclusions, and beg him to adopt or at least to examine them also. Children that walk in calico before open fires are not always burned to death; the instances to the contrary may be worth recording; but by no means if they are to be used as arguments against woollen frocks and high fenders.

I am not sure that this paper will escape another remark which it might be wished were founded in justice. It may be said that the facts are too generally known and acknowledged to require any formal argument or exposition, that there is nothing new in the positions advanced, and no need of laying additional statements before the Profession. But on turning to two works, one almost universally, and the other extensively appealed to as authority in this country, I see ample reason to overlook this objection. In the last edition of Dewees's Treatise on the "Diseases of Females," it is expressly said, "In this country, under no circumstance that puerperal fever has appeared hitherto, does it afford the slightest ground for the belief that it is contagious." In the "Philadelphia Practice of Midwifery" not one word can be found in the chapter devoted to this disease which would lead the reader to suspect that the idea of contagion had ever been entertained. It seems proper, therefore, to remind those who are in the habit of referring to these works for guidance, that there may possibly be some sources of danger they have slighted or omitted, quite as important as a trifling irregularity of diet, or a confined state of the bowels, and that whatever confidence a physician may have in his own mode of treatment, his services are of questionable value whenever he carries the bane as well as the antidote about his person.

The practical point to be illustrated is the following:

The disease known as Puerperal Fever is so far contagious as to be frequently carried from patient to patient by physicians and nurses.

Let me begin by throwing out certain incidental questions, which, without being absolutely essential, would render the subject more complicated, and by making such concessions and assumptions as may be fairly supposed to be without the pale of discussion.

1. It is granted that all the forms of what is called puerperal fever may not be, and probably are not, equally contagious or infectious. I do not enter into the distinctions which have been drawn by authors, because the facts do not appear to me sufficient to establish any absolute line of demarcation between such forms as may be propagated by contagion and those which are never so propagated. This general result I shall only support by the authority of Dr. Ramsbotham, who gives, as the result of his experience, that the same symptoms belong to what he calls the infectious and the sporadic forms of the disease, and the opinion of Armstrong in his original Essay. If others can show any such distinction, I leave it to them to do it. But there are cases enough that show the prevalence of the disease among the patients of a single practitioner when it was in no degree epidemic, in the proper sense of the term. I may refer to those of Mr. Roberton and of Dr. Peirson, hereafter to be cited, as examples.

2. I shall not enter into any dispute about the particular mode of infection, whether it be by the atmosphere the physician carries about him into the sick-chamber, or by the direct application of the virus to the absorbing surfaces with which his hand comes in contact. Many facts and opinions are in favor of each of these modes of transmission. But it is obvious that in the majority of cases it must be impossible to decide by which of these channels the disease is conveyed, from the nature of the intercourse between the physician and the patient.

3. It is not pretended that the contagion of puerperal fever must always be followed by the disease. It is true of all contagious diseases, that they frequently spare those who appear to be fully submitted to their influence. Even the vaccine virus, fresh from the subject, fails every day to produce its legitimate effect, though every precaution is taken to insure its action. This is still more remarkably the case with scarlet fever and some other diseases.

4. It is granted that the disease may be produced and variously modified by many causes besides contagion, and more especially by epidemic and endemic influences. But this is not peculiar to the disease in question. There is no doubt that small-pox is propagated to a great extent by contagion, yet it goes through the same periods of periodical increase and diminution which have been remarked in puer-

peral fever. If the question is asked how we are to reconcile the great variations in the mortality of puerperal fever in different seasons and places with the supposition of contagion, I will answer it by another question from Mr. Farr's letter to the Registrar-General. He makes the statement that "five die weekly of small-pox in the metropolis when the disease is not epidemic,"--and adds, "The problem for solution is,--Why do the five deaths become 10, 15, 20, 31, 58, 88, weekly, and then progressively fall through the same measured steps?"

5. I take it for granted, that if it can be shown that great numbers of lives have been and are sacrificed to ignorance or blindness on this point, no other error of which physicians or nurses may be occasionally suspected will be alleged in palliation of this; but that whenever and wherever they can be shown to carry disease and death instead of health and safety, the common instincts of humanity will silence every attempt to explain away their responsibility.

The treatise of Dr. Gordon of Aberdeen was published in the year 1795, being among the earlier special works upon the disease. A part of his testimony has been occasionally copied into other works, but his expressions are so clear, his experience is given with such manly distinctness and disinterested honesty, that it may be quoted as a model which might have been often followed with advantage.

"This disease seized such women only as were visited, or delivered by a practitioner, or taken care of by a nurse, who had previously attended patients affected with the disease."

"I had evident proofs of its infectious nature, and that the infection was as readily communicated as that of the small-pox or measles, and operated more speedily than any other infection with which I am acquainted."

"I had evident proofs that every person who had been with a patient in the puerperal fever became charged with an atmosphere of infection, which was communicated to every pregnant woman who happened to come within its sphere. This is not an assertion, but a fact, admitting of demonstration, as may be seen by a perusal of the foregoing table,"--referring to a table of seventy-seven cases, in many of which the channel of propagation was evident.

He adds, "It is a disagreeable declaration for me to mention, that I myself was the means of carrying the infection to a great number of women." He then enumerates a number of instances in which the disease was conveyed by midwives and others to the neighboring villages, and declares that "these facts fully prove that the cause of the puerperal fever, of which I treat, was a specific contagion, or infection, altogether unconnected with a noxious constitution of the atmosphere."

But his most terrible evidence is given in these words: "I ARRIVED AT THAT CERTAINTY IN THE MATTER, THAT I COULD VENTURE TO FORETELL WHAT WOMEN WOULD BE AFFECTED WITH THE DISEASE, UPON HEARING BY WHAT MIDWIFE THEY WERE TO BE DELIVERED, OR BY WHAT NURSE THEY WERE TO BE ATTENDED, DURING THEIR LYING-IN: AND ALMOST IN EVERY INSTANCE, MY PREDICTION WAS VERIFIED."

Even previously to Gordon, Mr. White of Manchester had said, "I am acquainted with two gentlemen in another town, where the whole business of midwifery is divided betwixt them, and it is very remarkable that one of them loses several patients every year of the puerperal fever, and the other never so much as meets with the disorder,"--a difference which he seems to attribute to their various modes of treatment. [On the Management of Lying-in Women, p. 120.]

Dr. Armstrong has given a number of instances in his Essay on Puerperal Fever, of the prevalence of the disease among the patients of a single practitioner. At Sunderland, "in all, forty-three cases occurred from the 1st of January to the 1st of October, when the disease ceased; and of this number forty were witnessed by Mr. Gregson and his assistant, Mr. Gregory, the remainder having been separately seen by three accoucheurs." There is appended to the London edition of this Essay, a letter from Mr. Gregson, in which that gentleman says, in reference to the great number of cases occurring in his practice, "The cause of this I cannot pretend fully to explain, but I should be wanting in common liberality if I were to make any hesitation in asserting, that the disease which appeared in my practice was highly contagious, and communicable from one puerperal woman to another." "It is customary among the lower and middle ranks of people to make frequent personal visits to puerperal women resident in the same neighborhood, and I have ample evidence for affirming that the infection of the disease was often carried about in that manner; and, however painful to my feelings, I must in candor declare, that it is very probable the contagion was conveyed, in some instances, by myself, though I took every possible care to prevent such a thing from happening, the moment that I ascertained that the distemper was infectious." Dr. Armstrong goes on to mention six other instances within his knowledge, in which the disease had at different times and places been limited, in the same singular manner, to the practice of individuals, while it existed scarcely if at all among the patients of others around them. Two of the gentlemen became so convinced of their conveying the contagion, that they withdrew for a time from practice.

I find a brief notice, in an American Journal, of another series of cases, first mentioned by Mr. Davies, in the "Medical Repository." This gentleman stated his conviction that the disease is contagious.

"In the autumn of 1822 he met with twelve cases, while his medical friends in the neighborhood did not meet with any, 'or at least very few.' He could attribute this circumstance to no other cause than his having been present at the examination, after death, of two cases, some time previous, and of his having imparted the disease to his patients, notwithstanding every precaution."

Dr. Gooch says, "It is not uncommon for the greater number of cases to occur in the practice of one man, whilst the other practitioners of the neighborhood, who are not more skilful or more busy, meet with few or none. A practitioner opened the body of a woman who had died of puerperal fever, and continued to wear the same clothes. A lady whom he delivered a few days afterwards was attacked with and died of a similar disease; two more of his lying-in patients, in rapid succession, met with the same fate; struck by the thought, that he might have carried contagion in his clothes, he instantly changed them, and 'met with no more cases of the kind.' A woman in the country, who was employed as washerwoman and nurse, washed the linen of one who had died of puerperal fever; the next lying-in patient she nursed died of the same disease; a third nursed by her met with the same fate, till the neighborhood, getting afraid of her, ceased to employ her."

In the winter of the year 1824, "Several instances occurred of its prevalence among the patients of particular practitioners, whilst others who were equally busy met with few or none. One instance of this kind was very remarkable. A general practitioner, in large midwifery practice, lost so many patients from puerperal fever, that he determined to deliver no more for some time, but that his partner should attend in his place. This plan was pursued for one month, during which not a case of the disease occurred in their practice. The elder practitioner, being then sufficiently recovered, returned to his practice, but the first patient he attended was attacked by the disease and died. A physician, who met him in consultation soon afterwards, about a case of a different kind, and who knew nothing of his misfortune, asked him whether puerperal fever was at all prevalent in his neighborhood, on which he burst into tears, and related the above circumstances.

"Among the cases which I saw this season in consultation, four occurred in one month in the practice of one medical man, and all of them terminated fatally." [Lond. Med. Gaz. May 2, 1835.]

Dr. Ramsbotham asserted, in a Lecture at the London Hospital, that he had known the disease spread through a particular district, or be confined to the practice of a particular person, almost every patient being attacked with it, while others had not a single case. It seemed capable, he thought, of conveyance, not only by common modes; but through the dress of the attendants upon the patient.

In a letter to be found in the "London Medical Gazette" for January, 1840, Mr. Roberton of Manchester makes the statement which I here give in a somewhat condensed form.

A midwife delivered a woman on the 4th of December, 1830, who died soon after with the symptoms of puerperal fever. In one month from this date the same midwife delivered thirty women, residing in different parts of an extensive suburb, of which number sixteen caught the disease and all died. These were the only cases which had occurred for a considerable time in Manchester. The other midwives connected with the same charitable institution as the woman already mentioned are twenty-five in number, and deliver, on an average, ninety women a week, or about three hundred and eighty a month. None of these women had a case of puerperal fever. "Yet all this time this woman was crossing the other midwives in every direction, scores of the patients of the charity being delivered by them in the very same quarters where her cases of fever were happening."

Mr. Roberton remarks, that little more than half the women she delivered during this month took the fever; that on some days all escaped, on others only one or more out of three or four; a circumstance similar to what is seen in other infectious maladies.

Dr. Blundell says, "Those who have never made the experiment can have but a faint conception how difficult it is to obtain the exact truth respecting any occurrence in which feelings and interests are concerned. Omitting particulars, then, I content myself with remarking, generally, that from more than one district I have received accounts of the prevalence of puerperal fever in the practice of some individuals, while its occurrence in that of others, in the same neighborhood, was not observed. Some, as I have been told, have lost ten, twelve, or a greater number of patients, in scarcely broken succession; like their evil genius, the puerperal fever has seemed to stalk behind them wherever they went. Some have deemed it prudent to retire for a time from practice. In fine, that this fever may occur spontaneously, I admit; that its infectious nature may be plausibly disputed, I do not deny; but I add, considerately, that in my own family I had rather that those I esteemed the most should be delivered, unaided, in a stable, by the manger-side, than that they should receive the best help, in the fairest apartment, but exposed to the vapors of this pitiless disease. Gossiping friends, wet-nurses, monthly nurses, the practitioner himself, these are the channels by which, as I suspect, the infection is principally conveyed."

At a meeting of the Royal Medical and Chirurgical Society, Dr. King mentioned that some years since a practitioner at Woolwich lost sixteen patients from puerperal fever in the same year. He was compelled to give up practice for one or two years, his business being divided among the neighboring practitioners. No case of puerperal fever occurred afterwards, neither had any of the neighboring surgeons any cases of this disease.

At the same meeting Mr. Hutchinson mentioned the occurrence of three consecutive cases of puerperal fever, followed subsequently by two others, all in the practice of one accoucheur.[Lancet, May 2, 1840.]

Dr. Lee makes the following statement: "In the last two weeks of September, 1827, five fatal cases of uterine inflammation came under our observation. All the individuals so attacked had been attended in labor by the same midwife, and no example of a febrile or inflammatory disease of a serious nature occurred during that period among the other patients of the Westminster General Dispensary, who had been attended by the other midwives belonging to that institution."

The recurrence of long series of cases like those I have cited, reported by those most interested to disbelieve in contagion, scattered along through an interval of half a century, might have been thought sufficient to satisfy the minds of all inquirers that here was something more than a singular coincidence. But if, on a more extended observation, it should be found that the same ominous groups of cases clustering about individual practitioners were observed in a remote country, at different times, and in widely separated regions, it would seem incredible that any should be found too prejudiced or indolent to accept the solemn truth knelled into their ears by the funeral bells from both sides of the ocean,--the plain conclusion that the physician and the disease entered, hand in hand, into the chamber of the unsuspecting patient.

That such series of cases have been observed in this country, and in this neighborhood, I proceed to show.

In Dr. Francis's "Notes to Denman's Midwifery," a passage is cited from Dr. Hosack, in which he refers to certain puerperal cases which proved fatal to several lying-in women, and in some of which the disease was supposed to be conveyed by the accoucheurs themselves.

A writer in the "New York Medical and Physical Journal" for October, 1829, in speaking of the occurrence of puerperal fever, confined to one man's practice, remarks, "We have known cases of this kind occur, though rarely, in New York."

I mention these little hints about the occurrence of such cases, partly because they are the first I have met with in American medical literature, but more especially because they serve to remind us that behind the fearful array of published facts there lies a dark list of similar events, unwritten in the records of science, but long remembered by many a desolated fireside.

Certainly nothing can be more open and explicit than the account given by Dr. Peirson of Salem, of the cases seen by him. In the first nineteen days of January, 1829, he had five consecutive cases of puerperal fever, every patient he attended being attacked, and the three first cases proving fatal. In March of the same year he had two moderate cases, in June, another case, and in July, another, which proved fatal. "Up to this period," he remarks, "I am not informed that a single case had occurred in the practice of any other physician. Since that period I have had no fatal case in my practice, although I have had several dangerous cases. I have attended in all twenty cases of this disease, of which four have been fatal. I am not aware that there has been any other case in the town of distinct puerperal peritonitis, although I am willing to admit my information may be very defective on this point. I have been told of some I 'mixed cases,' and 'morbid affections after delivery.'"

In the "Quarterly Summary of the Transactions of the College of Physicians of Philadelphia" may be found some most extraordinary developments respecting a series of cases occurring in the practice of a member of that body.

Dr. Condie called the attention of the Society to the prevalence, at the present time, of puerperal fever of a peculiarly insidious and malignant character. "In the practice of one gentleman extensively engaged as an obstetrician, nearly every female he has attended in confinement, during several weeks past, within the above limits" (the southern sections and neighboring districts), "had been attacked by the fever."

"An important query presents itself, the Doctor observed, in reference to the particular form of fever now prevalent. Is it, namely, capable of being propagated by contagion, and is a physician who has been in attendance upon a case of the disease warranted in continuing, without interruption, his practice as an obstetrician? Dr. C., although not a believer in the contagious character of many of those affections generally supposed to be propagated in this manner, has nevertheless become convinced by the facts that have fallen under his notice, that the puerperal fever now prevailing is capable of being communicated by contagion. How otherwise can be explained the very curious circumstance of the disease in one district being exclusively confined to the practice of a single physician, a Fellow of this College, extensively engaged in obstetrical practice,--while no instance of the disease has occurred in the patients under the care of any other accoucheur practising within the same district; scarcely a female that has been delivered for weeks past has escaped an attack?"

Dr. Rutter, the practitioner referred to, "observed that, after the occurrence of a number of cases of the disease in his practice, he had left the city and remained absent for a week, but on returning, no article of clothing he then wore having been used by him before, one of the very first cases of parturition he attended was followed by an attack of the fever, and terminated fatally; he cannot, readily, therefore, believe in the transmission of the disease from female to female, in the person or clothes of the physician."

The meeting at which these remarks were made was held on the 3d of May, 1842. In a letter dated December 20, 1842, addressed to Dr. Meigs, and to be found in the "Medical Examiner," he speaks of "those horrible cases of puerperal fever, some of which you did me the favor to see with me during the past summer," and talks of his experience in the disease, "now numbering nearly seventy cases, all of which have occurred within less than a twelvemonth past."

And Dr. Meigs asserts, on the same page, "Indeed, I believe that his practice in that department of the profession was greater than that of any other gentleman, which was probably the cause of his seeing a greater number of the cases." This from a professor of midwifery, who some time ago assured a gentleman whom he met in consultation, that the night on which they met was the eighteenth in succession that he himself had been summoned from his repose, seems hardly satisfactory.

I must call the attention of the inquirer most particularly to the Quarterly Report above referred to, and the letters of Dr. Meigs and Dr. Rutter, to be found in the "Medical Examiner." Whatever impression they may produce upon his mind, I trust they will at least convince him that there is some reason for looking into this apparently uninviting subject.

At a meeting of the College of Physicians just mentioned, Dr. Warrington stated, that a few days after assisting at an autopsy of puerperal peritonitis, in which he laded out the contents of the abdominal cavity with his hands, he was called upon to deliver three women in rapid succession. All of these women were attacked with different forms of what is commonly called puerperal fever. Soon after these he saw two other patients, both on the same day, with the same disease. Of these five patients two died.

At the same meeting, Dr. West mentioned a fact related to him by Dr. Samuel Jackson of Northumberland. Seven females, delivered by Dr. Jackson in rapid succession, while practising in Northumberland County, were all attacked with puerperal fever, and five of them died. "Women," he said, "who had expected me to attend upon them, now becoming alarmed, removed out of my reach, and others sent for a physician residing several miles distant. These women, as well as those attended by midwives; all did well; nor did we hear of any deaths in child-bed within a radius of fifty miles, excepting two, and these I afterwards ascertained to have been caused by other diseases." He underwent, as he thought, a thorough purification, and still his next patient was attacked with the disease and died. He was led to suspect that the contagion might have been carried in the gloves which he had worn in attendance upon the previous cases. Two months or more after this he had two other cases. He could find nothing to account for these, unless it were the instruments for giving enemata, which had been used in two of the former cases, and were employed by these patients. When the first case occurred, he was attending and dressing a limb extensively mortified from erysipelas, and went immediately to the accouchement with his clothes and gloves most thoroughly imbued with its effluvia. And here I may mention, that this very Dr. Samuel Jackson of Northumberland is one of Dr. Dewees's authorities against contagion.

The three following statements are now for the first time given to the public. All of the cases referred to occurred within this State, and two of the three series in Boston and its immediate vicinity.

I. The first is a series of cases which took place during the last spring in a town at some distance from this neighborhood. A physician of that town, Dr. C., had the following consecutive cases.

No. 1, delivered March 20, died March 24.
" 2, "   April 9, " April 14.
" 3, "   " 10, " " 14.
" 4, "   " 11, " " 18.
" 5, "   " 27, " May 3.
" 6, "   " 28, had some symptoms,(recovered.)
" 7, "   May 8, had some symptoms,(also recovered.)

These were the only cases attended by this physician during the period referred to. "They were all attended by him until their termination, with the exception of the patient No. 6, who fell into the hands of another physician on the 2d of May. (Dr. C. left town for a few days at this time.) Dr. C. attended cases immediately before and after the above-named periods, none of which, however, presented any peculiar symptoms of the disease."

About the 1st of July he attended another patient in a neighboring village, who died two or three days after delivery.

The first patient, it is stated, was delivered on the 20th of March. "On the 19th, Dr. C. made the autopsy of a man who died suddenly, sick only forty-eight hours;

had oedema of the thigh, and gangrene extending from a little above the ankle into the cavity of the abdomen." Dr. C. wounded himself, very slightly, in the right hand during the autopsy. The hand was quite painful the night following, during his attendance on the patient No. 1. He did not see this patient after the 20th, being confined to the house, and very sick from the wound just mentioned, from this time until the 3d of April.

Several cases of erysipelas occurred in the house where the autopsy mentioned above took place, soon after the examination. There were also many cases of erysipelas in town at the time of the fatal puerperal cases which have been mentioned.

The nurse who laid out the body of the patient No. 3 was taken on the evening of the same day with sore throat and erysipelas, and died in ten days from the first attack.

The nurse who laid out the body of the patient No. 4 was taken on the day following with symptoms like those of this patient, and died in a week, without any external marks of erysipelas.

"No other cases of similar character with those of Dr. C. occurred in the practice of any of the physicians in the town or vicinity at the time. Deaths following confinement have occurred in the practice of other physicians during the past year, but they were not cases of puerperal fever. No post-mortem examinations were held in any of these puerperal cases."

Some additional statements in this letter are deserving of insertion.

"A physician attended a woman in the immediate neighborhood of the cases numbered 2, 3, and 4. This patient was confined the morning of March 1st, and died on the night of March 7th. It is doubtful whether this should be considered a case of puerperal fever. She had suffered from canker, indigestion, and diarrhoea for a year previous to her delivery. Her complaints were much aggravated for two or three months previous to delivery; she had become greatly emaciated, and weakened to such an extent that it had not been expected that she would long survive her confinement, if indeed she reached that period. Her labor was easy enough; she flowed a good deal, seemed exceedingly prostrated, had ringing in the ears, and other symptoms of exhaustion; the pulse was quick and small. On the second and third day there was some tenderness and tumefaction of the abdomen, which increased somewhat on the fourth and fifth. He had cases in midwifery before and after this, which presented nothing peculiar."

It is also mentioned in the same letter, that another physician had a case during the last summer and another last fall, both of which recovered.

Another gentleman reports a case last December, a second case five weeks, and another three weeks since. All these recovered. A case also occurred very recently in the practice of a physician in the village where the eighth patient of Dr. C. resides, which proved fatal. "This patient had some patches of erysipelas on the legs and arms. The same physician has delivered three cases since, which have all done well. There have been no other cases in this town or its vicinity recently. There have been some few cases of erysipelas." It deserves notice that the partner of Dr. C., who attended the autopsy of the man above mentioned and took an active part in it; who also suffered very slightly from a prick under the thumb-nail received during the examination, had twelve cases of midwifery between March 26th and April 12th, all of which did well, and presented no peculiar symptoms. It should also be stated, that during these seventeen days he was in attendance on all the cases of erysipelas in the house where the autopsy had been performed.

I owe these facts to the prompt kindness of a gentleman whose intelligence and character are sufficient guaranty for their accuracy.

The two following letters were addressed to my friend Dr. Scorer, by the gentleman in whose practice the cases of puerperal fever occurred. His name renders it unnecessary to refer more particularly to these gentlemen, who on their part have manifested the most perfect freedom and courtesy in affording these accounts of their painful experience.

"January 28, 1843.

II.... "The time to which you allude was in 1830. The first case was in February, during a very cold time. She was confined the 4th, and died the 12th. Between the 10th and 28th of this month, I attended six women in labor, all of whom did well except the last, as also two who were confined March 1st and 5th. Mrs. E., confined February 28th, sickened, and died March 8th. The next day, 9th, I inspected the body, and the night after attended a lady, Mrs. B., who sickened, and died 16th. The 10th, I attended another, Mrs. G., who sickened, but recovered. March 16th, I went from Mrs. G.'s room to attend a Mrs. H., who sickened, and died 21st. The 17th, I inspected Mrs. B. On the 19th, I went directly from Mrs. H.'s room to attend another lady, Mrs. G., who also sickened, and died 22d. While Mrs. B. was sick, on 15th, I went directly from her room a few rods, and attended another woman, who was not sick. Up to 20th of this month I wore the same clothes. I now refused to attend any labor, and did not till April 21st, when, having thoroughly cleansed myself, I resumed my practice, and had no more puerperal fever.

"The cases were not confined to a narrow space. The two nearest were half a mile from each other, and half that distance from my residence. The others were from two to three miles apart, and nearly that distance from my residence. There were no other cases in their immediate vicinity which came to my knowledge. The general health of all the women was pretty good, and all the labors as good as common, except the first. This woman, in consequence of my not arriving in season, and the child being half-born at some time before I arrived, was very much exposed to the cold at the time of confinement, and afterwards, being confined in a very open, cold room. Of the six cases you perceive only one recovered.

"In the winter of 1817 two of my patients had puerperal fever, one very badly, the other not so badly. Both recovered. One other had swelled leg, or phlegmasia dolens, and one or two others did not recover as well as usual.

"In the summer of 1835 another disastrous period occurred in my practice. July 1st, I attended a lady in labor, who was afterwards quite ill and feverish; but at the time I did not consider her case a decided puerperal fever. On the 8th, I attended one who did well. On the 12th, one who was seriously sick. This was also an equivocal case, apparently arising from constipation and irritation of the rectum. These women were ten miles apart and five from my residence. On 15th and 20th, two who did well. On 25th, I attended another. This was a severe labor, and followed by unequivocal puerperal fever, or peritonitis. She recovered. August 2d and 3d, in about twenty-four hours I attended four persons. Two of them did very well; one was attacked with some of the common symptoms, which however subsided in a day or two, and the other had decided puerperal fever, but recovered. This woman resided five miles from me. Up to this time I wore the same coat. All my other clothes had frequently been changed. On 6th, I attended two women, one of whom was not sick at all; but the other, Mrs. L., was afterwards taken ill. On 10th, I attended a lady, who did very well. I had previously changed all my clothes, and had no garment on which had been in a puerperal room. On 12th, I was called to Mrs.

S., in labor. While she was ill, I left her to visit Mrs. L., one of the ladies who was confined on 6th. Mrs. L. had been more unwell than usual, but I had not considered her case anything more than common till this visit. I had on a surtout at this visit, which, on my return to Mrs. S., I left in another room. Mrs. S. was delivered on 13th with forceps. These women both died of decided puerperal fever.

"While I attended these women in their fevers, I changed my clothes, and washed my hands in a solution of chloride of lime after each visit. I attended seven women in labor during this period, all of whom recovered without sickness.

"In my practice I have had several single cases of puerperal fever, some of whom have died and some have recovered. Until the year 1830 I had no suspicion that the disease could be communicated from one patient to another by a nurse or midwife; but I now think the foregoing facts strongly favor that idea. I was so much convinced of this fact, that I adopted the plan before related.

"I believe my own health was as good as usual at each of the above periods. I have no recollections to the contrary.

"I believe I have answered all your questions. I have been more particular on some points perhaps than necessary; but I thought you could form your own opinion better than to take mine. In 1830 I wrote to Dr. Charming a more particular statement of my cases. If I have not answered your questions sufficiently, perhaps Dr. C. may have my letter to him, and you can find your answer there." [In a letter to myself, this gentleman also stated, "I do not recollect that there was any erysipelas or any other disease particularly prevalent at the time."]

"BOSTON, February 3, 1843.

III. "MY DEAR SIR,--I received a note from you last evening, requesting me to answer certain questions therein proposed, touching the cases of puerperal fever which came under my observation the past summer. It gives me pleasure to comply with your request, so far as it is in my power so to do, but, owing to the hurry in preparing for a journey, the notes of the cases I had then taken were lost or mislaid. The principal facts, however, are too vivid upon my recollection to be soon forgotten. I think, therefore, that I shall be able to give you all the information you may require.

"All the cases that occurred in my practice took place between the 7th of May and the 17th of June 1842.

"They were not confined to any particular part of the city. The first two cases were patients residing at the South End, the next was at the extreme North End, one living in Sea Street and the other in Roxbury. The following is the order in which they occurred:

"Case 1. Mrs. was confined on the 7th of May, at 5 o'clock, P. M., after a natural labor of six hours. At 12 o'clock at night, on the 9th (thirty-one hours after confinement), she was taken with severe chill, previous to which she was as comfortable as women usually are under the circumstances. She died on the 10th.

"Case 2. Mrs. was confined on the 10th of June (four weeks after Mrs. C.), at 11 A. M., after a natural, but somewhat severe labor of five hours. At 7 o'clock, on the morning of the 11th, she had a chill. Died on the 12th.

"Case 3. Mrs. , confined on the 14th of June, was comfortable until the 18th, when symptoms of puerperal fever were manifest. She died on the 20th.

"Case 4. Mrs. , confined June 17th, at 5 o'clock, A. M., was doing well until the morning of the 19th. She died on the evening of the 21st.

"Case 5. Mrs. was confined with her fifth child on the 17th of June, at 6 o'clock in the evening. This patient had been attacked with puerperal fever, at three of her previous confinements, but the disease yielded to depletion and other remedies without difficulty. This time, I regret to say, I was not so fortunate. She was not attacked, as were the other patients, with a chill, but complained of extreme pain in abdomen, and tenderness on pressure, almost from the moment of her confinement. In this as in the other cases, the disease resisted all remedies, and she died in great distress on the 22d of the same month. Owing to the extreme heat of the season, and my own indisposition, none of the subjects were examined after death. Dr. Channing, who was in attendance with me on the three last cases, proposed to have a post-mortem examination of the subject of case No. 5, but from some cause which I do not now recollect it was not obtained.

"You wish to know whether I wore the same clothes when attending the different cases. I cannot positively say, but I should think I did not, as the weather became warmer after the first two cases; I therefore think it probable that I made a change of at least a part of my dress. I have had no other case of puerperal fever in my own practice for three years, save those above related, and I do not remember to have lost a patient before with this disease. While absent, last July, I visited two patients sick with puerperal fever, with a friend of mine in the country. Both of them recovered.

"The cases that I have recorded were not confined to any particular constitution or temperament, but it seized upon the strong and the weak, the old and the young,--one being over forty years, and the youngest under eighteen years of age.... If the disease is of an erysipelatous nature, as many suppose, contagionists may perhaps find some ground for their belief in the fact, that, for two weeks previous to my first case of puerperal fever, I had been attending a severe case of erysipelas, and the infection may have been conveyed through me to the patient; but, on the other hand, why is not this the case with other physicians, or with the same physician at all times, for since my return from the country I have had a more inveterate case of erysipelas than ever before, and no difficulty whatever has attended any of my midwifery cases?"

I am assured, on unquestionable authority, that "About three years since, a gentleman in extensive midwifery business, in a neighboring State, lost in the course of a few weeks eight patients in child-bed, seven of them being undoubted cases of puerperal fever. No other physician of the town lost a single patient of this disease during the same period." And from what I have heard in conversation with some of our most experienced practitioners, I am inclined to think many cases of the kind might be brought to light by extensive inquiry.

This long catalogue of melancholy histories assumes a still darker aspect when we remember how kindly nature deals with the parturient female, when she is not immersed in the virulent atmosphere of an impure lying-in hospital, or poisoned in her chamber by the unsuspected breath of contagion. From all causes together, not more than four deaths in a thousand births and miscarriages happened in England and Wales during the period embraced by the first "Report of the Registrar-General." In the second Report the mortality was shown to be about five in one thousand. In the Dublin Lying-in Hospital, during the seven years of Dr. Collins's mastership, there was one case of puerperal fever to 178 deliveries, or less than six to the thousand, and one death from this disease in 278 cases, or between three and four to the thousand a yet during this period the disease was endemic in the hospital, and might have gone on to rival the horrors of the pestilence of the Maternite, had not the poison been destroyed by a thorough purification.

In private practice, leaving out of view the cases that are to be ascribed to the self-acting system of propagation, it would seem that the disease must be far from common. Mr. White of Manchester says, "Out of the whole number of lying-in patients whom I have delivered (and I may safely call it a great one), I have never lost one, nor to the best of my recollection has one been greatly endangered, by the puerperal, miliary, low nervous, putrid malignant, or milk fever." Dr. Joseph Clarke informed Dr. Collins, that in the course of forty-five years' most extensive practice he lost but four patients from this disease. One of the most eminent practitioners of Glasgow, who has been engaged in very extensive practice for upwards of a quarter of a century, testifies that he never saw more than twelve cases of real puerperal fever.[Lancet, May 4, 1833]

I have myself been told by two gentlemen practising in this city, and having for many years a large midwifery business, that they had neither of them lost a patient from this disease, and by one of them that he had only seen it in consultation with other physicians. In five hundred cases of midwifery, of which Dr. Storer has given an abstract in the first number of this Journal, there was only one instance of fatal puerperal peritonitis.

In the view of these facts, it does appear a singular coincidence, that one man or woman should have ten, twenty, thirty, or seventy cases of this rare disease following his or her footsteps with the keenness of a beagle, through the streets and lanes of a crowded city, while the scores that cross the same paths on the same errands know it only by name. It is a series of similar coincidences which has led us to consider the dagger, the musket, and certain innocent-looking white powders as having some little claim to be regarded as dangerous. It is the practical inattention to similar coincidences which has given rise to the unpleasant but often necessary documents called indictments, which has sharpened a form of the cephalotome sometimes employed in the case of adults, and adjusted that modification of the fillet which delivers the world of those who happen to be too much in the way while such striking coincidences are taking place.

I shall now mention a few instances in which the disease appears to have been conveyed by the process of direct inoculation.

Dr. Campbell of Edinburgh states that in October, 1821, he assisted at the postmortem examination of a patient who died with puerperal fever. He carried the pelvic viscera in his pocket to the class-room. The same evening he attended a woman in labor without previously changing his clothes; this patient died. The next morning he delivered a woman with the forceps; she died also, and of many others who were seized with the disease within a few weeks, three shared the same fate in succession.

In June, 1823, he assisted some of his pupils at the autopsy of a case of puerperal fever. He was unable to wash his hands with proper care, for want of the necessary accommodations. On getting home he found that two patients required his assistance. He went without further ablution, or changing his clothes; both these patients died with puerperal fever. This same Dr. Campbell is one of Dr. Churchill's authorities against contagion.

Mr. Roberton says that in one instance within his knowledge a practitioner passed the catheter for a patient with puerperal fever late in the evening; the same night he attended a lady who had the symptoms of the disease on the second day. In another instance a surgeon was called while in the act of inspecting the body of a woman who had died of this fever, to attend a labor; within forty-eight hours this patient was seized with the fever.'

On the 16th of March, 1831, a medical practitioner examined the body of a woman who had died a few days after delivery, from puerperal peritonitis. On the evening of the 17th he delivered a patient, who was seized with puerperal fever on the 19th, and died on the 24th. Between this period and the 6th of April, the same practitioner attended two other patients, both of whom were attacked with the same disease and died.

In the autumn of 1829 a physician was present at the examination of a case of puerperal fever, dissected out the organs, and assisted in sewing up the body. He had scarcely reached home when he was summoned to attend a young lady in labor. In sixteen hours she was attacked with the symptoms of puerperal fever, and narrowly escaped with her life.

In December, 1830, a midwife, who had attended two fatal cases of puerperal fever at the British Lying-in Hospital, examined a patient who had just been admitted, to ascertain if labor had commenced. This patient remained two days in the expectation that labor would come on, when she returned home and was then suddenly taken in labor and delivered before she could set out for the hospital. She went on favorably for two days, and was then taken with puerperal fever and died in thirty-six hours.

"A young practitioner, contrary to advice, examined the body of a patient who had died from puerperal fever; there was no epidemic at the time; the case appeared to be purely sporadic. He delivered three other women shortly afterwards; they all died with puerperal fever, the symptoms of which broke out very soon after labor. The patients of his colleague did well, except one, where he assisted to remove some coagula from the uterus; she was attacked in the same manner as those whom he had attended, and died also." The writer in the "British and Foreign Medical Review," from whom I quote this statement,--and who is no other than Dr. Rigby, adds, "We trust that this fact alone will forever silence such doubts, and stamp the well-merited epithet of 'criminal,' as above quoted, upon such attempts." [Brit. and For. Medical Review for Jan. 1842, p. 112.]

From the cases given by Mr. Ingleby, I select the following. Two gentlemen, after having been engaged in conducting the post-mortem examination of a case of puerperal fever, went in the same dress, each respectively, to a case of midwifery. "The one patient was seized with the rigor about thirty hours afterwards. The other patient was seized with a rigor the third morning after delivery. One recovered, one died." [Edin. Med. and Surg. Journal, April, 1838.]

One of these same gentlemen attended another woman in the same clothes two days after the autopsy referred to. "The rigor did not take place until the evening of the fifth day from the first visit. Result fatal." These cases belonged to a series of seven, the first of which was thought to have originated in a case of erysipelas. "Several cases of a mild character followed the foregoing seven, and their nature being now most unequivocal, my friend declined visiting all midwifery cases for a time, and there was no recurrence of the disease." These cases occurred in 1833. Five of them proved fatal. Mr. Ingleby gives another series of seven eases which occurred to a practitioner in 1836, the first of which was also attributed to his having opened several erysipelatous abscesses a short time previously.

I need not refer to the case lately read before this Society, in which a physician went, soon after performing an autopsy of a case of puerperal fever, to a woman in labor, who was seized with the same disease and perished. The forfeit of that error has been already paid.

At a meeting of the Medical and Chirurgical Society before referred to, Dr. Merriman related an instance occurring in his own practice, which excites a reasonable suspicion that two lives were sacrificed to a still less dangerous experiment. He was at the examination of a case of puerperal fever at two o'clock in the afternoon. He took care not to touch the body. At nine o'clock the same evening he attended a woman in labor; she was so nearly delivered that he had scarcely anything to do. The next morning she had severe rigors, and in forty-eight hours she was a corpse. Her infant had erysipelas and died in two days. [Lancet, May 2, 1840.]

In connection with the facts which have been stated, it seems proper to allude to the dangerous and often fatal effects which have followed from wounds received in the post-mortem examination of patients who have died of puerperal fever. The fact that such wounds are attended with peculiar risk has been long noticed. I find that Chaussier was in the habit of cautioning his students against the danger to which they were exposed in these dissections. [Stein, L'Art d'Accoucher, 1794; Dict. des Sciences Medicales, art. "Puerperal."] The head pharmacien of the Hotel Dieu, in his analysis of the fluid effused in puerperal peritonitis, says that practitioners are convinced of its deleterious qualities, and that it is very dangerous to apply it to the denuded skin. [Journal de Pharmacie, January, 1836.] Sir Benjamin Brodie speaks of it as being well known that the inoculation of lymph or pus from the peritoneum of a puerperal patient is often attended with dangerous and even fatal symptoms. Three cases in confirmation of this statement, two of them fatal, have been reported to this Society within a few months.

Of about fifty cases of injuries of this kind, of various degrees of severity, which I have collected from different sources, at least twelve were instances of infection from puerperal peritonitis. Some of the others are so stated as to render it probable that they may have been of the same nature. Five other cases were of peritoneal inflammation; three in males. Three were what was called enteritis, in one instance complicated with erysipelas; but it is well known that this term has been often used to signify inflammation of the peritoneum covering the intestines. On the other hand, no case of typhus or typhoid fever is mentioned as giving rise to dangerous consequences, with the exception of the single instance of an undertaker mentioned by Mr. Travers, who seems to have been poisoned by a fluid which exuded from the body. The other accidents were produced by dissection, or some other mode of contact with bodies of patients who had died of various affections. They also differed much in severity, the cases of puerperal origin being among the most formidable and fatal. Now a moment's reflection will show that the number of cases of serious consequences ensuing from the dissection of the bodies of those who had perished of puerperal fever is so vastly disproportioned to the relatively small number of autopsies made in this complaint as compared with typhus or pneumonia (from which last disease not one case of poisoning happened), and still more from all diseases put together, that the conclusion is irresistible that a most fearful morbid poison is often generated in the course of this disease. Whether or not it is sui generis, confined to this disease, or produced in some others, as, for instance, erysipelas, I need, not stop to inquire.

In connection with this may be taken the following statement of Dr. Rigby. "That the discharges from a patient under puerperal fever are in the highest degree contagious we have abundant evidence in the history of lying-in hospitals. The puerperal abscesses are also contagious, and may be communicated to healthy lying-in women by washing with the same sponge; this fact has been repeatedly proved in the Vienna Hospital; but they are equally communicable to women not pregnant; on more than one occasion the women engaged in washing the soiled bed-linen of the General Lying-in Hospital have been attacked with abscess in the fingers or hands, attended with rapidly spreading inflammation of the cellular tissue."

Now add to all this the undisputed fact, that within the walls of lying-in hospitals there is often generated a miasm, palpable as the chlorine used to destroy it, tenacious so as in some cases almost to defy extirpation, deadly in some institutions as the plague; which has killed women in a private hospital of London so fast that they were buried two in one coffin to conceal its horrors; which enabled Tonnelle to record two hundred and twenty-two autopsies at the Maternite of Paris; which has led Dr. Lee to express his deliberate conviction that the loss of life occasioned by these institutions completely defeats the objects of their founders; and out of this train of cumulative evidence, the multiplied groups of cases clustering about individuals, the deadly results of autopsies, the inoculation by fluids from the living patient, the murderous poison of hospitals,--does there not result a conclusion that laughs all sophistry to scorn, and renders all argument an insult?

I have had occasion to mention some instances in which there was an apparent relation between puerperal fever and erysipelas. The length to which this paper has extended does not allow me to enter into the consideration of this most important subject. I will only say, that the evidence appears to me altogether satisfactory that some most fatal series of puerperal fever have been produced by an infection originating in the matter or effluvia of erysipelas. In evidence of some connection between the two diseases, I need not go back to the older authors, as Pouteau or Gordon, but will content myself with giving the following references, with their dates; from which it will be seen that the testimony has been constantly coming before the profession for the last few years.

"London Cyclopaedia of Practical Medicine," article Puerperal Fever, 1833.

Mr. Ceeley's Account of the Puerperal Fever at Aylesbury. "Lancet," 1835.

Dr. Ramsbotham's Lecture. "London Medical Gazette," 1835.

Mr. Yates Ackerly's Letter in the same Journal, 1838.

Mr. Ingleby on Epidemic Puerperal Fever. "Edinburgh Medical and Surgical Journal," 1838.

Mr. Paley's Letter. "London Medical Gazette," 1839.

Remarks at the Medical and Chirurgical Society. "Lancet," 1840.

Dr. Rigby's "System of Midwifery." 1841.

"Nunneley on Erysipelas,"--a work which contains a large number of references on the subject. 1841.

"British and Foreign Quarterly Review," 1842.

Dr. S. Jackson of Northumberland, as already quoted from the Summary of the College of Physicians, 1842.

And lastly, a startling series of cases by Mr. Storrs of Doncaster, to be, found in the "American Journal of the Medical Sciences" for January, 1843.

The relation of puerperal fever with other continued fevers would seem to be remote and rarely obvious. Hey refers to two cases of synochus occurring in the Royal Infirmary of Edinburgh, in women who had attended upon puerperal patients. Dr. Collins refers to several instances in which puerperal fever has appeared to originate from a continued proximity to patients suffering with typhus.

Such occurrences as those just mentioned, though most important to be remembered and guarded against, hardly attract our notice in the midst of the gloomy facts by which they are surrounded. Of these facts, at the risk of fatiguing repetitions, I have summoned a sufficient number, as I believe, to convince the most incredulous that every attempt to disguise the truth which underlies them all is useless.

It is true that some of the historians of the disease, especially Hulme, Hull, and Leake, in England; Tonnelle, Duges, and Baudelocque, in France, profess not to have found puerperal fever contagious. At the most they give us mere negative facts, worthless against an extent of evidence which now overlaps the widest range of doubt, and doubles upon itself in the redundancy of superfluous demonstration. Examined in detail, this and much of the show of testimony brought up to stare the daylight of conviction out of countenance, proves to be in a great measure unmeaning and inapplicable, as might be easily shown were it necessary. Nor do I feel the necessity of enforcing the conclusion which arises spontaneously from the facts which have been enumerated, by formally citing the opinions of those grave authorities who have for the last half-century been sounding the unwelcome truth it has cost so many lives to establish.

"It is to the British practitioner," says Dr. Rigby, "that we are indebted for strongly insisting upon this important and dangerous character of puerperal fever."

The names of Gordon, John Clarke, Denman, Burns, Young, Hamilton, Haighton, Good, Waller; Blundell, Gooch, Ramsbotham, Douglas, Lee, Ingleby, Locock, Abercrombie, Alison; Travers, Rigby, and Watson, many of whose writings I have already referred to, may have some influence with those who prefer the weight of authorities to the simple deductions of their own reason from the facts laid before them. A few Continental writers have adopted similar conclusions. It gives me pleasure to remember, that while the doctrine has been unceremoniously discredited in one of the leading Journals, and made very light of by teachers in two of the principal Medical Schools, of this country, Dr. Channing has for many years inculcated, and enforced by examples, the danger to be apprehended and the precautions to be taken in the disease under consideration.

I have no wish to express any harsh feeling with regard to the painful subject which has come before us. If there are any so far excited by the story of these dreadful events that they ask for some word of indignant remonstrance to show that science does not turn the hearts of its followers into ice or stone, let me remind them that such words have been uttered by those who speak with an authority I could not claim. It is as a lesson rather than as a reproach that I call up the memory of these irreparable errors and wrongs. No tongue can tell the heart-breaking calamity they have caused; they have closed the eyes just opened upon a new world of love and happiness; they have bowed the strength of manhood into the dust; they have cast the helplessness of infancy into the stranger's arms, or bequeathed it, with less cruelty, the death of its dying parent. There is no tone deep enough for regret, and no voice loud enough for warning. The woman about to become a mother, or with her new-born infant upon her bosom, should be the object of trembling care and sympathy wherever she bears her tender burden, or stretches her aching limbs. The very outcast of the streets has pity upon her sister in degradation, when the seal of promised maternity is impressed upon her. The remorseless vengeance of the law, brought down upon its victim by a machinery as sure as destiny, is arrested in its fall at a word which reveals her transient claim for mercy. The solemn prayer of the liturgy singles out her sorrows from the multiplied trials of life, to plead for her in the hour of peril. God forbid that any member of the profession to which she trusts her life, doubly precious at that eventful period, should hazard it negligently, unadvisedly, or selfishly!

There may be some among those whom I address who are disposed to ask the question, What course are we to follow in relation to this matter? The facts are before them, and the answer must be left to their own judgment and conscience. If any should care to know my own conclusions, they are the following; and in taking the liberty to state them very freely and broadly, I would ask the inquirer to examine them as freely in the light of the evidence which has been laid before him.

1. A physician holding himself in readiness to attend cases of midwifery should never take any active part in the post-mortem examination of cases of puerperal fever.

2. If a physician is present at such autopsies, he should use thorough ablution, change every article of dress, and allow twenty-four hours or more to elapse before attending to any case of midwifery. It may be well to extend the same caution to cases of simple peritonitis.

3. Similar precautions should be taken after the autopsy or surgical treatment of cases of erysipelas, if the physician is obliged to unite such offices with his obstetrical duties, which is in the highest degree inexpedient.

4. On the occurrence of a single case of puerperal fever in his practice, the physician is bound to consider the next female he attends in labor, unless some weeks at least have elapsed, as in danger of being infected by him, and it is his duty to take every precaution to diminish her risk of disease and death.

5. If within a short period two cases of puerperal fever happen close to each other, in the practice of the same physician, the disease not existing or prevailing in the neighborhood, he would do wisely to relinquish his obstetrical practice for at least one month, and endeavor to free himself by every available means from any noxious influence he may carry about with him.

6. The occurrence of three or more closely connected cases, in the practice of one individual, no others existing in the neighborhood, and no other sufficient cause being alleged for the coincidence, is prima facie evidence that he is the vehicle of contagion.

7. It is the duty of the physician to take every precaution that the disease shall not be introduced by nurses or other assistants, by making proper inquiries concerning them, and giving timely warning of every suspected source of danger.

8. Whatever indulgence may be granted to those who have heretofore been the ignorant causes of so much misery, the time has come when the existence of a private pestilence in the sphere of a single physician should be looked upon, not as a misfortune, but a crime; and in the knowledge of such occurrences the duties of the practitioner to his profession should give way to his paramount obligations to society. ADDITIONAL REFERENCES AND CASES.

Fifth Annual Report of the Registrar-General of England.

1843. Appendix. Letter from William Farr, Esq.--Several new series of cases are given in the Letter of Mr. Stows, contained in the Appendix to this Report. Mr. Stows suggests precautions similar to those I have laid down, and these precautions are strongly enforced by Mr. Farr, who is, therefore, obnoxious to the same criticisms as myself.

Hall and Dexter, in Am. Journal of Med. Sc. for January, 1844.--Cases of puerperal fever seeming to originate in erysipelas.

Elkington, of Birmingham, in Provincial Med. Journal, cited in Am. Journ. Med. Sc. for April, 1844.--Six cases in less than a fortnight, seeming to originate in a case of erysipelas.

West's Reports, in Brit. and For. Med. Review for October, 1845, and January, 1847.--Affection of the arm, resembling malignant pustule, after removing the placenta of a patient who died from puerperal fever. Reference to cases at Wurzburg, as proving contagion, and to Keiller's cases in the Monthly Journal for February, 1846, as showing connection of puerperal fever and erysipelas.

Kneeland.--Contagiousness of Puerperal Fever. Am. Jour. Med. Se., January, 1846. Also, Connection between Puerperal Fever and Epidemic Erysipelas. Ibid., April, 1846.

Robert Storrs.--Contagious Effects of Puerperal Fever on the Male Subject; or on Persons not Child-bearing. (From Provincial Med. and Surg. Journal.) Am. Jour. Med. Sc., January, 184,6. Numerous cases. See also Dr. Reid's case in same Journal for April, 1846.

Routh's paper in Proc. of Royal Med. Chir. Soc., Am. Jour. Med. Sc., April, 1849, also in B. and F. Med. Chir. Review, April, 1850.

Hill, of Leuchars.--A Series of Cases illustrating the Contagious Nature of Erysipelas and of Puerperal Fever, and their Intimate Pathological Connection. (From Monthly Journal of Med. Sc.) Am. Jour. Med. Se., July, 1850.

Skoda on the Causes of Puerperal Fever. (Peritonitis in rabbits, from inoculation with different morbid secretions.) Am. Jour. Med. Se., October, 1850.

Arneth. Paper read before the National Academy of Medicine. Annales d'Hygiene, Tome LXV. 2e Partie. (Means of Disinfection proposed by M. "Semmeliveis" (Semmelweiss.) Lotions of chloride of lime and use of nail-brush before admission to lying-in wards. Alleged sudden and great decrease of mortality from puerperal fever. Cause of disease attributed to inoculation with cadaveric matters.) See also Routh's paper, mentioned above.

Moir. Remarks at a meeting of the Edinburgh Medico-Chirurgical Society. Refers to cases of Dr. Kellie, of Leith. Sixteen in succession, all fatal. Also to several instances of individual pupils having had a succession of cases in various quarters of the town, while others, practising as extensively in the same localities, had none. Also to several special cases not mentioned elsewhere. Am. Jour. Med. Se. for October, 1851. (From New Monthly Journal of Med. Science.)

Simpson.--Observations at a Meeting of the Edinburgh Obstetrical Society. (An "eminent gentleman," according to Dr. Meigs, whose "name is as well known in America as in (his) native land." Obstetrics. Phil. 1852, pp. 368, 375.) The student is referred to this paper for a valuable resume of many of the facts, and the necessary inferences, relating to this subject. Also for another series of cases, Mr. Sidey's, five or six in rapid succession. Dr. Simpson attended the dissection of two of Dr. Sidey's cases, and freely handled the diseased parts. His next four child-bed patients were affected with puerperal fever, and it was the first time he had seen it in practice. As Dr. Simpson is a gentleman (Dr. Meigs, as above), and as "a gentleman's hands are clean" (Dr. Meigs' Sixth Letter), it follows that a gentleman with clean hands may carry the disease. Am. Jour. Med. Sc., October, 1851.

Peddle.--The five or six cases of Dr. Sidey, followed by the four of Dr. Simpson, did not end the series. A practitioner in Leith having examined in Dr. Simpson's house, a portion of the uterus obtained from one of the patients, had immediately afterwards three fatal cases of puerperal fever. Dr. Veddie referred to two distinct series of consecutive cases in his own practice. He had since taken precautions, and not met with any such cases. Am. Jour. Med. Sc., October, 1851.

Copland. Considers it proved that puerperal fever maybe propagated by the hands and the clothes, or either, of a third person, the bed-clothes or body-clothes of a patient. Mentions a new series of cases, one of which he saw, with the practitioner who had attended them. She was the sixth he had had within a few days. All died. Dr. Copland insisted that contagion had caused these cases; advised precautionary measures, and the practitioner had no other cases for a considerable time. Considers it criminal, after the evidence adduced,--which he could have quadrupled,--and the weight of authority brought forward, for a practitioner to be the medium of transmitting contagion and death to his patients. Dr. Copland lays down rules similar to those suggested by myself, and is therefore entitled to the same epithet for so doing. Medical Dictionary, New York, 1852. Article, Puerperal States and Diseases.

If there is any appetite for facts so craving as to be yet unappeased,--Lesotho, necdum satiata,--more can be obtained. Dr. Hodge remarks that "the frequency and importance of this singular circumstance (that the disease is occasionally more prevalent with one practitioner than another) has been exceedingly overrated." More than thirty strings of cases, more than two hundred and fifty sufferers from puerperal fever, more than one hundred and thirty deaths appear as the results of a sparing estimate of such among the facts I have gleaned as could be numerically valued. These facts constitute, we may take it for granted, but a small fraction of those that have actually occurred. The number of them might be greater, but "'t is enough, 't will serve," in Mercutio's modest phrase, so far as frequency is concerned. For a just estimate of the importance of the singular circumstance, it might be proper to consult the languid survivors, the widowed husbands, and the motherless children, as well as "the unfortunate accoucheur."

CURRENTS AND COUNTER-CURRENTS IN MEDICAL SCIENCE

An Address delivered before the Massachusetts Medical Society, at the Annual Meeting, May 30, 1860.

"Facultate magis quam violentia."
HIPPOCRATES.

Our Annual Meeting never fails to teach us at least one lesson. The art whose province it is to heal and to save cannot protect its own ranks from the inroads of disease and the waste of the Destroyer.

Seventeen of our associates have been taken from us since our last Anniversary. Most of them followed their calling in the villages or towns that lie among the hills or along the inland streams. Only those who have lived the kindly, mutually dependent life of the country, can tell how near the physician who is the main reliance in sickness of all the families throughout a thinly settled region comes to the hearts of the people among whom he labors, how they value him while living, how they cherish his memory when dead. For these friends of ours who have gone before, there is now no more toil; they start from their slumbers no more at the cry of pain; they sally forth no more into the storms; they ride no longer over the lonely roads that knew them so well; their wheels are rusting on their axles or rolling with other burdens; their watchful eyes are closed to all the sorrows they lived to soothe. Not one of these was famous in the great world; some were almost unknown beyond their own immediate circle. But they have left behind them that loving remembrance which is better than fame, and if their epitaphs are chiselled briefly in stone, they are written at full length on living tablets in a thousand homes to which they carried their ever-welcome aid and sympathy.

One whom we have lost, very widely known and honored, was a leading practitioner of this city. His image can hardly be dimmed in your recollection, as he stood before you only three years ago, filling the same place with which I am now honored. To speak of him at all worthily, would be to write the history of professional success, won without special aid at starting, by toil, patience, good sense, pure character, and pleasing manners; won in a straight uphill ascent, without one breathing-space until he sat down, not to rest, but to die. If prayers could have shielded him from the stroke, if love could have drawn forth the weapon, and skill could have healed the wound, this passing tribute might have been left to other lips and to another generation.

Let us hope that our dead have at last found that rest which neither summer nor winter, nor day nor night, had granted to their unending earthly labors! And let us remember that our duties to our brethren do not cease when they become unable to share our toils, or leave behind them in want and woe those whom their labor had supported. It is honorable to the Profession that it has organized an Association a for the relief of its suffering members and their families; it owes this tribute to the ill-rewarded industry and sacrifices of its less fortunate brothers who wear out health and life in the service of humanity. I have great pleasure in referring to this excellent movement, which gives our liberal profession a chance to show its liberality, and serves to unite us all, the successful and those whom fortune has cast down, in the bonds of a true brotherhood.

A medical man, as he goes about his daily business after twenty years of practice, is apt to suppose that he treats his patients according to the teachings of his experience. No doubt this is true to some extent; to what extent depending much on the qualities of the individual. But it is easy to prove that the prescriptions of even wise physicians are very commonly founded on something quite different from experience. Experience must be based on the permanent facts of nature. But a glance at the prevalent modes of treatment of any two successive generations will show that there is a changeable as well as a permanent element in the art of healing; not merely changeable as diseases vary, or as new remedies are introduced, but changeable by the going out of fashion of special remedies, by the decadence of a popular theory from which their fitness was deduced, or other cause not more significant. There is no reason to suppose that the present time is essentially different in this respect from any other. Much, therefore, which is now very commonly considered to be the result of experience, will be recognized in the next, or in some succeeding generation, as no such result at all, but as a foregone conclusion, based on some prevalent belief or fashion of the time.

There are, of course, in every calling, those who go about the work of the day before them, doing it according to the rules of their craft, and asking no questions of the past or of the future, or of the aim and end to which their special labor is contributing. These often consider and call themselves practical men. They pull the oars of society, and have no leisure to watch the currents running this or that way; let theorists and philosophers attend to them. In the mean time, however, these currents are carrying the practical men, too, and all their work may be thrown away, and worse than thrown away, if they do not take knowledge of them and get out of the wrong ones and into the right ones as soon as they may. Sir Edward Parry and his party were going straight towards the pole in one of their arctic expeditions, travelling at the rate of ten miles a day. But the ice over which they travelled was drifting straight towards the equator, at the rate of twelve miles a day, and yet no man among them would have known that he was travelling two miles a day backward unless he had lifted his eyes from the track in which he was plodding. It is not only going backward that the plain practical workman is liable to, if he will not look up and look around; he may go forward to ends he little dreams of. It is a simple business for a mason to build up a niche in a wall; but what if, a hundred years afterwards when the wall is torn down, the skeleton of a murdered man drop out of the niche? It was a plain practical piece of carpentry for a Jewish artisan to fit two pieces of timber together according to the legal pattern in the time of Pontius Pilate; he asked no questions, perhaps, but we know what burden the cross bore on the morrow! And so, with subtler tools than trowels or axes, the statesman who works in policy without principle, the theologian who works in forms without a soul, the physician who, calling himself a practical man, refuses to recognize the larger laws which govern his changing practice, may all find that they have been building truth into the wall, and hanging humanity upon the cross.

The truth is, that medicine, professedly founded on observation, is as sensitive to outside influences, political, religious, philosophical, imaginative, as is the barometer to the changes of atmospheric density. Theoretically it ought to go on its own straightforward inductive path, without regard to changes of government or to fluctuations of public opinion. But look a moment while I clash a few facts together, and see if some sparks do not reveal by their light a closer relation between the Medical Sciences and the conditions of Society and the general thought of the time, than would at first be suspected.

Observe the coincidences between certain great political and intellectual periods and the appearance of illustrious medical reformers and teachers. It was in the age of Pericles, of Socrates, of Plato, of Phidias, that Hippocrates gave to medical knowledge the form which it retained for twenty centuries. With the world-conquering Alexander, the world-embracing Aristotle, appropriating anatomy and physiology, among his manifold spoils of study, marched abreast of his royal pupil to wider conquests. Under the same Ptolemies who founded the Alexandrian Library and Museum, and ordered the Septuagint version of the Hebrew Scriptures, the infallible Herophilus ["Contradicere Herophilo in anatomicis, est contradicere evangelium," was a saying of Fallopius.] made those six hundred dissections of which Tertullian accused him, and the sagacious Erasistratus introduced his mild antiphlogistic treatment in opposition to the polypharmacy and antidotal practice of his time. It is significant that the large-minded Galen should have been the physician and friend of the imperial philosopher Marcus Aurelius. The Arabs gave laws in various branches of knowledge to those whom their arms had invaded, or the terror of their spreading dominion had reached, and the point from which they started was, as Humboldt acknowledges, "the study of medicine, by which they long ruled the Christian Schools," and to which they added the department of chemical pharmacy.

Look at Vesalius, the contemporary of Luther. Who can fail to see one common spirit in the radical ecclesiastic and the reforming court-physician? Both still to some extent under the dominion of the letter: Luther holding to the real presence; Vesalius actually causing to be drawn and engraved two muscles which he knew were not found in the human subject, because they had been described by Galen, from dissections of the lower animals. Both breaking through old traditions in the search of truth; one, knife in hand, at the risk of life and reputation, the other at the risk of fire and fagot, with that mightier weapon which all the devils could not silence, though they had been thicker than the tiles on the house-tops. How much the physician of the Catholic Charles V. had in common with the great religious destructive, may be guessed by the relish with which he tells the story how certain Pavian students exhumed the body of an "elegans scortum," or lovely dame of ill repute, the favorite of a monk of the order of St. Anthony, who does not seem to have resisted temptation so well as the founder of his order. We have always ranked the physician Rabelais among the early reformers, but I do not know that Vesalius has ever been thanked for his hit at the morals of the religious orders, or for turning to the good of science what was intended for the "benefit of clergy."

Our unfortunate medical brother, Michael Servetus, the spiritual patient to whom the theological moxa was applied over the entire surface for the cure of his heresy, came very near anticipating Harvey. The same quickened thought of the time which led him to dispute the dogma of the Church, opened his mind to the facts which contradicted the dogmas of the Faculty.

Harvey himself was but the posthumous child of the great Elizabethan period. Bacon was at once his teacher and his patient. The founder of the new inductive philosophy had only been dead two years when the treatise on the Circulation, the first-fruit of the Restoration of Science, was given to the world.

And is it to be looked at as a mere accidental coincidence, that while Napoleon was modernizing the political world, Bichat was revolutionizing the science of life and the art that is based upon it; that while the young general was scaling the Alps, the young surgeon was climbing the steeper summits of unexplored nature; that the same year read the announcement of those admirable "Researches on Life and Death," and the bulletins of the battle of Marengo?

If we come to our own country, who can fail to recognize that Benjamin Rush, the most conspicuous of American physicians, was the intellectual offspring of the movement which produced the Revolution? "The same hand," says one of his biographers, "which subscribed the declaration of the political independence of these States, accomplished their emancipation from medical systems formed in foreign countries, and wholly unsuitable to the state of diseases in America."

Following this general course of remark, I propose to indicate in a few words the direction of the main intellectual current of the time, and to point out more particularly some of the eddies which tend to keep the science and art of medicine from moving with it, or even to carry them backwards.

The two dominant words of our time are law and average, both pointing to the uniformity of the order of being in which we live. Statistics have tabulated everything,--population, growth, wealth, crime, disease. We have shaded maps showing the geographical distribution of larceny and suicide. Analysis and classification have been at work upon all tangible and visible objects. The Positive Philosophy of Comte has only given expression to the observing and computing mind of the nineteenth century.

In the mean time, the great stronghold of intellectual conservatism, traditional belief, has been assailed by facts which would have been indicted as blasphemy but a few generations ago. Those new tables of the law, placed in the hands of the geologist by the same living God who spoke from Sinai to the Israelites of old, have remodelled the beliefs of half the civilized world. The solemn scepticism of science has replaced the sneering doubts of witty philosophers. The more positive knowledge we gain, the more we incline to question all that has been received without absolute proof.

As a matter of course, this movement has its partial reactions. The province of faith is claimed as a port free of entry to unsupported individual convictions. The tendency to question is met by the unanalyzing instinct of reverence. The old church calls back its frightened truants. Some who have lost their hereditary religious belief find a resource in the revelations of Spiritualism. By a parallel movement, some of those who have become medical infidels pass over to the mystic band of believers in the fancied miracles of Homoeopathy.

Under these influences transmitted to, or at least shared by, the medical profession, the old question between "Nature," so called, and "Art," or professional tradition, has reappeared with new interest. I say the old question, for Hippocrates stated the case on the side of "Nature" more than two thousand years ago. Miss Florence Nightingale,--and if I name her next to the august Father of the Healing Art, its noblest daughter well deserves that place of honor,--Miss Florence Nightingale begins her late volume with a paraphrase of his statement. But from a very early time to this there has always been a strong party against "Nature." Themison called the practice of Hippocrates "a meditation upon death." Dr. Rush says: "It is impossible to calculate the mischief which Hippocrates, has done, by first marking Nature with his name and afterwards letting her loose upon sick people. Millions have perished by her hands in all ages and countries." Sir John Forbes, whose defence of "Nature" in disease you all know, and to the testimonial in whose honor four of your Presidents have contributed, has been recently greeted, on retiring from the profession, with a wish that his retirement had been twenty years sooner, and the opinion that no man had done so much to destroy the confidence of the public in the medical profession.

In this Society we have had the Hippocratic and the Themisonic side fairly represented. The treatise of one of your early Presidents on the Mercurial Treatment is familiar to my older listeners. Others who have held the same office have been noted for the boldness of their practice, and even for partiality to the use of complex medication.

On the side of "Nature" we have had, first of all, that remarkable discourse on Self-Limited Diseases, [On Self-Limited Diseases. A Discourse delivered before the Massachusetts Medical Society, at their Annual Meeting, May 27, 1835. By Jacob Bigelow, M. D.] which has given the key-note to the prevailing medical tendency of this neighborhood, at least, for the quarter of a century since it was delivered. Nor have we forgotten the address delivered at Springfield twenty years later, [Search out the Secrets, of Nature. By Augustus A. Gould, M. D. Read at the Annual Meeting, June 27, 1855.] full of good sense and useful suggestions, to one of which suggestions we owe the learned, impartial, judicious, well-written Prize Essay of Dr. Worthington Hooker. [Rational Therapeutics. A Prize Essay. By Worthington Hooker, M. D., of New Haven. Boston. 1857.] We should not omit from the list the important address of another of our colleagues, [On the Treatment of Compound and Complicated Fractures. By William J. Walker, M. D. Read at the Annual Meeting, May 29, 1845.] showing by numerous cases the power of Nature in healing compound fractures to be much greater than is frequently supposed,--affording, indeed, more striking illustrations than can be obtained from the history of visceral disease, of the supreme wisdom, forethought, and adaptive dexterity of that divine Architect, as shown in repairing the shattered columns which support the living temple of the body.

We who are on the side of "Nature" please ourselves with the idea that we are in the great current in which the true intelligence of the time is moving. We believe that some who oppose, or fear, or denounce our movement are themselves caught in various eddies that set back against the truth. And we do most earnestly desire and most actively strive, that Medicine, which, it is painful to remember, has been spoken of as "the withered branch of science" at a meeting of the British Association, shall be at length brought fully to share, if not to lead, the great wave of knowledge which rolls with the tides that circle the globe.

If there is any State or city which might claim to be the American headquarters of the nature-trusting heresy, provided it be one, that State is Massachusetts, and that city is its capital. The effect which these doctrines have upon the confidence reposed in the profession is a matter of opinion. For myself, I do not believe this confidence can be impaired by any investigations which tend to limit the application of troublesome, painful, uncertain, or dangerous remedies. Nay, I will venture to say this, that if every specific were to fail utterly, if the cinchona trees all died out, and the arsenic mines were exhausted, and the sulphur regions were burned up, if every drug from the vegetable, animal, and mineral kingdom were to disappear from the market, a body of enlightened men, organized as a distinct profession, would be required just as much as now, and respected and trusted as now, whose province should be to guard against the causes of disease, to eliminate them if possible when still present, to order all the conditions of the patient so as to favor the efforts of the system to right itself, and to give those predictions of the course of disease which only experience can warrant, and which in so many cases relieve the exaggerated fears of sufferers and their friends, or warn them in season of impending danger. Great as the loss would be if certain active remedies could no longer be obtained, it would leave the medical profession the most essential part of it's duties, and all, and more than all, its present share of honors; for it would be the death-blow to charlatanism, which depends for its success almost entirely on drugs, or at least on a nomenclature that suggests them.

There is no offence, then, or danger in expressing the opinion, that, after all which has been said, the community is still overdosed: The best proof of it is, that "no families take so little medicine as those of doctors, except those of apothecaries, and that old practitioners are more sparing of active medicines than younger ones."

[Dr. James Jackson has kindly permitted me to make the following extract from a letter just received by him from Sir James Clark, and dated May 26, 1860: "As a physician advances in age, he generally, I think, places less confidence in the ordinary medical treatment than he did, not only during his early, but even his middle period of life."] The conclusion from these facts is one which the least promising of Dr. Howe's pupils in the mental department could hardly help drawing.

Part of the blame of over-medication must, I fear, rest with the profession, for yielding to the tendency to self-delusion, which seems inseparable from the practice of the art of healing. I need only touch on the common modes of misunderstanding or misapplying the evidence of nature.

First, there is the natural incapacity for sound observation, which is like a faulty ear in music. We see this in many persons who know a good deal about books, but who are not sharp-sighted enough to buy a horse or deal with human diseases.

Secondly, there is in some persons a singular inability to weigh the value of testimony; of which, I think, from a pretty careful examination of his books, Hahnemann affords the best specimen outside the walls of Bedlam.

The inveterate logical errors to which physicians have always been subject are chiefly these:

The mode of inference per enumerationem simplicem, in scholastic phrase; that is, counting only their favorable cases. This is the old trick illustrated in Lord Bacon's story of the gifts of the shipwrecked people, hung up in the temple.--Behold! they vowed these gifts to the altar, and the gods saved them. Ay, said a doubting bystander, but how many made vows of gifts and were shipwrecked notwithstanding? The numerical system is the best corrective of this and similar errors. The arguments commonly brought against its application to all matters of medical observation, treatment included, seem to apply rather to the tabulation of facts ill observed, or improperly classified, than to the method itself.

The post hoc ergo propter hoc error: he got well after taking my medicine; therefore in consequence of taking it.

The false induction from genuine facts of observation, leading to the construction of theories which are then deductively applied in the face of the results of direct observation. The school of Broussais has furnished us with a good example of this error.

And lastly, the error which Sir Thomas Browne calls giving "a reason of the golden tooth;" that is, assuming a falsehood as a fact, and giving reasons for it, commonly fanciful ones, as is constantly done by that class of incompetent observers who find their "golden tooth" in the fabulous effects of the homoeopathic materia medica,--which consists of sugar of milk and a nomenclature.

Another portion of the blame rests with the public itself, which insists on being poisoned. Somebody buys all the quack medicines that build palaces for the mushroom, say rather, the toadstool millionaires. Who is it? These people have a constituency of millions. The popular belief is all but universal that sick persons should feed on noxious substances. One of our members was called not long since to a man with a terribly sore mouth. On inquiry he found that the man had picked up a box of unknown pills, in Howard Street, and had proceeded to take them, on general principles, pills being good for people. They happened to contain mercury, and hence the trouble for which he consulted our associate.

The outside pressure, therefore, is immense upon the physician, tending to force him to active treatment of some kind. Certain old superstitions, still lingering in the mind of the public, and not yet utterly expelled from that of the profession, are at the bottom of this, or contribute to it largely. One of the most ancient is, that disease is a malignant agency, or entity, to be driven out of the body by offensive substances, as the smoke of the fish's heart and liver drove the devil out of Tobit's bridal chamber, according to the Apochrypha. Epileptics used to suck the blood from the wounds of dying gladiators. [Plinii Hist. Mundi. lib. xxviii. c. 4.] The Hon. Robert Boyle's little book was published some twenty or thirty years before our late President, Dr. Holyoke, was born. [A Collection of Choice and Safe Remedies. The Fifth Edition, corrected. London, 1712. Dr. Holyoke was born in 1728.] In it he recommends, as internal medicines, most of the substances commonly used as fertilizers of the soil. His "Album Graecum" is best left untranslated, and his "Zebethum Occidentale" is still more transcendentally unmentionable except in a strange dialect. It sounds odiously to us to hear him recommend for dysentery a powder made from "the sole of an old shoe worn by some man that walks much." Perhaps nobody here ever heard of tying a stocking, which had been worn during the day, round the neck at night for a sore throat. The same idea of virtue in unlovely secretions! [The idea is very ancient. "Sordes hominis" "Sudore et oleo medicinam facientibus."--

Plin. xxviii. 4.]

Even now the Homoeopathists have been introducing the venom of serpents, under the learned title of Lachesis, and outraging human nature with infusions of the pediculus capitis; that is, of course, as we understand their dilutions, the names of these things; for if a fine-tooth-comb insect were drowned in Lake Superior, we cannot agree with them in thinking that every drop of its waters would be impregnated with all the pedicular virtues they so highly value. They know what they are doing. They are appealing to the detestable old superstitious presumption in favor of whatever is nauseous and noxious as being good for the sick.

Again, we all occasionally meet persons stained with nitrate of silver, given for epilepsy. Read what Dr. Martin says, about the way in which it came to be used, in his excellent address before the Norfolk County Medical Society, and the evidence I can show, but have not time for now, and then say what you think of the practice which on such presumptions turns a white man as blue as the double-tattooed King of the Cannibal Islands! [Note A.]

If medical superstitions have fought their way down through all the rationalism and scepticism of the nineteenth century, of course the theories of the schools, supported by great names, adopted into the popular belief and incorporated with the general mass of misapprehension with reference to disease, must be expected to meet us at every turn in the shape of bad practice founded on false doctrine. A French patient complains that his blood heats him, and expects his doctor to bleed him. An English or American one says he is bilious, and will not be easy without a dose of calomel. A doctor looks at a patient's tongue, sees it coated, and says the stomach is foul; his head full of the old saburral notion which the extreme inflammation-doctrine of Broussais did so much to root out, but which still leads, probably, to much needless and injurious wrong of the stomach and bowels by evacuants, when all they want is to be let alone. It is so hard to get anything out of the dead hand of medical tradition! The mortmain of theorists extinct in science clings as close as that of ecclesiastics defunct in law.

One practical hint may not be out of place here. It seems to be sometimes forgotten, by those who must know the fact, that the tongue is very different, anatomically and physiologically, from the stomach. Its condition does not in the least imply a similar one of the stomach, which is a very different structure, covered with a different kind of epithelium, and furnished with entirely different secretions. A silversmith will, for a dollar, make a small hoe, of solid silver, which will last for centuries, and will give a patient more comfort, used for the removal of the accumulated epithelium and fungous growths which constitute the "fur," than many a prescription with a split-footed Rx before it, addressed to the parts out of reach.

I think more of this little implement on account of its agency in saving the Colony at Plymouth in the year 1623. Edward Winslow heard that Massasoit was sick and like to die. He found him with a houseful of people about him, women rubbing his arms and legs, and friends "making such a hellish noise" as they probably thought would scare away the devil of sickness. Winslow gave him some conserve, washed his mouth, scraped his tongue, which was in a horrid state, got down some drink, made him some broth, dosed him with an infusion of strawberry leaves and sassafras root, and had the satisfaction of seeing him rapidly recover. Massasoit, full of gratitude, revealed the plot which had been formed to destroy the colonists, whereupon the Governor ordered Captain Miles Standish to see to them; who thereupon, as everybody remembers, stabbed Pecksuot with his own knife, broke up the plot, saved the colony, and thus rendered Massachusetts and the Massachusetts Medical Society a possibility, as they now are a fact before us. So much for this parenthesis of the tongue-scraper, which helped to save the young colony from a much more serious scrape, and may save the Union yet, if a Presidential candidate should happen to be taken sick as Massasoit was, and his tongue wanted cleaning,--which process would not hurt a good many politicians, with or without a typhoid fever.

Again, see how the "bilious" theory works in every-day life here and now, illustrated by a case from actual life. A youthful practitioner, whose last molars have not been a great while cut, meets an experienced and noted physician in consultation. This is the case. A slender, lymphatic young woman is suckling two lusty twins, the intervals of suction being occupied on her part with palpitations, headaches, giddiness, throbbing in the head, and various nervous symptoms, her cheeks meantime getting bloodless, and her strength running away in company with her milk. The old experienced physician, seeing the yellowish waxy look which is common in anaemic patients, considers it a "bilious" case, and is for giving a rousing emetic. Of course, he has to be wheedled out of this, a recipe is written for beefsteaks and porter, the twins are ignominiously expelled from the anaemic bosom, and forced to take prematurely to the bottle, and this prolific mother is saved for future usefulness in the line of maternity.

The practice of making a profit on the medicine ordered has been held up to reprobation by one at least of the orators who have preceded me. That the effect of this has been ruinous in English practice I cannot doubt, and that in this country the standard of practice was in former generations lowered through the same agency is not unlikely. I have seen an old account-book in which the physician charged an extra price for gilding his rich patients' pills. If all medicine were very costly, and the expense of it always came out of the physician's fee, it would really be a less objectionable arrangement than this other most pernicious one. He would naturally think twice before he gave an emetic or cathartic which evacuated his own pocket, and be sparing of the cholagogues that emptied the biliary ducts of his own wallet, unless he were sure they were needed. If there is any temptation, it should not be in favor of giving noxious agents, as it clearly must be in the case of English druggists and "General Practitioners." The complaint against the other course is a very old one. Pliny, inspired with as truly Roman horror of quackery as the elder Cato,--who declared that the Greek doctors had sworn to exterminate all barbarians, including the Romans, with their drugs, but is said to have physicked his own wife to death, notwithstanding,--Pliny says, in so many words, that the cerates and cataplasms, plasters, collyria, and antidotes, so abundant in his time, as in more recent days, were mere tricks to make money.

A pretty strong eddy, then, or rather many eddies, setting constantly back from the current of sober observation of nature, in the direction of old superstitions and fancies, of exploded theories, of old ways of making money, which are very slow to pass out of fashion.

But there are other special American influences which we are bound to take cognizance of. If I wished to show a student the difficulties of getting at truth from medical experience, I would give him the history of epilepsy to read. If I wished him to understand the tendencies of the American medical mind, its sanguine enterprise, its self-confidence, its audacious handling of Nature, its impatience with her old-fashioned ways of taking time to get a sick man well, I would make him read the life and writings of Benjamin Rush. Dr. Rush thought and said that there were twenty times more intellect and a hundred times more knowledge in the country in 1799 than before the Revolution. His own mind was in a perpetual state of exaltation produced by the stirring scenes in which he had taken a part, and the quickened life of the time in which he lived. It was not the state to favor sound, calm observation. He was impatient, and Nature is profoundly imperturbable. We may adjust the beating of our hearts to her pendulum if we will and can, but we may be very sure that she will not change the pendulum's rate of going because our hearts are palpitating. He thought he had mastered yellow-fever. "Thank God," he said, "out of one hundred patients whom I have visited or prescribed for this day, I have lost none." Where was all his legacy of knowledge when Norfolk was decimated? Where was it when the blue flies were buzzing over the coffins of the unburied dead piled up in the cemetery of New Orleans, at the edge of the huge trenches yawning to receive them?

One such instance will do as well as twenty. Dr. Rush must have been a charming teacher, as he was an admirable man. He was observing, rather than a sound observer; eminently observing, curious, even, about all manner of things. But he could not help feeling as if Nature had been a good deal shaken by the Declaration of Independence, and that American art was getting to be rather too much for her,--especially as illustrated in his own practice. He taught thousands of American students, he gave a direction to the medical mind of the country more than any other one man; perhaps he typifies it better than any other. It has clearly tended to extravagance in remedies and trust in remedies, as in everything else. How could a people which has a revolution once in four years, which has contrived the Bowie-knife and the revolver, which has chewed the juice out of all the superlatives in the language in Fourth of July orations, and so used up its epithets in the rhetoric of abuse that it takes two great quarto dictionaries to supply the demand; which insists in sending out yachts and horses and boys to out-sail, out-run, out-fight, and checkmate all the rest of creation; how could such a people be content with any but "heroic" practice? What wonder that the stars and stripes wave over doses of ninety grains of sulphate of quinine, [More strictly, ninety-six grains in two hours. Dunglison's Practice, 1842, vol. ii. p. 520. Eighty grains in one dose. Ibid. p. 536. Ninety-six grains of sulphate of quinine are equal to eight ounces of good bark.--Wood & Bache.] and that the American eagle screams with delight to see three drachms of calomel given at a single mouthful?

Add to this the great number of Medical Journals, all useful, we hope, most of them necessary, we trust, many of them excellently well conducted, but which must find something to fill their columns, and so print all the new plans of treatment and new remedies they can get hold of, as the newspapers, from a similar necessity, print the shocking catastrophes and terrible murders.

Besides all this, here are we, the great body of teachers in the numberless medical schools of the Union, some of us lecturing to crowds who clap and stamp in the cities, some of us wandering over the country, like other professional fertilizers, to fecundate the minds of less demonstrative audiences at various scientific stations; all of us talking habitually to those supposed to know less than ourselves, and loving to claim as much for our art as we can, not to say for our own schools, and possibly indirectly for our own practical skill. Hence that annual crop of introductory lectures; the useful blossoming into the ornamental, as the cabbage becomes glorified in the cauliflower; that lecture-room literature of adjectives, that declamatory exaggeration, that splendid show of erudition borrowed from D'Israeli, and credited to Lord Bacon and the rest, which have suggested to our friends of the Medical Journals an occasional epigram at our expense. Hence the tendency in these productions, and in medical lectures generally, to overstate the efficacy of favorite methods of cure, and hence the premium offered for showy talkers rather than sagacious observers, for the men of adjectives rather than of nouns substantive in the more ambitious of these institutions.

Such are some of the eddies in which we are liable to become involved and carried back out of the broad stream of philosophical, or, in other words, truth-loving, investigations. The causes of disease, in the mean time, have been less earnestly studied in the eagerness of the search for remedies. Speak softly! Women have been borne out from an old-world hospital, two in one coffin, that the horrors of their prison-house might not be known, while the very men who were discussing the treatment of the disease were stupidly conveying the infection from bed to bed, as rat-killers carry their poisons from one household to another. Do not some of you remember that I have had to fight this private-pestilence question against a scepticism which sneered in the face of a mass of evidence such as the calm statisticians of the Insurance office could not listen to without horror and indignation? ["The

Contagiousness of Puerperal Fever."--N. E. Quar. Jour. of Medicine and Surgery, April, 1843. Reprinted, with Additions. Boston: Ticknor & Fields. 1855.] Have we forgotten what is told in one of the books published under our own sanction, that a simple measure of ventilation, proposed by Dr. John Clark, had saved more than sixteen thousand children's lives in a single hospital? How long would it have taken small doses of calomel and rhubarb to save as many children? These may be useful in prudent hands, but how insignificant compared to the great hygienic conditions! Causes, causes, and again causes,--more and more we fall back on these as the chief objects of our attention. The shortest system of medical practice that I know of is the oldest, but not the worst. It is older than Hippocrates, older than Chiron the Centaur. Nature taught it to the first mother when she saw her first-born child putting some ugly pebble or lurid berry into its mouth. I know not in what language it was spoken, but I know that in English it would sound thus: Spit it out!

Art can do something more than say this. It can sometimes reach the pebble or berry after it has been swallowed. But the great thing is to keep these things out of children's mouths, and as soon as they are beyond our reach, to be reasonable and patient with Nature, who means well, but does not like to hurry, and who took nine calendar months, more or less, to every mother's son among us, before she thought he was fit to be shown to the public.

Suffer me now to lay down a few propositions, whether old or new it matters little, not for your immediate acceptance, nor yet for your hasty rejection, but for your calm consideration.

But first, there are a number of terms which we are in the habit of using in a vague though not unintelligible way, and which it is as well now to define. These terms are the tools with which we are to work, and the first thing is to sharpen them. It is nothing to us that they have been sharpened a thousand times before; they always get dull in the using, and every new workman has a right to carry them to the grindstone and sharpen them to suit himself.

Nature, in medical language, as opposed to Art, means trust in the reactions of the living system against, ordinary normal impressions.

Art, in the same language, as opposed to Nature, means an intentional resort to extraordinary abnormal impressions for the relief of disease.

The reaction of the living system is the essence of both. Food is nothing, if there is no digestive act to respond to it. We cannot raise a blister on a dead man, or hope that a carminative forced between his lips will produce its ordinary happy effect.

Disease, dis-ease,--disturbed quiet, uncomfortableness,--means imperfect or abnormal reaction of the living system, and its more or less permanent results.

Food, in its largest sense, is whatever helps to build up the normal structures, or to maintain their natural actions.

Medicine, in distinction from food, is every unnatural or noxious agent applied for the relief of disease.

Physic means properly the Natural art, and Physician is only the Greek synonyme of Naturalist.

With these few explanations I proceed to unfold the propositions I have mentioned.

Disease and death, if we may judge by the records of creation, are inherently and essentially necessary in the present order of things. A perfect intelligence, trained by a perfect education, could do no more than keep the laws of the physical and spiritual universe. An imperfect intelligence, imperfectly taught,--and this is the condition of our finite humanity,--will certainly fail to keep all these laws perfectly. Disease is one of the penalties of one of the forms of such failure. It is prefigured in the perturbations of the planets, in the disintegration of the elemental masses; it has left its traces in the fossil organisms of extinct creations. [Professor Agassiz has kindly handed me the following note: "There are abnormal structures in animals of all ages anterior to the creation of mankind. Malformed specimens of Crinoids are known from the Triassic and Jurassic deposits. Malformed and diseased bones of tertiary mammalia have been collected in the caverns of Gailenreuth with traces of healing."]

But it is especially the prerogative, I had almost said privilege, of educated and domesticated beings, from man down to the potato, serving to teach them, and such as train them, the laws of life, and to get rid of those who will not mind or cannot be kept subject to these laws.

Disease, being always an effect, is always in exact proportion to the sum of its causes, as much in the case of Spigelius, who dies of a scratch, as in that of the man who recovers after an iron bar has been shot through his brain. The one prevalent failing of the medical art is to neglect the causes and quarrel with the effect.

There are certain general facts which include a good deal of what is called and treated as disease. Thus, there are two opposite movements of life to be seen in cities and elsewhere, belonging to races which, from various persistent causes, are breeding down and tending to run out, and to races which are breeding up, or accumulating vital capital,--a descending and an ascending series. Let me give an example of each; and that I may incidentally remove a common impression about this country as compared with the Old World, an impression which got tipsy with conceit and staggered into the attitude of a formal proposition in the work of Dr. Robert Knox, I will illustrate the downward movement from English experience, and the upward movement from a family history belonging to this immediate neighborhood.

Miss Nightingale speaks of "the fact so often seen of a great-grandmother, who was a tower of physical vigor, descending into a grandmother perhaps a little less vigorous, but still sound as a bell, and healthy to the core, into a mother languid and confined to her carriage and house; and lastly into a daughter sickly and confined to her bed." So much for the descending English series; now for the ascending American series.

Something more than one hundred and thirty years ago there graduated at Harvard College a delicate youth, who lived an invalid life and died at the age of about fifty. His two children were both of moderate physical power, and one of them diminutive in stature. The next generation rose in physical development, and reached eighty years of age and more in some of its members. The fourth generation was of fair average endowment. The fifth generation, great-great-grandchildren of the slender invalid, are several of, them of extraordinary bodily and mental power; large in stature, formidable alike with their brains and their arms, organized on a more extensive scale than either of their parents.

This brief account illustrates incidentally the fallacy of the universal-degeneration theory applied to American life; the same on which one of our countrymen has lately brought some very forcible facts to bear in a muscular discussion of which we have heard rather more than is good for us. But the two series, American and English, ascending and descending, were adduced with the main purpose of showing the immense difference of vital endowments in different strains of blood; a difference to which all ordinary medication is in all probability a matter of comparatively trivial purport. Many affections which art has to strive against might be easily shown to be vital to the well-being of society. Hydrocephalus, tabes mesenterica, and other similar maladies, are natural agencies which cut off the children of races that are sinking below the decent minimum which nature has established as the condition of viability, before they reach the age of reproduction. They are really not so much diseases, as manifestations of congenital incapacity for life; the race would be ruined if art could ever learn always to preserve the individuals subject to them. We must do the best we can for them, but we ought also to know what these "diseases" mean.

Again, invalidism is the normal state of many organizations. It can be changed to disease, but never to absolute health by medicinal appliances. There are many ladies, ancient and recent, who are perpetually taking remedies for irremediable pains and aches. They ought to have headaches and back-aches and stomach-aches; they are not well if they do not have them. To expect them to live without frequent twinges is like expecting a doctor's old chaise to go without creaking; if it did, we might be sure the springs were broken. There is no doubt that the constant demand for medicinal remedies from patients of this class leads to their over-use; often in the case of cathartics, sometimes in that of opiates. I have been told by an intelligent practitioner in a Western town, that the constant prescription of opiates by certain physicians in his vicinity has rendered the habitual use of that drug in all that region very prevalent; more common, I should think, than alcoholic drunkenness in the most intemperate localities of which I have known anything. A frightful endemic demoralization betrays itself in the frequency with which the haggard features and drooping shoulders of the opium-drunkards are met with in the streets.

The next proposition I would ask you to consider is this: The presumption always is that every noxious agent, including medicines proper, which hurts a well man, hurts a sick one. [Note B.]

Let me illustrate this proposition before you decide upon it. If it were known that a prize-fighter were to have a drastic purgative administered two or three days before a contest, or a large blister applied to his back, no one will question that it would affect the betting on his side unfavorably; we will say to the amount of five per cent. Now the drain upon the resources of the system produced in such a case must be at its minimum, for the subject is a powerful man, in the prime of life, and in admirable condition. If the drug or the blister takes five per cent. from his force of resistance, it will take at least as large a fraction from any invalid. But this invalid has to fight a champion who strikes hard but cannot be hit in return, who will press him sharply for breath, but will never pant himself while the wind can whistle through his fleshless ribs. The suffering combatant is liable to want all his stamina, and five per cent. may lose him the battle.

All noxious agents, all appliances which are not natural food or stimuli, all medicines proper, cost a patient, on the average, five per cent. of his vital force, let us say. Twenty times as much waste of force produced by any of them, that is, would exactly kill him, nothing less than kill him, and nothing more. If this, or something like this, is true, then all these medications are, prima facie, injurious.

In the game of Life-or-Death, Rouge et Noir, as played between the Doctor and the Sexton, this five per cent., this certain small injury entering into the chances is clearly the sexton's perquisite for keeping the green table, over which the game is played, and where he hoards up his gains. Suppose a blister to diminish a man's pain, effusion or dyspnoea to the saving of twenty per cent. in vital force; his profit from it is fifteen, in that case, for it always hurts him five to begin with, according to our previous assumption.

Presumptions are of vast importance in medicine, as in law. A man is presumed innocent until he is proved guilty. A medicine--that is, a noxious agent, like a blister, a seton, an emetic, or a cathartic --should always be presumed to be hurtful. It always is directly hurtful; it may sometimes be indirectly beneficial. If this presumption were established, and disease always assumed to be the innocent victim of circumstances, and not punishable by medicines, that is, noxious agents, or poisons, until the contrary was shown, we should not so frequently hear the remark commonly, perhaps erroneously, attributed to Sir Astley Cooper, but often repeated by sensible persons, that, on the whole, more harm than good is done by medication. Throw out opium, which the Creator himself seems to prescribe, for we often see the scarlet poppy growing in the cornfields, as if it were foreseen that wherever there is hunger to be fed there must also be pain to be soothed; throw out a few specifics which our art did not discover, and is hardly needed to apply [Note C.]; throw out wine, which is a food, and the vapors which produce the miracle of anaesthesia, and I firmly believe that if the whole materia medica, as now used, could be sunk to the bottom of the sea, it would be all the better for mankind,--and all the worse for the fishes.

But to justify this proposition, I must add that the injuries inflicted by over-medication are to a great extent masked by disease. Dr. Hooker believes that the typhus syncopatia of a preceding generation in New England "was often in fact a brandy and opium disease." How is a physician to distinguish the irritation produced by his blister from that caused by the inflammation it was meant to cure? How can he tell the exhaustion produced by his evacuants from the collapse belonging to the disease they were meant to remove?

Lastly, medication without insuring favorable hygienic conditions is like amputation without ligatures. I had a chance to learn this well of old, when physician to the Broad Street district of the Boston Dispensary. There, there was no help for the utter want of wholesome conditions, and if anybody got well under my care, it must have been in virtue of the rough-and-tumble constitution which emerges from the struggle for life in the street gutters, rather than by the aid of my prescriptions.

But if the materia medica were lost overboard, how much more pains would be taken in ordering all the circumstances surrounding the patient (as can be done everywhere out of the crowded pauper districts), than are taken now by too many who think they do their duty and earn their money when they write a recipe for a patient left in an atmosphere of domestic malaria, or to the most negligent kind of nursing! I confess that I should think my chance of recovery from illness less with Hippocrates for my physician and Mrs. Gamp for my nurse, than if I were in the hands of Hahnemann himself, with Florence Nightingale or good Rebecca Taylor to care for me.

If I am right in maintaining that the presumption is always against the use of noxious agents in disease, and if any whom I might influence should adopt this as a principle of practice, they will often find themselves embarrassed by the imperative demand of patients and their friends for such agents where a case is not made out against this standing presumption. I must be permitted to say, that I think the French, a not wholly uncivilized people, are in advance of the English and ourselves in the art of prescribing for the sick without hurting them. And I do confess that I think their varied ptisans and syrups are as much preferable to the mineral regimen of bug-poison and ratsbane, so long in favor on the other side of the Channel, as their art of preparing food for the table to the rude cookery of those hard-feeding and much-dosing islanders. We want a reorganized cuisine of invalidism perhaps as much as the culinary, reform, for which our lyceum lecturers, and others who live much at hotels and taverns, are so urgent. Will you think I am disrespectful if I ask whether, even in Massachusetts, a dose of calomel is not sometimes given by a physician on the same principle as that upon which a landlord occasionally prescribes bacon and eggs,--because he cannot think of anything else quite so handy? I leave my suggestion of borrowing a hint from French practice to your mature consideration.

I may, however, call your attention, briefly, to the singular fact, that English and American practitioners are apt to accuse French medical practice of inertness, and French surgical practice of unnecessary activity. Thus, Dr. Bostock considers French medical treatment, with certain exceptions, as "decidedly less effective" than that of his own country. Mr. S. Cooper, again, defends the simple British practice of procuring union by the first intention against the attacks of M. Roux and Baron Larrey. [Cooper's Surg. Diet. art. "Wounds." Yet Mr. John Bell gives the French surgeons credit for introducing this doctrine of adhesion, and accuses O'Halloran of "rudeness and ignorance," and "bold, uncivil language," in disputing their teaching. Princ. of Surgery, vol. i. p. 42. Mr. Hunter succeeded at last in naturalizing the doctrine and practice, but even he had to struggle against the perpetual jealousy of rivals, and died at length assassinated by an insult.] We have often heard similar opinions maintained by our own countrymen. While Anglo-American criticism blows hot or cold on the two departments of French practice, it is not, I hope, indecent to question whether all the wisdom is necessarily with us in both cases.

Our art has had two or three lessons which have a deep meaning to those who are willing to read them honestly. The use of water-dressings in surgery completed the series of reforms by which was abolished the "coarse and cruel practice" of the older surgeons, who with their dressings and acrid balsams, their tents and leaden tubes, "absolutely delayed the cure." The doctrine of Broussais, transient as was its empire, reversed the practice of half of Christendom for a season, and taught its hasty disciples to shun their old favorite remedies as mortal poisons. This was not enough permanently to shift the presumption about drugs where it belonged, and so at last, just as the sympathetic powder and the Unguentum Armarium came in a superstitious age to kill out the abuses of external over-medication, the solemn farce of Homoeopathy was enacted in the face of our own too credulous civilization, that under shelter of its pretences the "inward bruises" of over-drugged viscera might be allowed to heal by the first intention. Its lesson we must accept, whether we will or not; its follies we are tired of talking about. The security of the medical profession against this and all similar fancies is in the average constitution of the human mind with regard to the laws of evidence.

My friends and brothers in Art! There is nothing to be feared from the utterance of any seeming heresy to which you may have listened. I cannot compromise your collective wisdom. If I have strained the truth one hair's breadth for the sake of an epigram or an antithesis, you are accustomed to count the normal pulse-beats of sound judgment, and know full well how to recognize the fever-throbs of conceit and the nervous palpitations of rhetoric.

The freedom with which each of us speaks his thought in this presence, belongs in part to the assured position of the Profession in our Commonwealth, to the attitude of Science, which is always fearless, and to the genius of the soil on which we stand, from which Nature withheld the fatal gift of malaria only to fill it with exhalations that breed the fever of inquiry in our blood and in our brain. But mainly we owe the large license of speech we enjoy to those influences and privileges common to us all as self-governing Americans.

This Republic is the chosen home of minorities, of the less power in the presence of the greater. It is a common error to speak of our distinction as consisting in the rule of the majority. Majorities, the greater material powers, have always ruled before. The history of most countries has been that of majorities, mounted majorities, clad in iron, armed with death treading down the tenfold more numerous minorities. In the old civilizations they root themselves like oaks in the soil; men must live in their shadow or cut them down. With us the majority is only the flower of the passing noon, and the minority is the bud which may open in the next morning's sun. We must be tolerant, for the thought which stammers on a single tongue today may organize itself in the growing consciousness of the time, and come back to us like the voice of the multitudinous waves of the ocean on the morrow.

Twenty-five years have passed since one of your honored Presidents spoke to this Society of certain limitations to the power of our Art, now very generally conceded. Some were troubled, some were almost angry, thinking the Profession might suffer from such concessions. It has certainly not suffered here; if, as some affirm, it has lost respect anywhere, it was probably for other, and no doubt sufficient reasons.

Since that time the civilization of this planet has changed hands. Strike out of existence at this moment every person who was breathing on that day, May 27, 1835, and every institution of society, every art and every science would remain intact and complete in the living that would be left. Every idea the world then held has been since dissolved and recrystallized.

We are repeating the same process. Not to make silver shrines for our old divinities, even though by this craft we should have our wealth, was this Society organized and carried on by the good men and true who went before us. Not for this, but to melt the gold out of the past, though its dross should fly in dust to all the winds of heaven, to save all our old treasures of knowledge and mine deeply for new, to cultivate that mutual respect of which outward courtesy is the sign, to work together, to feel together, to take counsel together, and to stand together for the truth, now, always, here, everywhere; for this our fathers instituted, and we accept, the offices and duties of this time-honored Society.

BORDER LINES OF KNOWLEDGE IN SOME PROVINCES OF MEDICAL SCIENCE.

An Introductory Lecture delivered before the Medical Class of Harvard University, November 6, 1861.

[This Lecture appears as it would have been delivered had the time allowed been less strictly, limited. Passages necessarily omitted have been restored, and points briefly touched have been more fully considered. A few notes have been added for the benefit of that limited class of students who care to track an author through the highways and by-ways of his reading. I owe my thanks to several of my professional brethren who have communicated with me on subjects with which they are familiar; especially to Dr. John Dean, for the opportunity of profiting by his unpublished labors, and to Dr. Hasket Derby, for information and references to recent authorities relating to the anatomy and physiology of the eye.]

The entrance upon a new course of Lectures is always a period of interest to instructors and pupils. As the birth of a child to a parent, so is the advent of a new class to a teacher. As the light of the untried world to the infant, so is the dawning of the light resting over the unexplored realms of science to the student. In the name of the Faculty I welcome you, Gentlemen of the Medical Class, new-born babes of science, or lustier nurslings, to this morning of your medical life, and to the arms and the bosom of this ancient University. Fourteen years ago I stood in this place for the first time to address those who occupied these benches. As I recall these past seasons of our joint labors, I feel that they have been on the whole prosperous, and not undeserving of their prosperity.

For it has been my privilege to be associated with a body of true and faithful workers; I cannot praise them freely to their faces, or I should be proud to discourse of the harmonious diligence and the noble spirit in which they have toiled together, not merely to teach their several branches, but to elevate the whole standard of teaching.

I may speak with less restraint of those gentlemen who have aided me in the most laborious part of my daily duties, the Demonstrators, to whom the successive classes have owed so much of their instruction. They rise before me, the dead and the living, in the midst of the most grateful recollections. The fair, manly face and stately figure of my friend, Dr. Samuel Parkman, himself fit for the highest offices of teaching, yet willing to be my faithful assistant in the time of need, come back to me with the long sigh of regret for his early loss to our earthly companionship. Every year I speak the eulogy of Dr. Ainsworth's patient toil as I show his elaborate preparations: When I take down my "American Cyclopaedia" and borrow instruction from the learned articles of Dr. Kneeland, I cease to regret that his indefatigable and intelligent industry was turned into a broader channel. And what can I say too cordial of my long associated companion and friend, Dr. Hodges, whose admirable skill, working through the swiftest and surest fingers that ever held a scalpel among us, has delighted class after class, and filled our Museum with monuments which will convey his name to unborn generations?

This day belongs, however, not to myself and my recollections, but to all of us who teach and all of you who listen, whether experts in our specialties or aliens to their mysteries, or timid neophytes just entering the portals of the hall of science. Look in with me, then, while I attempt to throw some rays into its interior, which shall illuminate a few of its pillars and cornices, and show at the same time how many niches and alcoves remain in darkness.

SCIENCE is the topography of ignorance. From a few elevated points we triangulate vast spaces, inclosing infinite unknown details. We cast the lead, and draw up a little sand from abysses we may never reach with our dredges.

The best part of our knowledge is that which teaches us where knowledge leaves off and ignorance begins. Nothing more clearly separates a vulgar from a superior mind, than the confusion in the first between the little that it truly knows, on the one hand, and what it half knows and what it thinks it knows on the other.

That which is true of every subject is especially true of the branch of knowledge which deals with living beings. Their existence is a perpetual death and reanimation. Their identity is only an idea, for we put off our bodies many times during our lives, and dress in new suits of bones and muscles.

> "Thou art not thyself;
> For thou exist'st on many a thousand grains
> That issue out of dust."

If it is true that we understand ourselves but imperfectly in health, this truth is more signally manifested in disease, where natural actions imperfectly understood, disturbed in an obscure way by half-seen causes, are creeping and winding along in the dark toward their destined issue, sometimes using our remedies as safe stepping-stones, occasionally, it may be, stumbling over them as obstacles.

I propose in this lecture to show you some points of contact between our ignorance and our knowledge in several of the branches upon the study of which you are entering. I may teach you a very little directly, but I hope much more from the trains of thought I shall suggest. Do not expect too much ground to be covered in this rapid survey. Our task is only that of sending out a few pickets under the starry flag of science to the edge of that dark domain where the ensigns of the obstinate rebel, Ignorance, are flying undisputed. We are not making a reconnoissance in force, still less advancing with the main column. But here are a few roads along which we have to march together, and we wish to see clearly how far our lines extend, and where the enemy's outposts begin.

Before touching the branches of knowledge that deal with organization and vital functions, let us glance at that science which meets you at the threshold of your study, and prepares you in some measure to deal with the more complex problems of the living laboratory.

CHEMISTRY. includes the art of separating and combining the elements of matter, and the study of the changes produced by these operations. We can hardly say too much of what it has contributed to our knowledge of the universe and our power of dealing with its materials. It has given us a catalogue raisonne of the substances found upon our planet, and shown how everything living and dead is put together from them. It is accomplishing wonders before us every day, such as Arabian story-tellers used to string together in their fables. It spreads the sensitive film on the artificial retina which looks upon us through the optician's lens for a few seconds, and fixes an image that will outlive its original. It questions the light of the sun, and detects the vaporized metals floating around the great luminary,--iron, sodium, lithium, and the rest,--as if the chemist of our remote planet could fill his bell-glasses from its fiery atmosphere. It lends the power which flashes our messages in thrills that leave the lazy chariot of day behind them. It seals up a few dark grains in iron vases, and lo! at the touch of a single spark, rises in smoke and flame a mighty Afrit with a voice like thunder and an arm that shatters like an earthquake. The dreams of Oriental fancy have become the sober facts of our every-day life, and the chemist is the magician to whom we owe them.

To return to the colder scientific aspect of chemistry. It has shown us how bodies stand affected to each other through an almost boundless range of combinations. It has given us a most ingenious theory to account for certain fixed relations in these combinations. It has successfully eliminated a great number of proximate compounds, more or less stable, from organic structures. It has invented others which form the basis of long series of well-known composite substances. In fact, we are perhaps becoming overburdened with our list of proximate principles, demonstrated and hypothetical.

How much nearer have we come to the secret of force than Lully and Geber and the whole crew of juggling alchemists? We have learned a great deal about the how, what have we learned about the why?

Why does iron rust, while gold remains untarnished, and gold amalgamate, while iron refuses the alliance of mercury?

The alchemists called gold Sol, the sun, and iron Mars, and pleased themselves with fancied relations between these substances and the heavenly bodies, by which they pretended to explain the facts they observed. Some of their superstitions have lingered in practical medicine to the present day, but chemistry has grown wise enough to confess the fact of absolute ignorance.

What is it that makes common salt crystallize in the form of cubes, and saltpetre in the shape of six-sided prisms? We see no reason why it should not have been just the other way, salt in prisms and saltpetre in cubes, or why either should take an exact geometrical outline, any more than coagulating albumen.

But although we had given up attempting to explain the essential nature of affinities and of crystalline types, we might have supposed that we had at least fixed the identity of the substances with which we deal, and determined the laws of their combination. All at once we find that a simple substance changes face, puts off its characteristic qualities and resumes them at will;--not merely when we liquefy or vaporize a solid, or reverse the process; but that a solid is literally transformed into another solid under our own eyes. We thought we knew phosphorus. We warm a portion of it sealed in an empty tube, for about a week. It has become a brown infusible substance, which does not shine in the dark nor oxidate in the air. We heat it to 500 F., and it becomes common phosphorus again. We transmute sulphur in the same singular way. Nature, you know, gives us carbon in the shape of coal and in that of the diamond. It is easy to call these changes by the name allotropism, but not the less do they confound our hasty generalizations.

These facts of allotropism have some corollaries connected with them rather startling to us of the nineteenth century. There may be other transmutations possible besides those of phosphorus and sulphur. When Dr. Prout, in 1840, talked about azote and carbon being "formed" in the living system, it was looked upon as one of those freaks of fancy to which philosophers, like other men, are subject. But when Professor Faraday, in 1851, says, at a meeting of the British Association, that "his hopes are in the direction of proving that bodies called simple were really compounds, and may be formed artificially as soon as we are masters of the laws influencing their combinations,"--when he comes forward and says that he has tried experiments at transmutation, and means, if his life is spared, to try them again,--how can we be surprised at the popular story of 1861, that Louis Napoleon has established a gold-factory and is glutting the mints of Europe with bullion of his own making?

And so with reference to the law of combinations. The old maxim was, Corpora non agunt nisi soluta. If two substances, a and b, are inclosed in a glass vessel, c, we do not expect the glass to change them, unless a or b or the compound a b has the power of dissolving the glass. But if for a I take oxygen, for b hydrogen, and for c a piece of spongy platinum, I find the first two combine with the common signs of combustion and form water, the third in the mean time undergoing no perceptible change. It has played the part of the unwedded priest, who marries a pair without taking a fee or having any further relation with the parties. We call this catalysis, catalytic action, the action of presence, or by what learned name we choose. Give what name to it we will, it is a manifestation of power which crosses our established laws of combination at a very open angle of intersection. I think we may find an analogy for it in electrical induction, the disturbance of the equilibrium of the electricity of a body by the approach of a charged body to it, without interchange of electrical conditions between the two bodies. But an analogy is not an explanation, and why a few drops of yeast should change a saccharine mixture to carbonic acid and alcohol,--a little leaven leavening the whole lump,--not by combining with it, but by setting a movement at work, we not only cannot explain, but the fact is such an exception to the recognized laws of combination that Liebig is unwilling to admit the new force at all to which Berzelius had given the name so generally accepted.

The phenomena of isomerism, or identity of composition and proportions of constituents with difference of qualities, and of isomorphism, or identity of form in crystals which have one element substituted for another, were equally surprises to science; and although the mechanism by which they are brought about can be to a certain extent explained by a reference to the hypothetical atoms of which the elements are constituted, yet this is only turning the difficulty into a fraction with an infinitesimal denominator and an infinite numerator.

So far we have studied the working of force and its seeming anomalies in purely chemical phenomena. But we soon find that chemical force is developed by various other physical agencies,--by heat, by light, by electricity, by magnetism, by mechanical agencies; and, vice versa, that chemical action develops heat, light, electricity, magnetism, mechanical force, as we see in our matches, galvanic batteries, and explosive compounds. Proceeding with our experiments, we find that every kind of force is capable of producing all other kinds, or, in Mr. Faraday's language, that "the various forms under which the forces of matter are made manifest have a common origin, or, in other words, are so directly related and mutually dependent that they are convertible one into another."

Out of this doctrine naturally springs that of the conservation of force, so ably illustrated by Mr. Grove, Dr. Carpenter, and Mr. Faraday. This idea is no novelty, though it seems so at first sight. It was maintained and disputed among the giants of philosophy. Des Cartes and Leibnitz denied that any new motion originated in nature, or that any ever ceased to exist; all motion being in a circle, passing from one body to another, one losing what the other gained. Newton, on the other hand, believed that new motions were generated and existing ones destroyed. On the first supposition, there is a fixed amount of force always circulating in the universe. On the second, the total amount may be increasing or diminishing. You will find in the "Annual of Scientific Discovery" for 1858 a very interesting lecture by Professor Helmholtz of Bonn, in which it is maintained that a certain portion of force is lost in every natural process, being converted into unchangeable heat, so that the universe will come to a stand-still at last, all force passing into heat, and all heat into a state of equilibrium.

The doctrines of the convertibility or specific equivalence of the various forms of force, and of its conservation, which is its logical consequence, are very generally accepted, as I believe, at the present time, among physicists. We are naturally led to the question, What is the nature of force? The three illustrious philosophers just referred to agree in attributing the general movements of the universe to the immediate Divine action. The doctrine of "preestablished harmony" was an especial contrivance of Leibnitz to remove the Creator from unworthy association with the less divine acts of living beings. Obsolete as this expression sounds to our ears, the phrase laws of the universe, which we use so constantly with a wider application, appears to me essentially identical with it.

Force does not admit of explanation, nor of proper definition, any more than the hypothetical substratum of matter. If we assume the Infinite as omnipresent, omniscient, omnipotent, we cannot suppose Him excluded from any part of His creation, except from rebellious souls which voluntarily exclude Him by the exercise of their fatal prerogative of free-will. Force, then, is the act of immanent Divinity. I find no meaning in mechanical explanations. Newton's hypothesis of an ether filling the heavenly spaces does not, I confess, help my conceptions. I will, and the muscles of my vocal organs shape my speech. God wills, and the universe articulates His power, wisdom, and goodness. That is all I know. There is no bridge my mind can throw from the "immaterial" cause to the "material" effect.

The problem of force meets us everywhere, and I prefer to encounter it in the world of physical phenomena before reaching that of living actions. It is only the name for the incomprehensible cause of certain changes known to our consciousness, and assumed to be outside of it. For me it is the Deity Himself in action.

I can therefore see a large significance in the somewhat bold language of Burdach: "There is for me but one miracle, that of infinite existence, and but one mystery, the manner in which the finite proceeds from the infinite. So soon as we recognize this incomprehensible act as the general and primordial miracle, of which our reason perceives the necessity, but the manner of which our intelligence cannot grasp, so soon as we contemplate the nature known to us by experience in this light, there is for us no other impenetrable miracle or mystery."

Let us turn to a branch of knowledge which deals with certainties up to the limit of the senses, and is involved in no speculations beyond them. In certain points of view, HUMAN ANATOMY may be considered an almost exhausted science. From time to time some small organ which had escaped earlier observers has been pointed out,--such parts as the tensor tarsi, the otic ganglion, or the Pacinian bodies; but some of our best anatomical works are those which have been classic for many generations. The plates of the bones in Vesalius, three centuries old, are still masterpieces of accuracy, as of art. The magnificent work of Albinus on the muscles, published in 1747, is still supreme in its department, as the constant references of the most thorough recent treatise on the subject, that of Theile, sufficiently show. More has been done in unravelling the mysteries of the fasciae, but there has been a tendency to overdo this kind of material analysis. Alexander Thomson split them up into cobwebs, as you may see in the plates to Velpeau's Surgical Anatomy. I well remember how he used to shake his head over the coarse work of Scarpa and Astley Cooper,--as if Denner, who painted the separate hairs of the beard and pores of the skin in his portraits, had spoken lightly of the pictures of Rubens and Vandyk.

Not only has little been added to the catalogue of parts, but some things long known had become half-forgotten. Louis and others confounded the solitary glands of the lower part of the small intestine with those which "the great Brunner," as Haller calls him, described in 1687 as being found in the duodenum. The display of the fibrous structure of the brain seemed a novelty as shown by Spurzheim. One is startled to find the method anticipated by Raymond Vieussens nearly two centuries ago. I can hardly think Gordon had ever looked at his figures, though he names their author, when he wrote the captious and sneering article which attracted so much attention in the pages of the "Edinburgh Review."

This is the place, if anywhere, to mention any observations I could pretend to have made in the course of my teaching the structure of the human body. I can make no better show than most of my predecessors in this well-reaped field. The nucleated cells found connected with the cancellated structure of the bones, which I first pointed out and had figured in 1847, and have shown yearly from that time to the present, and the fossa masseterica, a shallow concavity on the ramus of the lower jaw, for the lodgment of the masseter muscle, which acquires significance when examined by the side of the deep cavity on the corresponding part in some carnivora to which it answers, may perhaps be claimed as deserving attention. I have also pleased myself by making a special group of the six radiating muscles which diverge from the spine of the axis, or second cervical vertebra, and by giving to it the name stella musculosa nuchae. But this scanty catalogue is only an evidence that one may teach long and see little that has not been noted by those who have gone before him. Of course I do not think it necessary to include rare, but already described anomalies, such as the episternal bones, the rectus sternalis, and other interesting exceptional formations I have encountered, which have shown a curious tendency to present themselves several times in the same season, perhaps because the first specimen found calls our attention to any we may subsequently meet with.

The anatomy of the scalpel and the amphitheatre was, then, becoming an exhausted branch of investigation. But during the present century the study of the human body has changed its old aspect, and become fertile in new observations. This rejuvenescence was effected by means of two principal agencies,--new methods and a new instrument.

Descriptive anatomy, as known from an early date, is to the body what geography is to the planet. Now geography was pretty well known so long ago as when Arrowsmith, who was born in 1750, published his admirable maps. But in that same year was born Werner, who taught a new way of studying the earth, since become familiar to us all under the name of Geology.

What geology has done for our knowledge of the earth, has been done for our knowledge of the body by that method of study to which is given the name of General Anatomy. It studies, not the organs as such, but the elements out of which the organs are constructed. It is the geology of the body, as that is the general anatomy of the earth. The extraordinary genius of Bichat, to whom more than any other we owe this new method of study, does not require Mr. Buckle's testimony to impress the practitioner with the importance of its achievements. I have heard a very wise physician question whether any important result had accrued to practical medicine from Harvey's discovery of the circulation. But Anatomy, Physiology, and Pathology have received a new light from this novel method of contemplating the living structures, which has had a vast influence in enabling the practitioner at least to distinguish and predict the course of disease. We know as well what differences to expect in the habits of a mucous and of a serous membrane, as what mineral substances to look for in the chalk or the coal measures. You have only to read Cullen's description of inflammation of the lungs or of the bowels, and compare it with such as you may find in Laennec or Watson, to see the immense gain which diagnosis and prognosis have derived from general anatomy.

The second new method of studying the human structure, beginning with the labors of Scarpa, Burns, and Colles, grew up principally during the first third of this century. It does not deal with organs, as did the earlier anatomists, nor with tissues, after the manner of Bichat. It maps the whole surface of the body into an arbitrary number of regions, and studies each region successively from the surface to the bone, or beneath it. This hardly deserves the name of a science, although Velpeau has dignified it with that title, but it furnishes an admirable practical way for the surgeon who has to operate on a particular region of the body to study that region. If we are buying a farm, we are not content with the State map or a geological chart including the estate in question. We demand an exact survey of that particular property, so that we may know what we are dealing with. This is just what regional, or, as it is sometimes called, surgical anatomy, does for the surgeon with reference to the part on which his skill is to be exercised. It enables him to see with the mind's eye through the opaque tissues down to the bone on which they lie, as if the skin were transparent as the cornea, and the organs it covers translucent as the gelatinous pulp of a medusa.

It is curious that the Japanese should have anticipated Europe in a kind of rude regional anatomy. I have seen a manikin of Japanese make traced all over with lines, and points marking their intersection. By this their doctors are guided in the performance of acupuncture, marking the safe places to thrust in needles, as we buoy out our ship-channels, and doubtless indicating to learned eyes the spots where incautious meddling had led to those little accidents of shipwreck to which patients are unfortunately liable.

A change of method, then, has given us General and Regional Anatomy. These, too, have been worked so thoroughly, that, if not exhausted, they have at least become to a great extent fixed and positive branches of knowledge. But the first of them, General Anatomy, would never, have reached this positive condition but for the introduction of that, instrument which I have mentioned as the second great aid to modern progress.

This instrument is the achromatic microscope. For the history of the successive steps by which it became the effective scientific implement we now possess, I must refer you to the work of Mr. Quekett, to an excellent article in the "Penny Cyclopaedia," or to that of Sir David Brewster in the "Encyclopaedia Britannica." It is a most interesting piece of scientific history, which shows how the problem which Biot in 1821 pronounced insolvable was in the course of a few years practically solved, with a success equal to that which Dollond had long before obtained with the telescope. It is enough for our purpose that we are now in possession of an instrument freed from all confusions and illusions, which magnifies a thousand diameters,--a million times in surface,--without serious distortion or discoloration of its object.

A quarter of a century ago, or a little more, an instructor would not have hesitated to put John Bell's "Anatomy" and Bostock's "Physiology" into a student's hands, as good authority on their respective subjects. Let us not be unjust to either of these authors. John Bell is the liveliest medical writer that I can remember who has written since the days of delightful old Ambroise Pare. His picturesque descriptions and bold figures are as good now as they ever were, and his book can never become obsolete. But listen to what John Bell says of the microscope:

"Philosophers of the last age had been at infinite pains to find the ultimate fibre of muscles, thinking to discover its properties in its form; but they saw just in proportion to the glasses which they used, or to their practice and skill in that art, which is now almost forsaken."

Dr. Bostock's work, neglected as it is, is one which I value very highly as a really learned compilation, full of original references. But Dr. Bostock says: "Much as the naturalist has been indebted to the microscope, by bringing into view many beings of which he could not otherwise have ascertained the existence, the physiologist has not yet derived any great benefit from the instrument."

These are only specimens of the manner in which the microscope and its results were generally regarded by the generation just preceding our own.

I have referred you to the proper authorities for the account of those improvements which about the year 1830 rendered the compound microscope an efficient and trustworthy instrument. It was now for the first time that a true general anatomy became possible. As early as 1816 Treviranus had attempted to resolve the tissues, of which Bichat had admitted no less than twenty-one, into their simple microscopic elements. How could such an attempt succeed, Henle well asks, at a time when the most extensively diffused of all the tissues, the areolar, was not at all understood? All that method could do had been accomplished by Bichat and his followers. It was for the optician to take the next step. The future of anatomy and physiology, as an enthusiastic micrologist of the time said, was in the hands of Messrs. Schieck and Pistor, famous opticians of Berlin.

In those earlier days of which I am speaking, all the points of minute anatomy were involved in obscurity. Some found globules everywhere, some fibres. Students disputed whether the conjunctiva extended over the cornea or not, and worried themselves over Gaultier de Claubry's stratified layers of the skin, or Breschet's blennogenous and chromatogenous organs. The dartos was a puzzle, the central spinal canal a myth, the decidua clothed in fable as much as the golden fleece. The structure of bone, now so beautifully made out,--even that of the teeth, in which old Leeuwenhoek, peeping with his octogenarian eyes through the minute lenses wrought with his own hands, had long ago seen the "pipes," as he called them,-- was hardly known at all. The minute structure of the viscera lay in the mists of an uncertain microscopic vision. The intimate recesses of the animal system were to the students of anatomy what the anterior of Africa long was to geographers, and the stories of microscopic explorers were as much sneered at as those of Bruce or Du Chailly, and with better reason.

Now what have we come to in our own day? In the first place, the minute structure of all the organs has been made out in the most satisfactory way. The special arrangements of the vessels and the ducts of all the glands, of the air-tubes and vesicles of the lungs, of the parts which make up the skin and other membranes, all the details of those complex parenchymatous organs which had confounded investigation so long, have been lifted out of the invisible into the sight of all observers. It is fair to mention here, that we owe a great deal to the art of minute injection, by which we are enabled to trace the smallest vessels in the midst of the tissues where they are distributed. This is an old artifice of anatomists. The famous Ruysch, who died a hundred and thirty years ago, showed that each of the viscera has its terminal vessels arranged in its own peculiar way; the same fact which you may see illustrated in Gerber's figures after the minute injections of Berres. I hope to show you many specimens of this kind in the microscope, the work of English and American hands. Professor Agassiz allows me also to make use of a very rich collection of injected preparations sent him by Professor Hyrtl, formerly of Prague, now of Vienna, for the proper exhibition of which I had a number of microscopes made expressly, by Mr. Grunow, during the past season. All this illustrates what has been done for the elucidation of the intimate details of formation of the organs.

But the great triumph of the microscope as applied to anatomy has been in the resolution of the organs and the tissues into their simple constituent anatomical elements. It has taken up general anatomy where Bichat left it. He had succeeded in reducing the structural language of nature to syllables, if you will permit me to use so bold an image. The microscopic observers who have come after him have analyzed these into letters, as we may call them,--the simple elements by the combination of which Nature spells out successively tissues, which are her syllables, organs which are her words, systems which are her chapters, and so goes on from the simple to the complex, until she binds up in one living whole that wondrous volume of power and wisdom which we call the human body.

The alphabet of the organization is so short and simple, that I will risk fatiguing your attention by repeating it, according to the plan I have long adopted.

A. Cells, either floating, as in the blood, or fixed, like those in the cancellated structure of bone, already referred to. Very commonly they have undergone a change of figure, most frequently a flattening which reduces them to scales, as in the epidermis and the epithelium.

B. Simple, translucent, homogeneous solid, such as is found at the back of the cornea, or forming the intercellular substance of cartilage.

C. The white fibrous element, consisting of very delicate, tenacious threads. This is the long staple textile substance of the body. It is to the organism what cotton is pretended to be to our Southern States. It pervades the whole animal fabric as areolar tissue, which is the universal packing and wrapping material. It forms the ligaments which bind the whole frame-work together. It furnishes the sinews, which are the channels of power. It enfolds every muscle. It wraps the brain in its hard, insensible folds, and the heart itself beats in a purse that is made of it.

D. The yellow elastic, fibrous element, the caoutchouc of the animal mechanism, which pulls things back into place, as the India-rubber band shuts the door we have opened.

E. The striped muscular fibre,--the red flesh, which shortens itself in obedience to the will, and thus produces all voluntary active motion.

F. The unstriped muscular fibre, more properly the fusiform-cell fibre, which carries on the involuntary internal movements.

G. The nerve-cylinder, a glassy tube, with a pith of some firmness, which conveys sensation to the brain and the principle which induces motion from it.

H. The nerve-corpuscle, the centre of nervous power.

I. The mucous tissue, as Virchow calls it, common in embryonic structures, seen in the vitreous humor of the adult.

To these add X, granules, of indeterminate shape and size, Y, for inorganic matters, such as the salts of bone and teeth, and Z, to stand as a symbol of the fluids, and you have the letters of what I have ventured to call the alphabet of the body.

But just as in language certain diphthongs and syllables are frequently recurring, so we have in the body certain secondary and tertiary combinations, which we meet more frequently than the solitary elements of which they are composed.

Thus A B, or a collection of cells united by simple structureless solid, is seen to be extensively employed in the body under the name of cartilage. Out of this the surfaces of the articulations and the springs of the breathing apparatus are formed. But when Nature came to the buffers of the spinal column (intervertebral disks) and the washers of the joints (semilunar fibrocartilages of the knee, etc.), she required more tenacity than common cartilage possessed. What did she do? What does man do in a similar case of need? I need hardly tell you. The mason lays his bricks in simple mortar. But the plasterer works some hair into the mortar which he is going to lay in large sheets on the walls. The children of Israel complained that they had no straw to make their bricks with, though portions of it may still be seen in the crumbling pyramid of Darshour, which they are said to have built. I visited the old house on Witch Hill in Salem a year or two ago, and there I found the walls coated with clay in which straw was abundantly mingled;--the old Judaizing witch-hangers copied the Israelites in a good many things. The Chinese and the Corsicans blend the fibres of amianthus in their pottery to give it tenacity. Now to return to Nature. To make her buffers and washers hold together in the shocks to which they would be subjected, she took common cartilage and mingled the white fibrous tissue with it, to serve the same purpose as the hair in the mortar, the straw in the bricks and in the plaster of the old wall, and the amianthus in the earthen vessels. Thus we have the combination A B C, or fibro-cartilage. Again, the bones were once only gristle or cartilage, A B. To give them solidity they were infiltrated with stone, in the form of salts of lime, an inorganic element, so that bone would be spelt out by the letters A, B, and Y.

If from these organic syllables we proceed to form organic words, we shall find that Nature employs three principal forms; namely, Vessels, Membranes, and Parenchyma, or visceral tissue. The most complex of them can be resolved into a combination of these few simple anatomical constituents.

Passing for a moment into the domain of PATHOLOGICAL ANATOMY, we find the same elements in morbid growths that we have met with in normal structures. The pus-corpuscle and the white blood-corpuscle can only be distinguished by tracing them to their origin. A frequent form of so-called malignant disease proves to be only a collection of altered epithelium-cells. Even cancer itself has no specific anatomical element, and the diagnosis of a cancerous tumor by the microscope, though tolerably sure under the eye of an expert, is based upon accidental, and not essential points,--the crowding together of the elements, the size of the cell-nuclei, and similar variable characters.

Let us turn to PHYSIOLOGY. The microscope, which has made a new science of the intimate structure of the organs, has at the same time cleared up many uncertainties concerning the mechanism of the special functions. Up to the time of the living generation of observers, Nature had kept over all her inner workshops the forbidding inscription, No Admittance! If any prying observer ventured to spy through his magnifying tubes into the mysteries of her glands and canals and fluids, she covered up her work in blinding mists and bewildering halos, as the deities of old concealed their favored heroes in the moment of danger.

Science has at length sifted the turbid light of her lenses, and blanched their delusive rainbows.

Anatomy studies the organism in space. Physiology studies it also in time. After the study of form and composition follows close that of action, and this leads us along back to the first moment of the germ, and forward to the resolution of the living frame into its lifeless elements. In this way Anatomy, or rather that branch of it which we call Histology, has become inseparably blended with the study of function. The connection between the science of life and that of intimate structure on the one hand, and composition on the other, is illustrated in the titles of two recent works of remarkable excellence,--"the Physiological Anatomy" of Todd and Bowman, and the "Physiological Chemistry" of Lehmann.

Let me briefly recapitulate a few of our acquisitions in Physiology, due in large measure to our new instruments and methods of research, and at the same time indicate the limits which form the permanent or the temporary boundaries of our knowledge. I will begin with the largest fact and with the most absolute and universally encountered limitation.

The "largest truth in Physiology" Mr. Paget considers to be "the development of ova through multiplication and division of their cells." I would state it more broadly as the agency of the cell in all living processes. It seems at present necessary to abandon the original idea of Schwann, that we can observe the building up of a cell from the simple granules of a blastema, or formative fluid. The evidence points rather towards the axiom, Omnis cellula a cellula; that is, the germ of a new cell is always derived from a preexisting cell. The doctrine of Schwann, as I remarked long ago (1844), runs parallel with the nebular theory in astronomy, and they may yet stand or fall together.

As we have seen Nature anticipating the plasterer in fibro-cartilage, so we see her beforehand with the glassblower in her dealings with the cell. The artisan blows his vitreous bubbles, large or small, to be used afterwards as may be wanted. So Nature shapes her hyaline vesicles and modifies them to serve the needs of the part where they are found. The artisan whirls his rod, and his glass bubble becomes a flattened disk, with its bull's-eye for a nucleus. These lips of ours are all glazed with microscopic tiles formed of flattened cells, each one of them with its nucleus still as plain and relatively as prominent, to the eye of the microscopist, as the bull's-eye in the old-fashioned windowpane. Everywhere we find cells, modified or unchanged. They roll in inconceivable multitudes (five millions and more to the cubic millimetre, according to Vierordt) as blood-disks through our vessels. A close-fitting mail of flattened cells coats our surface with a panoply of imbricated scales (more than twelve thousand millions), as Harting has computed, as true a defence against our enemies as the buckler of the armadillo or the carapace of the tortoise against theirs. The same little protecting organs pave all the great highways of the interior system. Cells, again, preside over the chemical processes which elaborate the living fluids; they change their form to become the agents of voluntary and involuntary motion; the soul itself sits on a throne of nucleated cells, and flashes its mandates through skeins of glassy filaments which once were simple chains of vesicles. And, as if to reduce the problem of living force to its simplest expression, we see the yolk of a transparent egg dividing itself in whole or in part, and again dividing and subdividing, until it becomes a mass of cells, out of which the harmonious diversity of the organs arranges itself, worm or man, as God has willed from the beginning.

This differentiation having been effected, each several part assumes its special office, having a life of its own adjusted to that of other parts and the whole. "Just as a tree constitutes a mass arranged in a definite manner, in which, in every single part, in the leaves as in the root, in the trunk as in the blossom, cells are discovered to be the ultimate elements, so is it also with the forms of animal life. Every animal presents itself as a sum of vital unities, every one of which manifests all the characteristics of life."

The mechanism is as clear, as unquestionable, as absolutely settled and universally accepted, as the order of movement of the heavenly bodies, which we compute backward to the days of the observatories on the plains of Shinar, and on the faith of which we regulate the movements of war and trade by the predictions of our ephemeris.

The mechanism, and that is all. We see the workman and the tools, but the skill that guides the work and the power that performs it are as invisible as ever. I fear that not every listener took the significance of those pregnant words in the passage I quoted from John Bell,--"thinking to discover its properties in its form." We have discovered the working bee in this great hive of organization. We have detected the cell in the very act of forming itself from a nucleus, of transforming itself into various tissues, of selecting the elements of various secretions. But why one cell becomes nerve and another muscle, why one selects bile and another fat, we can no more pretend to tell, than why one grape sucks out of the soil the generous juice which princes hoard in their cellars, and another the wine which it takes three men to drink,--one to pour it down, another to swallow it, and a third to hold him while it is going down. Certain analogies between this selecting power and the phenomena of endosmosis in the elective affinities of chemistry we can find, but the problem of force remains here, as everywhere, unsolved and insolable.

Do we gain anything by attempting to get rid of the idea of a special vital force because we find certain mutually convertible relations between forces in the body and out of it? I think not, any more than we should gain by getting rid of the idea and expression Magnetism because of its correlation with electricity. We may concede the unity of all forms of force, but we cannot overlook the fixed differences of its manifestations according to the conditions under which it acts. It is a mistake, however, to think the mystery is greater in an organized body than in any other. We see a stone fall or a crystal form, and there is nothing stranger left to wonder at, for we have seen the Infinite in action.

Just so far as we can recognize the ordinary modes of operation of the common forces of nature,--gravity, cohesion, elasticity, transudation, chemical action, and the rest,--we see the so-called vital acts in the light of a larger range of known facts and familiar analogies. Matteuecci's well-remembered lectures contain many and striking examples of the working of physical forces in physiological processes. Wherever rigid experiment carries us, we are safe in following this lead; but the moment we begin to theorize beyond our strict observation, we are in danger of falling into those mechanical follies which true science has long outgrown.

Recognizing the fact, then, that we have learned nothing but the machinery of life, and are no nearer to its essence, what is it that we have gained by this great discovery of the cell formation and function?

It would have been reward enough to learn the method Nature pursues for its own sake. If the sovereign Artificer lets us into his own laboratories and workshops, we need not ask more than the privilege of looking on at his work. We do not know where we now stand in the hierarchy of created intelligences. We were made a little lower than the angels. I speak it not irreverently; as the lower animals surpass man in some of their attributes, so it may be that not every angel's eye can see as broadly and as deeply into the material works of God as man himself, looking at the firmament through an equatorial of fifteen inches' aperture, and searching into the tissues with a twelfth of an inch objective.

But there are other positive gains of a more practical character. Thus we are no longer permitted to place the seat of the living actions in the extreme vessels, which are only the carriers from which each part takes what it wants by the divine right of the omnipotent nucleated cell. The organism has become, in the words already borrowed from Virchow, "a sum of vital unities." The strictum and laxum, the increased and diminished action of the vessels, out of which medical theories and methods of treatment have grown up, have yielded to the doctrine of local cell-communities, belonging to this or that vascular district, from which they help themselves, as contractors are wont to do from the national treasury.

I cannot promise to do more than to select a few of the points of contact between our ignorance and our knowledge which present particular interest in the existing state of our physiological acquisitions. Some of them involve the microscopic discoveries of which I have been speaking, some belong to the domain of chemistry, and some have relations with other departments of physical science.

If we should begin with the digestive function, we should find that the long-agitated question of the nature of the acid of the gastric juice is becoming settled in favor of the lactic. But the whole solvent agency of the digestive fluid enters into the category of that exceptional mode of action already familiar to us in chemistry as catalysis. It is therefore doubly difficult of explanation; first, as being, like all reactions, a fact not to be accounted for except by the imaginative appeal to "affinity," and secondly, as being one of those peculiar reactions provoked by an element which stands outside and looks on without compromising itself.

The doctrine of Mulder, so widely diffused in popular and scientific belief, of the existence of a common base of all albuminous substances, the so-called protein, has not stood the test of rigorous analysis. The division of food into azotized and non-azotized is no doubt important, but the attempt to show that the first only is plastic or nutritive, while the second is simply calorifacient, or heat-producing, fails entirely in the face of the facts revealed by the study of man in different climates, and of numerous experiments in the feeding of animals. I must return to this subject in connection with the respiratory function.

The sugar-making faculty of the liver is another "catalytic" mystery, as great as the rest of them, and no greater. Liver-tissue brings sugar out of the blood, or out of its own substance;--why?

Quia est in eo
Virtus saccharitiva.

Just what becomes of the sugar beyond the fact of its disappearance before it can get into the general circulation and sweeten our tempers, it is hard to say.

The pancreatic fluid makes an emulsion of the fat contained in our food, but just how the fatty particles get into the villi we must leave Brucke and Kolliker to settle if they can.

No one has shown satisfactorily the process by which the blood-corpuscles are formed out of the lymph-corpuscles, nor what becomes of them. These two questions are like those famous household puzzles,--Where do the flies come from? and, Where do the pins go to?

There is a series of organs in the body which has long puzzled physiologists,--organs of glandular aspect, but having no ducts,--the spleen, the thyroid and thymus bodies, and the suprarenal capsules. We call them vascular glands, and we believe that they elaborate colored and uncolored blood-cells; but just what changes they effect, and just how they effect them, it has proved a very difficult matter to determine. So of the noted glandules which form Peyer's patches, their precise office, though seemingly like those of the lymphatic glands, cannot be positively assigned, so far as I know, at the present time. It is of obvious interest to learn it with reference to the pathology of typhoid fever. It will be remarked that the coincidence of their changes in this disease with enlargement of the spleen suggests the idea of a similarity of function in these two organs.

The theories of the production of animal heat, from the times of Black, Lavoisier, and Crawford to those of Liebig, are familiar to all who have paid any attention to physiological studies. The simplicity of Liebig's views, and the popular form in which they have been presented, have given them wide currency, and incorporated them in the common belief and language of our text-books. Direct oxidation or combustion of the carbon and hydrogen contained in the food, or in the tissues themselves; the division of alimentary substances into respiratory, or non-azotized, and azotized,--these doctrines are familiar even to the classes in our high-schools. But this simple statement is boldly questioned. Nothing proves that oxygen combines (in the system) with hydrogen and carbon in particular, rather than with sulphur and azote. Such is the well-grounded statement of Robin and Verdeil. "It is very probable that animal heat is entirely produced by the chemical actions which take place in the organism, but the phenomenon is too complex to admit of our calculating it according to the quality of oxygen consumed." These last are the words of Regnault, as cited by Mr. Lewes, whose intelligent discussion of this and many of the most interesting physiological problems I strongly recommend to your attention.

This single illustration covers a wider ground than the special function to which it belongs. We are learning that the chemistry of the body must be studied, not simply by its ingesta and egesta, but that there is a long intermediate series of changes which must be investigated in their own light, under their own special conditions. The expression "sum of vital unities" applies to the chemical actions, as well as to other actions localized in special parts; and when the distinguished chemists whom I have just cited entitle their work a treatise on the immediate principles of the body, they only indicate the nature of that profound and subtile analysis which must take the place of all hasty generalizations founded on a comparison of the food with residual products.

I will only call your attention to the fact, that the exceptional phenomenon of the laboratory is the prevailing law of the organism. Nutrition itself is but one great catalytic process. As the blood travels its rounds, each part selects its appropriate element and transforms it to its own likeness. Whether the appropriating agent be cell or nucleus, or a structureless solid like the intercellular substance of cartilage, the fact of its presence determines the separation of its proper constituents from the circulating fluid, so that even when we are wounded bone is replaced by bone, skin by skin, and nerve by nerve.

It is hardly without a smile that we resuscitate the old question of the 'vis insita' of the muscular fibre, so famous in the discussions of Haller and his contemporaries. Speaking generally, I think we may say that Haller's doctrine is the one now commonly received; namely, that the muscles contract in virtue of their own inherent endowments. It is true that Kolliker says no perfectly decisive fact has been brought forward to prove that the striated muscles contract without having been acted on by nerves. Yet Mr. Bowman's observations on the contraction of isolated fibres appear decisive enough (unless we consider them invalidated by Dr. Lionel Beale's recent researches), tending to show that each elementary fibre is supplied with nerves; and as to the smooth muscular fibres, we have Virchow's statement respecting the contractility of those of the umbilical cord, where there is not a trace of any nerves.

In the investigation of the nervous system, anatomy and physiology have gone hand in hand. It is very singular that so important, and seemingly simple, a fact as the connection of the nerve-tubes, at their origin or in their course, with the nerve-cells, should have so long remained open to doubt, as you may see that it did by referring to the very complete work of Sharpey and Quain (edition of 1849), the histological portion of which is cordially approved by Kolliker himself.

Several most interesting points of the minute anatomy of the nervous centres have been laboriously and skilfully worked out by a recent graduate of this Medical School, in a monograph worthy to stand in line with those of Lockhart Clarke, Stilling, and Schroder van der Kolk. I have had the privilege of examining and of showing some of you a number of Dr. Dean's skilful preparations. I have no space to give even an abstract of his conclusions. I can only refer to his proof of the fact, that a single cell may send its processes into several different bundles of nerve-roots, and to his demonstration of the curved ascending and descending fibres from the posterior nerveroots, to reach what he has called the longitudinal columns of the cornea. I must also mention Dr. Dean's exquisite microscopic photographs from sections of the medulla oblongata, which appear to me to promise a new development, if not a new epoch, in anatomical art.

It having been settled that the nerve-tubes can very commonly be traced directly to the nerve-cells, the object of all the observers in this department of anatomy is to follow these tubes to their origin. We have an infinite snarl of telegraph wires, and we may be reasonably sure, that, if we can follow them up, we shall find each of them ends in a battery somewhere. One of the most interesting problems is to find the ganglionic origin of the great nerves of the medulla oblongata, and this is the end to which, by the aid of the most delicate sections, colored so as to bring out their details, mounted so as to be imperishable, magnified by the best instruments, and now self-recorded in the light of the truth-telling sunbeam, our fellow-student is making a steady progress in a labor which I think bids fair to rank with the most valuable contributions to histology that we have had from this side of the Atlantic.

It is interesting to see how old questions are incidentally settled in the course of these new investigations. Thus, Mr. Clarke's dissections, confirmed by preparations of Mr. Dean's which I have myself examined, placed the fact of the decussation of the pyramids--denied by Haller, by Morgagni, and even by Stilling--beyond doubt. So the spinal canal, the existence of which, at least in the adult, has been so often disputed, appears as a coarse and unequivocal anatomical fact in many of the preparations referred to.

While these studies of the structure of the cord have been going on, the ingenious and indefatigable Brown-Sequard has been investigating the functions of its different parts with equal diligence. The microscopic anatomists had shown that the ganglionic corpuscles of the gray matter of the cord are connected with each other by their processes, as well as with the nerve-roots. M. Brown-Sequard has proved by numerous experiments that the gray substance transmits sensitive impressions and muscular stimulation. The oblique ascending and descending fibres from the posterior nerve-roots, joining the "longitudinal columns of the cornua," account for the results of Brown-Sequard's sections of the posterior columns. The physiological experimenter has also made it evident that the decussation of the conductors of sensitive impressions has its seat in the spinal core, and not in the encephalon, as had been supposed. Not less remarkable than these results are the facts, which I with others of my audience have had the opportunity of observing, as shown by M. Brown-Sequard, of the artificial production of epilepsy in animals by injuring the spinal cord, and the induction of the paroxysm by pinching a certain portion of the skin. I would also call the student's attention to his account of the relations of the nervous centres to nutrition and secretion, the last of which relations has been made the subject of an extended essay by our fellow countryman, Dr. H. F. Campbell of Georgia.

The physiology of the spinal cord seems a simple matter as you study it in Longet. The experiments of Brown-Sequard have shown the problem to be a complex one, and raised almost as many doubts as they have solved questions; at any rate, I believe all lecturers on physiology agree that there is no part of their task they dread so much as the analysis of the evidence relating to the special offices of the different portions of the medulla spinalis. In the brain we are sure that we do not know how to localize functions; in the spinal cord, we think we do know something; but there are so many anomalies, and seeming contradictions, and sources of fallacy, that beyond the facts of crossed paralysis of sensation, and the conducting agency of the gray substance, I am afraid we retain no cardinal principles discovered since the development of the reflex function took its place by Sir Charles Bell's great discovery.

By the manner in which I spoke of the brain, you will see that I am obliged to leave phrenology sub Jove,--out in the cold,--as not one of the household of science. I am not one of its haters; on the contrary, I am grateful for the incidental good it has done. I love to amuse myself in its plaster Golgothas, and listen to the glib professor, as he discovers by his manipulations

"All that disgraced my betters met in me."

I loved of old to see square-headed, heavy-jawed Spurzheim make a brain flower out into a corolla of marrowy filaments, as Vieussens had done before him, and to hear the dry-fibred but human-hearted George Combe teach good sense under the disguise of his equivocal system. But the pseudo-sciences, phrenology and the rest, seem to me only appeals to weak minds and the weak points of strong ones. There is a pica or false appetite in many intelligences; they take to odd fancies in place of wholesome truth, as girls gnaw at chalk and charcoal. Phrenology juggles with nature. It is so adjusted as to soak up all evidence that helps it, and shed all that harms it. It crawls forward in all weathers, like Richard Edgeworth's hygrometer. It does not stand at the boundary of our ignorance, it seems to me, but is one of the will-o'-the-wisps of its undisputed central domain of bog and quicksand. Yet I should not have devoted so many words to it, did I not recognize the light it has thrown on human actions by its study of congenital organic tendencies. Its maps of the surface of the head are, I feel sure, founded on a delusion, but its studies of individual character are always interesting and instructive.

The "snapping-turtle" strikes after its natural fashion when it first comes out of the egg. Children betray their tendencies in their way of dealing with the breasts that nourish them; nay, lean venture to affirm, that long before they are born they teach their mothers something of their turbulent or quiet tempers.

"Castor gaudet equis, ovo proanatus eodem
Pugnis."

Strike out the false pretensions of phrenology; call it anthropology; let it study man the individual in distinction from man the abstraction, the metaphysical or theological lay-figure; and it becomes "the proper study of mankind," one of the noblest and most interesting of pursuits.

The whole physiology of the nervous system, from the simplest manifestation of its power in an insect up to the supreme act of the human intelligence working through the brain, is full of the most difficult yet profoundly interesting questions. The singular relations between electricity and nerve-force, relations which it has been attempted to interpret as meaning identity, in the face of palpable differences, require still more extended studies. You may be interested by Professor Faraday's statement of his opinion on the matter. "Though I am not satisfied that the nervous fluid is only electricity, still I think that the agent in the nervous system maybe an inorganic force; and if there be reason for supposing that magnetism is a higher relation of force than electricity, so it may well be imagined that the nervous power may be of a still more exalted character, and yet within the reach of experiment."

In connection with this statement, it is interesting to refer to the experiments of Helmholtz on the rapidity of transmission of the nervous actions. The rate is given differently in Valentin's report of these experiments and in that found in the "Scientific Annual" for 1858. One hundred and eighty to three hundred feet per second is the rate of movement assigned for sensation, but all such results must be very vaguely approximative. Boxers, fencers, players at the Italian game of morn, "prestidigitators," and all who depend for their success on rapidity of motion, know what differences there are in the personal equation of movement.

Reflex action, the mechanical sympathy, if I may so call it, of distant parts; Instinct, which is crystallized intelligence,--an absolute law with its invariable planes and angles introduced into the sphere of consciousness, as raphides are inclosed in the living cells of plants; Intellect,--the operation of the thinking principle through material organs, with an appreciable waste of tissue in every act of thought, so that our clergymen's blood has more phosphates to get rid of on Monday than on any other day of the week; Will,--theoretically the absolute determining power, practically limited in different degrees by the varying organization of races and individuals, annulled or perverted by different ill-understood organic changes; on all these subjects our knowledge is in its infancy, and from the study of some of them the interdict of the Vatican is hardly yet removed.

I must allude to one or two points in the histology and physiology of the organs of sense. The anterior continuation of the retina beyond the ora serrata has been a subject of much discussion. If H. Muller and Kolliker can be relied upon, this question is settled by recognizing that a layer of cells, continued from the retina, passes over the surface of the zonula Zinnii, but that no proper nervous element is so prolonged forward.

I observe that Kolliker calls the true nervous elements of the retina "the layer of gray cerebral substance." In fact, the ganglionic corpuscles of each eye may be considered as constituting a little brain, connected with the masses behind by the commissure, commonly called the optic nerve. We are prepared, therefore, to find these two little brains in the most intimate relations with each other, as we find the cerebral hemispheres. We know that they are directly connected by fibres that arch round through the chiasma.

I mention these anatomical facts to introduce a physiological observation of my own, first announced in one of the lectures before the Medical Class, subsequently communicated to the American Academy of Arts and Sciences, and printed in its "Transactions" for February 14, 1860. I refer to the apparent transfer of impressions from one retina to the other, to which I have given the name reflex vision. The idea was suggested to me in consequence of certain effects noticed in employing the stereoscope. Professor William B. Rodgers has since called the attention of the American Scientific Association to some facts bearing on the subject, and to a very curious experiment of Leonardo da Vinci's, which enables the observer to look through the palm of his hand (or seem to), as if it had a hole bored through it. As he and others hesitated to accept my explanation, I was not sorry to find recently the following words in the "Observations on Man" of that acute observer and thinker, David Hartley. "An impression made on the right eye alone by a single object may propagate itself into the left, and there raise up an image almost equal in vividness to itself; and consequently when we see with one eye only, we may, however, have pictures in both eyes." Hartley, in 1784, had anticipated many of the doctrines which have since been systematized into the theory of reflex actions, and with which I have attempted to associate this act of reflex vision. My sixth experiment, however, in the communication referred to, appears to me to be a crucial one, proving the correctness of my explanation, and I am not aware that it has been before instituted.

Another point of great interest connected with the physiology of vision, and involved for a long time in great obscurity, is that of the adjustment of the eye to different distances. Dr. Clay Wallace of New York, who published a very ingenious little book on the eye about twenty years ago, with vignettes reminding one of Bewick, was among the first, if not the first, to describe the ciliary muscle, to which the power of adjustment is generally ascribed. It is ascertained, by exact experiment with the phacueidoscope, that accommodation depends on change of form of the crystalline lens. Where the crystalline is wanting, as Mr. Ware long ago taught, no power of accommodation remains. The ciliary muscle is generally thought to effect the change of form of the crystalline. The power of accommodation is lost after the application of atropine, in consequence, as is supposed, of the paralysis of this muscle. This, I believe, is the nearest approach to a demonstration we have on this point.

I have only time briefly to refer to Professor Draper's most ingenious theory as to the photographic nature of vision, for an account of which I must refer to his original and interesting Treatise on Physiology.

It were to be wished that the elaborate and very interesting researches of the Marquis Corti, which have revealed such singular complexity of structure in the cochlea of the ear, had done more to clear up its doubtful physiology; but I am afraid we have nothing but hypotheses for the special part it plays in the act of hearing, and that we must say the same respecting the office of the semicircular canals.

The microscope has achieved some of its greatest triumphs in teaching us the changes which occur in the development of the embryo. No more interesting discovery stands recorded in the voluminous literature of this subject than the one originally announced by Martin Barry, afterwards discredited, and still later confirmed by Mr. Newport and others; namely the fact that the fertilizing filament reaches the interior of the ovum in various animals;--a striking parallel to the action of the pollen-tube in the vegetable. But beyond the mechanical facts all is mystery in the movements of organization, as profound as in the fall of a stone or the formation of a crystal.

To the chemist and the microscopist the living body presents the same difficulties, arising from the fact that everything is in perpetual change in the organism. The fibrine of the blood puzzles the one as much as its globules puzzle the other. The difference between the branches of science which deal with space only, and those which deal with space and time, is this: we have no glasses that can magnify time. The figure I here show you a was photographed from an object (pleurosigma angulatum) magnified a thousand diameters, or presenting a million times its natural surface. This other figure of the same object, enlarged from the one just shown, is magnified seven thousand diameters, or forty-nine million times in surface. When we can make the forty-nine millionth of a second as long as its integer, physiology and chemistry will approach nearer the completeness of anatomy.

Our reverence becomes more worthy, or, if you will, less unworthy of its Infinite Object in proportion as our intelligence is lifted and expanded to a higher and broader understanding of the Divine methods of action. If Galen called his heathen readers to admire, the power, the wisdom, the providence, the goodness of the "Framer of the animal body,"--if Mr. Boyle, the student of nature, as Addison and that friend of his who had known him for forty years tell us, never uttered the name of the Supreme Being without making a distinct pause in his speech, in token of his devout recognition of its awful meaning,--surely we, who inherit the accumulated wisdom of nearly two hundred years since the time of the British philosopher, and of almost two thousand since the Greek physician, may well lift our thoughts from the works we study to their great Artificer. These wonderful discoveries which we owe to that mighty little instrument, the telescope of the inner firmament with all its included worlds; these simple formulae by which we condense the observations of a generation in a single axiom; these logical analyses by which we fence out the ignorance we cannot reclaim, and fix the limits of our knowledge,--all lead us up to the inspiration of the Almighty, which gives understanding to the world's great teachers. To fear science or knowledge, lest it disturb our old beliefs, is to fear the influx of the Divine wisdom into the souls of our fellow-men; for what is science but the piecemeal revelation,--uncovering,--of the plan of creation, by the agency of those chosen prophets of nature whom God has illuminated from the central light of truth for that single purpose?

The studies which we have glanced at are preliminary in your education to the practical arts which make use of them,--the arts of healing,--surgery and medicine. The more you examine the structure of the organs and the laws of life, the more you will find how resolutely each of the cell-republics which make up the E pluribus unum of the body maintains its independence. Guard it, feed it, air it, warm it, exercise or rest it properly, and the working elements will do their best to keep well or to get well. What do we do with ailing vegetables? Dr. Warren, my honored predecessor in this chair, bought a country-place, including half of an old orchard. A few years afterwards I saw the trees on his side of the fence looking in good health, while those on the other side were scraggy and miserable. How do you suppose this change was brought about? By watering them with Fowler's solution? By digging in calomel freely about their roots? Not at all; but by loosening the soil round them, and supplying them with the right kind of food in fitting quantities.

Now a man is not a plant, or, at least, he is a very curious one, for he carries his soil in his stomach, which is a kind--of portable flower-pot, and he grows round it, instead of out of it. He has, besides, a singularly complex nutritive apparatus and a nervous system. But recollect the doctrine already enunciated in the language of Virchow, that an animal, like a tree, is a sum of vital unities, of which the cell is the ultimate element. Every healthy cell, whether in a vegetable or an animal, necessarily performs its function properly so long as it is supplied with its proper materials and stimuli. A cell may, it is true, be congenitally defective, in which case disease is, so to speak, its normal state. But if originally sound and subsequently diseased, there has certainly been some excess, deficiency, or wrong quality in the materials or stimuli applied to it. You remove this injurious influence and substitute a normal one; remove the baked coal-ashes, for instance, from the roots of a tree, and replace them with loam; take away the salt meat from the patient's table, and replace it with fresh meat and vegetables, and the cells of the tree or the man return to their duty.

I do not know that we ever apply to a plant any element which is not a natural constituent of the vegetable structure, except perhaps externally, for the accidental purpose of killing parasites. The whole art of cultivation consists in learning the proper food and conditions of plants, and supplying them. We give them water, earths, salts of various kinds such as they are made of, with a chance to help themselves to air and light. The farmer would be laughed at who undertook to manure his fields or his trees with a salt of lead or of arsenic. These elements are not constituents of healthy plants. The gardener uses the waste of the arsenic furnaces to kill the weeds in his walks.

If the law of the animal cell, and of the animal organism, which is built up of such cells, is like that of the vegetable, we might expect that we should treat all morbid conditions of any of the vital unities belonging to an animal in the same way, by increasing, diminishing, or changing its natural food or stimuli.

That is an aliment which nourishes; whatever we find in the organism, as a constant and integral element, either forming part of its structure, or one of the conditions of vital processes, that and that only deserves the name of aliment. I see no reason, therefore, why iron, phosphate of lime, sulphur, should not be considered food for man, as much as guano or poudrette for vegetables. Whether one or another of them is best in any given case,--whether they shall be taken alone or in combination, in large or small quantities, are separate questions. But they are elements belonging to the body, and even in moderate excess will produce little disturbance. There is no presumption against any of this class of substances, any more than against water or salt, provided they are used in fitting combinations, proportions, and forms.

But when it comes to substances alien to the healthy system, which never belong to it as normal constituents, the case is very different. There is a presumption against putting lead or arsenic into the human body, as against putting them into plants, because they do not belong there, any more than pounded glass, which, it is said, used to be given as a poison. The same thing is true of mercury and silver.

What becomes of these alien substances after they get into the system we cannot always tell. But in the case of silver, from the accident of its changing color under the influence of light, we do know what happens. It is thrown out, in part at least, under the epidermis, and there it remains to the patient's dying day. This is a striking illustration of the difficulty which the system finds in dealing with non-assimilable elements, and justifies in some measure the vulgar prejudice against mineral poisons.

I trust the youngest student on these benches will not commit the childish error of confounding a presumption against a particular class of agents with a condemnation of them. Mercury, for instance, is alien to the system, and eminently disturbing in its influence. Yet its efficacy in certain forms of specific disease is acknowledged by all but the most sceptical theorists. Even the esprit moqueur of Ricord, the Voltaire of pelvic literature, submits to the time-honored constitutional authority of this great panacea in the class of cases to which he has devoted his brilliant intelligence. Still, there is no telling what evils have arisen from the abuse of this mineral. Dr. Armstrong long ago pointed out some of them, and they have become matters of common notoriety. I am pleased, therefore, when I find so able and experienced a practitioner as Dr. Williams of this city proving that iritis is best treated without mercury, and Dr. Vanderpoel showing the same thing to be true for pericarditis.

Whatever elements nature does not introduce into vegetables, the natural food of all animal life,--directly of herbivorous, indirectly of carnivorous animals,--are to be regarded with suspicion. Arsenic-eating may seem to improve the condition of horses for a time,--and even of human beings, if Tschudi's stories can be trusted,--but it soon appears that its alien qualities are at war with the animal organization. So of copper, antimony, and other non-alimentary simple substances; everyone of them is an intruder in the living system, as much as a constable would be, quartered in our household. This does not mean that they may not, any of them, be called in for a special need, as we send for the constable when we have good reason to think we have a thief under our roof; but a man's body is his castle, as well as his house, and the presumption is that we are to keep our alimentary doors bolted against these perturbing agents.

Now the feeling is very apt to be just contrary to this. The habit has been very general with well-taught practitioners, to have recourse to the introduction of these alien elements into the system on the occasion of any slight disturbance. The tongue was a little coated, and mercury must be given; the skin was a little dry, and the patient must take antimony. It was like sending for the constable and the posse comitatus when there is only a carpet to shake or a refuse-barrel to empty. [Dr. James Johnson advises persons not ailing to take five grains of blue pill with one or two of aloes twice a week for three or four months in the year, with half a pint of compound decoction of sarsaparilla every day for the same period, to preserve health and prolong life. Pract. Treatise on Dis. of Liver, etc. p. 272.] The constitution bears slow poisoning a great deal better than might be expected; yet the most intelligent men in the profession have gradually got out of the habit of prescribing these powerful alien substances in the old routine way. Mr. Metcalf will tell you how much more sparingly they are given by our practitioners at the present time, than when he first inaugurated the new era of pharmacy among us. Still, the presumption in favor of poisoning out every spontaneous reaction of outraged nature is not extinct in those who are trusted with the lives of their fellow-citizens. "On examining the file of prescriptions at the hospital, I discovered that they were rudely written, and indicated a treatment, as they consisted chiefly of tartar emetic, ipecacuanha, and epsom salts, hardly favorable to the cure of the prevailing diarrhoea and dysenteries." In a report of a poisoning case now on trial, where we are told that arsenic enough was found in the stomach to produce death in twenty-four hours, the patient is said to have been treated by arsenic, phosphorus, bryonia, aconite, nux vomica, and muriatic acid,--by a practitioner of what school it may be imagined.

The traditional idea of always poisoning out disease, as we smoke out vermin, is now seeking its last refuge behind the wooden cannon and painted port-holes of that unblushing system of false scientific pretences which I do not care to name in a discourse addressed to an audience devoted to the study of the laws of nature in the light of the laws of evidence. It is extraordinary to observe that the system which, by its reducing medicine to a name and a farce, has accustomed all who have sense enough to see through its thin artifices to the idea that diseases get well without being "cured," should now be the main support of the tottering poison-cure doctrine. It has unquestionably helped to teach wise people that nature heals most diseases without help from pharmaceutic art, but it continues to persuade fools that art can arrest them all with its specifics.

It is worse than useless to attempt in any way to check the freest expression of opinion as to the efficacy of any or all of the "heroic" means of treatment employed by practitioners of different schools and periods. Medical experience is a great thing, but we must not forget that there is a higher experience, which tries its results in a court of a still larger jurisdiction; that, namely, in which the laws of human belief are summoned to the witness-box, and obliged to testify to the sources of error which beset the medical practitioner. The verdict is as old as the father of medicine, who announces it in the words, "judgment is difficult." Physicians differed so in his time, that some denied that there was any such thing as an art of medicine.

One man's best remedies were held as mischievous by another. The art of healing was like soothsaying, so the common people said; "the same bird was lucky or unlucky, according as he flew to the right or left."

The practice of medicine has undergone great changes within the period of my own observation. Venesection, for instance, has so far gone out of fashion, that, as I am told by residents of the New York Bellevue and the Massachusetts General Hospitals, it is almost obsolete in these institutions, at least in medical practice. The old Brunonian stimulating treatment has come into vogue again in the practice of Dr. Todd and his followers. The compounds of mercury have yielded their place as drugs of all work, and specifics for that very frequent subjective complaint, nescio quid faciam,--to compounds of iodine. [Sir Astley Cooper has the boldness,--or honesty,--to speak of medicines which "are given as much to assist the medical man as his patient." Lectures (London, 1832), p. 14.] Opium is believed in, and quinine, and "rum," using that expressive monosyllable to mean all alcoholic cordials. If Moliere were writing now, instead of saignare, purgare, and the other, he would be more like to say, Stimulare, opium dare et potassio-iodizare.

I have been in relation successively with the English and American evacuant and alterative practice, in which calomel and antimony figured so largely that, as you may see in Dr. Jackson's last "Letter," Dr. Holyoke, a good representative of sterling old-fashioned medical art, counted them with opium and Peruvian bark as his chief remedies; with the moderately expectant practice of Louis; the blood-letting "coup sur coup" of Bouillaud; the contra-stimulant method of Rasori and his followers; the anti-irritant system of Broussais, with its leeching and gum-water; I have heard from our own students of the simple opium practice of the renowned German teacher, Oppolzer; and now I find the medical community brought round by the revolving cycle of opinion to that same old plan of treatment which John Brown taught in Edinburgh in the last quarter of the last century, and Miner and Tully fiercely advocated among ourselves in the early years of the present. The worthy physicians last mentioned, and their antagonist Dr. Gallup, used stronger language than we of these degenerate days permit ourselves. "The lancet is a weapon which annually slays more than the sword," says Dr. Tully. "It is probable that, for forty years past, opium and its preparations have done seven times the injury they have rendered benefit, on the great scale of the world," says Dr. Gallup.

What is the meaning of these perpetual changes and conflicts of medical opinion and practice, from an early antiquity to our own time? Simply this: all "methods" of treatment end in disappointment of those extravagant expectations which men are wont to entertain of medical art. The bills of mortality are more obviously affected by drainage, than by this or that method of practice. The insurance companies do not commonly charge a different percentage on the lives of the patients of this or that physician. In the course of a generation, more or less, physicians themselves are liable to get tired of a practice which has so little effect upon the average movement of vital decomposition. Then they are ready for a change, even if it were back again to a method which has already been tried, and found wanting.

Our practitioners, or many of them, have got back to the ways of old Dr. Samuel Danforth, who, as it is well known, had strong objections to the use of the lancet. By and by a new reputation will be made by some discontented practitioner, who, tired of seeing patients die with their skins full of whiskey and their brains muddy with opium, returns to a bold antiphlogistic treatment, and has the luck to see a few patients of note get well under it. So of the remedies which have gone out of fashion and been superseded by others. It can hardly be doubted that they will come into vogue again, more or less extensively, under the influence of that irresistible demand for change just referred to.

Then will come the usual talk about a change in the character of disease, which has about as much meaning as that concerning "old-fashioned snow-storms." "Epidemic constitutions" of disease mean something, no doubt; a great deal as applied to malarious affections; but that the whole type of diseases undergoes such changes that the practice must be reversed from depleting to stimulating, and vice versa, is much less likely than that methods of treatment go out of fashion and come in again. If there is any disease which claims its percentage with reasonable uniformity, it is phthisis. Yet I remember that the reverend and venerable Dr. Prince of Salem told me one Commencement day, as I was jogging along towards Cambridge with him, that he recollected the time when that disease was hardly hardly known; and in confirmation of his statement mentioned a case in which it was told as a great event, that somebody down on "the Cape" had died of "a consumption." This story does not sound probable to myself, as I repeat it, yet I assure you it is true, and it shows how cautiously we must receive all popular stories of great changes in the habits of disease.

Is there no progress, then, but do we return to the same beliefs and practices which our forefathers wore out and threw away? I trust and believe that there is a real progress. We may, for instance, return in a measure to the Brunonian stimulating system, but it must be in a modified way, for we cannot go back to the simple Brunonian pathology, since we have learned too much of diseased action to accept its convenient dualism. So of other doctrines, each new Avatar strips them of some of their old pretensions, until they take their fitting place at last, if they have any truth in them, or disappear, if they were mere phantasms of the imagination.

In the mean time, while medical theories are coming in and going out, there is a set of sensible men who are never run away with by them, but practise their art sagaciously and faithfully in much the same way from generation to generation. From the time of Hippocrates to that of our own medical patriarch, there has been an apostolic succession of wise and good practitioners. If you will look at the first aphorism of the ancient Master you will see that before all remedies he places the proper conduct of the patient and his attendants, and the fit ordering of all the conditions surrounding him. The class of practitioners I have referred to have always been the most faithful in attending to these points. No doubt they have sometimes prescribed unwisely, in compliance with the prejudices of their time, but they have grown wiser as they have grown older, and learned to trust more in nature and less in their plans of interference. I believe common opinion confirms Sir James Clark's observation to this effect.

The experience of the profession must, I think, run parallel with that of the wisest of its individual members. Each time a plan of treatment or a particular remedy comes up for trial, it is submitted to a sharper scrutiny. When Cullen wrote his Materia Medica, he had seriously to assail the practice of giving burnt toad, which was still countenanced by at least one medical authority of note. I have read recently in some medical journal, that an American practitioner, whose name is known to the country, is prescribing the hoof of a horse for epilepsy. It was doubtless suggested by that old fancy of wearing a portion of elk's hoof hung round the neck or in a ring, for this disease. But it is hard to persuade reasonable people to swallow the abominations of a former period. The evidence which satisfied Fernelius will not serve one of our hospital physicians.

In this way those articles of the Materia Medica which had nothing but loathsomeness to recommend them have been gradually dropped, and are not like to obtain any general favor again with civilized communities. The next culprits to be tried are the poisons. I have never been in the least sceptical as to the utility of some of them, when properly employed. Though I believe that at present, taking the world at large, and leaving out a few powerful agents of such immense value that they rank next to food in importance, the poisons prescribed for disease do more hurt than good, I have no doubt, and never professed to have any, that they do much good in prudent and instructed hands. But I am very willing to confess a great jealousy of many agents, and I could almost wish to see the Materia Medica so classed as to call suspicion upon certain ones among them.

Thus the alien elements, those which do not properly enter into the composition of any living tissue, are the most to be suspected, --mercury, lead, antimony, silver, and the rest, for the reasons I have before mentioned. Even iodine, which, as it is found in certain plants, seems less remote from the animal tissues, gives unequivocal proofs from time to time that it is hostile to some portions of the glandular system.

There is, of course, less prima facie objection to those agents which consist of assimilable elements, such as are found making a part of healthy tissues. These are divisible into three classes,--foods, poisons, and inert, mostly because insoluble, substances. The food of one animal or of one human being is sometimes poison to another, and vice versa; inert substances may act mechanically, so as to produce the effect of poisons; but this division holds exactly enough for our purpose.

Strictly speaking, every poison consisting of assimilable elements may be considered as unwholesome food. It is rejected by the stomach, or it produces diarrhoea, or it causes vertigo or disturbance of the heart's action, or some other symptom for which the subject of it would consult the physician, if it came on from any other cause than taking it under the name of medicine. Yet portions of this unwholesome food which we call medicine, we have reason to believe, are assimilated; thus, castor-oil appears to be partially digested by infants, so that they require large doses to affect them medicinally. Even that deadliest of poisons, hydrocyanic acid, is probably assimilated, and helps to make living tissue, if it do not kill the patient, for the assimilable elements which it contains, given in the separate forms of amygdalin and emulsin, produce no disturbance, unless, as in Bernard's experiments, they are suffered to meet in the digestive organs. A medicine consisting of assimilable substances being then simply unwholesome food, we understand what is meant by those cumulative effects of such remedies often observed, as in the case of digitalis and strychnia. They are precisely similar to the cumulative effects of a salt diet in producing scurvy, or of spurred rye in producing dry gangrene. As the effects of such substances are a violence to the organs, we should exercise the same caution with regard to their use that we would exercise about any other kind of poisonous food,--partridges at certain seasons, for instance. Even where these poisonous kinds of food seem to be useful, we should still regard them with great jealousy. Digitalis lowers the pulse in febrile conditions. Veratrum viride does the same thing. How do we know that a rapid pulse is not a normal adjustment of nature to the condition it accompanies? Digitalis has gone out of favor; how sure are we that Veratrum viride will not be found to do more harm than good in a case of internal inflammation, taking the whole course of the disease into consideration? Think of the change of opinion with regard to the use of opium in delirium tremens (which you remember is sometimes called delirium vigilans), where it seemed so obviously indicated, since the publication of Dr. Ware's admirable essay. I respect the evidence of my contemporaries, but I cannot forget the sayings of the Father of medicine,--Ars longa, judicium difficile.

I am not presuming to express an opinion concerning Veratrum viride, which was little heard of when I was still practising medicine. I am only appealing to that higher court of experience which sits in judgment on all decisions of the lower medical tribunals, and which requires more than one generation for its final verdict.

Once change the habit of mind so long prevalent among practitioners of medicine; once let it be everywhere understood that the presumption is in favor of food, and not of alien substances, of innocuous, and not of unwholesome food, for the sick; that this presumption requires very strong evidence in each particular case to overcome it; but that, when such evidence is afforded, the alien substance or the unwholesome food should be given boldly, in sufficient quantities, in the same spirit as that with which the surgeon lifts his knife against a patient,--that is, with the same reluctance and the same determination,--and I think we shall have and hear much less of charlatanism in and out of the profession. The disgrace of medicine has been that colossal system of self-deception, in obedience to which mines have been emptied of their cankering minerals, the vegetable kingdom robbed of all its noxious growths, the entrails of animals taxed for their impurities, the poison-bags of reptiles drained of their venom, and all the inconceivable abominations thus obtained thrust down the throats of human beings suffering from some fault of organization, nourishment, or vital stimulation.

Much as we have gained, we have not yet thoroughly shaken off the notion that poison is the natural food of disease, as wholesome aliment is the support of health. Cowper's lines, in "The Task," show the matter-of-course practice of his time:

"He does not scorn it, who has long endured
A fever's agonies, and fed on drugs."

Dr. Kimball of Lowell, who has been in the habit of seeing a great deal more of typhoid fever than most practitioners, and whose surgical exploits show him not to be wanting in boldness or enterprise, can tell you whether he finds it necessary to feed his patients on drugs or not. His experience is, I believe, that of the most enlightened and advanced portion of the profession; yet I think that even in typhoid fever, and certainly in many other complaints, the effects of ancient habits and prejudices may still be seen in the practice of some educated physicians.

To you, young men, it belongs to judge all that has gone before you. You come nearer to the great fathers of modern medicine than some of you imagine. Three of my own instructors attended Dr. Rush's Lectures. The illustrious Haller mentions Rush's inaugural thesis in his "Bibliotheca Anatomica;" and this same Haller, brought so close to us, tells us he remembers Ruysch, then an old man, and used to carry letters between him and Boerhaave. Look through the history of medicine from Boerhaave to this present day. You will see at once that medical doctrine and practice have undergone a long series of changes. You will see that the doctrine and practice of our own time must probably change in their turn, and that, if we can trust at all to the indications of their course, it will be in the direction of an improved hygiene and a simplified treatment. Especially will the old habit of violating the instincts of the sick give place to a judicious study of these same instincts. It will be found that bodily, like mental insanity, is best managed, for the most part, by natural soothing agencies. Two centuries ago there was a prescription for scurvy containing "stercoris taurini et anserini par, quantitas trium magnarum nucum," of the hell-broth containing which "guoties-cumque sitit oeger, large bibit." When I have recalled the humane common-sense of Captain Cook in the matter of preventing this disease; when I have heard my friend, Mr. Dana, describing the avidity with which the scurvy-stricken sailors snuffed up the earthy fragrance of fresh raw potatoes, the food which was to supply the elements wanting to their spongy tissues, I have recognized that the perfection of art is often a return to nature, and seen in this single instance the germ of innumerable beneficent future medical reforms.

I cannot help believing that medical curative treatment will by and by resolve itself in great measure into modifications of the food, swallowed and breathed, and of the natural stimuli, and that less will be expected from specifics and noxious disturbing agents, either alien or assimilable. The noted mineral-waters containing iron, sulphur, carbonic acid, supply nutritious or stimulating materials to the body as much as phosphate of lime and ammoniacal compounds do to the cereal plants. The effects of a milk and vegetable diet, of gluten bread in diabetes, of cod-liver oil in phthisis, even of such audacious innovations as the water-cure and the grape-cure, are only hints of what will be accomplished when we have learned to discover what organic elements are deficient or in excess in a case of chronic disease, and the best way of correcting the abnormal condition, just as an agriculturist ascertains the wants of his crops and modifies the composition of his soil. In acute febrile diseases we have long ago discovered that far above all drug-medication is the use of mild liquid diet in the period of excitement, and of stimulant and nutritious food in that of exhaustion. Hippocrates himself was as particular about his barley-ptisan as any Florence Nightingale of our time could be.

The generation to which you, who are just entering the profession, belong, will make a vast stride forward, as I believe, in the direction of treatment by natural rather than violent agencies. What is it that makes the reputation of Sydenham, as the chief of English physicians? His prescriptions consisted principally of simples. An aperient or an opiate, a "cardiac" or a tonic, may be commonly found in the midst of a somewhat fantastic miscellany of garden herbs. It was not by his pharmaceutic prescriptions that he gained his great name. It was by daring to order fresh air for small-pox patients, and riding on horseback for consumptives, in place of the smothering system, and the noxious and often loathsome rubbish of the established schools. Of course Sydenham was much abused by his contemporaries, as he frequently takes occasion to remind his reader. "I must needs conclude," he says, "either that I am void of merit, or that the candid and ingenuous part of mankind, who are formed with so excellent a temper of mind as to be no strangers to gratitude, make a very small part of the whole." If in the fearless pursuit of truth you should find the world as ungracious in the nineteenth century as he found it in the seventeenth, you may learn a lesson of self-reliance from another utterance of the same illustrious physician: "'T is none of my business to inquire what other persons think, but to establish my own observations; in order to which, I ask no favor of the reader but to peruse my writings with temper."

The physician has learned a great deal from the surgeon, who is naturally in advance of him, because he has a better opportunity of seeing the effects of his remedies. Let me shorten one of Ambroise Pare's stories for you. There had been a great victory at the pass of Susa, and they were riding into the city. The wounded cried out as the horses trampled them under their hoofs, which caused good Ambroise great pity, and made him wish himself back in Paris. Going into a stable he saw four dead soldiers, and three desperately wounded, placed with their backs against the wall. An old campaigner came up.--"Can these fellows get well?" he said. "No!" answered the surgeon. Thereupon, the old soldier walked up to them and cut all their throats, sweetly, and without wrath (doulcement et sans cholere). Ambroise told him he was a bad man to do such a thing. "I hope to God;" he said, "somebody will do as much for me if I ever get into such a scrape" (accoustre de telle facon). "I was not much salted in those days" (bien doux de sel), says Ambroise, "and little acquainted with the treatment of wounds." However, as he tells us, he proceeded to apply boiling oil of Sambuc (elder) after the approved fashion of the time,--with what torture to the patient may be guessed. At last his precious oil gave out, and he used instead an insignificant mixture of his own contrivance. He could not sleep that night for fear his patients who had not been scalded with the boiling oil would be poisoned by the gunpowder conveyed into their wounds by the balls. To his surprise, he found them much better than the others the next morning, and resolved never again to burn his patients with hot oil for gun-shot wounds.

This was the beginning, as nearly as we can fix it, of that reform which has introduced plain water-dressings in the place of the farrago of external applications which had been a source of profit to apothecaries and disgrace to art from, and before, the time when Pliny complained of them. A young surgeon who was at Sudley Church, laboring among the wounded of Bull Run, tells me they had nothing but water for dressing, and he (being also doux de sel) was astonished to see how well the wounds did under that simple treatment.

Let me here mention a fact or two which may be of use to some of you who mean to enter the public service. You will, as it seems, have gun-shot wounds almost exclusively to deal with. Three different surgeons, the one just mentioned and two who saw the wounded of Big Bethel, assured me that they found no sabre-cuts or bayonet wounds. It is the rifle-bullet from a safe distance which pierces the breasts of our soldiers, and not the gallant charge of broad platoons and sweeping squadrons, such as we have been in the habit of considering the chosen mode of warfare of ancient and modern chivalry. [Sir Charles James Napier had the same experience in Virginia in 1813. "Potomac. We have nasty sort of fighting here, amongst creeks and bushes, and lose men without show." "Yankee never shows himself, he keeps in the thickest wood, fires and runs off."--"These five thousand in the open field might be attacked, but behind works it would be throwing away lives." He calls it "an inglorious warfare,"--says one of the leaders is "a little deficient in gumption,--but--still my opinion is, that if we tuck up our sleeves and lay our ears back we might thrash them; that is, if we caught them out of their trees, so as to slap at them with the bayonet."--Life, etc. vol. i. p. 218 et seq.]

Another fact parallels the story of the old campaigner, and may teach some of you caution in selecting your assistants. A chaplain told it to two of our officers personally known to myself. He overheard the examination of a man who wished to drive one of the "avalanche" wagons, as they call them. The man was asked if he knew how to deal with wounded men. "Oh yes," he answered; "if they're hit here," pointing to the abdomen, "knock 'em on the head,--they can't get well."

In art and outside of it you will meet the same barbarisms that Ambroise Pare met with,--for men differ less from century to century than we are apt to suppose; you will encounter the same opposition, if you attack any prevailing opinion, that Sydenham complained of. So far as possible, let not such experiences breed in you a contempt for those who are the subjects of folly or prejudice, or foster any love of dispute for its own sake. Should you become authors, express your opinions freely; defend them rarely. It is not often that an opinion is worth expressing, which cannot take care of itself. Opposition is the best mordant to fix the color of your thought in the general belief.

It is time to bring these crowded remarks to a close. The day has been when at the beginning of a course of Lectures I should have thought it fitting to exhort you to diligence and entire devotion to your tasks as students. It is not so now. The young man who has not heard the clarion-voices of honor and of duty now sounding throughout the land, will heed no word of mine. In the camp or the city, in the field or the hospital, under sheltering roof, or half-protecting canvas, or open sky, shedding our own blood or stanching that of our wounded defenders, students or teachers, whatever our calling and our ability, we belong, not to ourselves, but to our imperilled country, whose danger is our calamity, whose ruin would be our enslavement, whose rescue shall be our earthly salvation!

SCHOLASTIC AND BEDSIDE TEACHING.

An Introductory Lecture delivered before the Medical Class of Harvard University, November 6, 1867.

The idea is entertained by some of our most sincere professional brethren, that to lengthen and multiply our Winter Lectures will be of necessity to advance the cause of medical education. It is a fair subject for consideration whether they do not overrate the relative importance of that particular mode of instruction which forms the larger part of these courses.

As this School could only lengthen its lecture term at the expense of its "Summer Session," in which more direct, personal, and familiar teaching takes the place of our academic discourses, and in which more time can be given to hospitals, infirmaries, and practical instruction in various important specialties, whatever might be gained, a good deal would certainly be lost in our case by the exchange.

The most essential part of a student's instruction is obtained, as I believe, not in the lecture-room, but at the bedside. Nothing seen there is lost; the rhythms of disease are learned by frequent repetition; its unforeseen occurrences stamp themselves indelibly in the memory. Before the student is aware of what he has acquired, he has learned the aspects and course and probable issue of the diseases he has seen with his teacher, and the proper mode of dealing with them, so far as his master knows it. On the other hand, our ex cathedra prelections have a strong tendency to run into details which, however interesting they may be to ourselves and a few of our more curious listeners, have nothing in them which will ever be of use to the student as a practitioner. It is a perfectly fair question whether I and some other American Professors do not teach quite enough that is useless already. Is it not well to remind the student from time to time that a physician's business is to avert disease, to heal the sick, to prolong life, and to diminish suffering? Is it not true that the young man of average ability will find it as much as he can do to fit himself for these simple duties? Is it not best to begin, at any rate, by making sure of such knowledge as he will require in his daily walk, by no means discouraging him from any study for which his genius fits him when he once feels that he has become master of his chosen art.

I know that many branches of science are of the greatest value as feeders of our medical reservoirs. But the practising physician's office is to draw the healing waters, and while he gives his time to this labor he can hardly be expected to explore all the sources that spread themselves over the wide domain of science. The traveller who would not drink of the Nile until he had tracked it to its parent lakes, would be like to die of thirst; and the medical practitioner who would not use the results of many laborers in other departments without sharing their special toils, would find life far too short and art immeasurably too long.

We owe much to Chemistry, one of the most captivating as well as important of studies; but the medical man must as a general rule content himself with a clear view of its principles and a limited acquaintance with its facts; such especially as are pertinent to his pursuits. I am in little danger of underrating Anatomy or Physiology; but as each of these branches splits up into specialties, any one of which may take up a scientific life-time, I would have them taught with a certain judgment and reserve, so that they shall not crowd the more immediately practical branches. So of all the other ancillary and auxiliary kinds of knowledge, I would have them strictly subordinated to that particular kind of knowledge for which the community looks to its medical advisers.

A medical school is not a scientific school, except just so far as medicine itself is a science. On the natural history side, medicine is a science; on the curative side, chiefly an art. This is implied in Hufeland's aphorism: "The physician must generalize the disease and individualize the patient."

The coordinated and classified results of empirical observation, in distinction from scientific experiment, have furnished almost all we know about food, the medicine of health, and medicine, the food of sickness. We eat the root of the Solanum tuberosum and throw away its fruit; we eat the fruit of the Solanum Lycopersicum and throw away its root. Nothing but vulgar experience has taught us to reject the potato ball and cook the tomato. So of most of our remedies. The subchloride of mercury, calomel, is the great British specific; the protochloride of mercury, corrosive sublimate, kills like arsenic, but no chemist could have told us it would be so.

From observations like these we can obtain certain principles from which we can argue deductively to facts of a like nature, but the process is limited, and we are suspicious of all reasoning in that direction applied to the processes of healthy and diseased life. We are continually appealing to special facts. We are willing to give Liebig's artificial milk when we cannot do better, but we watch the child anxiously whose wet-nurse is a chemist's pipkin. A pair of substantial mammary glands has the advantage over the two hemispheres of the most learned Professor's brain, in the art of compounding a nutritious fluid for infants.

The bedside is always the true centre of medical teaching. Certain branches must be taught in the lecture-room, and will necessarily involve a good deal that is not directly useful to the future practitioner. But the over ambitious and active student must not be led away by the seduction of knowledge for its own sake from his principal pursuit. The humble beginner, who is alarmed at the vast fields of knowledge opened to him, may be encouraged by the assurance that with a very slender provision of science, in distinction from practical skill, he may be a useful and acceptable member of the profession to which the health of the community is intrusted.

To those who are not to engage in practice, the various pursuits of science hardly require to be commended. Only they must not be disappointed if they find many subjects treated in our courses as a medical class requires, rather than as a scientific class would expect, that is, with special limitations and constant reference to practical ends. Fortunately they are within easy reach of the highest scientific instruction. The business of a school like this is to make useful working physicians, and to succeed in this it is almost as important not to overcrowd the mind of the pupil with merely curious knowledge as it is to store it with useful information.

In this direction I have written my lecture, not to undervalue any form of scientific labor in its place, an unworthy thought from which I hope I need not defend myself,--but to discourage any undue inflation of the scholastic programme, which even now asks more of the student than the teacher is able to obtain from the great majority of those who present themselves for examination. I wish to take a hint in education from the Secretary of the Massachusetts Board of Agriculture, who regards the cultivation of too much land as a great defect in our New England farming. I hope that our Medical Institutions may never lay themselves open to the kind of accusation Mr. Lowe brings against the English Universities, when he says that their education is made up "of words that few understand and most will shortly forget; of arts that can never be used, if indeed they can even be learnt; of histories inapplicable to our times; of languages dead and even mouldy; of grammatical rules that never had living use and are only post mortem examinations; and of statements fagoted with utter disregard of their comparative value."

This general thought will be kept in view throughout my somewhat discursive address, which will begin with an imaginary clinical lesson from the lips of an historical personage, and close with the portrait from real life of one who, both as teacher and practitioner, was long loved and honored among us. If I somewhat overrun my hour, you must pardon me, for I can say with Pascal that I have not had the time to make my lecture shorter.

In the year 1647, that good man John Eliot, commonly called the Apostle Eliot, writing to Mr. Thomas Shepherd, the pious minister of Cambridge, referring to the great need of medical instruction for the Indians, used these words:

"I have thought in my heart that it were a singular good work, if the Lord would stirre up the hearts of some or other of his people in England to give some maintenance toward some Schoole or Collegiate exercise this way, wherein there should be Anatomies and other instructions that way, and where there might be some recompence given to any that should bring in any vegetable or other thing that is vertuous in the way of Physick.

"There is another reason which moves my thought and desires this way, namely that our young students in Physick may be trained up better then they yet bee, who have onely theoreticall knowledge, and are forced to fall to practise before ever they saw an Anatomy made, or duely trained up in making experiments, for we never had but one Anatomy in the countrey, which Mr. Giles Firman [Firmin] now in England, did make and read upon very well, but no more of that now."

Since the time of the Apostle Eliot the Lord has stirred up the hearts of our people to the building of many Schools and Colleges where medicine is taught in all its branches. Mr. Giles Firmin's "Anatomy" may be considered the first ancestor of a long line of skeletons which have been dangling and rattling in our lecture-rooms for more than a century.

Teaching in New England in 1647 was a grave but simple matter. A single person, combining in many cases, as in that of Mr. Giles Firmin, the offices of physician and preacher, taught what he knew to a few disciples whom he gathered about him. Of the making of that "Anatomy" on which my first predecessor in the branch I teach "did read very well" we can know nothing. The body of some poor wretch who had swung upon the gallows, was probably conveyed by night to some lonely dwelling at the outskirts of the village, and there by the light of flaring torches hastily dissected by hands that trembled over the unwonted task. And ever and anon the master turned to his book, as he laid bare the mysteries of the hidden organs; to his precious Vesalius, it might be, or his figures repeated in the multifarious volume of Ambroise Pare; to the Aldine octavo in which Fallopius recorded his fresh observations; or that giant folio of Spigelius just issued from the press of Amsterdam, in which lovely ladies display their viscera with a coquettish grace implying that it is rather a pleasure than otherwise to show the lace-like omentum, and hold up their appendices epiploicae as if they were saying "these are our jewels."

His teaching of medicine was no doubt chiefly clinical, and received with the same kind of faith as that which accepted his words from the pulpit. His notions of disease were based on what he had observed, seen always in the light of the traditional doctrines in which he was bred. His discourse savored of the weighty doctrines of Hippocrates, diluted by the subtle speculations of Galen, reinforced by the curious comments of the Arabian schoolmen as they were conveyed in the mellifluous language of Fernelius, blended, it may be, with something of the lofty mysticism of Van Helmont, and perhaps stealing a flavor of that earlier form of Homoeopathy which had lately come to light in Sir Kenelm Digby's "Discourse concerning the Cure of Wounds by the Sympathetic Powder."

His Pathology was mythology. A malformed foetus, as the readers of Winthrop's Journal may remember, was enough to scare the colonists from their propriety, and suggest the gravest fears of portended disaster. The student of the seventeenth century opened his Licetus and saw figures of a lion with the head of a woman, and a man with the head of an elephant. He had offered to his gaze, as born of a human mother, the effigy of a winged cherub, a pterocephalous specimen, which our Professor of Pathological Anatomy would hardly know whether to treat with the reverence due to its celestial aspect, or to imprison in one of his immortalizing jars of alcohol.

His pharmacopoeia consisted mainly of simples, such as the venerable "Herball" of Gerard describes and figures in abounding affluence. St. John's wort and Clown's All-heal, with Spurge and Fennel, Saffron and Parsley, Elder and Snake-root, with opium in some form, and roasted rhubarb and the Four Great Cold Seeds, and the two Resins, of which it used to be said that whatever the Tacamahaca has not cured, the Caranna will, with the more familiar Scammony and Jalap and Black Hellebore, made up a good part of his probable list of remedies. He would have ordered Iron now and then, and possibly an occasional dose of Antimony. He would perhaps have had a rheumatic patient wrapped in the skin of a wolf or a wild cat, and in case of a malignant fever with "purples" or petechiae, or of an obstinate king's evil, he might have prescribed a certain black powder, which had been made by calcining toads in an earthen pot; a choice remedy, taken internally, or applied to any outward grief.

Except for the toad-powder and the peremptory drastics, one might have borne up against this herb doctoring as well as against some more modern styles of medication. Barbeyrac and his scholar Sydenham had not yet cleansed the Pharmacopoeia of its perilous stuff, but there is no doubt that the more sensible physicians of that day knew well enough that a good honest herb-tea which amused the patient and his nurses was all that was required to carry him through all common disorders.

The student soon learned the physiognomy of disease by going about with his master; fevers, pleurisies, asthmas, dropsies, fluxes, small-pox, sore-throats, measles, consumptions. He saw what was done for them. He put up the medicines, gathered the herbs, and so learned something of materia medico and botany. He learned these few things easily and well, for he could give his whole attention to them. Chirurgery was a separate specialty. Women in child-birth were cared for by midwives. There was no chemistry deserving the name to require his study. He did not learn a great deal, perhaps, but what he did learn was his business, namely, how to take care of sick people.

Let me give you a picture of the old=fashioned way of instruction, by carrying you with me in imagination in the company of worthy Master Giles Firmin as he makes his round of visits among the good folk of Ipswich, followed by his one student, who shall answer to the scriptural name of Luke. It will not be for entertainment chiefly, but to illustrate the one mode of teaching which can never be superseded, and which, I venture to say, is more important than all the rest put together. The student is a green hand, as you will perceive.

In the first dwelling they come to, a stout fellow is bellowing with colic.

"He will die, Master, of a surety, methinks," says the timid youth in a whisper.

"Nay, Luke," the Master answers, "'t is but a dry belly-ache. Didst thou not mark that he stayed his roaring when I did press hard over the lesser bowels? Note that he hath not the pulse of them with fevers, and by what Dorcas telleth me there hath been no long shutting up of the vice naturales. We will steep certain comforting herbs which I will shew thee, and put them in a bag and lay them on his belly. Likewise he shall have my cordial julep with a portion of this confection which we do call Theriaca Andromachi, which hath juice of poppy in it, and is a great stayer of anguish. This fellow is at his prayers to-day, but I warrant thee he shall be swearing with the best of them to-morrow."

They jog along the bridle-path on their horses until they come to another lowly dwelling. They sit a while with a delicate looking girl in whom the ingenuous youth naturally takes a special interest. The good physician talks cheerfully with her, asks her a few questions. Then to her mother: "Good-wife, Margaret hath somewhat profited, as she telleth, by the goat's milk she hath taken night and morning. Do thou pluck a maniple--that is an handful--of the plant called Maidenhair, and make a syrup therewith as I have shewed thee. Let her take a cup full of the same, fasting, before she sleepeth, also before she riseth from her bed." And so they leave the house.

"What thinkest thou, Luke, of the maid we have been visiting?" "She seemeth not much ailing, Master, according to my poor judgment. For she did say she was better. And she had a red cheek and a bright eye, and she spake of being soon able to walk unto the meeting, and did seem greatly hopeful, but spare of flesh, methought, and her voice something hoarse, as of one that hath a defluxion, with some small coughing from a cold, as she did say. Speak I not truly, Master, that she will be well speedily?"

"Yea, Luke, I do think she shall be well, and mayhap speedily. But it is not here with us she shall be well. For that redness of the cheek is but the sign of the fever which, after the Grecians, we do call the hectical; and that shining of the eyes is but a sickly glazing, and they which do every day get better and likewise thinner and weaker shall find that way leadeth to the church-yard gate. This is the malady which the ancients did call tubes, or the wasting disease, and some do name the consumption. A disease whereof most that fall ailing do perish. This Margaret is not long for earth--but she knoweth it not, and still hopeth."

"Why, then, Master, didst thou give her of thy medicine, seeing that her ail is unto death?"

"Thou shalt learn, boy, that they which are sick must have somewhat wherewith to busy their thoughts. There be some who do give these tabid or consumptives a certain posset made with lime-water and anise and liquorice and raisins of the sun, and there be other some who do give the juice of craw-fishes boiled in barley-water with chicken-broth, but these be toys, as I do think, and ye shall find as good virtue, nay better, in this syrup of the simple called Maidenhair."

Something after this manner might Master Giles Firmin have delivered his clinical instructions. Somewhat in this way, a century and a half later, another New England physician, Dr. Edward Augustus Holyoke, taught a young man who came to study with him, a very diligent and intelligent youth, James Jackson by name, the same whose portrait in his advanced years hangs upon this wall, long the honored Professor of Theory and Practice in this Institution, of whom I shall say something in this Lecture. Our venerated Teacher studied assiduously afterwards in the great London Hospitals, but I think he used to quote his "old Master" ten times where he quoted Mr. Cline or Dr. Woodville once.

When I compare this direct transfer of the practical experience of a wise man into the mind of a student,--every fact one that he can use in the battle of life and death,--with the far off, unserviceable "scientific" truths that I and some others are in the habit of teaching, I cannot help asking myself whether, if we concede that our forefathers taught too little, there is not--a possibility that we may sometimes attempt to teach too much. I almost blush when I think of myself as describing the eight several facets on two slender processes of the palate bone, or the seven little twigs that branch off from the minute tympanic nerve, and I wonder whether my excellent colleague feels in the same way when he pictures himself as giving the constitution of neurin, which as he and I know very well is that of the hydrate of trimethyle-oxethyle-ammonium, or the formula for the production of alloxan, which, though none but the Professors and older students can be expected to remember it, is $C_{10} H_4 N_4 O_6 + 2HO, NO_5 = C_8 H_4 N_2 O_{10} + 2CO_2 + N_2 + NH_4 O, NO_5$.

I can bear the voice of some rough iconoclast addressing the Anatomist and the Chemist in tones of contemptuous indignation: "What is this stuff with which you are cramming the brains of young men who are to hold the lives of the community in their hands? Here is a man fallen in a fit; you can tell me all about the eight surfaces of the two processes of the palate bone, but you have not had the sense to loosen that man's neck-cloth, and the old women are all calling you a fool? Here is a fellow that has just swallowed poison. I want something to turn his stomach inside out at the shortest notice. Oh, you have forgotten the dose of the sulphate of zinc, but you remember the formula for the production of alloxan!"

"Look you, Master Doctor,--if I go to a carpenter to come and stop a leak in my roof that is flooding the house, do you suppose I care whether he is a botanist or not? Cannot a man work in wood without knowing all about endogens and exogens, or must he attend Professor Gray's Lectures before he can be trusted to make a box-trap? If my horse casts a shoe, do you think I will not trust a blacksmith to shoe him until I have made sure that he is sound on the distinction between the sesquioxide and the protosesquioxide of iron?"

--But my scientific labor is to lead to useful results by and by, in the next generation, or in some possible remote future.--

"Diavolo!" as your Dr. Rabelais has it,--answers the iconoclast,--"what is that to me and my colic, to me and my strangury? I pay the Captain of the Cunard steamship to carry me quickly and safely to Liverpool, not to make a chart of the Atlantic for after voyagers! If Professor Peirce undertakes to pilot me into Boston Harbor and runs me on Cohasset rocks, what answer is it to tell me that he is Superintendent of the Coast Survey? No, Sir! I want a plain man in a pea-jacket and a sou'wester, who knows the channel of Boston Harbor, and the rocks of Boston Harbor, and the distinguished Professor is quite of my mind as to the matter, for I took the pains to ask him before I ventured to use his name in the way of illustration."

I do not know how the remarks of the image-breaker may strike others, but

I feel that they put me on my defence with regard to much of my teaching. Some years ago I ventured to show in an introductory Lecture how very small a proportion of the anatomical facts taught in a regular course, as delivered by myself and others, had any practical bearing whatever on the treatment of disease. How can I, how can any medical teacher justify himself in teaching anything that is not like to be of practical use to a class of young men who are to hold in their hands the balance in which life and death, ease and anguish, happiness and wretchedness are to be daily weighed?

I hope we are not all wrong. Oftentimes in finding how sadly ignorant of really essential and vital facts and rules were some of those whom we had been larding with the choicest scraps of science, I have doubted whether the old one-man system of teaching, when the one man was of the right sort, did not turn out better working physicians than our more elaborate method. The best practitioner I ever knew was mainly shaped to excellence in that way. I can understand perfectly the regrets of my friend Dr. John Brown of Edinburgh, for the good that was lost with the old apprenticeship system. I understand as well Dr. Latham's fear "that many men of the best abilities and good education will be deterred from prosecuting physic as a profession, in consequence of the necessity indiscriminately laid upon all for impossible attainments."

I feel therefore impelled to say a very few words in defence of that system of teaching adopted in our Colleges, by which we wish to supplement and complete the instruction given by private individuals or by what are often called Summer Schools.

The reason why we teach so much that is not practical and in itself useful, is because we find that the easiest way of teaching what is practical and useful. If we could in any way eliminate all that would help a man to deal successfully with disease, and teach it by itself so that it should be as tenaciously rooted in the memory, as easily summoned when wanted, as fertile in suggestion of related facts, as satisfactory to the peremptory demands of the intelligence as if taught in its scientific connections, I think it would be our duty so to teach the momentous truths of medicine, and to regard all useless additions as an intrusion on the time which should be otherwise occupied.

But we cannot successfully eliminate and teach by itself that which is purely practical. The easiest and surest why of acquiring facts is to learn them in groups, in systems, and systematized knowledge is science. You can very often carry two facts fastened together more easily than one by itself, as a housemaid can carry two pails of water with a hoop more easily than one without it. You can remember a man's face, made up of many features, better than you can his nose or his mouth or his eye-brow. Scores of proverbs show you that you can remember two lines that rhyme better than one without the jingle. The ancients, who knew the laws of memory, grouped the seven cities that contended for the honor of being Homer's birthplace in a line thus given by Aulus Gellius:

Smurna, Rodos, Colophon, Salamin, Ios, Argos, Athenai.

I remember, in the earlier political days of Martin Van Buren, that Colonel Stone, of the "New York Commercial," or one of his correspondents, said that six towns of New York would claim in the same way to have been the birth-place of the "Little Magician," as he was then called; and thus he gave their names, any one of which I should long ago have forgotten, but which as a group have stuck tight in my memory from that day to this;

Catskill, Saugerties, Redhook, Kinderhook, Scaghticoke, Schodac.

If the memory gains so much by mere rhythmical association, how much more will it gain when isolated facts are brought together under laws and principles, when organs are examined in their natural connections, when structure is coupled with function, and healthy and diseased action are studied as they pass one into the other! Systematic, or scientific study is invaluable as supplying a natural kind of mnemonics, if for nothing else. You cannot properly learn the facts you want from Anatomy and Chemistry in any way so easily as by taking them in their regular order, with other allied facts, only there must be common sense exercised in leaving out a great deal which belongs to each of the two branches as pure science. The dullest of teachers is the one who does not know what to omit.

The larger aim of scientific training is to furnish you with principles to which you will be able to refer isolated facts, and so bring these within the range of recorded experience. See what the "London Times" said about the three Germans who cracked open John Bull Chatwood's strong-box at the Fair the other day, while the three Englishmen hammered away in vain at Brother Jonathan Herring's. The Englishmen represented brute force. The Germans had been trained to appreciate principle. The Englishman "knows his business by rote and rule of thumb"--science, which would "teach him to do in an hour what has hitherto occupied him two hours," "is in a manner forbidden to him." To this cause the "Times" attributes the falling off of English workmen in comparison with those of the Continent.

Granting all this, we must not expect too much from "science" as distinguished from common experience. There are ten thousand experimenters without special apparatus for every one in the laboratory. Accident is the great chemist and toxicologist. Battle is the great vivisector. Hunger has instituted researches on food such as no Liebig, no Academic Commission has ever recorded.

Medicine, sometimes impertinently, often ignorantly, often carelessly called "allopathy," appropriates everything from every source that can be of the slightest use to anybody who is ailing in any way, or like to be ailing from any cause. It learned from a monk how to use antimony, from a Jesuit how to cure agues, from a friar how to cut for stone, from a soldier how to treat gout, from a sailor how to keep off scurvy, from a postmaster how to sound the Eustachian tube, from a dairymaid how to prevent small-pox, and from an old market-woman how to catch the itch-insect. It borrowed acupuncture and the moxa from the Japanese heathen, and was taught the use of lobelia by the American savage. It stands ready to-day to accept anything from any theorist, from any empiric who can make out a good case for his discovery or his remedy. "Science" is one of its benefactors, but only one, out of many. Ask the wisest practising physician you know, what branches of science help him habitually, and what amount of knowledge relating to each branch he requires for his professional duties. He will tell you that scientific training has a value independent of all the special knowledge acquired. He will tell you that many facts are explained by studying them in the wider range of related facts to which they belong. He will gratefully recognize that the anatomist has furnished him with indispensable data, that the physiologist has sometimes put him on the track of new modes of treatment, that the chemist has isolated the active principles of his medicines, has taught him how to combine them, has from time to time offered him new remedial agencies, and so of others of his allies. But he will also tell you, if I am not mistaken, that his own branch of knowledge is so extensive and so perplexing that he must accept most of his facts ready made at their hands. He will own to you that in the struggle for life which goes on day and night in our thoughts as in the outside world of nature, much that he learned under the name of science has died out, and that simple homely experience has largely taken the place of that scholastic knowledge to which he and perhaps some of his instructors once attached a paramount importance.

This, then, is my view of scientific training as conducted in courses such as you are entering on. Up to a certain point I believe in set Lectures as excellent adjuncts to what is far more important, practical instruction at the bedside, in the operating room, and under the eye of the Demonstrator. But I am so far from wishing these courses extended, that I think some of them--suppose I say my own--would almost bear curtailing. Do you want me to describe more branches of the sciatic and crural nerves? I can take Fischer's plates, and lecturing on that scale fill up my whole course and not finish the nerves alone. We must stop somewhere, and for my own part I think the scholastic exercises of our colleges have already claimed their full share of the student's time without our seeking to extend them.

I trust I have vindicated the apparent inconsequence of teaching young students a good deal that seems at first sight profitless, but which helps them to learn and retain what is profitable. But this is an inquisitive age, and if we insist on piling up beyond a certain height knowledge which is in itself mere trash and lumber to a man whose life is to be one long fight with death and disease, there will be some sharp questions asked by and by, and our quick-witted people will perhaps find they can get along as well without the professor's cap as without the bishop's mitre and the monarch's crown.

I myself have nothing to do with clinical teaching. Yet I do not hesitate to say it is more essential than all the rest put together, so far as the ordinary practice of medicine is concerned; and this is by far the most important thing to be learned, because it deals with so many more lives than any other branch of the profession. So of personal instruction, such as we give and others give in the interval of lectures, much of it at the bedside, some of it in the laboratory, some in the microscope-room, some in the recitation-room, I think it has many advantages of its own over the winter course, and I do not wish to see it shortened for the sake of prolonging what seems to me long enough already.

If I am jealous of the tendency to expand the time given to the acquisition of curious knowledge, at the expense of the plain old-fashioned bedside teachings, I only share the feeling which Sydenham expressed two hundred years ago, using an image I have already borrowed. "He would be no honest and successful pilot who was to apply himself with less industry to avoid rocks and sands and bring his vessel safely home, than to search into the causes of the ebbing and flowing of the sea, which, though very well for a philosopher, is foreign to him whose business it is to secure the ship. So neither will a physician, whose province it is to cure diseases, be able to do so, though he be a person of great genius, who bestows less time on the hidden and intricate method of nature, and adapting his means thereto, than on curious and subtle speculation."

"Medicine is my wife and Science is my mistress," said Dr. Rush. I do not think that the breach of the seventh commandment can be shown to have been of advantage to the legitimate owner of his affections. Read what Dr. Elisha Bartlett says of him as a practitioner, or ask one of our own honored ex-professors, who studied under him, whether Dr. Rush had ever learned the meaning of that saying of Lord Bacon, that man is the minister and interpreter of Nature, or whether he did not speak habitually of Nature as an intruder in the sick room, from which his art was to expel her as an incompetent and a meddler.

All a man's powers are not too much for such a profession as Medicine. "He is a learned man," said old Parson Emmons of Franklin, "who understands one subject, and he is a very learned man who understands two subjects." Schonbein says he has been studying oxygen for thirty years. Mitscherlich said it took fourteen years to establish a new fact in chemistry. Aubrey says of Harvey, the discoverer of the circulation, that "though all his profession would allow him to be an excellent anatomist, I have never heard of any who admired his therapeutic way." My learned and excellent friend before referred to, Dr. Brown of Edinburgh, from whose very lively and sensible Essay, "Locke and Sydenham," I have borrowed several of my citations, contrasts Sir Charles Bell, the discoverer, the man of science, with Dr. Abercrombie, the master in the diagnosis and treatment of disease. It is through one of the rarest of combinations that we have in our Faculty a teacher on whom the scientific mantle of Bell has fallen, and who yet stands preeminent in the practical treatment of the class of diseases which his inventive and ardent experimental genius has illustrated. M. Brown-Sequard's example is as, eloquent as his teaching in proof of the advantages of well directed scientific investigation. But those who emulate his success at once as a discoverer and a practitioner must be content like him to limit their field of practice. The highest genius cannot afford in our time to forget the ancient precept, Divide et impera.

"I suppose I must go and earn this guinea," said a medical man who was sent for while he was dissecting an animal. I should not have cared to be his patient. His dissection would do me no good, and his thoughts would be too much upon it. I want a whole man for my doctor, not a half one. I would have sent for a humbler practitioner, who would have given himself entirely to me, and told the other--who was no less a man than John Hunter--to go on and finish the dissection of his tiger.

Sydenham's "Read Don Quixote" should be addressed not to the student, but to the Professor of today. Aimed at him it means, "Do not be too learned."

Do not think you are going to lecture to picked young men who are training themselves to be scientific discoverers. They are of fair average capacity, and they are going to be working doctors.

These young men are to have some very serious vital facts to deal with. I will mention a few of them.

Every other resident adult you meet in these streets is or will be more or less tuberculous. This is not an extravagant estimate, as very nearly one third of the deaths of adults in Boston last year were from phthisis. If the relative number is less in our other northern cities, it is probably in a great measure because they are more unhealthy; that is, they have as much, or nearly as much, consumption, but they have more fevers or other fatal diseases.

These heavy-eyed men with the alcoholized brains, these pallid youths with the nicotized optic ganglia and thinking-marrows brown as their own meerschaums, of whom you meet too many,--will ask all your wisdom to deal with their poisoned nerves and their enfeebled wills.

Nearly seventeen hundred children under five years of age died last year in this city. A poor human article, no doubt, in many cases, still, worth an attempt to save them, especially when we remember the effect of Dr. Clarke's suggestion at the Dublin Hospital, by which some twenty-five or thirty thousand children's lives have probably been saved in a single city.

Again, the complaint is often heard that the native population is not increasing so rapidly as in former generations. The breeding and nursing period of American women is one of peculiar delicacy and frequent infirmity. Many of them must require a considerable interval between the reproductive efforts, to repair damages and regain strength. This matter is not to be decided by an appeal to unschooled nature. It is the same question as that of the deformed pelvis,--one of degree. The facts of mal-vitalization are as much to be attended to as those of mal-formation. If the woman with a twisted pelvis is to be considered an exempt, the woman with a defective organization should be recognized as belonging to the invalid corps. We shudder to hear what is alleged as to the prevalence of criminal practices; if back of these there can be shown organic incapacity or overtaxing of too limited powers, the facts belong to the province of the practical physician, as well as of the moralist and the legislator, and require his gravest consideration.

Take the important question of bleeding. Is venesection done with forever? Six years ago it was said here in an introductory Lecture that it would doubtless come back again sooner or later. A fortnight ago I found myself in the cars with one of the most sensible and esteemed practitioners in New England. He took out his wallet and showed me two lancets, which he carried with him; he had never given up their use. This is a point you will have to consider.

Or, to mention one out of many questionable remedies, shall you give Veratrum Viride in fevers and inflammations? It makes the pulse slower in these affections. Then the presumption would naturally be that it does harm. The caution with reference to it on this ground was long ago recorded in the Lecture above referred to. See what Dr. John Hughes Bennett says of it in the recent edition of his work on Medicine. Nothing but the most careful clinical experience can settle this and such points of treatment.

These are all practical questions--questions of life and death, and every day will be full of just such questions. Take the problem of climate. A patient comes to you with asthma and wants to know where he can breathe; another comes to you with phthisis and wants to know where he can live. What boy's play is nine tenths of all that is taught in many a pretentious course of lectures, compared with what an accurate and extensive knowledge of the advantages and disadvantages of different residences in these and other complaints would be to a practising physician.

I saw the other day a gentleman living in Canada, who had spent seven successive winters in Egypt, with the entire relief of certain obscure thoracic symptoms which troubled him while at home. I saw, two months ago, another gentleman from Minnesota, an observer and a man of sense, who considered that State as the great sanatorium for all pulmonary complaints. If half our grown population are or will be more or less tuberculous, the question of colonizing Florida assumes a new aspect. Even within the borders of our own State, the very interesting researches of Dr. Bowditch show that there is a great variation in the amount of tuberculous disease in different towns, apparently connected with local conditions. The hygienic map of a State is quite as valuable as its geological map, and it is the business of every practising physician to know it thoroughly. They understand this in England, and send a patient with a dry irritating cough to Torquay or Penzance, while they send another with relaxed bronchial membranes to Clifton or Brighton. Here is another great field for practical study.

So as to the all-important question of diet. "Of all the means of cure at our command," says Dr. Bennett, "a regulation of the quantity and quality of the diet is by far the most powerful." Dr. MacCormac would perhaps except the air we breathe, for he thinks that impure air, especially in sleeping rooms, is the great cause of tubercle. It is sufficiently proved that the American,--the New Englander,--the Bostonian, can breed strong and sound children, generation after generation,--nay, I have shown by the record of a particular family that vital losses may be retrieved, and a feeble race grow to lusty vigor in this very climate and locality. Is not the question why our young men and women so often break down, and how they can be kept from breaking down, far more important for physicians to settle than whether there is one cranial vertebra, or whether there are four, or none?

--But I have a taste for the homologies, I want to go deeply into the subject of embryology, I want to analyze the protonihilates precipitated from pigeon's milk by the action of the lunar spectrum,--shall I not follow my star,--shall I not obey my instinct,--shall I not give myself to the lofty pursuits of science for its own sake?

Certainly you may, if you like. But take down your sign, or never put it up. That is the way Dr. Owen and Dr. Huxley, Dr. Agassiz and Dr. Jeffries Wyman, Dr. Gray and Dr. Charles T. Jackson settled the difficulty. We all admire the achievements of this band of distinguished doctors who do not practise. But we say of their work and of all pure science, as the French officer said of the charge of the six hundred at Balaclava, "C'est magnifique, mais ce n'est pas la guerre,"--it is very splendid, but it is not a practising doctor's business. His patient has a right to the cream of his life and not merely to the thin milk that is left after "science" has skimmed it off. The best a physician can give is never too good for the patient.

It is often a disadvantage to a young practitioner to be known for any accomplishment outside of his profession. Haller lost his election as Physician to the Hospital in his native city of Berne, principally on the ground that he was a poet. In his later years the physician may venture more boldly. Astruc was sixty-nine years old when he published his "Conjectures," the first attempt, we are told, to decide the authorship of the Pentateuch showing anything like a discerning criticism. Sir Benjamin Brodie was seventy years old before he left his physiological and surgical studies to indulge in psychological speculations. The period of pupilage will be busy enough in acquiring the knowledge needed, and the season of active practice will leave little leisure for any but professional studies.

Dr. Graves of Dublin, one of the first clinical teachers of our time, always insisted on his students' beginning at once to visit the hospital. At the bedside the student must learn to treat disease, and just as certainly as we spin out and multiply our academic prelections we shall work in more and more stuffing, more and more rubbish, more and more irrelevant, useless detail which the student will get rid of just as soon as he leaves us. Then the next thing will be a new organization, with an examining board of first-rate practical men, who will ask the candidate questions that mean business,--who will make him operate if he is to be a surgeon, and try him at the bedside if he is to be a physician,--and not puzzle him with scientific conundrums which not more than one of the questioners could answer himself or ever heard of since he graduated.

Or these women who are hammering at the gates on which is written "No admittance for the mothers of mankind," will by and by organize an institution, which starting from that skilful kind of nursing which Florence Nightingale taught so well, will work backwards through anodynes, palliatives, curatives, preventives, until with little show of science it imparts most of what is most valuable in those branches of the healing art it professes to teach. When that time comes, the fitness of women for certain medical duties, which Hecquet advocated in 1708, which Douglas maintained in 1736, which Dr. John Ware, long the honored Professor of Theory and Practice in this Institution, upheld within our own recollection in the face of his own recorded opinion to the contrary, will very possibly be recognized.

My advice to every teacher less experienced than myself would be, therefore: Do not fret over the details you have to omit; you probably teach altogether too many as it is. Individuals may learn a thing with once hearing it, but the only way of teaching a whole class is by enormous repetition, representation, and illustration in all possible forms. Now and then you will have a young man on your benches like the late Waldo Burnett,--not very often, if you lecture half a century. You cannot pretend to lecture chiefly for men like that,--a Mississippi raft might as well take an ocean-steamer in tow. To meet his wants you would have to leave the rest of your class behind and that you must not do. President Allen of Jefferson College says that his instruction has been successful in proportion as it has been elementary. It may be a humiliating statement, but it is one which I have found true in my own experience.

To the student I would say, that however plain and simple may be our teaching, he must expect to forget much which he follows intelligently in the lecture-room. But it is not the same as if he had never learned it. A man must get a thing before he can forget it. There is a great world of ideas we cannot voluntarily recall,--they are outside the limits of the will. But they sway our conscious thought as the unseen planets influence the movements of those within the sphere of vision. No man knows how much he knows,--how many ideas he has,--any more than he knows how many blood-globules roll in his veins. Sometimes accident brings back here and there one, but the mind is full of irrevocable remembrances and unthinkable thoughts, which take a part in all its judgments as indestructible forces. Some of you must feel your scientific deficiencies painfully after your best efforts. But every one can acquire what is most essential. A man of very moderate ability may be a good physician, if he devotes himself faithfully to the work. More than this, a positively dull man, in the ordinary acceptation of the term, sometimes makes a safer practitioner than one who has, we will say, five per cent. more brains than his average neighbor, but who thinks it is fifty per cent. more. Skulls belonging to this last variety of the human race are more common, I may remark, than specimens like the Neanderthal cranium, a cast of which you will find on the table in the Museum.

Whether the average talent be high or low, the Colleges of the land must make the best commodity they can out of such material as the country and the cities furnish them. The community must have Doctors as it must have bread. It uses up its Doctors just as it wears out its shoes, and requires new ones. All the bread need not be French rolls, all the shoes need not be patent leather ones; but the bread must be something that can be eaten, and the shoes must be something that can be worn. Life must somehow find food for the two forces that rub everything to pieces, or burn it to ashes,--friction and oxygen. Doctors are oxydable products, and the schools must keep furnishing new ones as the old ones turn into oxyds; some of first-rate quality that burn with a great light, some of a lower grade of brilliancy, some honestly, unmistakably, by the grace of God, of moderate gifts, or in simpler phrase, dull.

The public will give every honest and reasonably competent worker in the healing art a hearty welcome. It is on the whole very loyal to the Medical Profession. Three successive years have borne witness to the feeling with which this Institution, representing it in its educational aspect, is regarded by those who are themselves most honored and esteemed. The great Master of Natural Science bade the last year's class farewell in our behalf, in those accents which delight every audience. The Head of our ancient University honored us in the same way in the preceding season. And how can we forget that other occasion when the Chief Magistrate of the Commonwealth, that noble citizen whom we have just lost, large-souled, sweet-natured, always ready for every kind office, came among us at our bidding, and talked to us of our duties in words as full of wisdom as his heart was of goodness?

You have not much to fear, I think, from the fancy practitioners. The vulgar quackeries drop off, atrophied, one after another. Homoeopathy has long been encysted, and is carried on the body medical as quietly as an old wen. Every year gives you a more reasoning and reasonable people to deal with. See how it is in Literature. The dynasty of British dogmatists, after lasting a hundred years and more, is on its last legs. Thomas Carlyle, third in the line of descent, finds an audience very different from those which listened to the silver speech of Samuel Taylor Coleridge and the sonorous phrases of Samuel Johnson. We read him, we smile at his clotted English, his "swarmery" and other picturesque expressions, but we lay down his tirade as we do one of Dr. Cumming's interpretations of prophecy, which tells us that the world is coming to an end next week or next month, if the weather permits,--not otherwise,--feeling very sure that the weather will be unfavorable.

It is the same common-sense public you will appeal to. The less pretension you make, the better they will like you in the long run. I hope we shall make everything as plain and as simple to you as we can. I would never use a long word, even, where a short one would answer the purpose. I know there are professors in this country who "ligate" arteries. Other surgeons only tie them, and it stops the bleeding just as well. It is the familiarity and simplicity of bedside instruction which makes it so pleasant as well as so profitable. A good clinical teacher is himself a Medical School. We need not wonder that our young men are beginning to announce themselves not only as graduates of this or that College, but also as pupils of some one distinguished master.

I wish to close this Lecture, if you will allow me a few moments longer, with a brief sketch of an instructor and practitioner whose character was as nearly a model one in both capacities as I can find anywhere recorded.

Dr. JAMES JACKSON, Professor of the Theory and Practice of Medicine in this University from 1812 to 1846, and whose name has been since retained on our rolls as Professor Emeritus, died on the 27th of August last, in the ninetieth year of his age. He studied his profession, as I have already mentioned, with Dr. Holyoke of Salem, one of the few physicians who have borne witness to their knowledge of the laws of life by living to complete their hundredth year. I think the student took his Old Master, as he always loved to call him, as his model; each was worthy of the other, and both were bright examples to all who come after them.

I remember that in the sermon preached by Dr. Grazer after Dr. Holyoke's death, one of the points most insisted upon as characteristic of that wise and good old man was the perfect balance of all his faculties. The same harmonious adjustment of powers, the same symmetrical arrangement of life, the same complete fulfilment of every day's duties, without haste and without needless delay, which characterized the master, equally distinguished the scholar. A glance at the life of our own Old Master, if I can do any justice at all to his excellences, will give you something to carry away from this hour's meeting not unworthy to be remembered.

From December, 1797, to October, 1799, he remained with Dr. Holyoke as a student, a period which he has spoken of as a most interesting and most gratifying part of his life. After this he passed eight months in London, and on his return, in

October, 1800, he began business in Boston.

He had followed Mr. Cline, as I have mentioned, and was competent to practise Surgery. But he found Dr. John Collins Warren had already occupied the ground which at that day hardly called for more than one leading practitioner, and wisely chose the Medical branch of the profession. He had only himself to rely upon, but he had confidence in his prospects, conscious, doubtless, of his own powers, knowing his own industry and determination, and being of an eminently cheerful and hopeful disposition. No better proof of his spirit can be given than that, just a year from the time when he began to practise as a physician, he took that eventful step which in such a man implies that he sees his way clear to a position; he married a lady blessed with many gifts, but not bringing him a fortune to paralyze his industry.

He had not miscalculated his chances in life. He very soon rose into a good practice, and began the founding of that reputation which grew with his years, until he stood by general consent at the head of his chosen branch of the profession, to say the least, in this city and in all this region of country. His skill and wisdom were the last tribunal to which the sick and suffering could appeal. The community trusted and loved him, the profession recognized him as the noblest type of the physician. The young men whom he had taught wandered through foreign hospitals; where they learned many things that were valuable, and many that were curious; but as they grew older and began to think more of their ability to help the sick than their power of talking about phenomena, they began to look back to the teaching of Dr. Jackson, as he, after his London experience, looked back to that of Dr. Holyoke. And so it came to be at last that the bare mention of his name in any of our medical assemblies would call forth such a tribute of affectionate regard as is only yielded to age when it brings with it the record of a life spent in well doing.

No accident ever carries a man to eminence such as his in the medical profession. He who looks for it must want it earnestly and work for it vigorously; Nature must have qualified him in many ways, and education must have equipped him with various knowledge, or his reputation will evaporate before it reaches the noon-day blaze of fame. How did Dr. Jackson gain the position which all conceded to him? In the answer to this question some among you may find a key that shall unlock the gate opening on that fair field of the future of which all dream but which not all will ever reach.

First of all, he truly loved his profession. He had no intellectual ambitions outside of it, literary, scientific or political. To him it was occupation enough to apply at the bedside the best of all that he knew for the good of his patient; to protect the community against the inroads of pestilence; to teach the young all that he himself had been taught, with all that his own experience had added; to leave on record some of the most important results of his long observation.

With his patients he was so perfect at all points that it is hard to overpraise him. I have seen many noted British and French and American practitioners, but I never saw the man so altogether admirable at the bedside of the sick as Dr. James Jackson. His smile was itself a remedy better than the potable gold and the dissolved pearls that comforted the praecordia of mediaeval monarchs. Did a patient, alarmed without cause, need encouragement, it carried the sunshine of hope into his heart and put all his whims to flight, as David's harp cleared the haunted chamber of the sullen king. Had the hour come, not for encouragement, but for sympathy, his face, his voice, his manner all showed it, because his heart felt it. So gentle was he, so thoughtful, so calm, so absorbed in the case before him, not to turn round and look for a tribute to his sagacity, not to bolster himself in a favorite theory, but to find out all he could, and to weigh gravely and cautiously all that he found, that to follow him in his morning visit was not only to take a lesson in the healing art, it was learning how to learn, how to move, how to look, how to feel, if that can be learned. To visit with Dr. Jackson was a medical education.

He was very firm, with all his kindness. He would have the truth about his patients. The nurses found it out; and the shrewder ones never ventured to tell him anything but a straight story. A clinical dialogue between Dr. Jackson and Miss Rebecca Taylor, sometime nurse in the Massachusetts General Hospital, a mistress in her calling, was as good questioning and answering as one would be like to hear outside of the court-room.

Of his practice you can form an opinion from his book called "Letters to a Young Physician." Like all sensible men from the days of Hippocrates to the present, he knew that diet and regimen were more important than any drug or than all drugs put together. Witness his treatment of phthisis and of epilepsy. He retained, however, more confidence in some remedial agents than most of the younger generation would concede to them. Yet his materia medica was a simple one.

"When I first went to live with Dr. Holyoke," he says, "in 1797, showing me his shop, he said, 'There seems to you to be a great variety of medicines here, and that it will take you long to get acquainted with them, but most of them are unimportant. There are four which are equal to all the rest, namely, Mercury, Antimony, Bark and Opium.'" And Dr. Jackson adds, "I can only say of his practice, the longer I have lived, I have thought better and better of it." When he thought it necessary to give medicine, he gave it in earnest. He hated half-practice--giving a little of this or that, so as to be able to say that one had done something, in case a consultation was held, or a still more ominous event occurred. He would give opium, for instance, as boldly as the late Dr. Fisher of Beverly, but he followed the aphorism of the Father of Medicine, and kept extreme remedies for extreme cases.

When it came to the "non-naturals," as he would sometimes call them, after the old physicians,--namely, air, meat and drink, sleep and watching, motion and rest, the retentions and excretions, and the affections of the mind,--he was, as I have said, of the school of sensible practitioners, in distinction from that vast community of quacks, with or without the diploma, who think the chief end of man is to support apothecaries, and are never easy until they can get every patient upon a regular course of something nasty or noxious. Nobody was so precise in his directions about diet, air, and exercise, as Dr. Jackson. He had the same dislike to the a peu pres, the about so much, about so often, about so long, which I afterwards found among the punctilious adherents of the numerical system at La Pitie.

He used to insist on one small point with a certain philological precision, namely, the true meaning of the word "cure." He would have it that to cure a patient was simply to care for him. I refer to it as showing what his idea was of the relation of the physician to the patient. It was indeed to care for him, as if his life were bound up in him, to watch his incomings and outgoings, to stand guard at every avenue that disease might enter, to leave nothing to chance; not merely to throw a few pills and powders into one pan of the scales of Fate, while Death the skeleton was seated in the other, but to lean with his whole weight on the side of life, and shift the balance in its favor if it lay in human power to do it. Such devotion as this is only to be looked for in the man who gives himself wholly up to the business of healing, who considers Medicine itself a Science, or if not a science, is willing to follow it as an art,--the noblest of arts, which the gods and demigods of ancient religions did not disdain to practise and to teach.

The same zeal made him always ready to listen to any new suggestion which promised to be useful, at a period of life when many men find it hard to learn new methods and accept new doctrines. Few of his generation became so accomplished as he in the arts of direct exploration; coming straight from the Parisian experts, I have examined many patients with him, and have had frequent opportunities of observing his skill in percussion and auscultation.

One element in his success, a trivial one compared with others, but not to be despised, was his punctuality. He always carried two watches,--I doubt if he told why, any more than Dr. Johnson told what he did with the orange-peel,--but probably with reference to this virtue. He was as much to be depended upon at the appointed time as the solstice or the equinox. There was another point I have heard him speak of as an important rule with him; to come at the hour when he was expected; if he had made his visit for several days successively at ten o'clock, for instance, not to put it off, if he could possibly help it, until eleven, and so keep a nervous patient and an anxious family waiting for him through a long, weary hour.

If I should attempt to characterize his teaching, I should say that while it conveyed the best results of his sagacious and extended observation, it was singularly modest, cautious, simple, sincere. Nothing was for show, for self-love; there was no rhetoric, no declamation, no triumphant "I told you so," but the plain statement of a clear-headed honest man, who knows that he is handling one of the gravest subjects that interest humanity. His positive instructions were full of value, but the spirit in which he taught inspired that loyal love of truth which lies at the bottom of all real excellence.

I will not say that, during his long career, Dr. Jackson never made an enemy. I have heard him tell how, in his very early days, old Dr. Danforth got into a towering passion with him about some professional consultation, and exploded a monosyllable or two of the more energetic kind on the occasion. I remember that that somewhat peculiar personage, Dr. Waterhouse, took it hardly when Dr. Jackson succeeded to his place as Professor of Theory and Practice. A young man of Dr. Jackson's talent and energy could hardly take the position that belonged to him without crowding somebody in a profession where three in a bed is the common rule of the household. But he was a peaceful man and a peace-maker all his days. No man ever did more, if so much, to produce and maintain the spirit of harmony for which we consider our medical community as somewhat exceptionally distinguished.

If this harmony should ever be threatened, I could wish that every impatient and irritable member of the profession would read that beautiful, that noble Preface to the "Letters," addressed to John Collins Warren. I know nothing finer in the medical literature of all time than this Prefatory Introduction. It is a golden prelude, fit to go with the three great Prefaces which challenge the admiration of scholars,--Calvin's to his Institutes, De Thou's to his History, and Casaubon's to his Polybius,--not because of any learning or rhetoric, though it is charmingly written, but for a spirit flowing through it to which learning and rhetoric are but as the breath that is wasted on the air to the Mood that warms the heart.

Of a similar character is this short extract which I am permitted to make from a private letter of his to a dear young friend. He was eighty-three years old at the time of writing it.

"I have not loved everybody whom I have known, but I have striven to see the good points in the characters of all men and women. At first I must have done this from something in my own nature, for I was not aware of it, and yet was doing it without any plan, when one day, sixty years ago, a friend whom I loved and respected said this to me, 'Ah, James, I see that you are destined to succeed in the world, and to make friends, because you are so ready to see the good point in the characters of those you meet.'"

I close this imperfect notice of some features in the character of this most honored and beloved of physicians by applying to him the words which were written of William Heberden, whose career was not unlike his own, and who lived to the same patriarchal age.

"From his early youth he had always entertained a deep sense of religion, a consummate love of virtue, an ardent thirst after knowledge, and an earnest desire to promote the welfare and happiness of all mankind. By these qualities, accompanied with great sweetness of manners, he acquired the love and esteem of all good men, in a degree which perhaps very few have experienced; and after passing an active life with the uniform testimony of a good conscience, he became an eminent example of its influence, in the cheerfulness and serenity of his latest age."

Such was the man whom I offer to you as a model, young gentlemen, at the outset of your medical career. I hope that many of you will recognize some traits of your own special teachers scattered through various parts of the land in the picture I have drawn. Let me assure you that whatever you may learn in this or any other course of public lectures,--and I trust you will learn a great deal,--the daily guidance, counsel, example, of your medical father, for such the Oath of Hippocrates tells you to consider your preceptor, will, if he is in any degree like him of whom I have spoken, be the foundation on which all that we teach is reared, and perhaps outlive most of our teachings, as in Dr. Jackson's memory the last lessons that remained with him were those of his Old Master.

THE MEDICAL PROFESSION IN MASSACHUSETTS.

A Lecture of a Course by members of the Massachusetts Historical Society, delivered before the Lowell Institute, January 29, 1869.

The medical history of eight generations, told in an hour, must be in many parts a mere outline. The details I shall give will relate chiefly to the first century. I shall only indicate the leading occurrences, with the more prominent names of the two centuries which follow, and add some considerations suggested by the facts which have been passed in review.

A geographer who was asked to describe the tides of Massachusetts Bay, would have to recognize the circumstance that they are a limited manifestation of a great oceanic movement. To consider them apart from this, would be to localize a planetary phenomenon, and to provincialize a law of the universe. The art of healing in Massachusetts has shared more or less fully and readily the movement which, with its periods of ebb and flow, has been raising its level from age to age throughout the better part of Christendom. Its practitioners brought with them much of the knowledge and many of the errors of the Old World; they have always been in communication with its wisdom and its folly; it is not without interest to see how far the new conditions in which they found themselves have been favorable or unfavorable to the growth of sound medical knowledge and practice.

The state of medicine is an index of the civilization of an age and country,-- one of the best, perhaps, by which it can be judged. Surgery invokes the aid of all the mechanical arts. From the rude violences of the age of stone,--a relic of which we may find in the practice of Zipporah, the wife of Moses,--to the delicate operations of to-day upon patients lulled into temporary insensibility, is a progress which presupposes a skill in metallurgy and in the labors of the workshop and the laboratory it has taken uncounted generations to accumulate. Before the morphia which deadens the pain of neuralgia, or the quinine which arrests the fit of an ague, can find their place in our pharmacies, commerce must have perfected its machinery, and science must have refined its processes, through periods only to be counted by the life of nations. Before the means which nature and art have put in the hands of the medical practitioner can be fairly brought into use, the prejudices of the vulgar must be overcome, the intrusions of false philosophy must be fenced out, and the partnership with the priesthood dissolved. All this implies that freedom and activity of thought which belong only to the most advanced conditions of society; and the progress towards this is by gradations as significant of wide-spread changes, as are the varying states of the barometer of far-extended conditions of the atmosphere.

Apart, then, from its special and technical interest, my subject has a meaning which gives a certain importance, and even dignity, to details in themselves trivial and almost unworthy of record. A medical entry in Governor Winthrop's journal may seem at first sight a mere curiosity; but, rightly interpreted, it is a key to his whole system of belief as to the order of the universe and the relations between man and his Maker. Nothing sheds such light on the superstitions of an age as the prevailing interpretation and treatment of disease. When the touch of a profligate monarch was a cure for one of the most inveterate of maladies, when the common symptoms of hysteria were prayed over as marks of demoniacal possession, we might well expect the spiritual realms of thought to be peopled with still stranger delusions.

Let us go before the Pilgrims of the Mayflower, and look at the shores on which they were soon to land. A wasting pestilence had so thinned the savage tribes that it was sometimes piously interpreted as having providentially prepared the way for the feeble band of exiles. Cotton Mather, who, next to the witches, hated the "tawnies," "wild beasts," "blood-hounds," "rattlesnakes," "infidels," as in different places he calls the unhappy Aborigines, describes the condition of things in his lively way, thus: "The Indians in these Parts had newly, even about a Year or Two before, been visited with such a prodigious Pestilence; as carried away not a Tenth, but Nine Parts of Ten (yea't is said Nineteen of Twenty) among them so that the Woods were almost cleared of those pernicious Creatures to make Room for a better Growth."

What this pestilence was has been much discussed. It is variously mentioned by different early writers as "the plague," "a great and grievous plague," "a sore consumption," as attended with spots which left unhealed places on those who recovered, as making the "whole surface yellow as with a garment." Perhaps no disease answers all these conditions so well as smallpox. We know from different sources what frightful havoc it made among the Indians in after years,--in 1631, for instance, when it swept away the aboriginal inhabitants of "whole towns," and in 1633. We have seen a whole tribe, the Mandans, extirpated by it in our own day. The word "plague" was used very vaguely, as in the description of the "great sickness" found among the Indians by the expedition of 1622. This same great sickness could hardly have been yellow fever, as it occurred in the month of November. I cannot think, therefore, that either the scourge of the East or our Southern malarial pestilence was the disease that wasted the Indians. As for the yellowness like a garment, that is too familiar to the eyes of all who have ever looked on the hideous mask of confluent variola.

Without the presence or the fear of these exotic maladies, the forlorn voyagers of the Mayflower had sickness enough to contend with. At their first landing at Cape Cod, gaunt and hungry and longing for fresh food, they found upon the sandy shore "great mussel's, and very fat and full of sea-pearl." Sailors and passengers indulged in the treacherous delicacy; which seems to have been the sea-clam; and found that these mollusks, like the shell the poet tells of, remembered their august abode, and treated the way-worn adventurers to a gastric reminiscence of the heaving billows. In the mean time it blew and snowed and froze. The water turned to ice on their clothes, and made them many times like coats of iron. Edward Tilley had like to have "sounded" with cold. The gunner, too, was sick unto death, but "hope of trucking" kept him on his feet,--a Yankee, it should seem, when he first touched the shore of New England. Most, if not all, got colds and coughs, which afterwards turned to scurvy, whereof many died.

How can we wonder that the crowded and tempest-tossed voyagers, many of them already suffering, should have fallen before the trials of the first winter in Plymouth? Their imperfect shelter, their insufficient supply of bread, their salted food, now in unwholesome condition, account too well for the diseases and the mortality that marked this first dreadful season; weakness, swelling of the limbs, and other signs of scurvy, betrayed the want of proper nourishment and protection from the elements. In December six of their number died, in January eight, in

February, seventeen, in March thirteen. With the advance of spring the mortality diminished, the sick and lame began to recover, and the colonists, saddened but not disheartened, applied themselves to the labors of the opening year.

One of the most pressing needs of the early colonists must have been that of physicians and surgeons. In Mr. Savage's remarkable Genealogical Dictionary of the first settlers who came over before 1692 and their descendants to the third generation, I find scattered through the four crowded volumes the names of one hundred and thirty-four medical practitioners. Of these, twelve, and probably many more, practised surgery; three were barber-surgeons. A little incident throws a glimmer from the dark lantern of memory upon William Direly, one of these practitioners with the razor and the lancet. He was lost between Boston and Roxbury in a violent tempest of wind and snow; ten days afterwards a son was born to his widow, and with a touch of homely sentiment, I had almost said poetry, they called the little creature "Fathergone" Direly. Six or seven, probably a larger number, were ministers as well as physicians, one of whom, I am sorry to say, took to drink and tumbled into the Connecticut River, and so ended. One was not only doctor, but also schoolmaster and poet. One practised medicine and kept a tavern. One was a butcher, but calls himself a surgeon in his will, a union of callings which suggests an obvious pleasantry. One female practitioner, employed by her own sex,--Ann Moore,--was the precursor of that intrepid sisterhood whose cause it has long been my pleasure and privilege to advocate on all fitting occasions.

Outside of this list I must place the name of Thomas Wilkinson, who was complained of, is 1676, for practising contrary to law.

Many names in the catalogue of these early physicians have been associated, in later periods, with the practice of the profession, --among them, Boylston, Clark, Danforth, Homan, Jeffrey, Kittredge, Oliver, Peaslee, Randall, Shattuck, Thacher, Wellington, Williams, Woodward. Touton was a Huguenot, Burchsted a German from Silesia, Lunerus a German or a Pole; "Pighogg Churrergeon," I hope, for the honor of the profession, was only Peacock disguised under this alias, which would not, I fear, prove very attractive to patients.

What doctrines and practice were these colonists likely to bring, with them?

Two principal schools of medical practice prevailed in the Old World during the greater part of the seventeenth century. The first held to the old methods of

Galen: its theory was that the body, the microcosm, like the macrocosm, was made up of the four elements--fire, air, water, earth; having respectively the qualities hot, dry, moist, cold. The body was to be preserved in health by keeping each of these qualities in its natural proportion; heat, by the proper temperature; moisture, by the due amount of fluid; and so as to the rest. Diseases which arose from excess of heat were to be attacked by cooling remedies; those from excess of cold, by heating ones; and so of the other derangements of balance. This was truly the principle of contraries contrariis, which ill-informed persons have attempted to make out to be the general doctrine of medicine, whereas there is no general dogma other than this: disease is to be treated by anything that is proved to cure it. The means the Galenist employed were chiefly diet and vegetable remedies, with the use of the lancet and other depleting agents. He attributed the four fundamental qualities to different vegetables, in four different degrees; thus chicory was cold in the fourth degree, pepper was hot in the fourth, endive was cold and dry in the second, and bitter almonds were hot in the first and dry in the second degree. When we say "cool as a cucumber," we are talking Galenism. The seeds of that vegetable ranked as one of "the four greater cold seeds" of this system.

Galenism prevailed mostly in the south of Europe and France. The readers of Moliere will have no difficulty in recalling some of its favorite modes of treatment, and the abundant mirth he extracted from them.

These Galenists were what we should call "herb-doctors" to-day. Their insignificant infusions lost credit after a time; their absurdly complicated mixtures excited contempt, and their nauseous prescriptions provoked loathing and disgust. A simpler and bolder practice found welcome in Germany, depending chiefly on mineral remedies, mercury, antimony, sulphur, arsenic, and the use, sometimes the secret use, of opium. Whatever we think of Paracelsus, the chief agent in the introduction of these remedies, and whatever limits we may assign to the use of these long-trusted mineral drugs, there can be no doubt that the chemical school, as it was called, did a great deal towards the expurgation of the old, overloaded, and repulsive pharmacopoeia. We shall find evidence in the practice of our New-England physicians of the first century, that they often employed chemical remedies, and that, by the early part of the following century, their chief trust was in the few simple, potent drugs of Paracelsus.

We have seen that many of the practitioners of medicine, during the first century of New England, were clergymen. This relation between medicine and theology has existed from a very early period; from the Egyptian priest to the Indian medicine-man, the alliance has been maintained in one form or another. The partnership was very common among our British ancestors. Mr. Ward, the Vicar of Stratford-on-Avon, himself a notable example of the union of the two characters, writing about 1660, says,

"The Saxons had their blood-letters, but under the Normans physicke, begunne in England; 300 years agoe itt was not a distinct profession by itself, but practised by men in orders, witness Nicholas de Ternham, the chief English physician and Bishop of Durham; Hugh of Evesham, a physician and cardinal; Grysant, physician and pope; John Chambers, Dr. of Physick, was the first Bishop of Peterborough; Paul Bush, a bachelor of divinitie in Oxford, was a man well read in physick as well as divinitie, he was the first bishop of Bristol."

"Again in King Richard the Second's time physicians and divines were not distinct professions; for one Tydeman, Bishop of Landaph and Worcester, was physician to King Richard the Second."

This alliance may have had its share in creating and keeping up the many superstitions which have figured so largely in the history of medicine. It is curious to see that a medical work left in manuscript by the Rev. Cotton Mather and hereafter to be referred to, is running over with follies and superstitious fancies; while his contemporary and fellow-townsman, William Douglass, relied on the same few simple remedies which, through Dr. Edward Holyoke and Dr. James Jackson, have come down to our own time, as the most important articles of the materia medica.

Let us now take a general glance at some of the conditions of the early settlers; and first, as to the healthfulness of the climate. The mortality of the season that followed the landing of the Pilgrims at Plymouth has been sufficiently accounted for. After this, the colonists seem to have found the new country agreeing very well with their English constitutions. Its clear air is the subject of eulogy. Its dainty springs of sweet water are praised not only by Higginson and Wood, but even the mischievous Morton says, that for its delicate waters "Canaan came not near this country." There is a tendency to dilate on these simple blessings, which reminds one a little of the Marchioness in Dickens's story, with her orange-peel-and-water beverage.

Still more does one feel the warmth of coloring,--such as we expect from converts to a new faith, and settlers who want to entice others over to their clearings, when Winslow speaks, in 1621, of "abundance of roses, white, red, and damask; single, but very sweet indeed;" a most of all, however, when, in the same connection, he says, "Here are grapes white and red, and very sweet and strong also." This of our wild grape, a little vegetable Indian, which scalps a civilized man's mouth, as his animal representative scalps his cranium. But there is something quite charming in Winslow's picture of the luxury in which they are living. Lobsters, oysters, eels, mussels, fish and fowl, delicious fruit, including the grapes aforesaid,--if they only had "kine, horses, and sheep," he makes no question but men would live as contented here as in any part of the world. We cannot help admiring the way in which they took their trials, and made the most of their blessings.

"And how Content they were," says Cotton Mather, "when an Honest Man, as I have heard, inviting his Friends to a Dish of Clams, at the Table gave Thanks to Heaven, who had given them to suck the abundance of the Seas, and of the Treasures Aid in the Sands!"

Strangely enough, as it would seem, except for this buoyant determination to make the best of everything, they hardly appear to recognize the difference of the climate from that which they had left. After almost three years' experience, Winslow says, he can scarce distinguish New England from Old England, in respect of heat and cold, frost, snow, rain, winds, etc. The winter, he thinks (if there is a difference), is sharper and longer; but yet he may be deceived by the want of the comforts he enjoyed at home. He cannot conceive any climate to agree better with the constitution of the English, not being oppressed with extremity of heats, nor nipped by biting cold:

"By which means, blessed be God, we enjoy our health, notwithstanding those difficulties we have undergone, in such a measure as would have been admired, if we had lived in England with the like means."

Edward Johnson, after mentioning the shifts to which they were put for food, says,--

"And yet, methinks, our children are as cheerful, fat, and lusty, with feeding upon those mussels, clams, and other fish, as they were in England with their fill of bread."

Higginson, himself a dyspeptic, "continually in physic," as he says, and accustomed to dress in thick clothing, and to comfort his stomach with drink that was "both strong and stale,"--the "jolly good ale and old," I suppose, of free and easy Bishop Still's song,--found that he both could and did oftentimes drink New England water very well,--which he seems to look upon as a remarkable feat. He could go as lightclad as any, too, with only a light stuff cassock upon his shirt, and stuff breeches without linings. Two of his children were sickly: one,--little misshapen Mary,--died on the passage, and, in her father's words, "was the first in our ship that was buried in the bowels of the great Atlantic sea;" the other, who had been "most lamentably handled" by disease, recovered almost entirely "by the very wholesomeness of the air, altering, digesting, and drying up the cold and crude humors of the body." Wherefore, he thinks it a wise course for all cold complexions to come to take physic in New England, and ends with those often quoted words, that "a sup of New England's air is better than a whole draught of Old England's ale." Mr. Higginson died, however, "of a hectic fever," a little more than a year after his arrival.

The medical records which I shall cite show that the colonists were not exempt from the complaints of the Old World. Besides the common diseases to which their descendants are subject, there were two others, to say nothing of the dreaded small-pox, which later medical science has disarmed,--little known among us at the present day, but frequent among the first settlers. The first of these was the scurvy, already mentioned, of which Winthrop speaks in 1630, saying, that it proved fatal to those who fell into discontent, and lingered after their former conditions in England; the poor homesick creatures in fact, whom we so forget in our florid pictures of the early times of the little band in the wilderness. Many who were suffering from scurvy got well when the Lyon arrived from England, bringing store of juice of lemons. The Governor speaks of another case in 1644; and it seems probable that the disease was not of rare occurrence.

The other complaint from which they suffered, but which has nearly disappeared from among us, was intermittent fever, or fever and ague. I investigated the question as to the prevalence of this disease in New England, in a dissertation, which was published in a volume with other papers, in the year 1838. I can add little to the facts there recorded. One which escaped me was, that Joshua Scottow, in "Old Men's Tears," dated 1691, speaks of "shaking agues," as among the trials to which they had been subjected. The outline map of New England, accompanying the dissertation above referred to, indicates all the places where I had evidence that the disease had originated. It was plain enough that it used to be known in many localities where it has long ceased to be feared. Still it was and is remarkable to see what a clean bill of health in this particular respect our barren soil inherited with its sterility. There are some malarious spots on the edge of Lake Champlain, and there have been some temporary centres of malaria, within the memory of man, on one or more of our Massachusetts rivers, but these are harmless enough, for the most part, unless the millers dam them, when they are apt to retaliate with a whiff from their meadows, that sets the whole neighborhood shaking with fever and ague.

The Pilgrims of the Mayflower had with them a good physician, a man of standing, a deacon of their church, one whom they loved and trusted, Dr. Samuel Fuller. But no medical skill could keep cold and hunger and bad food, and, probably enough, desperate homesickness in some of the feebler sort, from doing their work. No detailed record remains of what they suffered or what was attempted for their relief during the first sad winter. The graves of those who died were levelled and sowed with grain that the losses of the little band might not be suspected by the savage tenants of the wilderness, and their story remains untold.

Of Dr. Fuller's practice, at a later period, we have an account in a letter of his to Governor Bradford, dated June, 1630. "I have been to Matapan" (now Dorchester), he says, "and let some twenty of those people blood." Such wholesale depletion as this, except with avowed homicidal intent, is quite unknown in these days; though I once saw the noted French surgeon, Lisfranc, in a fine phlebotomizing frenzy, order some ten or fifteen patients, taken almost indiscriminately, to be bled in a single morning.

Dr. Fuller's two visits to Salem, at the request of Governor Endicott, seem to have been very satisfactory to that gentleman. Morton, the wild fellow of Merry Mount, gives a rather questionable reason for the Governor's being so well pleased with the physician's doings. The names under which he mentions the two personages, it will be seen, are not intended to be complimentary. "Dr. Noddy did a great cure for Captain Littleworth. He cured him of a disease called a wife." William Gager, who came out with Winthrop, is spoken of as "a right godly man and skilful chyrurgeon, but died of a malignant fever not very long after his arrival."

Two practitioners of the ancient town of Newbury are entitled to special notice, for different reasons. The first is Dr. John Clark, who is said by tradition to have been the first regularly educated physician who resided in New England. His portrait, in close-fitting skull-cap, with long locks and venerable flowing beard, is familiar to our eyes on the wall of our Society's antechamber. His left hand rests upon a skull, his right hand holds an instrument which deserves a passing comment. It is a trephine, a surgical implement for cutting round pieces out of broken skulls, so as to get at the fragments which have been driven in, and lift them up. It has a handle like that of a gimlet, with a claw like a hammer, to lift with, I suppose, which last contrivance I do not see figured in my books. But the point I refer to is this: the old instrument, the trepan, had a handle like a wimble, what we call a brace or bit-stock. The trephine is not mentioned at all in Peter Lowe's book, London, 1634; nor in Wiseman's great work on Surgery, London, 1676; nor in the translation of Dionis, published by Jacob Tonson, in 1710. In fact it was only brought into more general use by Cheselden and Sharpe so late as the beginning of the last century. As John Clark died in 1661, it is remarkable to see the last fashion in the way of skull-sawing contrivances in his hands,--to say nothing of the claw on the handle, and a Hey's saw, so called in England, lying on the table by him, and painted there more than a hundred years before Hey was born. This saw is an old invention, perhaps as old as Hippocrates, and may be seen figured in the "Armamentarium Chirurgicum" of Scultetus, or in the Works of Ambroise Pare.

Dr. Clark is said to have received a diploma before he came, for skill in lithotomy. He loved horses, as a good many doctors do, and left a good property, as they all ought to do. His grave and noble presence, with the few facts concerning him, told with more or less traditional authority, give us the feeling that the people of Newbury, and afterwards of Boston, had a wise and skilful medical adviser and surgeon in Dr. John Clark.

The venerable town of Newbury had another physician who was less fortunate. The following is a court record of 1652:

"This is to certify whom it may concern, that we the subscribers, being called upon to testify against doctor William Snelling for words by him uttered, affirm that being in way of merry discourse, a health being drank to all friends, he answered,

"I'll pledge my friends,

And for my foes
A plague for their heels
And,'----
[a similar malediction on the other extremity of their feet.]
"Since when he hath affirmed that he only intended the proverb used in the west country, nor do we believe he intended otherwise.

"[Signed] WILLIAM THOMAS.

"THOMAS MILWARD."

"March 12th 1651, All which I acknowledge, and am sorry I did not expresse my intent, or that I was so weak as to use so foolish a proverb.

"[Signed] GULIELMUS SNELLING."

Notwithstanding this confession and apology, the record tells us that "William Snelling in his presentment for cursing is fined ten shillings and the fees of court."

I will mention one other name among those of the Fathers of the medical profession in New England. The "apostle" Eliot says, writing in 1647, "We never had but one anatomy in the country, which Mr. Giles Firman, now in England, did make and read upon very well."

Giles Firmin, as the name is commonly spelled, practised physic in this country for a time. He seems to have found it a poor business; for, in a letter to Governor Winthrop, he says, "I am strongly sett upon to studye divinitie: my studyes else must be lost, for physick is but a meene helpe."

Giles Firmin's Lectures on Anatomy were the first scientific teachings of the New World. While the Fathers were enlightened enough to permit such instructions, they were severe in dealing with quackery; for, in 1631, our court records show that one Nicholas Knopp, or Knapp, was sentenced to be fined or whipped "for taking upon him to cure the scurvey by a water of noe worth nor value, which he solde att a very deare rate." Empty purses or sore backs would be common with us to-day if such a rule were enforced.

Besides the few worthies spoken of, and others whose names I have not space to record, we must remember that there were many clergymen who took charge of the bodies as well as the souls of their patients, among them two Presidents of Harvard College, Charles Chauncy and Leonard Hoar,--and Thomas Thacher, first minister of the "Old South," author of the earliest medical treatises printed in the country,[A Brief Rule to Guide the Common People in Small pox and Measles. 1674.] whose epitaph in Latin and Greek, said to have been written by Eleazer, an "Indian Youth" and a member of the Senior Class of Harvard College, may be found in the "Magnalia." I miss this noble savage's name in our triennial catalogue; and as there is many a slip between the cup and lip, one is tempted to guess that he may have lost his degree by some display of his native instinct,--possibly a flourish of the tomahawk or scalping-knife. However this may have been, the good man he celebrated was a notable instance of the Angelical Conjunction, as the author of the "Magnalia" calls it, of the offices of clergyman and medical practitioner.

Michael Wigglesworth, author of the "Day of Doom," attended the sick, "not only as a Pastor, but as a Physician too, and this, not only in his own town, but also in all those of the vicinity." Mather says of the sons of Charles Chauncy, "All of these did, while they had Opportunity, Preach the Gospel; and most, if not all of them, like their excellent Father before them, had an eminent skill in physick added unto their other accomplishments," etc. Roger Williams is said to have saved many in a kind of pestilence which swept away many Indians.

To these names must be added, as sustaining a certain relation to the healing art, that of the first Governor Winthrop, who is said by John Cotton to have been "Help for our Bodies by Physick [and] for our Estates by Law," and that of his son, the Governor of Connecticut, who, as we shall see, was as much physician as magistrate.

I had submitted to me for examination, in 1862, a manuscript found among the Winthrop Papers, marked with the superscription, "For my worthy friend Mr. Wintrop," dated in 1643, London, signed Edward Stafford, and containing medical directions and prescriptions. It may be remembered by some present that I wrote a report on this paper, which was published in the "Proceedings" of this Society. Whether the paper was written for Governor John Winthrop of Massachusetts, or for his son, Governor John of Connecticut, there is no positive evidence that I have been able to obtain. It is very interesting, however, as giving short and simple practical directions, such as would be most like to be wanted and most useful, in the opinion of a physician in repute of that day.

The diseases prescribed for are plague, small-pox, fevers, king's evil, insanity, falling-sickness, and the like; with such injuries as broken bones, dislocations, and burning with gunpowder. The remedies are of three kinds: simples, such as St. John's wort, Clown's all-heal, elder, parsley, maidenhair, mineral drugs, such as lime, saltpetre, Armenian bole, crocus metallorum, or sulphuret of antimony; and thaumaturgic or mystical, of which the chief is, "My black powder against the plague, small-pox; purples, all sorts of feavers; Poyson; either, by Way of Prevention or after Infection." This marvellous remedy was made by putting live toads into an earthen pot so as to half fill it, and baking and burning them "in the open ayre, not in an house,"--concerning which latter possibility I suspect Madam Winthrop would have had something to say,--until they could be reduced by pounding, first into a brown, and then into a black, powder. Blood-letting in some inflammations, fasting in the early stage of fevers, and some of those peremptory drugs with which most of us have been well acquainted in our time, the infragrant memories of which I will not pursue beyond this slight allusion, are among his remedies.

The Winthrops, to one of whom Dr. Stafford's directions were addressed, were the medical as well as the political advisers of their fellow-citizens for three or four successive generations. One of them, Governor John of Connecticut, practised so extensively, that, but for his more distinguished title in the State, he would have been remembered as the Doctor. The fact that he practised in another colony, for the most part, makes little difference in the value of the records we have of his medical experience, which have fortunately been preserved, and give a very fair idea, in all probability, of the way in which patients were treated in Massachusetts, when they fell into intelligent and somewhat educated hands, a little after the middle of the seventeenth century:

I have before me, while writing, a manuscript collection of the medical cases treated by him, and recorded at the time in his own hand, which has been intrusted to me by our President, his descendant.

They are generally marked Hartford, and extend from the year 1657 to 1669. From these, manuscripts, and from the letters printed in the Winthrop Papers published by our Society, I have endeavored to obtain some idea of the practice of Governor John Winthrop, Junior. The learned eye of Mr. Pulsifer would have helped me, no doubt, as it has done in other cases; but I have ventured this time to attempt finding my own way among the hieroglyphics of these old pages. By careful comparison of many prescriptions, and by the aid of Schroder, Salmon, Culpeper, and other old compilers, I have deciphered many of his difficult paragraphs with their mysterious recipes.

The Governor employed a number of the simples dear to ancient women, --elecampane and elder and wormwood and anise and the rest; but he also employed certain mineral remedies, which he almost always indicates by their ancient symbols, or by a name which should leave them a mystery to the vulgar. I am now prepared to reveal the mystic secrets of the Governor's beneficent art, which rendered so many good and great as well as so many poor and dependent people his debtors,--at least, in their simple belief,--for their health and their lives.

His great remedy, which he gave oftener than any other, was nitre; which he ordered in doses of twenty or thirty grains to adults, and of three grains to infants. Measles, colics, sciatica, headache, giddiness, and many other ailments, all found themselves treated, and I trust bettered, by nitre; a pretty safe medicine in moderate doses, and one not likely to keep the good Governor awake at night, thinking whether it might not kill, if it did not cure. We may say as much for spermaceti, which he seems to have considered "the sovereign'st thing on earth" for inward bruises, and often prescribes after falls and similar injuries.

One of the next remedies, in point of frequency, which he was in the habit of giving, was (probably diaphoretic) antimony; a mild form of that very active metal, and which, mild as it was, left his patients very commonly with a pretty strong conviction that they had been taking something that did not exactly agree with them. Now and then he gave a little iron or sulphur or calomel, but very rarely; occasionally, a good, honest dose of rhubarb or jalap; a taste of stinging horseradish, oftener of warming guiacum; sometimes an anodyne, in the shape of mithridate,--the famous old farrago, which owed its virtue to poppy juice; [This is the remedy which a Boston divine tried to simplify. See Electuarium Novum Alexipharmacum, by Rev. Thomas Harward, lecturer at the Royal Chappell. Boston, 1732. This tract is in our Society's library.] very often, a harmless powder of coral; less frequently, an inert prescription of pleasing amber; and (let me say it softly within possible hearing of his honored descendant), twice or oftener,--let us hope as a last resort,--an electuary of millipedes,--sowbugs, if we must give them their homely English name. One or two other prescriptions, of the many unmentionable ones which disgraced the pharmacopoeia of the seventeenth century, are to be found, but only in very rare instances, in the faded characters of the manuscript.

The excellent Governor's accounts of diseases are so brief, that we get only a very general notion of the complaints for which he prescribed. Measles and their consequences are at first more prominent than any other one affection, but the common infirmities of both sexes and of all ages seem to have come under his healing hand. Fever and ague appears to have been of frequent occurrence.

His published correspondence shows that many noted people were in communication with him as his patients. Roger Williams wants a little of his medicine for Mrs. Weekes's daughter; worshipful John Haynes is in receipt of his powders; troublesome Captain Underhill wants "a little white vitterall" for his wife, and something to cure his wife's friend's neuralgia, (I think his wife's friend's husband had a little rather have had it sent by the hands of Mrs. Underhill, than by those of the gallant and discursive captain); and pious John Davenport says, his wife "tooke but one halfe of one of the papers" (which probably contained the medicine he called rubila), "but could not beare the taste of it, and is discouraged from taking any more;" and honored William Leete asks for more powders for his "poore little daughter Graciana," though he found it "hard to make her take it," delicate, and of course sensitive, child as she was, languishing and dying before her time, in spite of all the bitter things she swallowed,--God help all little children in the hands of dosing doctors and howling dervishes! Restless Samuel Gorton, now tamed by the burden of fourscore and two years, writes so touching an account of his infirmities, and expresses such overflowing gratitude for the relief he has obtained from the Governor's prescriptions, wondering how "a thing so little in quantity, so little in sent, so little in taste, and so little to sence in operation, should beget and bring forth such efects," that we repent our hasty exclamation, and bless the memory of the good Governor, who gave relief to the worn-out frame of our long-departed brother, the sturdy old heretic of Rhode Island.

What was that medicine which so frequently occurs in the printed letters under the name of "rubila"? It is evidently a secret remedy, and, so far as I know, has not yet been made out. I had almost given it up in despair, when I found what appears to be a key to the mystery. In the vast multitude of prescriptions contained in the manuscripts, most of them written in symbols, I find one which I thus interpret:

"Four grains of (diaphoretic) antimony, with twenty grains of nitre, with a little salt of tin, making rubila." Perhaps something was added to redden the powder, as he constantly speaks of "rubifying" or "viridating" his prescriptions; a very common practice of prescribers, when their powders look a little too much like plain salt or sugar.

Waitstill Winthrop, the Governor's son, "was a skilful physician," says Mr. Sewall, in his funeral sermon; "and generously gave, not only his advice, but also his Medicines, for the healing of the Sick, which, by the Blessing of God, were made successful for the recovery of many." "His son John, a member of the Royal Society, speaks of himself as 'Dr. Winthrop,' and mentions one of his own prescriptions in a letter to Cotton Mather." Our President tells me that there was an heirloom of the ancient skill in his family, within his own remembrance, in the form of a certain precious eye-water, to which the late President John Quincy Adams ascribed rare virtue, and which he used to obtain from the possessor of the ancient recipe.

These inherited prescriptions are often treasured in families, I do not doubt, for many generations. When I was yet of trivial age, and suffering occasionally, as many children do, from what one of my Cambridgeport schoolmates used to call the "ager,"--meaning thereby toothache or face-ache,--I used to get relief from a certain plaster which never went by any other name in the family than "Dr. Oliver."

Dr. James Oliver was my great-great-grandfather, graduated in 1680, and died in 1703. This was, no doubt, one of his nostrums; for nostrum, as is well known, means nothing more than our own or my own particular medicine, or other possession or secret, and physicians in old times used to keep their choice recipes to themselves a good deal, as we have had occasion to see.

Some years ago I found among my old books a small manuscript marked "James Oliver. This Book Begun Aug. 12, 1685." It is a rough sort of account-book, containing among other things prescriptions for patients, and charges for the same, with counter-charges for the purchase of medicines and other matters. Dr. Oliver practised in Cambridge, where may be seen his tomb with inscriptions, and with sculptured figures that look more like Diana of the Ephesians, as given in Calmet's Dictionary, than like any angels admitted into good society here or elsewhere.

I do not find any particular record of what his patients suffered from, but I have carefully copied out the remedies he mentions, and find that they form a very respectable catalogue. Besides the usual simples, elder, parsley, fennel, saffron, snakeroot, wormwood, I find the Elixir Proprietatis, with other elixire and cordials, as if he rather fancied warming medicines; but he called in the aid of some of the more energetic remedies, including iron, and probably mercury, as he bought two pounds of it at one time.

The most interesting item is his bill against the estate of Samuel Pason of Roxbury, for services during his last illness. He attended this gentleman,--for such he must have been, by the amount of physic which he took, and which his heirs paid for,--from June 4th, 1696, to September 3d of the same year, three months. I observe he charges for visits as well as for medicines, which is not the case in most of his bills. He opens the attack with a carminative appeal to the visceral conscience, and follows it up with good hard-hitting remedies for dropsy,--as I suppose the disease would have been called,--and finishes off with a rallying dose of hartshorn and iron.

It is a source of honest pride to his descendant that his bill, which was honestly paid, as it seems to have been honorably earned, amounted to the handsome total of seven pounds and two shillings. Let me add that he repeatedly prescribes plaster, one of which was very probably the "Dr. Oliver" that soothed my infant griefs, and for which I blush to say that my venerated ancestor received from Goodman Hancock the painfully exiguous sum of no pounds, no shillings, and sixpence.

I have illustrated the practice of the first century, from the two manuscripts I have examined, as giving an impartial idea of its every-day methods. The Governor, Johannes Secundus, it is fair to remember, was an amateur practitioner, while my ancestor was a professed physician. Comparing their modes of treatment with the many scientific follies still prevailing in the Old World, and still more with the extraordinary theological superstitions of the community in which they lived, we shall find reason, I think, to consider the art of healing as in a comparatively creditable state during the first century of New England.

In addition to the evidence as to methods of treatment furnished by the manuscripts I have cited, I subjoin the following document, to which my attention was called by Dr. Shurtleff, our present Mayor. This is a letter of which the original is to be found in vol. lxix. page 10 of the "Archives" preserved at the State House in Boston. It will be seen that what the surgeon wanted consisted chiefly of opiates, stimulants, cathartics, plasters, and materials for bandages. The complex and varied formulae have given place to simpler and often more effective forms of the same remedies; but the list and the manner in which it is made out are proofs of the good sense and schooling of the surgeon, who, it may be noted, was in such haste that he neglected all his stops. He might well be in a hurry, as on the very day upon which he wrote, a great body of Indians--supposed to be six or seven hundred--appeared before Hatfield; and twenty-five resolute young men of Hadley, from which town he wrote, crossed the river and drove them away.

HADLY May 30: 76

Mr RAWSON Sr

What we have recd by Tho: Houey the past month is not the chiefest of our wants as you have love for poor wounded I pray let us not want for these following medicines if you have not a speedy conveyance of them I pray send on purpose they are those things mentioned in my former letter but to prevent future mistakes I have wrote them att large wee have great want with the greatest halt and speed let us be supplyed. Sr Yr Sert WILL LOCHS.

(Endorsed)

Mr. Lockes Letter Recd from the Governor 13 Jane & acquainted ye Council with it but could not obtain any thing to be sent in answer thereto. 13 June 1676.

I have given some idea of the chief remedies used by our earlier physicians, which were both Galenic and chemical; that is, vegetable and mineral. They, of course, employed the usual perturbing medicines which Montaigne says are the chief reliance of their craft. There were, doubtless, individual practitioners who employed special remedies with exceptional boldness and perhaps success. Mr. Eliot is spoken of, in a letter of William Leete to Winthrop, Junior, as being under Mr. Greenland's mercurial administrations. The latter was probably enough one of these specialists.

There is another class of remedies which appears to have been employed occasionally, but, on the whole, is so little prominent as to imply a good deal of common sense among the medical practitioners, as compared with the superstitions prevailing around them. I have said that I have caught the good Governor, now and then, prescribing the electuary of millipedes; but he is entirely excused by the almost incredible fact that they were retained in the materia medica so late as when

Rees's Cyclopaedia was published, and we there find the directions formerly given by the College of Edinburgh for their preparation. Once or twice we have found him admitting still more objectionable articles into his materia medica; in doing which, I am sorry to say that he could plead grave and learned authority. But these instances are very rare exceptions in a medical practice of many years, which is, on the whole, very respectable, considering the time and circumstances.

Some remedies of questionable though not odious character appear occasionally to have been employed by the early practitioners, but they were such as still had the support of the medical profession. Governor John Winthrop, the first, sends for East Indian bezoar, with other commodities he is writing for. Governor Endicott sends him one he had of Mr. Humfrey. I hope it was genuine, for they cheated infamously in the matter of this concretion, which ought to come out of an animal's stomach, but the real history of which resembles what is sometimes told of modern sausages.

There is a famous law-case of James the First's time, in which a goldsmith sold a hundred pounds' worth of what he called bezoar, which was proved to be false, and the purchaser got a verdict against him. Governor Endicott also sends Winthrop a unicorn's horn, which was the property of a certain Mrs. Beggarly, who, in spite of her name, seems to have been rich in medical knowledge and possessions. The famous Thomas Bartholinus wrote a treatise on the virtues of this fabulous-sounding remedy, which was published in 1641, and republished in 1678.

The "antimonial cup," a drinking vessel made of that metal, which, like our quassia-wood cups, might be filled and emptied in saecula saeculorum without exhausting its virtues, is mentioned by Matthew Cradock, in a letter to the elder Winthrop, but in a doubtful way, as it was thought, he says, to have shortened the days of Sir Nathaniel Riche; and Winthrop himself, as I think, refers to its use, calling it simply "the cup." An antimonial cup is included in the inventory of Samuel Seabury, who died 1680, and is valued at five shillings. There is a treatise entitled "The Universall Remedy, or the Vertues of the Antimoniall Cup, By John Evans, Minister and Preacher of God's Word, London, 1634," in our own Society's library.

One other special remedy deserves notice, because of native growth. I do not know when Culver's root, Leptandra Virginica of our National Pharmacopoeia, became noted, but Cotton Mather, writing in 1716 to John Winthrop of New London, speaks of it as famous for the cure of consumptions, and wishes to get some of it, through his mediation, for Katharine, his eldest daughter. He gets it, and gives it to the "poor damsel," who is languishing, as he says, and who dies the next month,--all the sooner, I have little doubt, for this uncertain and violent drug, with which the meddlesome pedant tormented her in that spirit of well-meant but restless quackery, which could touch nothing without making mischief, not even a quotation, and yet proved at length the means of bringing a great blessing to our community, as we shall see by and by; so does Providence use our very vanities and infirmities for its wise purposes.

Externally, I find the practitioners on whom I have chiefly relied used the plasters of Paracelsus, of melilot, diachylon, and probably diaphoenicon, all well known to the old pharmacopoeias, and some of them to the modern ones,--to say nothing of "my yellow salve," of Governor John, the second, for the composition of which we must apply to his respected descendant.

The authors I find quoted are Barbette's Surgery, Camerarius on Gout, and Wecherus, of all whom notices may be found in the pages of Haller and Vanderlinden; also, Reed's Surgery, and Nicholas Culpeper's Practice of Physic and Anatomy, the last as belonging to Samuel Seabury, chirurgeon, before mentioned. Nicholas Culpeper was a shrewd charlatan, and as impudent a varlet as ever prescribed for a colic; but knew very well what he was about, and badgers the College with great vigor. A copy of Spigelius's famous Anatomy, in the Boston Athenaeum, has the names of Increase and Samuel Mather written in it, and was doubtless early overhauled by the youthful Cotton, who refers to the great anatomist's singular death, among his curious stories in the "Magnalia," and quotes him among nearly a hundred authors whom he cites in his manuscript "The Angel of Bethesda." Dr. John Clark's "books and instruments, with several chirurgery materials in the closet," a were valued in his inventory at sixty pounds; Dr. Matthew Fuller, who died in 1678, left a library valued at ten pounds; and a surgeon's chest and drugs valued at sixteen pounds.'

Here we leave the first century and all attempts at any further detailed accounts of medicine and its practitioners. It is necessary to show in a brief glance what had been going on in Europe during the latter part of that century, the first quarter of which had been made illustrious in the history of medical science by the discovery of the circulation.

Charles Barbeyrac, a Protestant in his religion, was a practitioner and teacher of medicine at Montpellier. His creed was in the way of his obtaining office; but the young men followed his instructions with enthusiasm. Religious and scientific freedom breed in and in, until it becomes hard to tell the family of one from that of the other. Barbeyrac threw overboard the old complex medical farragos of the pharmacopoeias, as his church had disburdened itself of the popish ceremonies.

Among the students who followed his instructions were two Englishmen: one of them, John Locke, afterwards author of an "Essay on the Human Understanding," three years younger than his teacher; the other, Thomas Sydenham, five years older. Both returned to England. Locke, whose medical knowledge is borne witness to by Sydenham, had the good fortune to form a correct opinion on a disease from which the Earl of Shaftesbury was suffering, which led to an operation that saved his life. Less felicitous was his experience with a certain ancilla culinaria virgo,--which I am afraid would in those days have been translated kitchen-wench, instead of lady of the culinary department,--who turned him off after she had got tired of him, and called in another practitioner. [Locke and Sydenham, p. 124. By John Brown, M. D. Edinburgh, 1866.] This helped, perhaps, to spoil a promising doctor, and make an immortal metaphysician. At any rate, Locke laid down the professional wig and cane, and took to other studies.

The name of Thomas Sydenham is as distinguished in the history of medicine as that of John Locke in philosophy. As Barbeyrac was found in opposition to the established religion, as Locke took the rational side against orthodox Bishop Stillingfleet, so Sydenham went with Parliament against Charles, and was never admitted a Fellow by the College of Physicians, which, after he was dead, placed his bust in their hall by the side of that of Harvey.

What Sydenham did for medicine was briefly this he studied the course of diseases carefully, and especially as affected by the particular season; to patients with fever he gave air and cooling drinks, instead of smothering and heating them, with the idea of sweating out their disease; he ordered horseback exercise to consumptives; he, like his teacher, used few and comparatively simple remedies; he did not give any drug at all, if he thought none was needed, but let well enough alone. He was a sensible man, in short, who applied his common sense to diseases which he had studied with the best light of science that he could obtain.

The influence of the reform he introduced must have been more or less felt in this country, but not much before the beginning of the eighteenth century, as his great work was not published until 1675, and then in Latin. I very strongly suspect that there was not so much to reform in the simple practice of the physicians of the new community, as there was in that of the learned big-wigs of the "College," who valued their remedies too much in proportion to their complexity, and the extravagant and fantastic ingredients which went to their making.

During the memorable century which bred and bore the Revolution, the medical profession gave great names to our history. But John Brooks belonged to the State, and Joseph Warren belongs to the country and mankind, and to speak of them would lead me beyond my limited--subject. There would be little pleasure in dwelling on the name of Benjamin Church; and as for the medical politicians, like Elisha Cooke in the early part of the century, or Charles Jarvis, the bald eagle of Boston, in its later years, whether their practice was heroic or not, their patients were, for he is a bold man who trusts one that is making speeches and coaxing voters, to meddle with the internal politics of his corporeal republic.

One great event stands out in the medical history of this eighteenth century; namely, the introduction of the practice of inoculation for small-pox. Six epidemics of this complaint had visited Boston in the course of a hundred years. Prayers had been asked in the churches for more than a hundred sick in a single day, and this many times. About a thousand persons had died in a twelvemonth, we are told, and, as we may infer, chiefly from this cause.

In 1721, this disease, after a respite of nineteen years, again appeared as an epidemic. In that year it was that Cotton Mather, browsing, as was his wont, on all the printed fodder that came within reach of his ever-grinding mandibles, came upon an account of inoculation as practised in Turkey, contained in the "Philosophical Transactions." He spoke of it to several physicians, who paid little heed to his story; for they knew his medical whims, and had probably been bored, as we say now-a-days, many of them, with listening to his "Angel of Bethesda," and satiated with his speculations on the Nishmath Chajim.

The Reverend Mather,--I use a mode of expression he often employed when speaking of his honored brethren,--the Reverend Mather was right this time, and the irreverent doctors who laughed at him were wrong. One only of their number disputes his claim to giving the first impulse to the practice, in Boston. This is what that person says: "The Small-Pox spread in Boston, New England, A.1721, and the Reverend Dr. Cotton Mather, having had the use of these Communications from Dr. William Douglass (that is, the writer of these words); surreptitiously, without the knowledge of his Informer, that he might have the honour of a New fangled notion, sets an Undaunted Operator to work, and in this Country about 290 were inoculated."

All this has not deprived Cotton Mather of the credit of suggesting, and a bold and intelligent physician of the honor of carrying out, the new practice. On the twenty-seventh day of June, 1721, Zabdiel Boylston of Boston inoculated his only son for smallpox,--the first person ever submitted to the operation in the New World. The story of the fierce resistance to the introduction of the practice; of how Boylston was mobbed, and Mather had a hand-grenade thrown in at his window; of how William Douglass, the Scotchman, "always positive, and sometimes accurate," as was neatly said of him, at once depreciated the practice and tried to get the credit of suggesting it, and how Lawrence Dalhonde, the Frenchman, testified to its destructive consequences; of how Edmund Massey, lecturer at St. Albans, preached against sinfully endeavoring to alter the course of nature by presumptuous interposition, which he would leave to the atheist and the scoffer, the heathen and unbeliever, while in the face of his sermon, afterwards reprinted in Boston, many of our New England clergy stood up boldly in defence of the practice,--all this has been told so well and so often that I spare you its details. Set this good hint of Cotton Mather against that letter of his to John Richards, recommending the search after witch-marks, and the application of the water-ordeal, which means throw your grandmother into the water, if she has a mole on her arm;--if she swims, she is a witch and must be hanged; if she sinks, the Lord have mercy on her soul!

Thus did America receive this great discovery, destined to save thousands of lives, via Boston, from the hands of one of our own Massachusetts physicians.

The year 1735 was rendered sadly memorable by the epidemic of the terrible disease known as "throat distemper," and regarded by many as the same as our "diphtheria." Dr. Holyoke thinks the more general use of mercurials in inflammatory complaints dates from the time of their employment in this disease, in which they were thought to have proved specially useful.

At some time in the course of this century medical practice had settled down on four remedies as its chief reliance. I must repeat an incident which I have related in another of these Essays. When Dr. Holyoke, nearly seventy years ago, received young Mr. James Jackson as his student, he showed him the formidable array of bottles, jars, and drawers around his office, and then named the four remedies referred to as being of more importance than all the rest put together. These were "Mercury, Antimony, Opium, and Peruvian Bark." I doubt if either of them remembered that, nearly seventy years before, in 1730, Dr. William Douglass, the disputatious Scotchman, mentioned those same four remedies, in the dedication of his quarrelsome essay on inoculation, as the most important ones in the hands of the physicians of his time.

In the "Proceedings" of this Society for the year 1863 is a very pleasant paper by the late Dr. Ephraim Eliot, giving an account of the leading physicians of Boston during the last quarter of the last century. The names of Lloyd, Gardiner, Welsh, Rand, Bulfinch, Danforth, John Warren, Jeffries, are all famous in local history, and are commemorated in our medical biographies. One of them, at least, appears to have been more widely known, not only as one of the first aerial voyagers, but as an explorer in the almost equally hazardous realm of medical theory. Dr. John Jeffries, the first of that name, is considered by Broussais as a leader of medical opinion in America, and so referred to in his famous "Examen des Doctrines Medicales."

Two great movements took place in this eighteenth century, the effect of which has been chiefly felt in our own time; namely, the establishment of the Massachusetts Medical Society, and the founding of the Medical School of Harvard University.

The third century of our medical history began with the introduction of the second great medical discovery of modern times,--of all time up to that date, I may say,--once more via Boston, if we count the University village as its suburb, and once more by one of our Massachusetts physicians. In the month of July, 1800, Dr. Benjamin Waterhouse of Cambridge submitted four of his own children to the new process of vaccination,--the first persons vaccinated, as Dr. Zabdiel Boylston's son had been the first person inoculated in the New World.

A little before the first half of this century was completed, in the autumn of

1846, the great discovery went forth from the Massachusetts General Hospital, which repaid the debt of America to the science of the Old World, and gave immortality to the place of its origin in the memory and the heart of mankind. The production of temporary insensibility at will--tuto, cito, jucunde, safely, quickly, pleasantly--is one of those triumphs over the infirmities of our mortal condition which change the aspect of life ever afterwards. Rhetoric can add nothing to its glory; gratitude, and the pride permitted to human weakness, that our Bethlehem should have been chosen as the birthplace of this new embodiment of the divine mercy, are all we can yet find room for.

The present century has seen the establishment of all those great charitable institutions for the cure of diseases of the body and of the mind, which our State and our city have a right to consider as among the chief ornaments of their civilization.

The last century had very little to show, in our State, in the way of medical literature. The worthies who took care of our grandfathers and great-grandfathers, like the Revolutionary heroes, fought (with disease) and bled (their patients) and died (in spite of their own remedies); but their names, once familiar, are heard only at rare intervals. Honored in their day, not unremembered by a few solitary students of the past, their memories are going sweetly to sleep in the arms of the patient old dry-nurse, whose "blackdrop" is the never-failing anodyne of the restless generations of men. Except the lively controversy on inoculation, and floating papers in journals, we have not much of value for that long period, in the shape of medical records.

But while the trouble with the last century is to find authors to mention, the trouble of this would be to name all that we find. Of these, a very few claim unquestioned preeminence.

Nathan Smith, born in Rehoboth, Mass., a graduate of the Medical School of our University, did a great work for the advancement of medicine and surgery in New England, by his labors as teacher and author, greater, it is claimed by some, than was ever done by any other man. The two Warrens, of our time, each left a large and permanent record of a most extended surgical practice. James Jackson not only educated a whole generation by his lessons of wisdom, but bequeathed some of the most valuable results of his experience to those who came after him, in a series of letters singularly pleasant and kindly as well as instructive. John Ware, keen and cautious, earnest and deliberate, wrote the two remarkable essays which have identified his name, for all time, with two important diseases, on which he has shed new light by his original observations.

I must do violence to the modesty of the living by referring to the many important contributions to medical science by Dr. Jacob Bigelow, and especially to his discourse on "Self-limited Diseases," an address which can be read in a single hour, but the influence of which will be felt for a century.

Nor would the profession forgive me if I forgot to mention the admirable museum of pathological anatomy, created almost entirely by the hands of Dr. John Barnard Swett Jackson, and illustrated by his own printed descriptive catalogue, justly spoken of by a distinguished professor in the University of Pennsylvania as the most important contribution which had ever been made in this country to the branch to which it relates.

When we look at the literature of mental disease, as seen in hospital reports and special treatises, we can mention the names of Wyman, Woodward, Brigham, Bell, and Ray, all either natives of Massachusetts or placed at the head of her institutions for the treatment of the insane.

We have a right to claim also one who is known all over the civilized world as a philanthropist, to us as a townsman and a graduate of our own Medical School, Dr. Samuel Gridley Howe, the guide and benefactor of a great multitude who were born to a world of inward or of outward darkness.

I cannot pass over in silence the part taken by our own physicians in those sanitary movements which are assuming every year greater importance. Two diseases especially have attracted attention, above all others, with reference to their causes and prevention; cholera, the "black death" of the nineteenth century, and consumption, the white plague of the North, both of which have been faithfully studied and reported on by physicians of our own State and city. The cultivation of medical and surgical specialties, which is fast becoming prevalent, is beginning to show its effects in the literature of the profession, which is every year growing richer in original observations and investigations.

To these benefactors who have labored for us in their peaceful vocation, we must add the noble army of surgeons, who went with the soldiers who fought the battles of their country, sharing many of their dangers, not rarely falling victims to fatigue, disease, or the deadly volleys to which they often exposed themselves in the discharge of their duties.

The pleasant biographies of the venerable Dr. Thacher, and the worthy and kind-hearted gleaner, Dr. Stephen W. Williams, who came after him, are filled with the names of men who served their generation well, and rest from their labors, followed by the blessing of those for whom they endured the toils and fatigues inseparable from their calling. The hardworking, intelligent country physician more especially deserves the gratitude of his own generation, for he rarely leaves any permanent record in the literature of his profession. Books are hard to obtain; hospitals, which are always centres of intelligence, are remote; thoroughly educated and superior men are separated by wide intervals; and long rides, though favorable to reflection, take up much of the time which might otherwise be given to the labors of the study. So it is that men of ability and vast experience, like the late Dr. Twitchell, for instance, make a great and deserved reputation, become the oracles of large districts, and yet leave nothing, or next to nothing, by which their names shall be preserved from blank oblivion.

One or two other facts deserve mention, as showing the readiness of our medical community to receive and adopt any important idea or discovery. The new science of Histology, as it is now called, was first brought fully before the profession of this country by the translation of Bichat's great work, "Anatomie Generale," by the late Dr. George Hayward.

The first work printed in this country on Auscultation,--that wonderful art of discovering disease, which, as it were, puts a window in the breast, through which the vital organs can be seen, to all intents and purposes, was the manual published anonymously by "A Member of the Massachusetts Medical Society."

We are now in some slight measure prepared to weigh the record of the medical profession in Massachusetts, and pass our judgment upon it. But in-order to do justice to the first generation of practitioners, we must compare what we know of their treatment of disease with the state of the art in England, and the superstitions which they saw all around them in other departments of knowledge or belief.

English medical literature must have been at a pretty low ebb when Sydenham recommended Don Quixote to Sir Richard Blackmore for professional reading. The

College Pharmacopoeia was loaded with the most absurd compound mixtures, one of the most complex of which (the same which the Reverend Mr. Harward, "Lecturer at the Royal Chappel in Boston," tried to simplify), was not dropped until the year 1801. Sir Kenelm Digby was playing his fantastic tricks with the Sympathetic powder, and teaching Governor Winthrop, the second, how to cure fever and ague, which some may like to know. "Pare the patient's nails; put the parings in a little bag, and hang the bag round the neck of a live eel, and put him in a tub of water. The eel will die, and the patient will recover."

Wiseman, the great surgeon, was discoursing eloquently on the efficacy of the royal touch in scrofula. The founder of the Ashmolean Museum at Oxford, consorting with alchemists and astrologers, was treasuring the manuscripts of the late pious Dr. Richard Napier, in which certain letters (Rx Ris) were understood to mean Responsum Raphaelis,--the answer of the angel Raphael to the good man's medical questions. The illustrious Robert Boyle was making his collection of choice and safe remedies, including the sole of an old shoe, the thigh bone of a hanged man, and things far worse than these, as articles of his materia medica. Dr. Stafford, whose paper of directions to his "friend, Mr. Wintrop," I cited, was probably a man of standing in London; yet toad-powder was his sovereign remedy.

See what was the state of belief in other matters among the most intelligent persons of the colonies, magistrates and clergymen. Jonathan Brewster, son of the church-elder, writes the wildest letters to John Winthrop about alchemy,--"mad for making gold as the Lynn rock-borers are for finding it."

Remember the theology and the diabology of the time. Mr. Cotton's Theocracy was a royal government, with the King of kings as its nominal head, but with an upper chamber of saints, and a tremendous opposition in the lower house; the leader of which may have been equalled, but cannot have been surpassed by any of our earth-born politicians. The demons were prowling round the houses every night, as the foxes were sneaking about the hen-roosts. The men of Gloucester fired whole flasks of gunpowder at devils disguised as Indians and Frenchmen.

How deeply the notion of miraculous interference with the course of nature was rooted, is shown by the tenacity of the superstition about earthquakes. We can hardly believe that our Professor Winthrop, father of the old judge and the "squire," whom many of us Cambridge people remember so well, had to defend himself against the learned and excellent Dr. Prince, of the Old South Church, for discussing their phenomena as if they belonged to the province of natural science:

Not for the sake of degrading the aspect of the noble men who founded our State, do I refer to their idle beliefs and painful delusions, but to show against what influences the common sense of the medical profession had to assert itself.

Think, then, of the blazing stars, that shook their horrid hair in the sky; the phantom ship, that brought its message direct from the other world; the story of the mouse and the snake at Watertown; of the mice and the prayer-book; of the snake in church; of the calf with two heads; and of the cabbage in the perfect form of a cutlash,--all which innocent occurrences were accepted or feared as alarming portents.

We can smile at these: but we cannot smile at the account of unhappy Mary Dyer's malformed offspring; or of Mrs. Hutchinson's domestic misfortune of similar character, in the story of which the physician, Dr. John Clark of Rhode Island, alone appears to advantage; or as we read the Rev. Samuel Willard's fifteen alarming pages about an unfortunate young woman suffering with hysteria. Or go a little deeper into tragedy, and see poor Dorothy Talby, mad as Ophelia, first admonished, then whipped; at last, taking her own little daughter's life; put on trial, and standing mute, threatened to be pressed to death, confessing, sentenced, praying to be beheaded; and none the less pitilessly swung from the fatal ladder.

The cooper's crazy wife--crazy in the belief that she has committed the unpardonable sin--tries to drown her child, to save it from misery; and the poor lunatic, who would be tenderly cared for to-day in a quiet asylum, is judged to be acting under the instigation of Satan himself. Yet, after all, what can we say, who put Bunyan's "Pilgrim's Progress," full of nightmare dreams of horror, into all our children's hands; a story in which the awful image of the man in the cage might well turn the nursery where it is read into a madhouse?

The miserable delusion of witchcraft illustrates, in a still more impressive way, the false ideas which governed the supposed relation of men with the spiritual world. I have no doubt many physicians shared in these superstitions. Mr. Upham says they--that is, some of them--were in the habit of attributing their want of success to the fact, that an "evil hand" was on their patient. The temptation was strong, no doubt, when magistrates and ministers and all that followed their lead were contented with such an explanation. But how was it in Salem, according to Mr. Upham's own statement? Dr. John Swinnerton was, he says, for many years the principal physician of Salem. And he says, also, "The Swinnerton family were all along opposed to Mr. Parris, and kept remarkably clear from the witchcraft delusion." Dr. John Swinnerton--the same, by the way, whose memory is illuminated by a ray from the genius of Hawthorne--died the very year before the great witchcraft explosion took place. But who can doubt that it was from him that the family had learned to despise and to resist the base superstition; or that Bridget Bishop, whose house he rented, as Mr. Upham tells me, the first person hanged in the time of the delusion, would have found an efficient protector in her tenant, had he been living, to head the opposition of his family to the misguided clergymen and magistrates?

I cannot doubt that our early physicians brought with them many Old-World medical superstitions, and I have no question that they were more or less involved in the prevailing errors of the community in which they lived. But, on the whole, their record is a clean one, so far as we can get at it; and where it is questionable we must remember that there must have been many little-educated persons among them; and that all must have felt, to some extent, the influence of those sincere and devoted but unsafe men, the physic-practising clergymen, who often used spiritual means as a substitute for temporal ones, who looked upon a hysteric patient as possessed by the devil, and treated a fractured skull by prayers and plasters, following the advice of a ruling elder in opposition to the "unanimous opinion of seven surgeons."

To what results the union of the two professions was liable to lead, may be seen by the example of a learned and famous person, who has left on record the product of his labors in the double capacity of clergyman and physician.

I have had the privilege of examining a manuscript of Cotton Mather's relating to medicine, by the kindness of the librarian of the American Antiquarian Society, to which society it belongs. A brief notice of this curious document may prove not uninteresting.

It is entitled "The Angel of Bethesda: an Essay upon the Common Maladies of Mankind, offering, first, the sentiments of Piety," etc., etc., and "a collection of plain but potent and Approved REMEDIES for the Maladies." There are sixty-six "Capsula's," as he calls them, or chapters, in his table of contents; of which, five--from the fifteenth to the nineteenth, inclusive--are missing. This is a most unfortunate loss, as the eighteenth capsula treated of agues, and we could have learned from it something of their degree of frequency in this part of New England. There is no date to the manuscript; which, however, refers to a case observed Nov. 14, 1724.

The divine takes precedence of the physician in this extraordinary production. He begins by preaching a sermon at his unfortunate patient. Having thrown him into a cold sweat by his spiritual sudorific, he attacks him with his material remedies, which are often quite as unpalatable. The simple and cleanly practice of Sydenham, with whose works he was acquainted, seems to have been thrown away upon him. Everything he could find mentioned in the seventy or eighty authors he cites, all that the old women of both sexes had ever told him of, gets into his text, or squeezes itself into his margin.

Evolving disease out of sin, he hates it, one would say, as he hates its cause, and would drive it out of the body with all noisome appliances. "Sickness is in Fact Flagellum Dei pro peccatis mundi." So saying, he encourages the young mother whose babe is wasting away upon her breast with these reflections:

"Think; oh the grievous Effects of Sin! This wretched Infant has not arrived unto years of sense enough, to sin after the similitude of the transgression committed by Adam. Nevertheless the Transgression of Adam, who had all mankind Foederally, yea, Naturally, in him, has involved this Infant in the guilt of it. And the poison of the old serpent, which infected Adam when he fell into his Transgression, by hearkening to the Tempter, has corrupted all mankind, and is a seed unto such diseases as this Infant is now laboring under. Lord, what are we, and what are our children, but a Generation of Vipers?"

Many of his remedies are at least harmless, but his pedantry and utter want of judgment betray themselves everywhere. He piles his prescriptions one upon another, without the least discrimination. He is run away with by all sorts of fancies and superstitions. He prescribes euphrasia, eye-bright, for disease of the eyes; appealing confidently to the strange old doctrine of signatures, which inferred its use from the resemblance of its flower to the organ of vision. For the scattering of wens, the efficacy of a Dead Hand has been out of measure wonderful. But when he once comes to the odious class of remedies, he revels in them like a scarabeus. This allusion will bring us quite near enough to the inconceivable abominations with which he proposed to outrage the sinful stomachs of the unhappy confederates and accomplices of Adam.

It is well that the treatise was never printed, yet there are passages in it worth preserving. He speaks of some remedies which have since become more universally known:

"Among the plants of our soyl, Sir William Temple singles out Five [Six] as being of the greatest virtue and most friendly to health: and his favorite plants, Sage, Rue, Saffron, Alehoof, Garlick, and Elder."

"But these Five [Six] plants may admitt of some competitors. The QUINQUINA--How celebrated: Immoderately, Hyperbolically celebrated!"

Of Ipecacuanha, he says,--"This is now in its reign; the most fashionable vomit."

"I am not sorry that antimonial emetics begin to be disused."

He quotes "Mr. Lock" as recommending red poppy-water and abstinence from flesh as often useful in children's diseases.

One of his "Capsula's" is devoted to the animalcular origin of diseases, at the end of which he says, speaking of remedies for this supposed source of our distempers:

"Mercury we know thee: But we are afraid thou wilt kill us too, if we employ thee to kill them that kill us.

"And yett, for the cleansing of the small Blood Vessels, and making way for the free circulation of the Blood and Lymph--there is nothing like Mercurial Deobstruents."

From this we learn that mercury was already in common use, and the subject of the same popular prejudice as in our own time.

His poetical turn shows itself here and there:

"O Nightingale, with a Thorn at thy Breast; Under the trouble of a Cough, what can be more proper than such thoughts as these?"...

If there is pathos in this, there is bathos in his apostrophe to the millipede, beginning "Poor sowbug!" and eulogizing the healing virtues of that odious little beast; of which he tells us to take "half a pound, putt 'em alive into a quart or two of wine," with saffron and other drugs, and take two ounces twice a day.

The "Capsula" entitled "Nishmath Chajim" was printed in 1722, at New London, and is in the possession of our own Society. He means, by these words, something like the Archxus of Van Helmont, of which he discourses in a style wonderfully resembling that of Mr. Jenkinson in the "Vicar of Wakefield." "Many of the Ancients thought there was much of a Real History in the Parable, and their Opinion was that there is, DIAPHORA KATA TAS MORPHAS, A Distinction (and so a Resemblance) of men as to their Shapes after Death." And so on, with Ireaeus, Tertullian, Thespesius, and "the TA TONE PSEUCONE CROMATA," in the place of "Sanconiathon, Manetho, Berosus," and "Anarchon ara kai ateleutaion to pan."

One other passage deserves notice, as it relates to the single medical suggestion which does honor to Cotton Mather's memory. It does not appear that he availed himself of the information which he says, he obtained from his slave, for such I suppose he was.

In his appendix to "Variolae Triumphatae," he says,--

"There has been a wonderful practice lately used in several parts of the world, which indeed is not yet become common in our nation.

"I was first informed of it by a Garamantee servant of my own, long before I knew that any Europeans or Asiaticks had the least acquaintance with it, and some years before I was enriched with the communications of the learned Foreigners, whose accounts I found agreeing with what I received of my servant, when he shewed me the Scar of the Wound made for the operation; and said, That no person ever died of the smallpox, in their countrey, that had the courage to use it.

"I have since met with a considerable Number of these Africans, who all agree in one story; That in their countrey grandy-many dy of the small-pox: But now they learn this way: people take juice of smallpox and cutty-skin and put in a Drop; then by'nd by a little sicky, sicky: then very few little things like small-pox; and nobody dy of it; and nobody have small-pox any more. Thus, in Africa, where the poor creatures dy of the smallpox like Rotten Sheep, a merciful God has taught them an Infallible preservative. 'T is a common practice, and is attended with a constant success."

What has come down to us of the first century of medical practice, in the hands of Winthrop and Oliver, is comparatively simple and reasonable. I suspect that the conditions of rude, stern life, in which the colonists found themselves in the wilderness, took the nonsense out of them, as the exigencies of a campaign did out of our physicians and surgeons in the late war. Good food and enough of it, pure air and water, cleanliness, good attendance, an anaesthetic, an opiate, a stimulant, quinine, and two or three common drugs, proved to be the marrow of medical treatment; and the fopperies of the pharmacopoeia went the way of embroidered shirts and white kid gloves and malacca joints, in their time of need. "Good wine is the best cordiall for her," said Governor John Winthrop, Junior, to Samuel Symonds, speaking of that gentleman's wife,--just as Sydenham, instead of physic, once ordered a roast chicken and a pint of canary for his patient in male hysterics.

But the profession of medicine never could reach its full development until it became entirely separated from that of divinity. The spiritual guide, the consoler in affliction, the confessor who is admitted into the secrets of our souls, has his own noble sphere of duties; but the healer of men must confine himself solely to the revelations of God in nature, as he sees their miracles with his own eyes. No doctrine of prayer or special providence is to be his excuse for not looking straight at secondary causes, and acting, exactly so far as experience justifies him, as if he were himself the divine agent which antiquity fabled him to be. While pious men were praying--humbly, sincerely, rightly, according to their knowledge--over the endless succession of little children dying of spasms in the great Dublin Hospital, a sagacious physician knocked some holes in the walls of the ward, let God's blessed air in on the little creatures, and so had already saved in that single hospital, as it was soberly calculated thirty years ago, more than sixteen thousand lives of these infant heirs of immortality. [Collins's Midwifery, p. 312. Published by order of the Massachusetts Medical Society. Boston, 1841.]

Let it be, if you will, that the wise inspiration of the physician was granted in virtue of the clergyman's supplications. Still, the habit of dealing with things seen generates another kind of knowledge, and another way of thought, from that of dealing with things unseen; which knowledge and way of thought are special means granted by Providence, and to be thankfully accepted.

The mediaeval ecclesiastics expressed a great truth in that saying, so often quoted, as carrying a reproach with it: "Ubi tres medici, duo athei,"--"Where there are three physicians, there are two atheists."

It was true then, it is true to-day, that the physician very commonly, if not very generally, denies and repudiates the deity of ecclesiastical commerce. The Being whom Ambroise Pare meant when he spoke those memorable words, which you may read over the professor's chair in the French School of Medicine, "Te le pensay, et Dieu le guarit," "I dressed his wound, and God healed it,"--is a different being from the God that scholastic theologians have projected from their consciousness, or shaped even from the sacred pages which have proved so plastic in their hands. He is a God who never leaves himself without witness, who repenteth him of the evil, who never allows a disease or an injury, compatible with the enjoyment of life, to take its course without establishing an effort, limited by certain fixed conditions, it is true, but an effort, always, to restore the broken body or the shattered mind. In the perpetual presence of this great Healing Agent, who stays the bleeding of wounds, who knits the fractured bone, who expels the splinter by a gentle natural process, who walls in the inflammation that might involve the vital organs, who draws a cordon to separate the dead part from the living, who sends his three natural anaesthetics to the over-tasked frame in due order, according to its need,--sleep, fainting, death; in this perpetual presence, it is doubtless hard for the physician to realize the theological fact of a vast and permanent sphere of the universe, where no organ finds itself in its natural medium, where no wound heals kindly, where the executive has abrogated the pardoning power, and mercy forgets its errand; where the omnipotent is unfelt save in malignant agencies, and the omnipresent is unseen and unrepresented; hard to accept the God of Dante's "Inferno," and of Bunyan's caged lunatic. If this is atheism, call three, instead of two of the trio, atheists, and it will probably come nearer the truth.

 I am not disposed to deny the occasional injurious effect of the materializing influences to which the physician is subjected. A spiritual guild is absolutely necessary to keep him, to keep us all, from becoming the "fingering slaves" that Wordsworth treats with such shrivelling scorn. But it is well that the two callings have been separated, and it is fitting that they remain apart. In settling the affairs of the late concern, I am afraid our good friends remain a little in our debt. We lent them our physician Michael Servetus in fair condition, and they returned him so damaged by fire as to be quite useless for our purposes. Their Reverend Samuel Willard wrote us a not over-wise report of a case of hysteria; and our Jean Astruc gave them (if we may trust Dr. Smith's Dictionary of the Bible) the first discerning criticism on the authorship of the Pentateuch. Our John Locke enlightened them with his letters concerning toleration; and their Cotton Mather obscured our twilight with his "Nishmath Chajim."

Yet we must remember that the name of Basil Valentine, the monk, is associated with whatever good and harm we can ascribe to antimony; and that the most remarkable of our specifics long bore the name of "Jesuit's Bark," from an old legend connected with its introduction. "Frere Jacques," who taught the lithotomists of Paris, owes his ecclesiastical title to courtesy, as he did not belong to a religious order.

Medical science, and especially the study of mental disease, is destined, I believe, to react to much greater advantage on the theology of the future than theology has acted on medicine in the past. The liberal spirit very generally prevailing in both professions, and the good understanding between their most enlightened members, promise well for the future of both in a community which holds every point of human belief, every institution in human hands, and every word written in a human dialect, open to free discussion today, to-morrow, and to the end of time. Whether the world at large will ever be cured of trusting to specifics as a substitute for observing the laws of health, and to mechanical or intellectual formula as a substitute for character, may admit of question. Quackery and idolatry are all but immortal.

We can find most of the old beliefs alive amongst us to-day, only having changed their dresses and the social spheres in which they thrive. We think the quarrels of Galenists and chemists belong to the past, forgetting that Thomsonism has its numerous apostles in our community; that it is common to see remedies vaunted as purely vegetable, and that the prejudice against "mineral poisons," especially mercury, is as strong in many quarters now as it was at the beginning of the seventeenth century. Names are only air, and blow away with a change of wind; but beliefs are rooted in human wants and weakness, and die hard. The oaks of Dodona are prostrate, and the shrine of Delphi is desolate; but the Pythoness and the Sibyl may be consulted in Lowell Street for a very moderate compensation. Nostradamus and Lilly seem impossible in our time; but we have seen the advertisements of an astrologer in our Boston papers year after year, which seems to imply that he found believers and patrons. You smiled when I related Sir Kenelm Digby's prescription with the live eel in it; but if each of you were to empty his or her pockets, would there not roll out, from more than one of them, a horse-chestnut, carried about as a cure for rheumatism? The brazen head of Roger Bacon is mute; but is not "Planchette" uttering her responses in a hundred houses of this city? We think of palmistry or chiromancy as belonging to the days of Albertus Magnus, or, if existing in our time, as given over to the gypsies; but a very distinguished person has recently shown me the line of life, and the line of fortune, on the palm of his hand, with a seeming confidence in the sanguine predictions of his career which had been drawn from them. What shall we say of the plausible and well-dressed charlatans of our own time, who trade in false pretences, like Nicholas Knapp of old, but without any fear of being fined or whipped; or of the many follies and inanities, imposing on the credulous part of the community, each of them gaping with eager, open mouth for a gratuitous advertisement by the mention of its foolish name in any respectable connection?

I turn from this less pleasing aspect of the common intelligence which renders such follies possible, to close the honorable record of the medical profession in this, our ancient Commonwealth.

We have seen it in the first century divided among clergymen, magistrates, and regular practitioners; yet, on the whole, for the time, and under the circumstances, respectable, except where it invoked supernatural agencies to account for natural phenomena.

In the second century it simplified its practice, educated many intelligent practitioners, and began the work of organizing for concerted action, and for medical teaching.

In this, our own century, it has built hospitals, perfected and multiplied its associations and educational institutions, enlarged and created museums, and challenged a place in the world of science by its literature.

In reviewing the whole course of its history we read a long list of honored names, and a precious record written in private memories, in public charities, in permanent contributions to medical science, in generous sacrifices for the country. We can point to our capital as the port of entry for the New World of the great medical discoveries of two successive centuries, and we can claim for it the triumph over the most dreaded foe that assails the human body,--a triumph which the annals of the race can hardly match in three thousand years of medical history.

THE YOUNG PRACTITIONER

[A Valedictory Address delivered to the Graduating Class of the Bellevue Hospital College, March 2, 1871.]

The occasion which calls us together reminds us not a little of that other ceremony which unites a man and woman for life. The banns have already been pronounced which have wedded our young friends to the profession of their choice. It remains only to address to them some friendly words of cheering counsel, and to bestow upon them the parting benediction.

This is not the time for rhetorical display or ambitious eloquence. We must forget ourselves, and think only of them. To us it is an occasion; to them it is an epoch. The spectators at the wedding look curiously at the bride and bridegroom; at the bridal veil, the orange-flower garland, the giving and receiving of the ring; they listen for the tremulous "I will," and wonder what are the mysterious syllables the clergyman whispers in the ear of the married maiden. But to the newly-wedded pair what meaning in those words, "for better, for worse," "in sickness and in health," "till death us do part!" To the father, to the mother, who know too well how often the deadly nightshade is interwoven with the wreath of orange-blossoms, how empty the pageant, how momentous the reality!

You will not wonder that I address myself chiefly to those who are just leaving academic life for the sterner struggle and the larger tasks of matured and instructed manhood. The hour belongs to them; if others find patience to listen, they will kindly remember that, after all, they are but as the spectators at the wedding, and that the priest is thinking less of them than of their friends who are kneeling at the altar.

I speak more directly to you, then, gentlemen of the graduating class. The days of your education, as pupils of trained instructors, are over. Your first harvest is all garnered. Henceforth you are to be sowers as well as reapers, and your field is the world. How does your knowledge stand to-day? What have you gained as a permanent possession? What must you expect to forget? What remains for you yet to learn? These are questions which it may interest you to consider.

There is another question which must force itself on the thoughts of many among you: "How am I to obtain patients and to keep their confidence?" You have chosen a laborious calling, and made many sacrifices to fit yourselves for its successful pursuit. You wish to be employed that you may be useful, and that you may receive the reward of your industry. I would take advantage of these most receptive moments to give you some hints which may help you to realize your hopes and expectations. Such is the outline of the familiar talk I shall offer you.

Your acquaintance with some of the accessory branches is probably greater now than it will be in a year from now,--much greater than it will by ten years from now. The progress of knowledge, it may be feared, or hoped, will have outrun the text-books in which you studied these branches. Chemistry, for instance, is very apt to spoil on one's hands. "Nous avons change tout cela" might serve as the standing motto of many of our manuals. Science is a great traveller, and wears her shoes out pretty fast, as might be expected.

You are now fresh from the lecture-room and the laboratory. You can pass an examination in anatomy, physiology, chemistry, materia medica, which the men in large practice all around you would find a more potent sudorific than any in the Pharmacopceia. These masters of the art of healing were once as ready with their answers as you are now, but they have got rid of a great deal of the less immediately practical part of their acquisitions, and you must undergo the same depleting process. Hard work will train it off, as sharp exercise trains off the fat of a prize-fighter.

Yet, pause a moment before you infer that your teachers must have been in fault when they furnished you with mental stores not directly convertible to practical purposes, and likely in a few years to lose their place in your memory. All systematic knowledge involves much that is not practical, yet it is the only kind of knowledge which satisfies the mind, and systematic study proves, in the long-run, the easiest way of acquiring and retaining facts which are practical. There are many things which we can afford to forget, which yet it was well to learn. Your mental condition is not the same as if you had never known what you now try in vain to recall. There is a perpetual metempsychosis of thought, and the knowledge of to-day finds a soil in the forgotten facts of yesterday. You cannot see anything in the new season of the guano you placed last year about the roots of your climbing plants, but it is blushing and breathing fragrance in your trellised roses; it has scaled your porch in the bee-haunted honey-suckle; it has found its way where the ivy is green; it is gone where the woodbine expands its luxuriant foliage.

Your diploma seems very broad to-day with your list of accomplishments, but it begins to shrink from this hour like the Peau de Chagrin of Balzac's story. Do not worry about it, for all the while there will be making out for you an ampler and fairer parchment, signed by old Father Time himself as President of that great University in which experience is the one perpetual and all-sufficient professor.

Your present plethora of acquirements will soon cure itself. Knowledge that is not wanted dies out like the eyes of the fishes of the Mammoth Cave. When you come to handle life and death as your daily business, your memory will of itself bid good-by to such inmates as the well-known foramina of the sphenoid bone and the familiar oxides of methyl-ethylamyl-phenyl-ammonium. Be thankful that you have once known them, and remember that even the learned ignorance of a nomenclature is something to have mastered, and may furnish pegs to hang facts upon which would otherwise have strewed the floor of memory in loose disorder.

But your education has, after all, been very largely practical. You have studied medicine and surgery, not chiefly in books, but at the bedside and in the operating amphitheatre. It is the special advantage of large cities that they afford the opportunity of seeing a great deal of disease in a short space of time, and of seeing many cases of the same kind of disease brought together. Let us not be unjust to the claims of the schools remote from the larger centres of population. Who among us has taught better than Nathan Smith, better than Elisha Bartlett? who teaches better than some of our living contemporaries who divide their time between city and country schools? I am afraid we do not always do justice to our country brethren, whose merits are less conspicuously exhibited than those of the great city physicians and surgeons, such especially as have charge of large hospitals. There are modest practitioners living in remote rural districts who are gifted by nature with such sagacity and wisdom, trained so well in what is most essential to the practice of their art, taught so thoroughly by varied experience, forced to such manly self-reliance by their comparative isolation, that, from converse with them alone, from riding with them on their long rounds as they pass from village to village, from talking over cases with them, putting up their prescriptions, watching their expedients, listening to their cautions, marking the event of their predictions, hearing them tell of their mistakes, and now and then glory a little in the detection of another's blunder, a young man would find himself better fitted for his real work than many who have followed long courses of lectures and passed a showy examination. But the young man is exceptionally fortunate who enjoys the intimacy of such a teacher. And it must be confessed that the great hospitals, infirmaries, and dispensaries of large cities, where men of well-sifted reputations are in constant attendance, are the true centres of medical education. No students, I believe, are more thoroughly aware of this than those who have graduated at this institution. Here, as in all our larger city schools, the greatest pains are taken to teach things as well as names. You have entered into the inheritance of a vast amount of transmitted skill and wisdom, which you have taken, warm, as it were, with the life of your well-schooled instructors. You have not learned all that art has to teach you, but you are safer practitioners today than were many of those whose names we hardly mention without a genuflection. I had rather be cared for in a fever by the best-taught among you than by the renowned Fernelius or the illustrious Boerhaave, could they come back to us from that better world where there are no physicians needed, and, if the old adage can be trusted, not many within call. I had rather have one of you exercise his surgical skill upon me than find myself in the hands of a resuscitated Fabricius Hildanus, or even of a wise Ambroise Pare, revisiting earth in the light of the nineteenth century.

You will not accuse me of underrating your accomplishments. You know what to do for a child in a fit, for an alderman in an apoplexy, for a girl that has fainted, for a woman in hysterics, for a leg that is broken, for an arm that is out of joint, for fevers of every color, for the sailor's rheumatism, and the tailor's cachexy. In fact you do really know so much at this very hour, that nothing but the searching test of time can fully teach you the limitations of your knowledge.

Of some of these you will permit me to remind you. You will never have outgrown the possibility of new acquisitions, for Nature is endless in her variety. But even the knowledge which you may be said to possess will be a different thing after long habit has made it a part of your existence. The tactus eruditus extends to the mind as well as to the finger-ends. Experience means the knowledge gained by habitual trial, and an expert is one who has been in the habit of trying. This is the kind of knowledge that made Ulysses wise in the ways of men. Many cities had he seen, and known the minds of those who dwelt in them. This knowledge it was that Chaucer's Shipman brought home with him from the sea--

"In many a tempest had his berd be shake."

This is the knowledge we place most confidence in, in the practical affairs of life.

Our training has two stages. The first stage deals with our intelligence, which takes the idea of what is to be done with the most charming ease and readiness. Let it be a game of billiards, for instance, which the marker is going to teach us. We have nothing to do but to make this ball glance from that ball and hit that other ball, and to knock that ball with this ball into a certain caecal sacculus or diverticulum which our professional friend calls a pocket. Nothing can be clearer; it is as easy as "playing upon this pipe," for which Hamlet gives Guildenstern such lucid directions. But this intelligent Me, who steps forward as the senior partner in our dual personality, turns out to be a terrible bungler. He misses those glancing hits which the hard-featured young professional person calls "carroms," and insists on pocketing his own ball instead of the other one.

It is the unintelligent Me, stupid as an idiot, that has to try a thing a thousand times before he can do it, and then never knows how he does it, that at last does it well. We have to educate ourselves through the pretentious claims of intellect, into the humble accuracy of instinct, and we end at last by acquiring the dexterity, the perfection, the certainty, which those masters of arts, the bee and the spider, inherit from Nature.

Book-knowledge, lecture-knowledge, examination-knowledge, are all in the brain. But work-knowledge is not only in the brain, it is in the senses, in the muscles, in the ganglia of the sympathetic nerves,--all over the man, as one may say, as instinct seems diffused through every part of those lower animals that have no such distinct organ as a brain. See a skilful surgeon handle a broken limb; see a wise old physician smile away a case that looks to a novice as if the sexton would soon be sent for; mark what a large experience has done for those who were fitted to profit by it, and you will feel convinced that, much as you know, something is still left for you to learn.

May I venture to contrast youth and experience in medical practice, something in the way the man painted the lion, that is, the lion under?

The young man knows the rules, but the old man knows-the exceptions. The young man knows his patient, but the old man knows also his patient's family, dead and alive, up and down for generations. He can tell beforehand what diseases their unborn children will be subject to, what they will die of if they live long enough, and whether they had better live at all, or remain unrealized possibilities, as belonging to a stock not worth being perpetuated. The young man feels uneasy if he is not continually doing something to stir up his patient's internal arrangements. The old man takes things more quietly, and is much more willing to let well enough alone: All these superiorities, if such they are,'you must wait for time to bring you. In the meanwhile (if we will let the lion be uppermost for a moment), the young man's senses are quicker than those of his older rival. His education in all the accessory branches is more recent, and therefore nearer the existing condition of knowledge. He finds it easier than his seniors to accept the improvements which every year is bringing forward. New ideas build their nests in young men's brains. "Revolutions are not made by men in spectacles," as I once heard it remarked, and the first whispers of a new truth are not caught by those who begin to feel the need of an ear-trumpet. Granting all these advantages to the young man, he ought, nevertheless, to go on improving, on the whole, as a medical practitioner, with every year, until he has ripened into a well-mellowed maturity. But, to improve, he must be good for something at the start. If you ship a poor cask of wine to India and back, if you keep it a half a century, it only grows thinner and sharper.

You are soon to enter into relations with the public, to expend your skill and knowledge for its benefit, and find your support in the rewards of your labor. What kind of a constituency is this which is to look to you as its authorized champions in the struggle of life against its numerous enemies?

In the first place, the persons who seek the aid of the physician are very honest and sincere in their wish to get rid of their complaints, and, generally speaking, to live as long as they can. However attractively the future is painted to them, they are attached to the planet with which they are already acquainted. They are addicted to the daily use of this empirical and unchemical mixture which we call air; and would hold on to it as a tippler does to his alcoholic drinks. There is nothing men will not do, there is nothing they have not done, to recover their health and save their lives. They have submitted to be half-drowned in water, and half-choked with gases, to be buried up to their chins in earth, to be seared with hot irons like galley-slaves, to be crimped with knives, like cod-fish, to have needles thrust into their flesh, and bonfires kindled on their skin, to swallow all sorts of abominations, and to pay for all this, as if to be singed and scalded were a costly privilege, as if blisters were a blessing, and leeches were a luxury. What more can be asked to prove their honesty and sincerity?

This same community is very intelligent with respect to a great many subjects-commerce, mechanics, manufactures, politics. But with regard to medicine it is hopelessly ignorant and never finds it out. I do not know that it is any worse in this country than in Great Britain, where Mr. Huxley speaks very freely of "the utter ignorance of the simplest laws of their own animal life, which prevails among even the most highly educated persons." And Cullen said before him "Neither the acutest genius nor the soundest judgment will avail in judging of a particular science, in regard to which they have not been exercised. I have been obliged to please my patients sometimes with reasons, and I have found that any will pass, even with able divines and acute lawyers; the same will pass with the husbands as with the wives." If the community could only be made aware of its own utter ignorance, and incompetence to form opinions on medical subjects, difficult enough to those who give their lives to the study of them, the practitioner would have an easier task. But it will form opinions of its own, it cannot help it, and we cannot blame it, even though we know how slight and deceptive are their foundations.

This is the way it happens: Every grown-up person has either been ill himself or had a friend suffer from illness, from which he has recovered. Every sick person has done something or other by somebody's advice, or of his own accord, a little before getting better. There is an irresistible tendency to associate the thing done, and the improvement which followed it, as cause and effect. This is the great source of fallacy in medical practice. But the physician has some chance of correcting his hasty inference. He thinks his prescription cured a single case of a particular complaint; he tries it in twenty similar cases without effect, and sets down the first as probably nothing more than a coincidence. The unprofessional experimenter or observer has no large experience to correct his hasty generalization. He wants to believe that the means he employed effected his cure. He feels grateful to the person who advised it, he loves to praise the pill or potion which helped him, and he has a kind of monumental pride in himself as a living testimony to its efficacy. So it is that you will find the community in which you live, be it in town or country, full of brands plucked from the burning, as they believe, by some agency which, with your better training, you feel reasonably confident had nothing to do with it. Their disease went out of itself, and the stream from the medical fire-annihilator had never even touched it.

You cannot and need not expect to disturb the public in the possession of its medical superstitions. A man's ignorance is as much his private property, and as precious in his own eyes, as his family Bible. You have only to open your own Bible at the ninth chapter of St. John's Gospel, and you will find that the logic of a restored patient was very simple then, as it is now, and very hard to deal with. My clerical friends will forgive me for poaching on their sacred territory, in return for an occasional raid upon the medical domain of which they have now and then been accused.

A blind man was said to have been restored to sight by a young person whom the learned doctors of the Jewish law considered a sinner, and, as such, very unlikely to have been endowed with a divine gift of healing. They visited the patient repeatedly, and evidently teased him with their questions about the treatment, and their insinuations about the young man, until he lost his temper. At last he turned sharply upon them: "Whether he be a sinner or no, I know not: one thing I know, that, whereas I was blind, now I see."

This is the answer that always has been and always will be given by most persons when they find themselves getting well after doing anything, no matter what,--recommended by anybody, no matter whom. Lord Bacon, Robert Boyle, Bishop Berkeley, all put their faith in panaceas which we should laugh to scorn. They had seen people get well after using them. Are we any wiser than those great men? Two years ago, in a lecture before the Massachusetts Historical Society, I mentioned this recipe of Sir Kenelm Digby for fever and ague: Pare the patient's nails; put the parings in a little bag, and hang the bag round the neck of a live eel, and place him in a tub of water. The eel will die, and the patient will recover.

Referring to this prescription in the course of the same lecture, I said: "You smiled when I related Sir Kenehn Digby's prescription, with the live eel in it; but if each of you were to empty his or her pockets, would there not roll out, from more than one of them, a horse-chestnut, carried about as a cure for rheumatism?" Nobody saw fit to empty his or her pockets, and my question brought no response. But two months ago I was in a company of educated persons, college graduates every one of them, when a gentleman, well known in our community, a man of superior ability and strong common-sense, on the occasion of some talk arising about rheumatism, took a couple of very shiny horse-chestnuts from his breeches-pocket, and laid them on the table, telling us how, having suffered from the complaint in question, he had, by the advice of a friend, procured these two horse-chestnuts on a certain time a year or more ago, and carried them about him ever since; from which very day he had been entirely free from rheumatism.

This argument, from what looks like cause and effect, whether it be so or not, is what you will have to meet wherever you go, and you need not think you can answer it. In the natural course of things some thousands of persons must be getting well or better of slight attacks of colds, of rheumatic pains, every week, in this city alone. Hundreds of them do something or other in the way of remedy, by medical or other advice, or of their own motion, and the last thing they do gets the credit of the recovery. Think what a crop of remedies this must furnish, if it were all harvested!

Experience has taught, or will teach you, that most of the wonderful stories patients and others tell of sudden and signal cures are like Owen Glendower's story of the portents that announced his birth. The earth shook at your nativity, did it? Very likely, and

"So it would have done,
At the same season, if your mother's cat

Had kittened, though yourself had ne'er been born."

You must listen more meekly than Hotspur did to the babbling Welshman, for ignorance is a solemn and sacred fact, and, like infancy, which it resembles, should be respected. Once in a while you will have a patient of sense, born with the gift of observation, from whom you may learn something. When you find yourself in the presence of one who is fertile of medical opinions, and affluent in stories of marvellous cures,--of a member of Congress whose name figures in certificates to the value of patent medicines, of a voluble dame who discourses on the miracles she has wrought or seen wrought with the little jokers of the sugar-of-milk globule-box, take out your watch and count the pulse; also note the time of day, and charge the price of a visit for every extra fifteen, or, if you are not very busy, every twenty minutes. In this way you will turn what seems a serious dispensation into a double blessing, for this class of patients loves dearly to talk, and it does them a deal of good, and you feel as if you had earned your money by the dose you have taken, quite as honestly as by any dose you may have ordered.

You must take the community just as it is, and make the best of it. You wish to obtain its confidence; there is a short rule for doing this which you will find useful,--deserve it. But, to deserve it in full measure, you must unite many excellences, natural and acquired.

As the basis of all the rest, you must have all those traits of character which fit you to enter into the most intimate and confidential relations with the families of which you are the privileged friend and counsellor. Medical Christianity, if I may use such a term, is of very early date. By the oath of Hippocrates, the practitioner of ancient times bound himself to enter his patient's house with the sole purpose of doing him good, and so to conduct himself as to avoid the very appearance of evil. Let the physician of to-day begin by coming up to this standard, and add to it all the more recently discovered virtues and graces.

A certain amount of natural ability is requisite to make you a good physician, but by no means that disproportionate development of some special faculty which goes by the name of genius. A just balance of the mental powers is a great deal more likely to be useful than any single talent, even were it the power of observation; in excess. For a mere observer is liable to be too fond of facts for their own sake, so that, if he told the real truth, he would confess that he takes more pleasure in a post-mortem examination which shows him what was the matter with a patient, than in a case which insists on getting well and leaving him in the dark as to its nature. Far more likely to interfere with the sound practical balance of the mind is that speculative, theoretical tendency which has made so many men noted in their day, whose fame has passed away with their dissolving theories. Read Dr. Bartlett's comparison of the famous Benjamin Rush with his modest fellow-townsman Dr. William Currie, and see the dangers into which a passion for grandiose generalizations betrayed a man of many admirable qualities.

I warn you against all ambitious aspirations outside of your profession. Medicine is the most difficult of sciences and the most laborious of arts. It will task all your powers of body and mind if you are faithful to it. Do not dabble in the muddy sewer of politics, nor linger by the enchanted streams of literature, nor dig in far-off fields for the hidden waters of alien sciences. The great practitioners are generally those who concentrate all their powers on their business. If there are here and there brilliant exceptions, it is only in virtue of extraordinary gifts, and industry to which very few are equal.

To get business a man mast really want it; and do you suppose that when you are in the middle of a heated caucus, or half-way through a delicate analysis, or in the spasm of an unfinished ode, your eyes rolling in the fine frenzy of poetical composition, you want to be called to a teething infant, or an ancient person groaning under the griefs of a lumbago? I think I have known more than one young man whose doctor's sign proclaimed his readiness to serve mankind in that capacity, but who hated the sound of a patient's knock, and as he sat with his book or his microscope, felt exactly as the old party expressed himself in my friend Mr. Brownell's poem--

"All I axes is, let me alone."

The community soon finds out whether you are in earnest, and really mean business, or whether you are one of those diplomaed dilettanti who like the amusement of quasi medical studies, but have no idea of wasting their precious time in putting their knowledge in practice for the benefit of their suffering fellow-creatures.

The public is a very incompetent judge of your skill and knowledge, but it gives its confidence most readily to those who stand well with their professional brethren, whom they call upon when they themselves or their families are sick, whom they choose to honorable offices, whose writings and teachings they hold in esteem. A man may be much valued by the profession and yet have defects which prevent his becoming a favorite practitioner, but no popularity can be depended upon as permanent which is not sanctioned by the judgment of professional experts, and with these you will always stand on your substantial merits.

What shall I say of the personal habits you must form if you wish for success? Temperance is first upon the list. Intemperance in a physician partakes of the guilt of homicide, for the muddled brain may easily make a fatal blunder in a prescription and the unsteady hand transfix an artery in an operation. Tippling doctors have been too common in the history of medicine. Paracelsus was a sot, Radcliffe was much too fond of his glass, and Dr. James Hurlbut of Wethersfield, Connecticut, a famous man in his time, used to drink a square bottle of rum a day, with a corresponding allowance of opium to help steady his nerves. We commonly speak of a man as being the worse for liquor, but I was asking an Irish laborer one day about his doctor, who, as he said, was somewhat given to drink. "I like him best when he's a little that way," he said; "then I can spake to him." I pitied the poor patient who could not venture to allude to his colic or his pleurisy until his physician was tipsy.

There are personal habits of less gravity than the one I have mentioned which it is well to guard against, or, if they are formed, to relinquish. A man who may be called at a moment's warning into the fragrant boudoir of suffering loveliness should not unsweeten its atmosphere with reminiscences of extinguished meerschaums. He should remember that the sick are sensitive and fastidious, that they love the sweet odors and the pure tints of flowers, and if his presence is not like the breath of the rose, if his hands are not like the leaf of the lily, his visit may be unwelcome, and if he looks behind him he may see a window thrown open after he has left the sick-chamber. I remember too well the old doctor who sometimes came to help me through those inward griefs to which childhood is liable. "Far off his coming "--shall I say "shone," and finish the Miltonic phrase, or leave the verb to the happy conjectures of my audience? Before him came a soul-subduing whiff of ipecacuanha, and after him lingered a shuddering consciousness of rhubarb. He had lived so much among his medicaments that he had at last become himself a drug, and to have him pass through a sick-chamber was a stronger dose than a conscientious disciple of Hahnemann would think it safe to administer.

Need I remind you of the importance of punctuality in your engagements, and of the worry and distress to patients and their friends which the want of it occasions? One of my old teachers always carried two watches, to make quite sure of being exact, and not only kept his appointments with the regularity of a chronometer, but took great pains to be at his patient's house at the time when he had reason to believe he was expected, even if no express appointment was made. It is a good rule; if you call too early, my lady's hair may not be so smooth as could be wished, and, if you keep her waiting too long, her hair may be smooth, but her temper otherwise.

You will remember, of course, always to get the weather-gage of your patient. I mean, to place him so that the light falls on his face and not on yours. It is a kind of, ocular duel that is about to take place between you; you are going to look through his features into his pulmonary and hepatic and other internal machinery, and he is going to look into yours quite as sharply to see what you think about his probabilities for time or eternity.

No matter how hard he stares at your countenance, he should never be able to read his fate in it. It should be cheerful as long as there is hope, and serene in its gravity when nothing is left but resignation. The face of a physician, like that of a diplomatist, should be impenetrable. Nature is a benevolent old hypocrite; she cheats the sick and the dying with illusions better than any anodynes. If there are cogent reasons why a patient should be undeceived, do it deliberately and advisedly, but do not betray your apprehensions through your tell-tale features.

We had a physician in our city whose smile was commonly reckoned as being worth five thousand dollars a year to him, in the days, too, of moderate incomes. You cannot put on such a smile as that any more than you can get sunshine without sun; there was a tranquil and kindly nature under it that irradiated the pleasant face it made one happier to meet on his daily rounds. But you can cultivate the disposition, and it will work its way through to the surface, nay, more,--you can try to wear a quiet and encouraging look, and it will react on your disposition and make you like what you seem to be, or at least bring you nearer to its own likeness.

Your patient has no more right to all the truth you know than he has to all the medicine in your saddlebags, if you carry that kind of cartridge-box for the ammunition that slays disease. He should get only just so much as is good for him. I have seen a physician examining a patient's chest stop all at once, as he brought out a particular sound with a tap on the collarbone, in the attitude of a pointer who has just come on the scent or sight of a woodcock. You remember the Spartan boy, who, with unmoved countenance, hid the fox that was tearing his vitals beneath his mantle. What he could do in his own suffering you must learn to do for others on whose vital organs disease has fastened its devouring teeth. It is a terrible thing to take away hope, even earthly hope, from a fellow-creature. Be very careful what names you let fall before your patient. He knows what it means when you tell him he has tubercles or Bright's disease, and, if he hears the word carcinoma, he will certainly look it out in a medical dictionary, if he does not interpret its dread significance on the instant. Tell him he has asthmatic symptoms, or a tendency to the gouty diathesis, and he will at once think of all the asthmatic and gouty old patriarchs he has ever heard of, and be comforted. You need not be so cautious in speaking of the health of rich and remote relatives, if he is in the line of succession.

Some shrewd old doctors have a few phrases always on hand for patients that will insist on knowing the pathology of their complaints without the slightest capacity of understanding the scientific explanation. I have known the term "spinal irritation" serve well on such occasions, but I think nothing on the whole has covered so much ground, and meant so little, and given such profound satisfaction to all parties, as the magnificent phrase "congestion of the portal system."

Once more, let me recommend you, as far as possible, to keep your doubts to yourself, and give the patient the benefit of your decision. Firmness, gentle firmness, is absolutely necessary in this and certain other relations. Mr. Rarey with Cruiser, Richard with Lady Ann, Pinel with his crazy people, show what steady nerves can do with the most intractable of animals, the most irresistible of despots, and the most unmanageable of invalids.

If you cannot acquire and keep the confidence of your patient, it is time for you to give place to some other practitioner who can. If you are wise and diligent, you can establish relations with the best of them which they will find it very hard to break. But, if they wish to employ another person, who, as they think, knows more than you do, do not take it as a personal wrong. A patient believes another man can save his life, can restore him to health, which, as he thinks, you have not the skill to do. No matter whether the patient is right or wrong, it is a great impertinence to think you have any property in him. Your estimate of your own ability is not the question, it is what the patient thinks of it. All your wisdom is to him like the lady's virtue in Raleigh's song:

"If she seem not chaste to me,
What care I how chaste she be?"

What I call a good patient is one who, having found a good physician, sticks to him till he dies. But there are many very good people who are not what I call good patients. I was once requested to call on a lady suffering from nervous and other symptoms. It came out in the preliminary conversational skirmish, half medical, half social, that I was the twenty-sixth member of the faculty into whose arms, professionally speaking, she had successively thrown herself. Not being a believer in such a rapid rotation of scientific crops, I gently deposited the burden, commending it to the care of number twenty-seven, and, him, whoever he might be, to the care of Heaven.

If there happened to be among my audience any person who wished to know on what principles the patient should choose his physician, I should give him these few precepts to think over:

Choose a man who is personally agreeable, for a daily visit from an intelligent, amiable, pleasant, sympathetic person will cost you no more than one from a sloven or a boor, and his presence will do more for you than any prescription the other will order.

Let him be a man of recognized good sense in other matters, and the chance is that he will be sensible as a practitioner.

Let him be a man who stands well with his professional brethren, whom they approve as honest, able, courteous.

Let him be one whose patients are willing to die in his hands, not one whom they go to for trifles, and leave as soon as they are in danger, and who can say, therefore, that he never loses a patient.

Do not leave the ranks of what is called the regular profession, unless you wish to go farther and fare worse, for you may be assured that its members recognize no principle which hinders their accepting any remedial agent proved to be useful, no matter from what quarter it comes. The difficulty is that the stragglers, organized under fantastic names in pretentious associations, or lurking in solitary dens behind doors left ajar, make no real contributions to the art of healing. When they bring forward a remedial agent like chloral, like the bromide of potassium, like ether, used as an anesthetic, they will find no difficulty in procuring its recognition.

Some of you will probably be more or less troubled by the pretensions of that parody of mediaeval theology which finds its dogma of hereditary depravity in the doctrine of psora, its miracle of transubstantiation in the mystery of its triturations and dilutions, its church in the people who have mistaken their century, and its priests in those who have mistaken their calling. You can do little with persons who are disposed to accept these curious medical superstitions. The saturation-point of individual minds with reference to evidence, and especially medical evidence, differs, and must always continue to differ, very widely. There are those whose minds are satisfied with the decillionth dilution of a scientific proof. No wonder they believe in the efficacy of a similar attenuation of bryony or pulsatilla. You have no fulcrum you can rest upon to lift an error out of such minds as these, often highly endowed with knowledge and talent, sometimes with genius, but commonly richer in the imaginative than the observing and reasoning faculties.

Let me return once more to the young graduate. Your relations to your professional brethren may be a source of lifelong happiness and growth in knowledge and character, or they may make you wretched and end by leaving you isolated from those who should be your friends and counsellors. The life of a physician becomes ignoble when he suffers himself to feed on petty jealousies and sours his temper in perpetual quarrels. You will be liable to meet an uncomfortable man here and there in the profession,--one who is so fond of being in hot water that it is a wonder all the albumen in his body is not coagulated. There are common barrators among doctors as there are among lawyers,--stirrers up of strife under one pretext and another, but in reality because they like it. They are their own worst enemies, and do themselves a mischief each time they assail their neighbors. In my student days I remember a good deal of this Donnybrook-Fair style of quarrelling, more especially in Paris, where some of the noted surgeons were always at loggerheads, and in one of our lively Western cities. Soon after I had set up an office, I had a trifling experience which may serve to point a moral in this direction. I had placed a lamp behind the glass in the entry to indicate to the passer-by where relief from all curable infirmities was to be sought and found. Its brilliancy attracted the attention of a devious youth, who dashed his fist through the glass and upset my modest luminary. All he got by his vivacious assault was that he left portions of integument from his knuckles upon the glass, had a lame hand, was very easily identified, and had to pay the glazier's bill. The moral is that, if the brilliancy of another's reputation excites your belligerent instincts, it is not worth your while to strike at it, without calculating which of you is likely to suffer most, if you do.

You may be assured that when an ill-conditioned neighbor is always complaining of a bad taste in his mouth and an evil atmosphere about him, there is something wrong about his own secretions. In such cases there is an alterative regimen of remarkable efficacy: it is a starvation-diet of letting alone. The great majority of the profession are peacefully inclined. Their pursuits are eminently humanizing, and they look with disgust on the personalities which intrude themselves into the placid domain of an art whose province it is to heal and not to wound.

The intercourse of teacher and student in a large school is necessarily limited, but it should be, and, so far as my experience goes, it is, eminently cordial and kindly. You will leave with regret, and hold in tender remembrance, those who have taken you by the hand at your entrance on your chosen path, and led you patiently and faithfully, until the great gates at its end have swung upon their hinges, and the world lies open before you. That venerable oath to which I have before referred bound the student to regard his instructor in the light of a parent, to treat his children like brothers, to succor him in his day of need. I trust the spirit of the oath of Hippocrates is not dead in the hearts of the students of to-day. They will remember with gratitude every earnest effort, every encouraging word, which has helped them in their difficult and laborious career of study. The names they read on their diplomas will recall faces that are like family-portraits in their memory, and the echo of voices they have listened to so long will linger in their memories far into the still evening of their lives.

One voice will be heard no more which has been familiar to many among you. It is not for me, a stranger to these scenes, to speak his eulogy. I have no right to sadden this hour by dwelling on the deep regrets of friendship, or to bid the bitter tears of sorrow flow afresh. Yet I cannot help remembering what a void the death of such a practitioner as your late instructor must leave in the wide circle of those who leaned upon his counsel and assistance in their hour of need, in a community where he was so widely known and esteemed, in a school where he bore so important a part. There is no exemption from the common doom for him who holds the shield to protect others. The student is called from his bench, the professor from his chair, the practitioner in his busiest period hears a knock more peremptory than any patient's midnight summons, and goes on that unreturning visit which admits of no excuse, and suffers no delay. The call of such a man away from us is the bereavement of a great family. Nor can we help regretting the loss for him of a bright and cheerful earthly future; for the old age of a physician is one of the happiest periods of his life. He is loved and cherished for what he has been, and even in the decline of his faculties there are occasions when his experience is still appealed to, and his trembling hands are looked to with renewing hope and trust, as being yet able to stay the arm of the destroyer.

But if there is so much left for age, how beautiful, how inspiring is the hope of youth! I see among those whom I count as listeners one by whose side I have sat as a fellow-teacher, and by whose instructions I have felt myself not too old to profit. As we borrowed him from your city, I must take this opportunity of telling you that his zeal, intelligence, and admirable faculty as an instructor were heartily and universally recognized among us. We return him, as we trust, uninjured, to the fellow-citizens who have the privilege of claiming him as their own.

And now, gentlemen of the graduating class, nothing remains but for me to bid you, in the name of those for whom I am commissioned and privileged to speak, farewell as students, and welcome as practitioners. I pronounce the two benedictions in the same breath, as the late king's demise and the new king's accession are proclaimed by the same voice at the same moment. You would hardly excuse me if I stooped to any meaner dialect than the classical and familiar language of your prescriptions, the same in which your title to the name of physician is, if, like our own institution, you follow the ancient usage, engraved upon your diplomas.

Valete, JUVENES, artis medicae studiosi; valete, discipuli, valete, filii!
Salvete, VIRI, artis medicae magister; Salvete amici; salvete fratres!

MEDICAL LIBRARIES.

[Dedicatory Address at the opening of the Medical Library in Boston, December 3, 1878.]

It is my appointed task, my honorable privilege, this evening, to speak of what has been done by others. No one can bring his tribute of words into the presence of great deeds, or try with them to embellish the memory of any inspiring achievement, without feeling and leaving with others a sense of their insufficiency. So felt Alexander when he compared even his adored Homer with the hero the poet had sung. So felt Webster when he contrasted the phrases of rhetoric with the eloquence of patriotism and of self-devotion. So felt Lincoln when on the field of Gettysburg he spoke those immortal words which Pericles could not have bettered, which Aristotle could not have criticised. So felt he who wrote the epitaph of the builder of the dome which looks down on the crosses and weathercocks that glitter over London.

We are not met upon a battle-field, except so far as every laborious achievement means a victory over opposition, indifference, selfishness, faintheartedness, and that great property of mind as well as matter,--inertia. We are not met in a cathedral, except so far as every building whose walls are lined with the products of useful and ennobling thought is a temple of the Almighty, whose inspiration has given us understanding. But we have gathered within walls which bear testimony to the self-sacrificing, persevering efforts of a few young men, to whom we owe the origin and development of all that excites our admiration in this completed enterprise; and I might consider my task as finished if I contented myself with borrowing the last word of the architect's epitaph and only saying, Look around you!

The reports of the librarian have told or will tell you, in some detail, what has been accomplished since the 21st of December, 1874, when six gentlemen met at the house of Dr. Henry Ingersoll Bowditch to discuss different projects for a medical library. In less than four years from that time, by the liberality of associations and of individuals, this collection of nearly ten thousand volumes, of five thousand pamphlets, and of one hundred and twenty-five journals, regularly received,--all worthily sheltered beneath this lofty roof,--has come into being under our eyes. It has sprung up, as it were; in the night like a mushroom; it stands before us in full daylight as lusty as an oak, and promising to grow and flourish in the perennial freshness of an evergreen.

To whom does our profession owe this already large collection of books, exceeded in numbers only by four or five of the most extensive medical libraries in the country, and lodged in a building so well adapted to its present needs? We will not point out individually all those younger members of the profession who have accomplished what their fathers and elder brethren had attempted and partially achieved. We need not write their names on these walls, after the fashion of those civic dignitaries who immortalize themselves on tablets of marble and gates of iron. But their contemporaries know them well, and their descendants will not forget them,--the men who first met together, the men who have given their time and their money, the faithful workers, worthy associates of the strenuous agitator who gave no sleep to his eyes, no slumber to his eyelids, until he had gained his ends; the untiring, imperturbable, tenacious, irrepressible, all-subduing agitator who neither rested nor let others rest until the success of the project was assured. If, against his injunctions, I name Dr. James Read Chadwick, it is only my revenge for his having kept me awake so often and so long while he was urging on the undertaking in which he has been preeminently active and triumphantly successful.

We must not forget the various medical libraries which preceded this: that of an earlier period, when Boston contained about seventy regular practitioners, the collection afterwards transferred to the Boston Athenaeum; the two collections belonging to the University; the Treadwell Library at the Massachusetts General Hospital; the collections of the two societies, that for Medical Improvement and that for Medical Observation; and more especially the ten thousand volumes relating to medicine belonging to our noble public city library,--too many blossoms on the tree of knowledge, perhaps, for the best fruit to ripen. But the Massachusetts Medical Society now numbers nearly four hundred members in the city of Boston. The time had arrived for a new and larger movement. There was needed a place to which every respectable member of the medical profession could obtain easy access; where, under one roof, all might find the special information they were seeking; where the latest medical intelligence should be spread out daily as the shipping news is posted on the bulletins of the exchange; where men engaged in a common pursuit could meet, surrounded by the mute oracles of science and art; where the whole atmosphere should be as full of professional knowledge as the apothecary's shop is of the odor of his medicaments. This was what the old men longed for,--the prophets and kings of the profession, who

"Desired it long,
But died without the sight."

This is what the young men and those who worked under their guidance undertook to give us. And now such a library, such a reading-room, such an exchange, such an intellectual and social meeting place, we behold a fact, plain before us. The medical profession of our city, and, let us add, of all those neighboring places which it can reach with its iron arms, is united as never before by the commune vinculum, the common bond of a large, enduring, ennobling, unselfish interest. It breathes a new air of awakened intelligence. It marches abreast of the other learned professions, which have long had their extensive and valuable centralized libraries; abreast of them, but not promising to be content with that position. What glorifies a town like a cathedral? What dignifies a province like a university? What illuminates a country like its scholarship, and what is the nest that hatches scholars but a library?

The physician, some may say, is a practical man and has little use for all this book-learning. Every student has heard Sydenham's reply to Sir Richard Blackmore's question as to what books he should read,--meaning medical books. "Read Don Quixote," was his famous answer. But Sydenham himself made medical books and may be presumed to have thought those at least worth reading. Descartes was asked where was his library, and in reply held up the dissected body of an animal.

But Descartes made books, great books, and a great many of them. A physician of common sense without erudition is better than a learned one without common sense, but the thorough master of his profession must have learning added to his natural gifts.

It is not necessary to maintain the direct practical utility of all kinds of learning. Our shelves contain many books which only a certain class of medical scholars will be likely to consult. There is a dead medical literature, and there is a live one. The dead is not all ancient, the live is not all modern. There is none, modern or ancient, which, if it has no living value for the student, will not teach him something by its autopsy. But it is with the live literature of his profession that the medical practitioner is first of all concerned.

Now there has come a great change in our time over the form in which living thought presents itself. The first printed books,--the incunabula,--were inclosed in boards of solid oak, with brazen clasps and corners; the boards by and by were replaced by pasteboard covered with calf or sheepskin; then cloth came in and took the place of leather; then the pasteboard was covered with paper instead of cloth; and at this day the quarterly, the monthly, the weekly periodical in its flimsy unsupported dress of paper, and the daily journal, naked as it came from the womb of the press, hold the larger part of the fresh reading we live upon. We must have the latest thought in its latest expression; the page must be newly turned like the morning bannock; the pamphlet must be newly opened like the ante-prandial oyster.

Thus a library, to meet the need of our time, must take, and must spread out in a convenient form, a great array of periodicals. Our active practitioners read these by preference over almost everything else. Our specialists, more particularly, depend on the month's product, on the yearly crop of new facts, new suggestions, new contrivances, as much as the farmer on the annual yield of his acres. One of the first wants, then, of the profession is supplied by our library in its great array of periodicals from many lands, in many languages. Such a number of medical periodicals no private library would have room for, no private person would pay for, or flood his tables with if they were sent him for nothing. These, I think, with the reports of medical societies and the papers contributed to them, will form the most attractive part of our accumulated medical treasures. They will be also one of our chief expenses, for these journals must be bound in volumes and they require a great amount of shelf-room; all this, in addition to the cost of subscription for those which are not furnished us gratuitously.

It is true that the value of old scientific periodicals is, other things being equal, in the inverse ratio of their age, for the obvious reason that what is most valuable in the earlier volumes of a series is drained off into the standard works with which the intelligent practitioner is supposed to be familiar. But no extended record of facts grows too old to be useful, provided only that we have a ready and sure way of getting at the particular fact or facts we are in search of.

And this leads me to speak of what I conceive to be one of the principal tasks to be performed by the present and the coming generation of scholars, not only in the medical, but in every department of knowledge. I mean the formation of indexes, and more especially of indexes to periodical literature.

This idea has long been working in the minds of scholars, and all who have had occasion to follow out any special subject. I have a right to speak of it, for I long ago attempted to supply the want of indexes in some small measure for my own need. I had a very complete set of the "American Journal of the Medical Sciences;" an entire set of the "North American Review," and many volumes of the reprints of the three leading British quarterlies. Of what use were they to me without general indexes? I looked them all through carefully and made classified lists of all the articles I thought I should most care to read. But they soon outgrew my lists. The "North American Review" kept filling up shelf after shelf, rich in articles which I often wanted to consult, but what a labor to find them, until the index of Mr. Gushing, published a few months since, made the contents of these hundred and twenty volumes as easily accessible as the words in a dictionary! I had a copy of good Dr. Abraham Rees's Cyclopaedia, a treasure-house to my boyhood which has not lost its value for me in later years. But where to look for what I wanted? I wished to know, for instance, what Dr. Burney had to say about singing. Who would have looked for it under the Italian word cantare? I was curious to learn something of the etchings of Rembrandt, and where should I find it but under the head "Low Countries, Engravers of the,"--an elaborate and most valuable article of a hundred double-columned close-printed quarto pages, to which no reference, even, is made under the title Rembrandt.

There was nothing to be done, if I wanted to know where that which I specially cared for was to be found in my Rees's Cyclopaedia, but to look over every page of its forty-one quarto volumes and make out a brief list of matters of interest which I could not find by their titles, and this I did, at no small expense of time and trouble.

Nothing, therefore, could be more pleasing to me than to see the attention which has been given of late years to the great work of indexing. It is a quarter of a century since Mr. Poole published his "Index to Periodical Literature," which it is much to be hoped is soon to appear in a new edition, grown as it must be to formidable dimensions by the additions of so long a period. The "British and Foreign Medical Review," edited by the late Sir John Forties, contributed to by Huxley, Carpenter, Laycock, and others of the most distinguished scientific men of Great Britain, has an index to its twenty-four volumes, and by its aid I find this valuable series as manageable as a lexicon. The last edition of the "Encyclopaedia Britannica" had a complete index in a separate volume, and the publishers of Appletons' "American Cyclopaedia" have recently issued an index to their useful work, which must greatly add to its value. I have already referred to the index to the "North American Review," which to an American, and especially to a New Englander, is the most interesting and most valuable addition of its kind to our literary apparatus since the publication of Mr. Allibone's "Dictionary of Authors." I might almost dare to parody Mr. Webster's words in speaking of Hamilton, to describe what Mr. Gushing did for the solemn rows of back volumes of our honored old Review which had been long fossilizing on our shelves: "He touched the dead corpse of the 'North American,' and it sprang to its feet." A library of the best thought of the best American scholars during the greater portion of the century was brought to light by the work of the indexmaker as truly as were the Assyrian tablets by the labors of Layard.

A great portion of the best writing and reading literary, scientific, professional, miscellaneous--comes to us now, at stated intervals, in paper covers. The writer appears, as it were, in his shirt-sleeves. As soon as he has delivered his message the book-binder puts a coat on his back, and he joins the forlorn brotherhood of "back volumes," than which, so long as they are unindexed, nothing can be more exasperating. Who wants a lock without a key, a ship without a rudder, a binnacle without a compass, a check without a signature, a greenback without a goldback behind it?

I have referred chiefly to the medical journals, but I would include with these the reports of medical associations, and those separate publications which, coming in the form of pamphlets, heap themselves into chaotic piles and bundles which are worse than useless, taking up a great deal of room, and frightening everything away but mice and mousing antiquarians, or possibly at long intervals some terebrating specialist.

Arranged, bound, indexed, all these at once become accessible and valuable. I will take the first instance which happens to suggest itself. How many who know all about osteoblasts and the experiments of Ollier, and all that has grown out of them, know where to go for a paper by the late Dr. A. L. Peirson of Salem, published in the year 1840, under the modest title, Remarks on Fractures? And if any practitioner who has to deal with broken bones does not know that most excellent and practical essay, it is a great pity, for it answers very numerous questions which will be sure to suggest themselves to the surgeon and the patient as no one of the recent treatises, on my own shelves, at least, can do.

But if indexing is the special need of our time in medical literature, as in every department of knowledge, it must be remembered that it is not only an immense labor, but one that never ends. It requires, therefore, the cooperation of a large number of individuals to do the work, and a large amount of money to pay for making its results public through the press. When it is remembered that the catalogue of the library of the British Museum is contained in nearly three thousand large folios of manuscript, and not all its books are yet included, the task of indexing any considerable branch of science or literature looks as if it were well nigh impossible. But many hands make light work. An "Index Society" has been formed in England, already numbering about one hundred and seventy members. It aims at "supplying thorough indexes to valuable works and collections which have hitherto lacked them; at issuing indexes to the literature of special subjects; and at gathering materials for a general reference index." This society has published a little treatise setting forth the history and the art of indexing, which I trust is in the hands of some of our members, if not upon our shelves.

Something has been done in the same direction by individuals in our own country, as we have already seen. The need of it in the department of medicine is beginning to be clearly felt. Our library has already an admirable catalogue with cross references, the work of a number of its younger members cooperating in the task. A very intelligent medical student, Mr. William D. Chapin, whose excellent project is indorsed by well-known New York physicians and professors, proposes to publish a yearly index to original communications in the medical journals of the United States, classified by authors and subjects. But it is from the National Medical Library at Washington that we have the best promise and the largest expectations. That great and growing collection of fifty thousand volumes is under the eye and hand of a librarian who knows books and how to manage them. For libraries are the standing armies of civilization, and an army is but a mob without a general who can organize and marshal it so as to make it effective. The "Specimen Fasciculus of a Catalogue of the National Medical Library," prepared under the direction of Dr. Billings, the librarian, would have excited the admiration of Haller, the master scholar in medical science of the last century, or rather of the profession in all centuries, and if carried out as it is begun will be to the nineteenth all and more than all that the three Bibliothecae--Anatomica, Chirurgica, and Medicinae-Practicae-- were to the eighteenth century. I cannot forget the story that Agassiz was so fond of telling of the king of Prussia and Fichte. It was after the humiliation and spoliation of the kingdom by Napoleon that the monarch asked the philosopher what could be done to regain the lost position of the nation. "Found a great university, Sire," was the answer, and so it was that in the year 1810 the world-renowned University of Berlin came into being. I believe that we in this country can do better than found a national university, whose professors shall be nominated in caucuses, go in and out, perhaps, like postmasters, with every change of administration, and deal with science in the face of their constituency as the courtier did with time when his sovereign asked him what o'clock it was: "Whatever hour your majesty pleases." But when we have a noble library like that at Washington, and a librarian of exceptional qualifications like the gentleman who now holds that office, I believe that a liberal appropriation by Congress to carry out a conscientious work for the advancement of sound knowledge and the bettering of human conditions, like this which Dr. Billings has so well begun, would redound greatly to the honor of the nation. It ought to be willing to be at some charge to make its treasures useful to its citizens, and, for its own sake, especially to that class which has charge of health, public and private. This country abounds in what are called "self-made men," and is justly proud of many whom it thus designates. In one sense no man is self-made who breathes the air of a civilized community. In another sense every man who is anything other than a phonograph on legs is self-made. But if we award his just praise to the man who has attained any kind of excellence without having had the same advantages as others whom, nevertheless, he has equalled or surpassed, let us not be betrayed into undervaluing the mechanic's careful training to his business, the thorough and laborious education of the scholar and the professional man.

Our American atmosphere is vocal with the flippant loquacity of half knowledge. We must accept whatever good can be got out of it, and keep it under as we do sorrel and mullein and witchgrass, by enriching the soil, and sowing good seed in plenty; by good teaching and good books, rather than by wasting our time in talking against it. Half knowledge dreads nothing but whole knowledge.

I have spoken of the importance and the predominance of periodical literature, and have attempted to do justice to its value. But the almost exclusive reading of it is not without its dangers. The journals contain much that is crude and unsound; the presumption; it might be maintained, is against their novelties, unless they come from observers of established credit. Yet I have known a practitioner,--perhaps more than one,--who was as much under the dominant influence of the last article he had read in his favorite medical journal as a milliner under the sway of the last fashion-plate. The difference between green and seasoned knowledge is very great, and such practitioners never hold long enough to any of their knowledge to have it get seasoned.

It is needless to say, then, that all the substantial and permanent literature of the profession should be represented upon our shelves. Much of it is there already, and as one private library after another falls into this by the natural law of gravitation, it will gradually acquire all that is most valuable almost without effort. A scholar should not be in a hurry to part with his books. They are probably more valuable to him than they can be to any other individual. What Swedenborg called "correspondence" has established itself between his intelligence and the volumes which wall him within their sacred inclosure. Napoleon said that his mind was as if furnished with drawers,--he drew out each as he wanted its contents, and closed it at will when done with them. The scholar's mind, to use a similar comparison, is furnished with shelves, like his library. Each book knows its place in the brain as well as against the wall or in the alcove. His consciousness is doubled by the books which encircle him, as the trees that surround a lake repeat themselves in its unruffled waters. Men talk of the nerve that runs to the pocket, but one who loves his books, and has lived long with them, has a nervous filament which runs from his sensorium to every one of them. Or, if I may still let my fancy draw its pictures, a scholar's library is to him what a temple is to the worshipper who frequents it. There is the altar sacred to his holiest experiences. There is the font where his new-born thought was baptized and first had a name in his consciousness. There is the monumental tablet of a dead belief, sacred still in the memory of what it was while yet alive. No visitor can read all this on the lettered backs of the books that have gathered around the scholar, but for him, from the Aldus on the lowest shelf to the Elzevir on the highest, every volume has a language which none but he can interpret. Be patient with the book-collector who loves his companions too well to let them go. Books are not buried with their owners, and the veriest book-miser that ever lived was probably doing far more for his successors than his more liberal neighbor who despised his learned or unlearned avarice. Let the fruit fall with the leaves still clinging round it. Who would have stripped Southey's walls of the books that filled them, when, his mind no longer capable of taking in their meaning, he would still pat and fondle them with the vague loving sense of what they had once been to him,--to him, the great scholar, now like a little child among his playthings?

We need in this country not only the scholar, but the virtuoso, who hoards the treasures which he loves, it may be chiefly for their rarity and because others who know more than he does of their value set a high price upon them. As the wine of old vintages is gently decanted out of its cobwebbed bottles with their rotten corks into clean new receptacles, so the wealth of the New World is quietly emptying many of the libraries and galleries of the Old World into its newly formed collections and newly raised edifices. And this process must go on in an accelerating ratio. No Englishman will be offended if I say that before the New Zealander takes his stand on a broken arch of London Bridge to sketch the ruins of St. Paul's in the midst of a vast solitude, the treasures of the British Museum will have found a new shelter in the halls of New York or Boston. No Catholic will think hardly of my saying that before the Coliseum falls, and with it the imperial city, whose doom prophecy has linked with that of the almost eternal amphitheatre, the marbles, the bronzes, the paintings, the manuscripts of the Vatican will have left the shores of the Tiber for those of the Potomac, the Hudson, the Mississippi, or the Sacramento. And what a delight in the pursuit of the rarities which the eager book-hunter follows with the scent of a beagle!

Shall I ever forget that rainy day in Lyons, that dingy bookshop, where I found the Aetius, long missing from my Artis bledicae Principes, and where I bought for a small pecuniary consideration, though it was marked rare, and was really tres rare, the Aphorisms of Hippocrates, edited by and with a preface from the hand of Francis Rabelais? And the vellum-bound Tulpius, which I came upon in Venice, afterwards my only reading when imprisoned in quarantine at Marseilles, so that the two hundred and twenty-eight cases he has recorded are, many of them, to this day still fresh in my memory. And the Schenckius,--the folio filled with casus rariores, which had strayed in among the rubbish of the bookstall on the boulevard,--and the noble old Vesalius with its grand frontispiece not unworthy of Titian, and the fine old Ambroise Pare, long waited for even in Paris and long ago, and the colossal Spigelius with his eviscerated beauties, and Dutch Bidloo with its miracles of fine engraving and bad dissection, and Italian Mascagni, the despair of all would-be imitators, and pre-Adamite John de Ketam, and antediluvian Berengarius Carpensis,--but why multiply names, every one of which brings back the accession of a book which was an event almost like the birth of an infant?

A library like ours must exercise the largest hospitality. A great many books may be found in every large collection which remind us of those apostolic looking old men who figure on the platform at our political and other assemblages. Some of them have spoken words of wisdom in their day, but they have ceased to be oracles; some of them never had any particularly important message for humanity, but they add dignity to the meeting by their presence; they look wise, whether they are so or not, and no one grudges them their places of honor. Venerable figure-heads, what would our platforms be without you?

Just so with our libraries. Without their rows of folios in creamy vellum, or showing their black backs with antique lettering of tarnished gold, our shelves would look as insufficient and unbalanced as a column without its base, as a statue without its pedestal. And do not think they are kept only to be spanked and dusted during that dreadful period when their owner is but too thankful to become an exile and a wanderer from the scene of single combats between dead authors and living housemaids. Men were not all cowards before Agamemnon or all fools before the days of Virchow and Billroth. And apart from any practical use to be derived from the older medical authors, is there not a true pleasure in reading the accounts of great discoverers in their own words? I do not pretend to hoist up the Bibliotheca Anatomica of Mangetus and spread it on my table every day. I do not get out my great Albinus before every lecture on the muscles, nor disturb the majestic repose of Vesalius every time I speak of the bones he has so admirably described and figured. But it does please me to read the first descriptions of parts to which the names of their discoverers or those who have first described them have become so joined that not even modern science can part them; to listen to the talk of my old volume as Willis describes his circle and Fallopius his aqueduct and Varolius his bridge and Eustachius his tube and Monro his foramen,--all so well known to us in the human body; it does please me to know the very words in which Winslow described the opening which bears his name, and Glisson his capsule and De Graaf his vesicle; I am not content until I know in what language Harvey announced his discovery of the circulation, and how Spigelius made the liver his perpetual memorial, and Malpighi found a monument more enduring than brass in the corpuscles of the spleen and the kidney. But after all, the readers who care most for the early records of medical science and art are the specialists who are dividing up the practice of medicine and surgery as they were parcelled out, according to Herodotus, by the Egyptians. For them nothing is too old, nothing is too new, for to their books of all others is applicable the saying of D'Alembert that the author kills himself in lengthening out what the reader kills himself in trying to shorten.

There are practical books among these ancient volumes which can never grow old. Would you know how to recognize "male hysteria" and to treat it, take down your Sydenham; would you read the experience of a physician who was himself the subject of asthma, and who, notwithstanding that, in the words of Dr. Johnson, "panted on till ninety," you will find it in the venerable treatise of Sir John Floyer; would you listen to the story of the King's Evil cured by the royal touch, as told by a famous chirurgeon who fully believed in it, go to Wiseman; would you get at first hand the description of the spinal disease which long bore his name, do not be startled if I tell you to go to Pott,--to Percival Pott, the great surgeon of the last century.

There comes a time for every book in a library when it is wanted by somebody. It is but a few weeks since one of the most celebrated physicians in the country wrote to me from a great centre of medical education to know if I had the works of Sanctorius, which he had tried in vain to find. I could have lent him the "Medicina Statica," with its frontispiece showing Sanctorius with his dinner on the table before him, in his balanced chair which sunk with him below the level of his banquet-board when he had swallowed a certain number of ounces,--an early foreshadowing of Pettenkofer's chamber and quantitative physiology,--but the "Opera Omnia" of Sanctorius I had never met with, and I fear he had to do without it.

I would extend the hospitality of these shelves to a class of works which we are in the habit of considering as being outside of the pale of medical science, properly so called, and sometimes of coupling with a disrespectful name. Such has always been my own practice. I have welcomed Culpeper and Salmon to my bookcase as willingly as Dioscorides or Quincy, or Paris or Wood and Bache. I have found a place for St. John Long, and read the story of his trial for manslaughter with as much interest as the laurel-water case in which John Hunter figured as a witness. I would give Samuel Hahnemann a place by the side of Samuel Thomson. Am I not afraid that some student of imaginative turn and not provided with the needful cerebral strainers without which all the refuse of gimcrack intelligences gets into the mental drains and chokes them up,--am I not afraid that some such student will get hold of the "Organon" or the "Maladies Chroniques" and be won over by their delusions, and so be lost to those that love him as a man of common sense and a brother in their high calling? Not in the least. If he showed any symptoms of infection I would for once have recourse to the principle of similia similibus. To cure him of Hahnemann I would prescribe my favorite homoeopathic antidote, Okie's Bonninghausen. If that failed, I would order Grauvogl as a heroic remedy, and if he survived that uncured, I would give him my blessing, if I thought him honest, and bid him depart in peace. For me he is no longer an individual. He belongs to a class of minds which we are bound to be patient with if their Maker sees fit to indulge them with existence. We must accept the conjuring ultra-ritualist, the dreamy second adventist, the erratic spiritualist, the fantastic homoeopathist, as not unworthy of philosophic study; not more unworthy of it than the squarers of the circle and the inventors of perpetual motion, and the other whimsical visionaries to whom De

Morgan has devoted his most instructive and entertaining "Budget of Paradoxes." I hope, therefore, that our library will admit the works of the so-called Eclectics, of the Thomsonians, if any are in existence, of the Clairvoyants, if they have a literature, and especially of the Homoeopathists. This country seems to be the place for such a collection, which will by and by be curious and of more value than at present, for Homoeopathy seems to be following the pathological law of erysipelas, fading out where it originated as it spreads to new regions. At least I judge so by the following translated extract from a criticism of an American work in the "Homoeopatische Rundschau" of Leipzig for October, 1878, which I find in the "Homoeopathic Bulletin" for the month of November just passed: "While we feel proud of the spread and rise of Homoeopathy across the ocean, and while the Homoeopathic works reaching us from there, and published in a style such as is unknown in Germany, bear eloquent testimony to the eminent activity of our transatlantic colleagues, we are overcome by sorrowful regrets at the position Homoeopathy occupies in Germany. Such a work [as the American one referred to] with us would be impossible; it would lack the necessary support."

By all means let our library secure a good representation of the literature of Homoeopathy before it leaves us its "sorrowful regrets" and migrates with its sugar of milk pellets, which have taken the place of the old pilulae micae panis, to Alaska, to "Nova Zembla, or the Lord knows where."

What shall I say in this presence of the duties of a Librarian? Where have they ever been better performed than in our own public city library, where the late Mr. Jewett and the living Mr. Winsor have shown us what a librarian ought to be,--the organizing head, the vigilant guardian, the seeker's index, the scholar's counsellor? His work is not merely that of administration, manifold and laborious as its duties are. He must have a quick intelligence and a retentive memory. He is a public carrier of knowledge in its germs. His office is like that which naturalists attribute to the bumble-bee,--he lays up little honey for himself, but he conveys the fertilizing pollen from flower to flower. Our undertaking, just completed,--and just begun--has come at the right time, not a day too soon. Our practitioners need a library like this, for with all their skill and devotion there is too little genuine erudition, such as a liberal profession ought to be able to claim for many of its members. In reading the recent obituary notices of the late Dr. Geddings of South Carolina, I recalled what our lamented friend Dr. Coale used to tell me of his learning and accomplishments, and I could not help reflecting how few such medical scholars we had to show in Boston or New England. We must clear up this unilluminated atmosphere, and here,--here is the true electric light which will irradiate its darkness.

The public will catch the rays reflected from the same source of light, and it needs instruction on the great subjects of health and disease,--needs it sadly. It is preyed upon by every kind of imposition almost without hindrance. Its ignorance and prejudices react upon the profession to the great injury of both. The jealous feeling, for instance, with regard to such provisions for the study of anatomy as are sanctioned by the laws in this State and carried out with strict regard to those laws, threatens the welfare, if not the existence of institutions for medical instruction wherever it is not held in check by enlightened intelligence. And on the other hand the profession has just been startled by a verdict against a physician, ruinous in its amount,--enough to drive many a hard-working young practitioner out of house and home,--a verdict which leads to the fear that suits for malpractice may take the place of the panel game and child-stealing as a means of extorting money. If the profession in this State, which claims a high standard of civilization, is to be crushed and ground beneath the upper millstone of the dearth of educational advantages and the lower millstone of ruinous penalties for what the ignorant ignorantly shall decide to be ignorance, all I can say is

God save the Commonhealth of Massachusetts!

Once more, we cannot fail to see that just as astrology has given place to astronomy, so theology, the science of Him whom by searching no man can find out, is fast being replaced by what we may not improperly call theonomy, or the science of the laws according to which the Creator acts. And since these laws find their fullest manifestations for us, at least, in rational human natures, the study of anthropology is largely replacing that of scholastic divinity. We must contemplate our Maker indirectly in human attributes as we talk of Him in human parts of speech. And this gives a sacredness to the study of man in his physical, mental, moral, social, and religious nature which elevates the faithful students of anthropology to the dignity of a priesthood, and sheds a holy light on the recorded results of their labors, brought together as they are in such a collection as this which is now spread out before us.

Thus, then, our library is a temple as truly as the dome-crowned cathedral hallowed by the breath of prayer and praise, where the dead repose and the living worship. May it, with all its treasures, be consecrated like that to the glory of God, through the contributions it shall make to the advancement of sound knowledge, to the relief of human suffering, to the promotion of harmonious relations between the members of the two noble professions which deal with the diseases of the soul and with those of the body, and to the common cause in which all good men are working, the furtherance of the well-being of their fellow-creatures!

NOTE.--As an illustration of the statement in the last paragraph but one, I take the following notice from the "Boston Daily Advertiser," of December 4th, the day after the delivery of the address: "Prince Lucien Bonaparte is now living in London, and is devoting himself to the work of collecting the creeds of all religions and sects, with a view to their classification,--his object being simply scientific or anthropological."

Since delivering the address, also, I find a leading article in the "Cincinnati Lancet and Clinic" of November 30th, headed "The Decadence of Homoeopathy," abundantly illustrated by extracts from the "Homoeopathic Times," the leading American organ of that sect.

In the New York "Medical Record" of the same date, which I had not seen before the delivery of my address, is an account of the action of the Homoeopathic Medical Society of Northern New York, in which Hahnemann's theory of "dynamization" is characterized in a formal resolve as "unworthy the confidence of the Homoeopathic profession."

It will be a disappointment to the German Homoeopathists to read in the "Homoeopathic Times" such a statement as the following: "Whatever the influences have been which have checked the outward development of Homoeopathy, it is plainly evident that the Homoeopathic school, as regards the number of its openly avowed representatives, has attained its majority, and has begun to decline both in this country and in England."

All which is an additional reason for making a collection of the incredibly curious literature of Homoeopathy before that pseudological inanity has faded out like so many other delusions.

SOME OF MY EARLY TEACHERS

[A Farewell Address to the Medical School of Harvard University, November 28, 1882.]

I had intended that the recitation of Friday last should be followed by a few parting words to my class and any friends who might happen to be in the lecture-room. But I learned on the preceding evening that there was an expectation, a desire, that my farewell should take a somewhat different form; and not to disappoint the wishes of those whom I was anxious to gratify, I made up my mind to appear before you with such hasty preparation as the scanty time admitted.

There are three occasions upon which a human being has a right to consider himself as a centre of interest to those about him: when he is christened, when he is married, and when he is buried. Every one is the chief personage, the hero, of his own baptism, his own wedding, and his own funeral.

There are other occasions, less momentous, in which one may make more of himself than under ordinary circumstances he would think it proper to do; when he may talk about himself, and tell his own experiences, in fact, indulge in a more or less egotistic monologue without fear or reproach.

I think I may claim that this is one of those occasions. I have delivered my last anatomical lecture and heard my class recite for the last time. They wish to hear from me again in a less scholastic mood than that in which they have known me. Will you not indulge me in telling you something of my own story?

This is the thirty-sixth Course of Lectures in which I have taken my place and performed my duties as Professor of Anatomy. For more than half of my term of office I gave instruction in Physiology, after the fashion of my predecessors and in the manner then generally prevalent in our schools, where the physiological laboratory was not a necessary part of the apparatus of instruction. It was with my hearty approval that the teaching of Physiology was constituted a separate department and made an independent Professorship. Before my time, Dr. Warren had taught Anatomy, Physiology, and Surgery in the same course of Lectures, lasting only three or four months. As the boundaries of science are enlarged, new divisions and subdivisions of its territories become necessary. In the place of six Professors in 1847, when I first became a member of the Faculty, I count twelve upon the Catalogue before me, and I find the whole number engaged in the work of instruction in the Medical School amounts to no less than fifty.

Since I began teaching in this school, the aspect of many branches of science has undergone a very remarkable transformation. Chemistry and Physiology are no longer what they were, as taught by the instructors of that time. We are looking forward to the synthesis of new organic compounds; our artificial madder is already in the market, and the indigo-raisers are now fearing that their crop will be supplanted by the manufactured article. In the living body we talk of fuel supplied and work done, in movement, in heat, just as if we were dealing with a machine of our own contrivance.

A physiological laboratory of to-day is equipped with instruments of research of such ingenious contrivance, such elaborate construction, that one might suppose himself in a workshop where some exquisite fabric was to be wrought, such as Queens love to wear, and Kings do not always love to pay for. They are, indeed, weaving a charmed web, for these are the looms from which comes the knowledge that clothes the nakedness of the intellect. Here are the mills that grind food for its hunger, and "is not the life more than meat, and the body than raiment?"

But while many of the sciences have so changed that the teachers of the past would hardly know them, it has not been so with the branch I teach, or, rather, with that division of it which is chiefly taught in this amphitheatre. General anatomy, or histology, on the other hand, is almost all new; it has grown up, mainly, since I began my medical studies. I never saw a compound microscope during my years of study in Paris. Individuals had begun to use the instrument, but I never heard it alluded to by either Professors or students. In descriptive anatomy I have found little to unlearn, and not a great deal that was both new and important to learn. Trifling additions are made from year to year, not to be despised and not to be overvalued. Some of the older anatomical works are still admirable, some of the newer ones very much the contrary. I have had recent anatomical plates brought me for inspection, and I have actually button-holed the book-agent, a being commonly as hard to get rid of as the tar-baby in the negro legend, that I might put him to shame with the imperial illustrations of the bones and muscles in the great folio of Albinus, published in 1747, and the unapproached figures of the lymphatic system of Mascagni, now within a very few years of a century old, and still copied, or, rather, pretended to be copied, in the most recent works on anatomy.

I am afraid that it is a good plan to get rid of old Professors, and I am thankful to hear that there is a movement for making provision for those who are left in need when they lose their offices and their salaries. I remember one of our ancient Cambridge Doctors once asked me to get into his rickety chaise, and said to me, half humorously, half sadly, that he was like an old horse,--they had taken off his saddle and turned him out to pasture. I fear the grass was pretty short where that old servant of the public found himself grazing. If I myself needed an apology for holding my office so long, I should find it in the fact that human anatomy is much the same study that it was in the days of Vesalius and Fallopius, and that the greater part of my teaching was of such a nature that it could never become antiquated.

Let me begin with my first experience as a medical student. I had come from the lessons of Judge Story and Mr. Ashmun in the Law School at Cambridge. I had been busy, more or less, with the pages of Blackstone and Chitty, and other textbooks of the first year of legal study. More or less, I say, but I am afraid it was less rather than more. For during that year I first tasted the intoxicating pleasure of authorship. A college periodical, conducted by friends of mine, still undergraduates, tempted me into print, and there is no form of lead-poisoning which more rapidly and thoroughly pervades the blood and bones and marrow than that which reaches the young author through mental contact with type-metal. Qui a bu, boira,--he who has once been a drinker will drink again, says the French proverb. So the man or woman who has tasted type is sure to return to his old indulgence sooner or later. In that fatal year I had my first attack of authors' lead-poisoning, and I have never got quite rid of it from that day to this. But for that I might have applied myself more diligently to my legal studies, and carried a green bag in place of a stethoscope and a thermometer up to the present day.

What determined me to give up Law and apply myself to Medicine I can hardly say, but I had from the first looked upon that year's study as an experiment. At any rate, I made the change, and soon found myself introduced to new scenes and new companionships.

I can scarcely credit my memory when I recall the first impressions produced upon me by sights afterwards become so familiar that they could no more disturb a pulse-beat than the commonest of every-day experiences. The skeleton, hung aloft like a gibbeted criminal, looked grimly at me as I entered the room devoted to the students of the school I had joined, just as the fleshless figure of Time, with the hour-glass and scythe, used to glare upon me in my childhood from the "New England Primer." The white faces in the beds at the Hospital found their reflection in my own cheeks, which lost their color as I looked upon them. All this had to pass away in a little time; I had chosen my profession, and must meet its painful and repulsive aspects until they lost their power over my sensibilities.

The private medical school which I had joined was one established by Dr. James Jackson, Dr. Walter Channing, Dr. John Ware, Dr. Winslow Lewis, and Dr. George W. Otis. Of the first three gentlemen I have either spoken elsewhere or may find occasion to speak hereafter. The two younger members of this association of teachers were both graduates of our University, one of the year 1819, the other of 1818.

Dr. Lewis was a great favorite with students. He was a man of very lively temperament, fond of old books and young people, open-hearted, free-spoken, an enthusiast in teaching, and especially at home in that apartment of the temple of science where nature is seen in undress, the anthropotomic laboratory, known to common speech as the dissecting-room. He had that quality which is the special gift of the man born for a teacher,--the power of exciting an interest in that which he taught. While he was present the apartment I speak of was the sunniest of studios in spite of its mortuary spectacles. Of the students I met there I best remember James Jackson, Junior, full of zeal and playful as a boy, a young man whose early death was a calamity to the profession of which he promised to be a chief ornament; the late Reverend J. S. C. Greene, who, as the prefix to his name signifies, afterwards changed his profession, but one of whose dissections I remember looking upon with admiration; and my friend Mr. Charles Amory, as we call him, Dr. Charles Amory, as he is entitled to be called, then, as now and always, a favorite with all about him. He had come to us from the schools of Germany, and brought with him recollections of the teachings of Blumenbach and the elder Langenbeck, father of him whose portrait hangs in our Museum. Dr. Lewis was our companion as well as our teacher. A good demonstrator is,--I will not say as important as a good Professor in the teaching of Anatomy, because I am not sure that he is not more important. He comes into direct personal relations with the students,--he is one of them, in fact, as the Professor cannot be from the nature of his duties. The Professor's chair is an insulating stool, so to speak; his age, his knowledge, real or supposed, his official station, are like the glass legs which support the electrician's piece of furniture, and cut it off from the common currents of the floor upon which it stands. Dr. Lewis enjoyed teaching and made his students enjoy being taught. He delighted in those anatomical conundrums to answer which keeps the student's eyes open and his wits awake. He was happy as he dexterously performed the tour de maitre of the old barber-surgeons, or applied the spica bandage and taught his scholars to do it, so neatly and symmetrically that the aesthetic missionary from the older centre of civilization would bend over it in blissful contemplation, as if it were a sunflower. Dr. Lewis had many other tastes, and was a favorite, not only with students, but in a wide circle, professional, antiquarian, masonic, and social.

Dr. Otis was less widely known, but was a fluent and agreeable lecturer, and esteemed as a good surgeon.

I must content myself with this glimpse at myself and a few of my fellow-students in Boston. After attending two courses of Lectures in the school of the University, I went to Europe to continue my studies.

You may like to hear something of the famous Professors of Paris in the days when I was a student in the Ecole de Medicine, and following the great Hospital teachers.

I can hardly believe my own memory when I recall the old practitioners and Professors who were still going round the hospitals when I mingled with the train of students that attended the morning visits. See that bent old man who is groping his way through the wards of La Charity. That is the famous Baron Boyer, author of the great work on surgery in nine volumes, a writer whose clearness of style commends his treatise to general admiration, and makes it a kind of classic. He slashes away at a terrible rate, they say, when he gets hold of the subject of fistula in its most frequent habitat,--but I never saw him do more than look as if he wanted to cut a good dollop out of a patient he was examining. The short, square, substantial man with iron-gray hair, ruddy face, and white apron is Baron Larrey, Napoleon's favorite surgeon, the most honest man he ever saw,--it is reputed that he called him. To go round the Hotel des Invalides with Larrey was to live over the campaigns of Napoleon, to look on the sun of Austerlitz, to hear the cannons of Marengo, to struggle through the icy waters of the Beresina, to shiver in the snows of the Russian retreat, and to gaze through the battle smoke upon the last charge of the red lancers on the redder field of Waterloo. Larrey was still strong and sturdy as I saw him, and few portraits remain printed in livelier colors on the tablet of my memory.

Leave the little group of students which gathers about Larrey beneath the gilded dome of the Invalides and follow me to the Hotel Dieu, where rules and reigns the master-surgeon of his day, at least so far as Paris and France are concerned,-- the illustrious Baron Dupuytren. No man disputed his reign, some envied his supremacy. Lisfranc shrugged his shoulders as he spoke of "ce grand homme de l'autre cots de la riviere," that great man on the other side of the river, but the great man he remained, until he bowed before the mandate which none may disobey. "Three times," said Bouillaud, "did the apoplectic thunderbolt fall on that robust brain,"-- it yielded at last as the old bald cliff that is riven and crashes down into the valley. I saw him before the first thunderbolt had descended: a square, solid man, with a high and full-domed head, oracular in his utterances, indifferent to those around him, sometimes, it was said, very rough with them. He spoke in low, even tones, with quiet fluency, and was listened to with that hush of rapt attention which I have hardly seen in any circle of listeners unless when such men as ex-President John Quincy Adams or Daniel Webster were the speakers. I do not think that Dupuytren has left a record which explains his influence, but in point of fact he dominated those around him in a remarkable manner. You must have all witnessed something of the same kind. The personal presence of some men carries command with it, and their accents silence the crowd around them, when the same words from other lips might fall comparatively unheeded.

As for Lisfranc, I can say little more of him than that he was a great drawer of blood and hewer of members. I remember his ordering a wholesale bleeding of his patients, right and left, whatever might be the matter with them, one morning when a phlebotomizing fit was on him. I recollect his regretting the splendid guardsmen of the old Empire,--for what? because they had such magnificent thighs to amputate. I got along about as far as that with him, when I ceased to be a follower of M. Lisfranc.

The name of Velpeau must have reached many of you, for he died in 1867, and his many works made his name widely known. Coming to Paris in wooden shoes, starving, almost, at first, he raised himself to great eminence as a surgeon and as an author, and at last obtained the Professorship to which his talents and learning entitled him. His example may be an encouragement to some of my younger hearers who are born, not with the silver spoon in their mouths, but with the two-tined iron fork in their hands. It is a poor thing to take up their milk porridge with in their young days, but in after years it will often transfix the solid dumplings that roll out of the silver spoon. So Velpeau found it. He had not what is called genius, he was far from prepossessing in aspect, looking as if he might have wielded the sledge-hammer (as I think he had done in early life) rather than the lancet, but he had industry, determination, intelligence, character, and he made his way to distinction and prosperity, as some of you sitting on these benches and wondering anxiously what is to become of you in the struggle for life will have done before the twentieth century has got halfway through its first quarter. A good sound head over a pair of wooden shoes is a great deal better than a wooden head belonging to an owner who cases his feet in calf-skin, but a good brain is not enough without a stout heart to fill the four great conduits which carry at once fuel and fire to that mightiest of engines.

How many of you who are before me are familiarly acquainted with the name of Broussais, or even with that of Andral? Both were lecturing at the Ecole de Medicine, and I often heard them. Broussais was in those days like an old volcano, which has pretty nearly used up its fire and brimstone, but is still boiling and bubbling in its interior, and now and then sends up a spirt of lava and a volley of pebbles. His theories of gastro-enteritis, of irritation and inflammation as the cause of disease, and the practice which sprang from them, ran over the fields of medicine for a time like flame over the grass of the prairies. The way in which that knotty-featured, savage old man would bring out the word irritation--with rattling and rolling reduplication of the resonant letter r--might have taught a lesson in articulation to

Salvini. But Broussais's theory was languishing and well-nigh become obsolete, and this, no doubt, added vehemence to his defence of his cherished dogmas.

Old theories, and old men who cling to them, must take themselves out of the way as the new generation with its fresh thoughts and altered habits of mind comes forward to take the place of that which is dying out. This was a truth which the fiery old theorist found it very hard to learn, and harder to bear, as it was forced upon him. For the hour of his lecture was succeeded by that of a younger and far more popular professor. As his lecture drew towards its close, the benches, thinly sprinkled with students, began to fill up; the doors creaked open and banged back oftener and oftener, until at last the sound grew almost continuous, and the voice of the lecturer became a leonine growl as he strove in vain to be heard over the noise of doors and footsteps.

Broussais was now sixty-two years old. The new generation had outgrown his doctrines, and the Professor for whose hour the benches had filled themselves belonged to that new generation. Gabriel Andral was little more than half the age of Broussais, in the full prime and vigor of manhood at thirty-seven years. He was a rapid, fluent, fervid, and imaginative speaker, pleasing in aspect and manner,--a strong contrast to the harsh, vituperative old man who had just preceded him. His Clinique Medicale is still valuable as a collection of cases, and his researches on the blood, conducted in association with Gavarret, contributed new and valuable facts to science. But I remember him chiefly as one of those instructors whose natural eloquence made it delightful to listen to him. I doubt if I or my fellow-students did full justice either to him or to the famous physician of Hotel Dieu, Chomel. We had addicted ourselves almost too closely to the words of another master, by whom we were ready to swear as against all teachers that ever were or ever would be.

This object of our reverence, I might almost say idolatry, was one whose name is well known to most of the young men before me, even to those who may know comparatively little of his works and teachings. Pierre Charles Alexandre Louis, at the age of forty-seven, as I recall him, was a tall, rather spare, dignified personage, of serene and grave aspect, but with a pleasant smile and kindly voice for the student with whom he came into personal relations. If I summed up the lessons of Louis in two expressions, they would be these; I do not hold him answerable for the words, but I will condense them after my own fashion in French, and then give them to you, expanded somewhat, in English:

Formez toujours des idees nettes.
Fuyez toujours les a peu pres.

Always make sure that you form a distinct and clear idea of the matter you are considering.

Always avoid vague approximations where exact estimates are possible; about so many,--about so much, instead of the precise number and quantity.

Now, if there is anything on which the biological sciences have prided themselves in these latter years it is the substitution of quantitative for qualitative formulae. The "numerical system," of which Louis was the great advocate, if not the absolute originator, was an attempt to substitute series of carefully recorded facts, rigidly counted and closely compared, for those never-ending records of vague, unverifiable conclusions with which the classics of the healing art were overloaded. The history of practical medicine had been like the story of the Danaides. "Experience" had been, from time immemorial, pouring its flowing treasures into buckets full of holes. At the existing rate of supply and leakage they would never be filled; nothing would ever be settled in medicine. But cases thoroughly recorded and mathematically analyzed would always be available for future use, and when accumulated in sufficient number would lead to results which would be trustworthy, and belong to science.

You young men who are following the hospitals hardly know how much you are indebted to Louis. I say nothing of his Researches on Phthisis or his great work on Typhoid Fever. But I consider his modest and brief Essay on Bleeding in some Inflammatory Diseases, based on cases carefully observed and numerically analyzed, one of the most important written contributions to practical medicine, to the treatment of internal disease, of this century, if not since the days of Sydenham. The lancet was the magician's wand of the dark ages of medicine. The old physicians not only believed in its general efficacy as a wonder-worker in disease, but they believed that each malady could be successfully attacked from some special part of the body,--the strategic point which commanded the seat of the morbid affection. On a figure given in the curious old work of John de Ketam, no less than thirty-eight separate places are marked as the proper ones to bleed from, in different diseases. Even Louis, who had not wholly given up venesection, used now and then to order that a patient suffering from headache should be bled in the foot, in preference to any other part.

But what Louis did was this: he showed by a strict analysis of numerous cases that bleeding did not strangle,--jugulate was the word then used,--acute diseases, more especially pneumonia. This was not a reform,--it was a revolution. It was followed up in this country by the remarkable Discourse of Dr. Jacob Bigelow upon Self-Limited Diseases, which has, I believe, done more than any other work or essay in our own language to rescue the practice of medicine from the slavery to the drugging system which was a part of the inheritance of the profession.

Yes, I say, as I look back on the long hours of the many days I spent in the wards and in the autopsy room of La Pitie, where Louis was one of the attending physicians,--yes, Louis did a great work for practical medicine. Modest in the presence of nature, fearless in the face of authority, unwearying in the pursuit of truth, he was a man whom any student might be happy and proud to claim as his teacher and his friend, and yet, as I look back on the days when I followed his teachings, I feel that I gave myself up too exclusively to his methods of thought and study.

There is one part of their business which certain medical practitioners are too apt to forget; namely, that what they should most of all try to do is to ward off disease, to alleviate suffering, to preserve life, or at least to prolong it if possible. It is not of the slightest interest to the patient to know whether three or three and a quarter cubic inches of his lung are hepatized. His mind is not occupied with thinking of the curious problems which are to be solved by his own autopsy,--whether this or that strand of the spinal marrow is the seat of this or that form of degeneration. He wants something to relieve his pain, to mitigate the anguish of dyspnea, to bring back motion and sensibility to the dead limb, to still the tortures of neuralgia. What is it to him that you can localize and name by some uncouth term the disease which you could not prevent and which you cannot cure? An old woman who knows how to make a poultice and how to put it on, and does it tuto, eito, jucunde, just when and where it is wanted, is better,--a thousand times better in many cases,--than a staring pathologist, who explores and thumps and doubts and guesses, and tells his patient be will be better tomorrow, and so goes home to tumble his books over and make out a diagnosis.

But in those days, I, like most of my fellow students, was thinking much more of "science" than of practical medicine, and I believe if we had not clung so closely to the skirts of Louis and had followed some of the courses of men like Trousseau,--therapeutists, who gave special attention to curative methods, and not chiefly to diagnosis,--it would have been better for me and others. One thing, at any rate, we did learn in the wards of Louis. We learned that a very large proportion of diseases get well of themselves, without any special medication,--the great fact formulated, enforced, and popularized by Dr. Jacob Bigelow in the Discourse referred to. We unlearned the habit of drugging for its own sake. This detestable practice, which I was almost proscribed for condemning somewhat too epigrammatically a little more than twenty years ago, came to us, I suspect, in a considerable measure from the English "general practitioners," a sort of prescribing apothecaries. You remember how, when the city was besieged, each artisan who was called upon in council to suggest the best means of defence recommended the articles he dealt in: the carpenter, wood; the blacksmith, iron; the mason, brick; until it came to be a puzzle to know which to adopt. Then the shoemaker said, "Hang your walls with new boots," and gave good reasons why these should be the best of all possible defences. Now the "general practitioner" charged, as I understand, for his medicine, and in that way got paid for his visit. Wherever this is the practice, medicine is sure to become a trade, and the people learn to expect drugging, and to consider it necessary, because drugs are so universally given to the patients of the man who gets his living by them.

It was something to have unlearned the pernicious habit of constantly giving poisons to a patient, as if they were good in themselves, of drawing off the blood which he would want in his struggle with disease, of making him sore and wretched with needless blisters, of turning his stomach with unnecessary nauseous draught and mixtures,--only because he was sick and something must be done. But there were positive as well as negative facts to be learned, and some of us, I fear, came home rich in the negatives of the expectant practice, poor in the resources which many a plain country practitioner had ready in abundance for the relief and the cure of disease. No one instructor can be expected to do all for a student which he requires. Louis taught us who followed him the love of truth, the habit of passionless listening to the teachings of nature, the most careful and searching methods of observation, and the sure means of getting at the results to be obtained from them in the constant employment of accurate tabulation. He was not a showy, or eloquent, or, I should say, a very generally popular man, though the favorite, almost the idol, of many students, especially Genevese and Bostonians. But he was a man of lofty and admirable scientific character, and his work will endure in its influences long after his name is lost sight of save to the faded eyes of the student of medical literature.

Many other names of men more or less famous in their day, and who were teaching while I was in Paris, come up before me. They are but empty sounds for the most part in the ears of persons of not more than middle age. Who of you knows anything of Richerand, author of a very popular work on Physiology, commonly put into the student's hands when I first began to ask for medical text-books? I heard him lecture once, and have had his image with me ever since as that of an old, worn-out man,--a venerable but dilapidated relic of an effete antiquity. To verify this impression I have just looked out the dates of his birth and death, and find that he was eighteen years younger than the speaker who is now addressing you. There is a terrible parallax between the period before thirty and that after threescore and ten, as two men of those ages look, one with naked eyes, one through his spectacles, at the man of fifty and thereabout. Magendie, I doubt not you have all heard of. I attended but one of his lectures. I question if one here, unless some contemporary of my own has strayed into the amphitheatre,--knows anything about Marjolin. I remember two things about his lectures on surgery, the deep tones of his voice as he referred to his oracle,--the earlier writer, Jean Louis Petit,--and his formidable snuffbox. What he taught me lies far down, I doubt not, among the roots of my knowledge, but it does not flower out in any noticeable blossoms, or offer me any very obvious fruits. Where now is the fame of Bouillaud, Professor and Deputy, the Sangrado of his time? Where is the renown of Piorry, percussionist and poet, expert alike in the resonances of the thoracic cavity and those of the rhyming vocabulary?--I think life has not yet done with the vivacious Ricord, whom I remember calling the Voltaire of pelvic literature,--a sceptic as to the morality of the race in general, who would have submitted Diana to treatment with his mineral specifics, and ordered a course of blue pills for the vestal virgins.

Ricord was born at the beginning of the century, and Piorry some years earlier. Cruveilhier, who died in 1874, is still remembered by his great work on pathological anatomy; his work on descriptive anatomy has some things which I look in vain for elsewhere. But where is Civiale,--where are Orfila, Gendrin, Rostan, Biett, Alibert,--jolly old Baron Alibert, whom I remember so well in his broad-brimmed hat, worn a little jauntily on one side, calling out to the students in the court-yard of the Hospital St. Louis, "Enfans de la methode naturelle, etes-vous tous ici?" "Children of the natural method [his own method of classification of skin diseases,] are you all here?" All here, then, perhaps; all where, now?

My show of ghosts is over. It is always the same story that old men tell to younger ones, some few of whom will in their turn repeat the tale, only with altered names, to their children's children.

> Like phantoms painted on the magic slide,
> Forth from the darkness of the past we glide,
> As living shadows for a moment seen
> In airy pageant on the eternal screen,
> Traced by a ray from one unchanging flame,
> Then seek the dust and stillness whence we came.

Dr. Benjamin Waterhouse, whom I well remember, came back from Leyden, where he had written his Latin graduating thesis, talking of the learned Gaubius and the late illustrious Boerhaave and other dead Dutchmen, of whom you know as much, most of you, as you do of Noah's apothecary and the family physician of Methuselah, whose prescriptions seem to have been lost to posterity. Dr. Lloyd came back to Boston full of the teachings of Cheselden and Sharpe, William Hunter, Smellie, and Warner; Dr. James Jackson loved to tell of Mr. Cline and to talk of Mr. John Hunter; Dr. Reynolds would give you his recollections of Sir Astley Cooper and Mr. Abernethy; I have named the famous Frenchmen of my student days; Leyden, Edinburgh, London, Paris, were each in turn the Mecca of medical students, just as at the present day Vienna and Berlin are the centres where our young men crowd for instruction. These also must sooner or later yield their precedence and pass the torch they hold to other hands. Where shall it next flame at the head of the long procession? Shall it find its old place on the shores of the Gulf of Salerno, or shall it mingle its rays with the northern aurora up among the fiords of Norway,--or shall it be borne across the Atlantic and reach the banks of the Charles, where Agassiz and Wyman have taught, where Hagen still teaches, glowing like his own Lampyris splendidula, with enthusiasm, where the first of American botanists and the ablest of American surgeons are still counted in the roll of honor of our great University?

Let me add a few words which shall not be other than cheerful, as I bid farewell to this edifice which I have known so long. I am grateful to the roof which has sheltered me, to the floors which have sustained me, though I have thought it safest always to abstain from anything like eloquence, lest a burst of too emphatic applause might land my class and myself in the cellar of the collapsing structure, and bury us in the fate of Korah, Dathan, and Abiram. I have helped to wear these stairs into hollows,--stairs which I trod when they were smooth and level, fresh from the plane. There are just thirty-two of them, as there were five and thirty years ago, but they are steeper and harder to climb, it seems to me, than they were then. I remember that in the early youth of this building, the late Dr. John K. Mitchell, father of our famous Dr. Weir Mitchell, said to me as we came out of the Demonstrator's room, that some day or other a whole class would go heels over head down this graded precipice, like the herd told of in Scripture story. This has never happened as yet; I trust it never will. I have never been proud of the apartment beneath the seats, in which my preparations for lecture were made. But I chose it because I could have it to myself, and I resign it, with a wish that it were more worthy of regret, into the hands of my successor, with my parting benediction. Within its twilight precincts I have often prayed for light, like Ajax, for the daylight found scanty entrance, and the gaslight never illuminated its dark recesses. May it prove to him who comes after me like the cave of the Sibyl, out of the gloomy depths of which came the oracles which shone with the rays of truth and wisdom!

This temple of learning is not surrounded by the mansions of the great and the wealthy. No stately avenues lead up to its facades and porticoes. I have sometimes felt, when convoying a distinguished stranger through its precincts to its door, that he might question whether star-eyed Science had not missed her way when she found herself in this not too attractive locality. I cannot regret that we--you, I should say--are soon to migrate to a more favored region, and carry on your work as teachers and as learners in ampler halls and under far more favorable conditions.

I hope that I may have the privilege of meeting you there, possibly may be allowed to add my words of welcome to those of my former colleagues, and in that pleasing anticipation I bid good-by to this scene of my long labors, and, for the present at least, to the friends with whom I have been associated.

APPENDUM

NOTES TO THE ADDRESS ON CURRENTS AND COUNTER CURRENTS IN MEDICAL SCIENCE.

Some passages contained in the original manuscript of the Address, and omitted in the delivery on account of its length, are restored in the text or incorporated with these Notes.

NOTE A.--

There is good reason to doubt whether the nitrate of silver has any real efficacy in epilepsy. It has seemed to cure many cases, but epilepsy is a very uncertain disease, and there is hardly anything which has not been supposed to cure it. Dr. Copland cites many authorities in its favor, most especially Lombard's cases. But De la Berge and Monneret (Comp. de Med. Paris), 1839, analyze these same cases, eleven in number, and can only draw the inference of a very questionable value in the supposed remedy. Dr. James Jackson says that relief of epilepsy is not to be attained by any medicine with which he is acquainted, but by diet. (Letters to a Young Physician, p. 67.) Guy Patin, Dean of the Faculty of Paris, Professor at the Royal College, Author of the Antimonial Martyrology, a wit and a man of sense and learning, who died almost two hundred years ago, had come to the same conclusion, though the chemists of his time boasted of their remedies. "Did, you ever see a case of epilepsy cured by nitrate of silver?" I said to one of the oldest and most experienced surgeons in this country. "Never," was his instant reply. Dr. Twitchell's experience was very similar. How, then, did nitrate of silver come to be given for epilepsy? Because, as Dr. Martin has so well reminded us, lunatics were considered formerly to be under the special influence of Luna, the moon (which Esquirol, be it observed, utterly denies), and lunar caustic, or nitrate of silver, is a salt of that metal which was called luna from its whiteness, and of course must be in the closest relations with the moon. It follows beyond all reasonable question that the moon's metal, silver, and its preparations, must be the specific remedy for moonblasted maniacs and epileptics!

Yet the practitioner who prescribes the nitrate of silver supposes he is guided by the solemn experience of the past, instead of by its idle fancies. He laughs at those old physicians who placed such confidence in the right hind hoof of an elk as a remedy for the same disease, and leaves the record of his own belief in a treatment quite as fanciful and far more objectionable, written in indelible ink upon a living tablet where he who runs may read it for a whole generation, if nature spares his walking advertisement so long.

NOTE B.--

The presumption that a man is innocent until he is proved guilty, does not mean that there are no rogues, but lays the onus probandi on the party to which it properly belongs. So with this proposition. A noxious agent should never be employed in sickness unless there is ample evidence in the particular case to overcome the general presumption against all such agents, and the evidence is very apt to be defective.

The miserable delusion of Homoeopathy builds itself upon an axiom directly the opposite of this; namely, that the sick are to be cured by poisons. Similia similibus curantur means exactly this. It is simply a theory of universal poisoning, nullified in practice by the infinitesimal contrivance. The only way to kill it and all similar fancies, and to throw every quack nostrum into discredit, is to root out completely the suckers of the old rotten superstition that whatever is odious or noxious is likely to be good for disease. The current of sound practice with ourselves is, I believe, setting fast in the direction I have indicated in the above proposition. To uphold the exhibition of noxious agents in disease, as the rule, instead of admitting them cautiously and reluctantly as the exception, is, as I think, an eddy of opinion in the direction of the barbarism out of which we believe our art is escaping. It is only through the enlightened sentiment and action of the Medical Profession that the community can be brought to acknowledge that drugs should always be regarded as evils.

It is true that some suppose, and our scientific and thoughtful associate, Dr. Gould, has half countenanced the opinion, that there may yet be discovered a specific for every disease. Let us not despair of the future, but let us be moderate in our expectations. When an oil is discovered that will make a bad watch keep good time; when a recipe is given which will turn an acephalous foetus into a promising child; when a man can enter the second time into his mother's womb and give her back the infirmities which twenty generations have stirred into her blood, and infused into his own through hers, we may be prepared to enlarge the National Pharmacopoeia with a list of specifics for everything but old age,--and possibly for that also.

NOTE C.--

The term specific is used here in its ordinary sense, without raising the question of the propriety of its application to these or other remedies.

The credit of introducing Cinchona rests between the Jesuits, the Countess of Chinchon, the Cardinal de Lugo, and Sir Robert Talbor, who employed it as a secret remedy. (Pereira.) Mercury as an internal specific remedy was brought into use by that impudent and presumptuous quack, as he was considered, Paracelsus. (Encyc. Brit. art. "Paracelsus.") Arsenic was introduced into England as a remedy for intermittents by Dr. Fowler, in consequence of the success of a patent medicine, the Tasteless Ague Drops, which were supposed, "probably with reason," to be a preparation of that mineral. (Rees's Cyc. art. "Arsenic.") Colchicum came into notice in a similar way, from the success of the Eau Medicinale of M. Husson, a French military officer. (Pereira.) Iodine was discovered by a saltpetre manufacturer, but applied by a physician in place of the old remedy, burnt sponge, which seems to owe its efficacy to it. (Dunglison, New Remedies.) As for Sulphur, "the common people have long used it as an ointment" for scabies. (Rees's Cyc. art. "Scabies.") The modern cantiscorbutic regimen is credited to Captain Cook. "To his sagacity we are indebted for the first impulse to those regulations by which scorbutus is so successfully prevented in our navy." (Lond. Cyc. Prac. Med. art. "Scorbutus.") Iron and various salts which enter into the normal composition of the human body do not belong to the materia medica by our definition, but to the materia alimentaria.

For the first introduction of iron as a remedy, see Pereira, who gives a very curious old story.

The statement in the text concerning a portion of the materia medica stands exactly as delivered, and is meant exactly as it stands. No denunciation of drugs, as sparingly employed by a wise physician, was or is intended. If, however, as Dr. Gould stated in his "valuable and practical discourse" to which the Massachusetts Medical Society "listened with profit as well as interest," "Drugs, in themselves considered, may always be regarded as evils,"--any one who chooses may question whether the evils from their abuse are, on the whole, greater or less than the undoubted benefits obtained from their proper use. The large exception of opium, wine, specifics, and anaesthetics, made in the text, takes off enough from the useful side, as I fully believe, to turn the balance; so that a vessel containing none of these, but loaded with antimony, strychnine, acetate of lead, aloes, aconite, lobelia, lapis infernalis, stercus diaboli, tormentilla, and other approved, and, in skilful hands, really useful remedies, brings, on the whole, more harm than good to the port it enters.

It is a very narrow and unjust view of the practice of medicine, to suppose it to consist altogether in the use of powerful drugs, or of drugs of any kind. Far from it. "The physician may do very much for the welfare of the sick, more than others can do, although he does not, even in the major part of cases, undertake to control and overcome the disease by art. It was with these views that I never reported any patient cured at our hospital. Those who recovered their health were reported as well; not implying that they were made so by the active treatment they had received there. But it was to be understood that all patients received in that house were to be cured, that is, taken care of." (Letters to a Young Physician, by James Jackson, M. D., Boston, 1855.)

"Hygienic rules, properly enforced, fresh air, change of air, travel, attention to diet, good and appropriate food judiciously regulated, together with the administration of our tonics, porter, ale, wine, iron, etc., supply the diseased or impoverished system with what Mr. Gull, of St. Bartholomew's Hospital, aptly calls the 'raw material of the blood;' and we believe that if any real improvement has taken place in medical practice, independently of those truly valuable contributions we have before described, it is in the substitution of tonics, stimulants, and general management, for drastic cathartics, for bleeding, depressing agents, including mercury, tartar emetics, etc., so much in vogue during the early part even of this century." (F. P. Porcher, in Charleston Med. Journal and Review for January, 1860.)

www.bookjungle.com *email: sales@bookjungle.com fax: 630-214-0564 mail: Book Jungle PO Box 2226 Champaign, IL 61825*

The Codes Of Hammurabi And Moses
W. W. Davies

The discovery of the Hammurabi Code is one of the greatest achievements of archaeology, and is of paramount interest, not only to the student of the Bible, but also to all those interested in ancient history...

Religion   **ISBN:** *1-59462-338-4*   *Pages:132*
MSRP $12.95

QTY

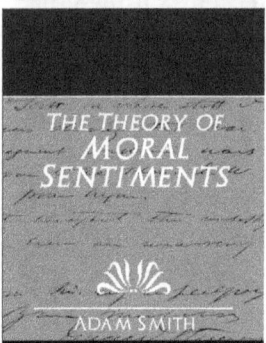

The Theory of Moral Sentiments
Adam Smith

This work from 1749. contains original theories of conscience amd moral judgment and it is the foundation for systemof morals.

Philosophy   **ISBN:** *1-59462-777-0*   *Pages:536*
MSRP $19.95

QTY

Jessica's First Prayer
Hesba Stretton

In a screened and secluded corner of one of the many railway-bridges which span the streets of London there could be seen a few years ago, from five o'clock every morning until half past eight, a tidily set-out coffee-stall, consisting of a trestle and board, upon which stood two large tin cans, with a small fire of charcoal burning under each so as to keep the coffee boiling during the early hours of the morning when the work-people were thronging into the city on their way to their daily toil...

Childrens   **ISBN:** *1-59462-373-2*   *Pages:84*
MSRP $9.95

QTY

My Life and Work
Henry Ford

Henry Ford revolutionized the world with his implementation of mass production for the Model T automobile. Gain valuable business insight into his life and work with his own auto-biography... "We have only started on our development of our country we have not as yet, with all our talk of wonderful progress, done more than scratch the surface. The progress has been wonderful enough but..."

Biographies/   **ISBN:** *1-59462-198-5*   *Pages:300*
MSRP $21.95

QTY

www.bookjungle.com *email: sales@bookjungle.com fax: 630-214-0564 mail: Book Jungle PO Box 2226 Champaign, IL 61825*

The Art of Cross-Examination
Francis Wellman

QTY

I presume it is the experience of every author, after his first book is published upon an important subject, to be almost overwhelmed with a wealth of ideas and illustrations which could readily have been included in his book, and which to his own mind, at least, seem to make a second edition inevitable. Such certainly was the case with me; and when the first edition had reached its sixth impression in five months, I rejoiced to learn that it seemed to my publishers that the book had met with a sufficiently favorable reception to justify a second and considerably enlarged edition. ...

Reference   ISBN: *1-59462-647-2*   Pages:412   *MSRP $19.95*

On the Duty of Civil Disobedience
Henry David Thoreau

QTY

Thoreau wrote his famous essay, On the Duty of Civil Disobedience, as a protest against an unjust but popular war and the immoral but popular institution of slave-owning. He did more than write—he declined to pay his taxes, and was hauled off to gaol in consequence. Who can say how much this refusal of his hastened the end of the war and of slavery?

Law   ISBN: *1-59462-747-9*   Pages:48   *MSRP $7.45*

Dream Psychology Psychoanalysis for Beginners
Sigmund Freud

QTY

Sigmund Freud, born Sigismund Schlomo Freud (May 6, 1856 - September 23, 1939), was a Jewish-Austrian neurologist and psychiatrist who co-founded the psychoanalytic school of psychology. Freud is best known for his theories of the unconscious mind, especially involving the mechanism of repression; his redefinition of sexual desire as mobile and directed towards a wide variety of objects; and his therapeutic techniques, especially his understanding of transference in the therapeutic relationship and the presumed value of dreams as sources of insight into unconscious desires.

Psychology   ISBN: *1-59462-905-6*   Pages:196   *MSRP $15.45*

The Miracle of Right Thought
Orison Swett Marden

QTY

Believe with all of your heart that you will do what you were made to do. When the mind has once formed the habit of holding cheerful, happy, prosperous pictures, it will not be easy to form the opposite habit. It does not matter how improbable or how far away this realization may see, or how dark the prospects may be, if we visualize them as best we can, as vividly as possible, hold tenaciously to them and vigorously struggle to attain them, they will gradually become actualized, realized in the life. But a desire, a longing without endeavor, a yearning abandoned or held indifferently will vanish without realization.

Self Help   ISBN: *1-59462-644-8*   Pages:360   *MSRP $25.45*

www.bookjungle.com email: sales@bookjungle.com fax: 630-214-0564 mail: Book Jungle PO Box 2226 Champaign, IL 61825

QTY

	Title	ISBN	Price
☐	**The Rosicrucian Cosmo-Conception Mystic Christianity** by *Max Heindel*	ISBN: 1-59462-188-8	$38.95
	The Rosicrucian Cosmo-conception is not dogmatic, neither does it appeal to any other authority than the reason of the student. It is: not controversial, but is: sent forth in the, hope that it may help to clear...	New Age/Religion Pages 646	
☐	**Abandonment To Divine Providence** by *Jean-Pierre de Caussade*	ISBN: 1-59462-228-0	$25.95
	"The Rev. Jean Pierre de Caussade was one of the most remarkable spiritual writers of the Society of Jesus in France in the 18th Century. His death took place at Toulouse in 1751. His works have gone through many editions and have been republished...	Inspirational/Religion Pages 400	
☐	**Mental Chemistry** by *Charles Haanel*	ISBN: 1-59462-192-6	$23.95
	Mental Chemistry allows the change of material conditions by combining and appropriately utilizing the power of the mind. Much like applied chemistry creates something new and unique out of careful combinations of chemicals the mastery of mental chemistry...	New Age Pages 354	
☐	**The Letters of Robert Browning and Elizabeth Barret Barrett 1845-1846 vol II** by *Robert Browning* and *Elizabeth Barrett*	ISBN: 1-59462-193-4	$35.95
		Biographies Pages 596	
☐	**Gleanings In Genesis (volume I)** by *Arthur W. Pink*	ISBN: 1-59462-130-6	$27.45
	Appropriately has Genesis been termed "the seed plot of the Bible" for in it we have, in germ form, almost all of the great doctrines which are afterwards fully developed in the books of Scripture which follow...	Religion/Inspirational Pages 420	
☐	**The Master Key** by *L. W. de Laurence*	ISBN: 1-59462-001-6	$30.95
	In no branch of human knowledge has there been a more lively increase of the spirit of research during the past few years than in the study of Psychology, Concentration and Mental Discipline. The requests for authentic lessons in Thought Control, Mental Discipline and...	New Age/Business Pages 422	
☐	**The Lesser Key Of Solomon Goetia** by *L. W. de Laurence*	ISBN: 1-59462-092-X	$9.95
	This translation of the first book of the "Lernegton" which is now for the first time made accessible to students of Talismanic Magic was done, after careful collation and edition, from numerous Ancient Manuscripts in Hebrew, Latin, and French...	New Age/Occult Pages 92	
☐	**Rubaiyat Of Omar Khayyam** by *Edward Fitzgerald*	ISBN: 1-59462-332-5	$13.95
	Edward Fitzgerald, whom the world has already learned, in spite of his own efforts to remain within the shadow of anonymity, to look upon as one of the rarest poets of the century, was born at Bredfield, in Suffolk, on the 31st of March, 1809. He was the third son of John Purcell...	Music Pages 172	
☐	**Ancient Law** by *Henry Maine*	ISBN: 1-59462-128-4	$29.95
	The chief object of the following pages is to indicate some of the earliest ideas of mankind, as they are reflected in Ancient Law, and to point out the relation of those ideas to modern thought.	Religion/History Pages 452	
☐	**Far-Away Stories** by *William J. Locke*	ISBN: 1-59462-129-2	$19.45
	"Good wine needs no bush, but a collection of mixed vintages does. And this book is just such a collection. Some of the stories I do not want to remain buried for ever in the museum files of dead magazine-numbers an author's not unpardonable vanity..."	Fiction Pages 272	
☐	**Life of David Crockett** by *David Crockett*	ISBN: 1-59462-250-7	$27.45
	"Colonel David Crockett was one of the most remarkable men of the times in which he lived. Born in humble life, but gifted with a strong will, an indomitable courage, and unremitting perseverance...	Biographies/New Age Pages 424	
☐	**Lip-Reading** by *Edward Nitchie*	ISBN: 1-59462-206-X	$25.95
	Edward B. Nitchie, founder of the New York School for the Hard of Hearing, now the Nitchie School of Lip-Reading, Inc, wrote "LIP-READING Principles and Practice". The development and perfecting of this meritorious work on lip-reading was an undertaking...	How-to Pages 400	
☐	**A Handbook of Suggestive Therapeutics, Applied Hypnotism, Psychic Science** by *Henry Munro*	ISBN: 1-59462-214-0	$24.95
		Health/New Age/Health/Self-help Pages 376	
☐	**A Doll's House: and Two Other Plays** by *Henrik Ibsen*	ISBN: 1-59462-112-8	$19.95
	Henrik Ibsen created this classic when in revolutionary 1848 Rome. Introducing some striking concepts in playwriting for the realist genre, this play has been studied the world over.	Fiction/Classics/Plays 308	
☐	**The Light of Asia** by *sir Edwin Arnold*	ISBN: 1-59462-204-3	$13.95
	In this poetic masterpiece, Edwin Arnold describes the life and teachings of Buddha. The man who was to become known as Buddha to the world was born as Prince Gautama of India but he rejected the worldly riches and abandoned the reigns of power when...	Religion/History/Biographies Pages 170	
☐	**The Complete Works of Guy de Maupassant** by *Guy de Maupassant*	ISBN: 1-59462-157-8	$16.95
	"For days and days, nights and nights, I had dreamed of that first kiss which was to consecrate our engagement, and I knew not on what spot I should put my lips..."	Fiction/Classics Pages 240	
☐	**The Art of Cross-Examination** by *Francis L. Wellman*	ISBN: 1-59462-309-0	$26.95
	Written by a renowned trial lawyer, Wellman imparts his experience and uses case studies to explain how to use psychology to extract desired information through questioning.	How-to/Science/Reference Pages 408	
☐	**Answered or Unanswered?** by *Louisa Vaughan* Miracles of Faith in China	ISBN: 1-59462-248-5	$10.95
		Religion Pages 112	
☐	**The Edinburgh Lectures on Mental Science (1909)** by *Thomas*	ISBN: 1-59462-008-3	$11.95
	This book contains the substance of a course of lectures recently given by the writer in the Queen Street Hall, Edinburgh. Its purpose is to indicate the Natural Principles governing the relation between Mental Action and Material Conditions...	New Age/Psychology Pages 148	
☐	**Ayesha** by *H. Rider Haggard*	ISBN: 1-59462-301-5	$24.95
	Verily and indeed it is the unexpected that happens! Probably if there was one person upon the earth from whom the Editor of this, and of a certain previous history, did not expect to hear again...	Classics Pages 380	
☐	**Ayala's Angel** by *Anthony Trollope*	ISBN: 1-59462-352-X	$29.95
	The two girls were both pretty, but Lucy who was twenty-one who supposed to be simple and comparatively unattractive, whereas Ayala was credited, as her Bombwhat romantic name might show, with poetic charm and a taste for romance. Ayala when her father died was nineteen...	Fiction Pages 484	
☐	**The American Commonwealth** by *James Bryce*	ISBN: 1-59462-286-8	$34.45
	An interpretation of American democratic political theory. It examines political mechanics and society from the perspective of Scotsman James Bryce	Politics Pages 572	
☐	**Stories of the Pilgrims** by *Margaret P. Pumphrey*	ISBN: 1-59462-116-0	$17.95
	This book explores pilgrims religious oppression in England as well as their escape to Holland and eventual crossing to America on the Mayflower, and their early days in New England...	History Pages 268	

www.bookjungle.com email: sales@bookjungle.com fax: 630-214-0564 mail: Book Jungle PO Box 2226 Champaign, IL 61825

QTY

The Fasting Cure by *Sinclair Upton* ISBN: *1-59462-222-1* **$13.95**
In the Cosmopolitan Magazine for May, 1910, and in the Contemporary Review (London) for April, 1910, I published an article dealing with my experiences in fasting. I have written a great many magazine articles, but never one which attracted so much attention... *New Age/Self Help/Health Pages 164*

Hebrew Astrology by *Sepharial* ISBN: *1-59462-308-2* **$13.45**
In these days of advanced thinking it is a matter of common observation that we have left many of the old landmarks behind and that we are now pressing forward to greater heights and to a wider horizon than that which represented the mind-content of our progenitors... *Astrology Pages 144*

Thought Vibration or The Law of Attraction in the Thought World ISBN: *1-59462-127-6* **$12.95**
by *William Walker Atkinson* *Psychology/Religion Pages 144*

Optimism by *Helen Keller* ISBN: *1-59462-108-X* **$15.95**
Helen Keller was blind, deaf, and mute since 19 months old, yet famously learned how to overcome these handicaps, communicate with the world, and spread her lectures promoting optimism. An inspiring read for everyone... *Biographies/Inspirational Pages 84*

Sara Crewe by *Frances Burnett* ISBN: *1-59462-360-0* **$9.45**
In the first place, Miss Minchin lived in London. Her home was a large, dull, tall one, in a large, dull square, where all the houses were alike, and all the sparrows were alike, and where all the door-knockers made the same heavy sound... *Childrens/Classic Pages 88*

The Autobiography of Benjamin Franklin by *Benjamin Franklin* ISBN: *1-59462-135-7* **$24.95**
The Autobiography of Benjamin Franklin has probably been more extensively read than any other American historical work, and no other book of its kind has had such ups and downs of fortune. Franklin lived for many years in England, where he was agent... *Biographies/History Pages 332*

Name	
Email	
Telephone	
Address	
City, State ZIP	

☐ Credit Card   ☐ Check / Money Order

Credit Card Number	
Expiration Date	
Signature	

Please Mail to: Book Jungle
PO Box 2226
Champaign, IL 61825
or Fax to: 630-214-0564

ORDERING INFORMATION

web: *www.bookjungle.com*
email: *sales@bookjungle.com*
fax: *630-214-0564*
mail: *Book Jungle PO Box 2226 Champaign, IL 61825*
or PayPal *to sales@bookjungle.com*

Please contact us for bulk discounts

DIRECT-ORDER TERMS

20% Discount if You Order Two or More Books
Free Domestic Shipping!
Accepted: Master Card, Visa, Discover, American Express

www.ingramcontent.com/pod-product-compliance
Lightning Source LLC
Chambersburg PA
CBHW081209230426
43666CB00015B/2688